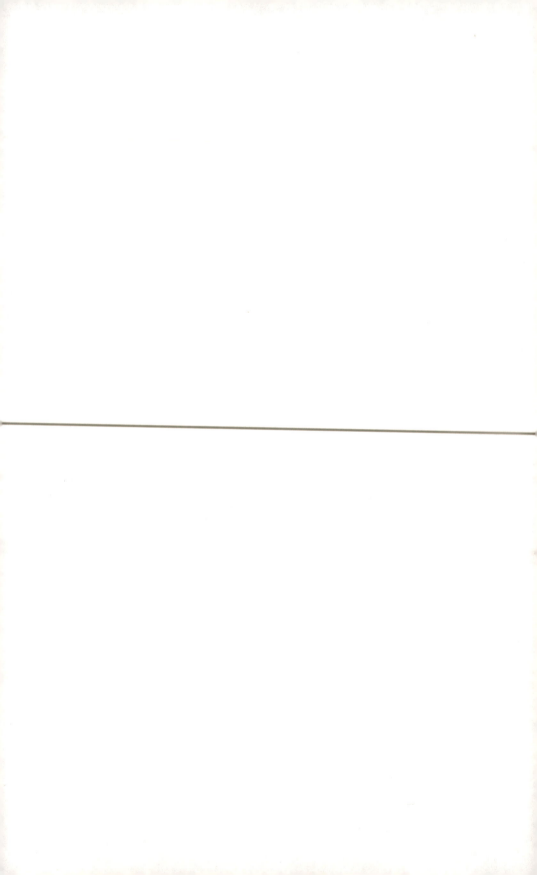

MARIGOLD

MARIGOLD

THE MUSIC OF BILLY MAYERL

Peter Dickinson

OXFORD

UNIVERSITY PRESS

OXFORD
UNIVERSITY PRESS

Great Clarendon Street, Oxford OX2 6DP

Oxford University Press is a department of the University of Oxford.
It furthers the University's objective of excellence in research, scholarship,
and education by publishing worldwide in

Oxford New York

Athens Auckland Bangkok Bogotá Buenos Aires Calcutta
Cape Town Chennai Dar es Salaam Delhi Florence Hong Kong Istanbul
Karachi Kuala Lumpur Madrid Melbourne Mexico City Mumbai
Nairobi Paris São Paulo Singapore Taipei Tokyo Toronto Warsaw

with associated companies in Berlin Ibadan

Oxford is a registered trade mark of Oxford University Press
in the UK and in certain other countries

Published in the United States
by Oxford University Press Inc., New York

Text © Peter Dickinson 1999
Discography © John Watson 1999
List of Works © Alex Hassan 1999

The moral rights of the author have been asserted
Database right Oxford University Press (maker)

First published 1999

British Library Cataloguing in Publication Data

Data available

Library of Congress Cataloging in Publication Data

Data available

ISBN 0-19-816213-8

1 3 5 7 9 10 8 6 4 2

Typeset in Jansen Text
by Cambrian Typesetters, Frimley, Surrey
Printed in Great Britain
on acid-free paper by
Bookcraft (Bath) Ltd., Midsomer Norton

ACKNOWLEDGEMENTS

My earliest acknowledgement must be to my father, Frank Dickinson (1906–78), the contact lens pioneer, who used to play Billy Mayerl's piano music with such skill and infectious enjoyment for as long as I can remember. It was only after his death that I began to recognize the quality of what had previously seemed to me to be ephemeral entertainment music. I learnt to take the musical world complete from my study of American music and the courses I ran at Keele University, where I was first Professor and Head of Department from 1974 to 1984 and set up a Centre for American Music. I played plenty of Joplin and other rags in my American programmes with my sister, the mezzo-soprano Meriel Dickinson, and later came to regard Mayerl as a kind of English Joplin of novelty piano.

Then I am indebted to all those whose interviews formed the basis for my BBC Radio 3 documentary—'Billy Mayerl: a Formula for Success'—which was broadcast twice in 1996. I am especially grateful to Ann Stanger for starting the project in 1982, when several crucial contacts were still alive. Later Derek Drescher and Robin Cherry took it over with dedicated enthusiasm and brought it to completion. Amongst those interviewed, first place must go to Mrs Mayerl, then Leslie Osborne and Van Phillips—both colleagues of Mayerl's—and, from a later generation, the pianists Sir Richard Rodney Bennett and William Davies. Later on Reginald Leopold and Mrs Doris Dargie joined in as well as Mayerl's pupils Josie Steele and Monty Warlock. Luckily both Mayerl's secretaries at the School, those splendid octogenarians Mrs E. A. McInerney (Miss Eve Hooper) and Mrs Vicky Matkin (Miss Vesta Harrison), were available and invaluable.

I am also indebted to members of Billy Mayerl's family. Fred and Hilda Mayerl gave me leads I could not have obtained in any other way. In particular they enabled me to trace Julian Norris, son of Billy's sister Johanna, who provided valuable information and found two unique photographs. Very special thanks must go to Dr Richard Head. He was one of the first to be interviewed and made his entire collection of recordings and material available to me on my visits to Selsea. Ever since 1982 he has taken a personal interest in the project and I owe him a great deal for his generous encouragement.

Bruce Phillips, at OUP until 1998, has always admired Mayerl and has been consistently supportive to me through frustrating delays covering more than a decade. I am particularly grateful to the fine American pianist and collector, Alex Hassan, for access to his splendid list of works and to John Watson for his discography and other fruits of his research. Both of them have also helped with detailed information. The contribution of those who have read all or part of the book at different stages has been invaluable—Professor Stephen Banfield, Professor Cyril Ehrlich, Sir Richard Rodney Bennett, Mark Tucker, and John Archer, whose first biographical study of Mayerl was included in M. Harth (ed.), *Lightning Fingers* (Paradise Press, 1995), and who generously shared his research with me. I have also had valuable assistance from Mike Lorenzini at the Billy Mayerl Society. Along with John Watson, he arranged for the production of the CD for this book, where the technical work was done by Philip Legg.

There is now a long list of individuals who have helped in various capacities and I shall have to put in the usual apologies to anyone I have inadvertently left out. It has been difficult, sometimes impossible, to trace information required, but I have been copiously assisted all along in an atmosphere of helpful co-operation, which characterizes the community of those interested in Mayerl.

My Czech research assistant, Marta Jones, worked in Prague to try to find details of the Mayerl family. Help also came from the staff of the Institute of Musicology at the Academy of Sciences of the Czech Republic in Prague, the Charles Ferdinand Universities and the Czech High Schools of Technical Studies. Several genealogists have been involved in the search for Mayerl's antecedents, including Tony Halstead and Paul Chennell. Karl Kroeger gave me a list of American Mayerls—none replied to letters. Both sides of Billy Mayerl's family have worked on tracing his ancestors. Patrick Howat helped me by finding Christian Mayerl, of Karlsruhe, who tried to find Mayerl's paternal roots through family connections in Germany and Austria, but finally without success. On the maternal side, Hans Petri contacted Willem Umbach, of Heino in Holland, who undertook research there and managed to locate the origins of Elise Mayerl's family. Many more have helped with details. Maria Jefferis and Maggi Simpson at the *Melody Maker*; Kate Ferguson at the Zoological Society of London; Peter Bond, archivist of the Savage Club; Rosemary Ashbee and Susan Scott at the Savoy Hotel Archive; Nick Dellow for information about bands at the Savoy; the staff at the BBC's Written Archives Centre at Caversham, especially Caroline Cornish and later Jacqueline Kavanagh for permission to quote from BBC archives; Geoffrey Lester at the BBC Library for trying to find the collection of Mayerl material which R. G. Howarth catalogued in 1972 and which has now disappeared; Reginald Phillips, Mrs Mayerl's accountant and friend; Jerome Farrell, archivist for Hammersmith and Fulham and later Westminster, for details about the Mayerl and Umbach families in London; Clare Colvin at the English National Opera archives for details from Coliseum programmes;

Carol Detmon at the Greater London Record Office for trying to find archives of schools attended by Mayerl; the Performing Right Society, especially Amanda Arnold for providing figures for Mayerl's PRS earnings and Huntley Leonard and colleagues for providing details of his PRS titles; Ernest Tomlinson for details of the Light Music Society in the 1950s; Terry Wilkinson at the Midland Gershwin Mayerl Society for letting me see correspondence relating to Mayerl; Malcolm Walker at the *Gramophone* for information from files; Andrew Lamb for details of songs; Kate Woodhouse for scouring the passenger lists of steamship companies at the Public Records Office; Kieran Conry at the Catholic Media Office; Edmund A. Stanbrook, who shared details of his personal research; Enid Foster at the Garrick Club Library; F. G. L. O. Van Kretschmar for help with Dutch translation; Mary Worthington, my dedicated copy-editor, and the staff at OUP; and Peter Gammond whose excellent *Oxford Companion to Popular Music* I have consulted more often than any other volume in connection with this book.

I am grateful to the Office for National Statistics for providing me with tables of their long-term indicator of prices of consumer goods and services. These cannot be precise figures but, rounded off, have been provided in the text and in Appendix 3 to give a rough idea of equivalents in modern cash terms.

I should like to thank my colleagues in the Music Department at Keele University for their support in developing teaching and research in the field of popular music. I must also thank Goldsmiths College of the University of London, where I was Professor and Head of the Music Department from 1991 to 1997, for a term's study leave in the autumn of 1994 largely to advance work on this book. Three generations of my family have taken an interest in my work—especially my mother Muriel Dickinson and my sister Meriel—and, as in everything worthwhile I have done in the past thirty-five years, I am overwhelmingly grateful to my wife Bridget.

PETER DICKINSON

Aldeburgh, Suffolk

Contents

Contents of CD

The Discography gives the numbers of records originally issued as 78s, which can be traced there by the date of the actual recording.

Six Pianolettes (1925)

1. *The Jazz Master* (2′ 54″), 24 Sept. 1925
2. *The Jazz Mistress* (2′ 28″), 24 Sept. 1925
3. *Eskimo Shivers* (2′ 25″), 24 Sept. 1925
4. *All-of-a-Twist* (2′ 33″), 24 Sept. 1925
5. *Virginia Creeper* (2′ 33″), 12 Nov. 1925
6. *Jazzaristrix* (2′ 52″), 12 Nov. 1925

Four Piano Exaggerations (1926)

7. *Loose Elbows* (3′ 16″), 3 Mar. 1926
8. *Antiquary* (2′ 44″), 3 Mar. 1926
9. *Jack-in-the-Box* (2′ 25″), 26 Aug. 1926
10. *Sleepy Piano* (2′ 27″), 26 Aug. 1926

11. *Marigold*: solo (2′ 25″), 7 Oct. 1927
12. *Marigold*: duet with Mrs. Mayerl (2′ 49″), 31 Aug. 1934
13. *Chop-sticks* (1′ 44″), 7 Oct. 1927
14. *Hollyhock* (1′ 40″), 7 Oct. 1927
15. *Honky-Tonk* (2′ 36″), 11 Oct. 1928

Puppet's Suite (1927)

16. *Golliwog* (1′ 40″), 25 Aug. 1927
17. *Judy* (2′ 11″), 25 Aug. 1927
18. *Punch* (2′ 08″), 7 Oct. 1927

19. *Limehouse Blues*: transcription of song by Philip Braham (2′ 21″), 1 May 1936

Four Aces Suite (1933)

20. *Ace of Clubs* (1′ 38″), 12 Dec. 1933
21. *Ace of Diamonds* (0′ 50″), 12 Dec. 1933
22. *Ace of Hearts* (1′ 36″), 12 Dec. 1933
23. *Ace of Spades* (2′ 16″), 12 Dec. 1933

24. *Railroad Rhythm* (2′ 35″), 19 May 1939
25. *Harp of the Winds* (2′ 54″), 19 May 1939

LIST OF ILLUSTRATIONS

(between pp. 142 and 143)

It has not been possible to trace the copyright holders of the photographs. The publishers would be glad to hear from any such unacknowledged copyright holders.

List of Music Examples

All Mayerl unless otherwise stated. Dates are those of publication.

Music Example Acknowledgements

The author and publisher wish to thank the following copyright holders: Exx. 2, 4, 6, 7, 9, and 13 are reproduced by permission of Keith Prowse Music Publishing Co., London WC2H 0EA; Ex. 3 is reproduced by permission of Lawrence Wright Music Co. Ltd., London WC2H 0EA; Exx. 5 and 8 (copyright 1929 by Boosey & Co. Ltd.) are reproduced by permission of Boosey & Hawkes Music Publishers Ltd.; Exx. 11 and 12, copyright Victoria Music Publishing Company (1935), are reproduced by permission of International Music Publication Ltd.; Ex. 14, copyright Ascherberg, Hopwood & Crewe Ltd./Warner-Chappell Music Ltd., is reproduced by permission of IMP Ltd.

Chronology

1871	Birth of Mayerl's father, Joseph Mayerl (musician), son of Anton (musician), in Austria.
1881	*5 January*: Birth of Mayerl's mother, Elise Umbach, daughter of Adam August Umbach (musician in the Seventh Infantry) and Johanna Francisca Theodora (née Stockman), at 'S-Hertogenbosch, Holland.
1896	*24 March*: birth of Mayerl's future wife, Ermenegilda (Gilda, Gil, and later mostly Jill) Bernini, at Via Dietro le Chiesa, Minori, Salerno, Italy.
1899	*26 August*: marriage of Mayerl's parents, Joseph Mayerl and Elise Umbach, at St Pancras Parish Church, London. Address of both parties given as 47 Tottenham Court Road, London.
1901	*20 December*: birth of Mayerl's sister, Johanna Elisa, at 15 Harrington St., Regents Park, St Pancras, London.
1902	*31 May*: birth of William (Billy) Joseph Mayerl at 53 Tottenham Court Rd., St Pancras, London.
1910	*2 October*: birth of Mayerl's brother, Frederick August, at 26 Beauclere Rd., South Hammersmith, Fulham, London.
1911	Mayerl first listed as a student at Trinity College of Music, London, continuing for the academic years of 1912, 1913, 1914.
1915	Mayerl leaves Trinity College and works in cinemas during these years.
1919	Mayerl's first known publication, *Egyptian Suite* for piano. Gershwin records his *Novelette in Fourths* on a Welte Mignon roll.
1920	Mayerl plays with David de Groot's Orchestra at the Piccadilly Hotel during this period.
1921	Mayerl almost certainly meets Bert Ralton at the Polygon Hotel in Southampton who engages him to play with the Savoy Havana.
1922	*May*: Mayerl officially replaces John Firman as pianist in the Savoy Havana Band, but had been playing with them earlier. He started recording with the Band in about July.
1923	*19 April*: marriage of William Joseph Mayerl and Ermenegilda Bernini at the Register Office, Hammersmith, London.
1924	*16 August*: Mayerl, now living at 4 Roland Gardens, SW7, sails for New York with Geoffrey Clayton, leaving Southampton on the *Aquitania*. *22 December*: Mayerl's maternal grandfather, Adam August Umbach of 85 Shaftesbury Rd., Hammersmith, dies in Glasgow.

1925   *3 January; 24 January; 10 March; 28 October;* and *9 December*: Savoy Bands
        play at the Queen's Hall, but the sensation created by the first concert de-
        clines.
        The Jazz Master, first in set of *Six Pianolettes*, published by Keith Prowse,
        Mayerl's principal publisher for the next thirty years.
        19 April: Mayerl and his wife, living at 30 Catherine St., Buckingham Gate,
        London SW1 send out their wedding anniversary party invitation.
        15 June: Gershwin plays *Rhapsody in Blue* for the first time in this country in
        a broadcast concert at the Savoy Hotel.
        24 September: Mayerl makes his first records for HMV—four of the
        Pianolettes.
        28 October: Mayerl plays *Rhapsody in Blue* at the Queen's Hall.
        October: Mayerl's 'lightning fingers' are filmed by a slow-motion camera.

1926   *January*: Mayerl announces in the *Melody Maker* that he is leaving the
        Savoy and launching the Billy Mayerl School.
        March: the School (Modern Postal Tuition Ltd.) is set up at 29 Oxford St.
        May: Billy Mayerl and his Orchestra begin recording for Vocalion.
        July: Mayerl launches four-year partnership with Gwen Farrar at the
        Coliseum.
        October: Mayerl's photograph is on the front cover of the *Melody Maker* and
        three articles by him appear in the following months.
        The Billy Mayerl Salon Syncopators launched, with Ron Gray as
        pianist/leader.
        4 November: Billy Mayerl's Vocalion Dance band at the Queen's Hall.

1927   *17 January*: Bert Ralton dies through a shooting accident in South Africa.
        Marigold composed and published: recorded for Columbia on 7 October.

1929   *20 February*: William Mayerl of Jazzaristrix, Cranbourne Gardens,
        Golders Green, Middlesex, makes a will leaving everything to his wife.

1930   Mayerl is with the Co-Optimists in their final period, although ill for some
        of this time.
        30 August: Mayerl, still writing from 30 Catherine St., accepts membership
        of the Savage Club, remaining a member until his death.
        30 October: *Nippy*, Mayerl's first full-length musical, opens at the Prince
        Edward Theatre, London, with Binnie Hale in the lead.

1931   *20 May*: *The Millionaire Kid* opens at the Gaiety Theatre.
        29 October: the Mayerls move to Hampstead.

1932   Billy Mayerl School moves to Steinway Hall, 1–2 George St., London W1.

1934   *January*: First issue of the *Billy Mayerl Club Magazine*.
        Mayerl takes the role of a composer in the film, *Without You*.
        31 March: *Sporting Love* with Mayerl conducting, opens at the Gaiety
        Theatre and goes on tour.

1935   *February*: Mayerl plays the world's largest piano, a Challen, before Her
        Majesty the Queen at the British Industries Fair, Olympia.

12 November: *Twenty to One* opens at the Alhambra Theatre.

Mayerl writes songs for films, *Honeymoon for Three* and *Cheer Up*, and conducts his band in Noel Gay's *Love Lies*.

1936   *23 September*: *Over She Goes* opens at the Saville Theatre.

The Mayerls living at Marigold Lodge, 18 West Heath Close, Hampstead.

Mayerl joins the Zoological Society of London, resigning in 1947.

19 December: Mayerl takes cruise to West Africa on *SS Atlantis*, returning on 11 January 1937.

1937   *February*: Mayerl starts weekly broadcasts for Radio Luxemburg.

13 April: Mayerl takes part in *Savoy Memories* on BBC London National.

21 June: Fred Mayerl marries Hilda Bray.

Four articles signed by Mayerl appear in *Tit-bits*: 'A Master of Jazz writes his own Story' 19, 26 June; 3, 10 July.

11 July: Gershwin dies.

14 September: *Crazy Days* opens at the Shaftesbury Theatre.

21 November: death of Mayerl's father, Joseph Mayerl of 54 Richmond Gardens, Hammersmith, London W14.

8 December: Laddie Cliff dies.

1938   *9 February*: the Mayerls leave for Sweden. He meets the Stockholm Club and plays on *Radiotjanst*.

12 February: death of Mayerl's mother, Elise Mayerl of 54 Richmond Gardens, Hammersmith, London W14.

1939   *19 May*: South London and Surrey Branch Meeting attended by Billy and Jill (the only one she had visited so far apart from Sweden) as well as Fred and Hilda Mayerl.

4 July: West London Branch Meeting again attended by Billy and Fred and their wives.

3 November: *Runaway Love*, put on by Billy Mayerl Enterprises and accompanied by Billy Mayerl and his Challen Multitone Piano Orchestra, opens at the Saville Theatre.

1940   *7 February*: the Billy Mayerl School moves to 10 New Bond St., W1.

The Mayerls take a house in Maidenhead.

29 March: Billy Mayerl School (Modern Postal Tuition Ltd.) officially liquidated.

Mayerl directs Billy Mayerl and his Grosvenor House Band, based at the hotel in Park Lane, London W1.

4 December: *A Happy Birthday* opens in Slough.

1941   The Mayerls are living at Grosvenor House into 1944.

1944   Mayerl ill from mid-1944 to mid-1945.

The Mayerls living since Christmas 1944 at Chellow Dene, Buccleuch Rd., Bournemouth.

1945   Mayerl resigns from Grosvenor House by 20 April and is now 'available for broadcasting'.

1946   Mayerl signs BBC long-term contract from 13 January 1946 to 12 March 1949; the Mayerls living at Marigold Lodge, 2 Telegraph Hill, New Platts Lane, Hampstead, NW3.

1949   *23 March*: the Mayerls leave for a year's tour of Australia and New Zealand initially with Stanley Holloway on the *SS Orcades*.

1950   The Mayerls return by early January and are at 505 Nelson House, Dolphin Square, SW1, then have moved by February to 18 Avenue Mansions, Finchley Rd., London NW3, where they remain until at least 1955; a revived but slender Billy Mayerl School operates from 407a Edgware Rd., W2.

1951   Mayerl signs another BBC long-term contract from 24 June 1951 to 3 November 1956.

1952   The Billy Mayerl School operates from 395a Edgware Rd., London W2.

1953   *July*: Mayerl on European tour, including Stockholm.
        31 August: Mayerl joins the Musicians Union after being black-listed for a month.

1956   Mayerl joins protest against Copyright Bill, signing a letter to *The Times* on 3 April along with Benjamin Britten, Vivian Ellis, Arthur Benjamin, Howard Ferguson, and Racine Fricker.

1957   The Mayerls are living at Marigold Lodge, Pyebush Lane, Beaconsfield, Bucks.

1958   *21 April*: Mayerl interviewed by Roy Plomley on *Desert Island Discs*.

1959   Mayerl seriously ill at St Joseph's Nursing Home, Beaconsfield.
        25 March at 8.00 p.m.: Billy Mayerl dies at home.
        31 March at 11.00 a.m.: Billy Mayerl cremated at Golders Green Crematorium.
        14 June: BBC Home Service tribute broadcast with London Theatre Orchestra/Reginald Kilbey and William Davies.

1961   *30 June*: The Billy Mayerl School Ltd. officially liquidated.

1963   Mrs Mayerl founds the Billy Mayerl Bursary at Trinity College of Music.

1968   *2 January*: Mayerl's sister, Johanna Elisa, dies.

1974   The Billy Mayerl Circle is formed with H. Nichols as Secretary, Mrs Jill Mayerl as Patron, and Leslie Osborne as President. Seventeen Newsletters published from Summer 1974 to Spring 1978 with R. J. Howarth as editor.

1975   Richard Rodney Bennett records eight Mayerl solos on Polydor LP 2460–245.

1984   *21 August*: Mrs Mayerl dies at Brighton General Hospital.
        29 August: Mrs Mayerl cremated at Downs Crematorium, Brighton.

1987   *Marigold: Piano Impressions of Billy Mayerl*—the first of Eric Parkin's extensive Mayerl series appears on Chandos, later on Priory and Shellwood.
        October: the Midland Gershwin Mayerl Society formed, organized by C. T. Wilkinson.

1989   *Loose Elbows*—Mayerl anthology by Susan Tomes appears on Virgin.

1992   The Billy Mayerl Society formed, with Eric Parkin and Susan Tomes as Patrons, journal edited by Mike Harth and headquarters at Mike Lorenzini's house, Shellwood, St Leonards Road, Thames Ditton, Surrey KT7 0RN.
         9 June: Billy Mayerl: the Marigold Man, 90th anniversary tribute by Steve Race, researched and produced by Steve Edwards on BBC Radio 2.

1994   The first of Eric Parkin's series of Mayerl transcriptions appears on Priory.

1995   The first book about Mayerl published—*Lightning Fingers: Billy Mayerl, the Man and his Music, a Symposium* edited by Mike Harth, Paradise Press.

1996   Three programmes of Billy Mayerl on BBC Radio 3. *Billy Mayerl: A Formula for Success*, BBC Radio 3 documentary by Peter Dickinson, produced by Derek Drescher with technical assistance from Robin Cherry, broadcast on 11 February and repeated on 24 August followed in each case by two programmes of Mayerl's music.

1997   Shellwood Productions record label started by Mike Lorenzini. First release is Billy Mayerl Rediscoveries Vol. 1 by Alex Hassan.

1998   Eric Parkin's tenth CD of Mayerl's piano music appears.

Introduction

AMERICAN music started to have an impact in England as long ago as the 1840s. Minstrel shows, based on blacked-up white performers caricaturing African Americans were organized in the USA early in that decade and reached London well before the end of it. The popularity of such shows was phenomenal and enduring. After the American Civil War (1861–5) Blacks themselves increasingly took part. They were obviously more authentic in their portrayals, but the whole enterprise remained in the context of entertainment stereotypes. Something more serious, and equally magnetic, came with the discovery of Black spirituals. The Jubilee Singers, of Fisk University, Nashville, were the pioneers and they became celebrities, touring Europe in the 1870s.

For more than a century the whole world has sung the songs of Stephen Foster and stepped out to the marches of Sousa. But the next wave of the American invasion of Europe was ragtime, which was known in sheet music from the late 1890s, appeared in British music halls, and developed into a dance craze well before the First World War (1914–18). These were the years when Irving Berlin, with *Alexander's Ragtime Band* and countless other songs, became the most successful American song-writer, a position he retained until well after the Second World War. Dances based on ragtime included the cakewalk, the boston, the turkey-trot, the bunny-hug, and the grizzly-bear, many of them popularized on both sides of the Atlantic by Irene and Vernon Castle. The American musicians to conquer Britain on this wave were the Original American Ragtime Octette, a vaudeville team, who opened at the London Hippodrome in 1912 and were so popular that they stayed in England for five years. They set a new style for syncopated dance music in Britain which came to full fruition with the famous bands at London's Savoy Hotel after the war.

Billy Mayerl (1902–59) was born into the London of King Edward VII in the year when the South African war against the Boers ended, a year after the death of Queen Victoria. Edwardian Britain inherited Victorian prosperity, but the years leading up to the First World War in 1914, like those leading up to the Second World War in 1939, were dominated by looming international conflict. The first period was that of Mayerl's adolescence: in the second he was a celebrity. His 1920s persona as the pianist with the 'lightning fingers' captured exactly the frantic pace of the dance-crazed, flapper-infested jazz age of the Bright Young Things.

He was the first prominent British performer and composer to master the implications of the American idiom in a virtuoso piano style all his own. Today, as pianist, composer, celebrity, and educator he is emerging as a seminal figure in British music operating in the gap between classical music and jazz and flowering during the inter-war period.

Mayerl made his initial impact as a dazzling performer: everyone regarded him as a sensation. His old friend and contemporary Leslie Osborne explained: 'Everybody knew Billy Mayerl. He was the pianist's god.'[1] A younger colleague, William Davies, who worked with him at the BBC in his last years, confirmed this in similar terminology: 'There was nobody to touch Billy Mayerl. He was God: he was No. 1!'[2] Sir Richard Rodney Bennett revived interest in Mayerl in 1975 when he put some of his pieces on the other side of an LP of Gershwin's Songbook and later said: 'He was head and shoulders above anybody else. He was so witty and original and the tunes were so intriguing and touching.'[3]

In 1991 Alan Rusbridger introduced Mayerl unusually precisely to readers of the *Guardian*:

The music holds you instantly but you can't quite place it. It's not exactly jazz, nor is it Stravinsky playing at jazz. It's too harmonically sophisticated and dazzling to be Scott Joplin; it's too pianistic to be Gershwin. The harmonies *are* Gershwinesque, though there are occasional shades of Ravel and a bit of John Ireland in there too. But then a stride bass breaks in, more Fats Waller than Art Tatum.[4]

1993, the British pianist and broadcaster, Steve Race, summed him up:

Billy wasn't exactly a serious composer: he certainly wasn't a jazz composer, nor a pop-song writer. The truth is that he invented a whole enchanting musical world of his own—somewhere between syncopation, salon, novelty, light music. All words which have now fallen into disuse. But Mayerl's music is as vital, fresh and full of delight as ever.[5]

Mayerl was a product of unique circumstances, arising from an interaction of coincidences which on closer examination look more like a preordained pattern. To start with he was born into a family with professional musicians on both sides but, unlike his father and maternal grandfather who played melody instruments, he took up the most popular instrument of the period—the piano. This was a fortunate choice since, as so often in musical history, the keyboard is a focus for experiment under the control of one player—look at developments

---

[1] L. Osborne, interview with Peter Dickinson, 11 Aug. 1981.
[2] W. Davies, interview with Ann Stangar, 17 Sept. 1982.
[3] R. R. Bennett, interview with Peter Dickinson, 22 Oct. 1981.
[4] A. Rusbridger, 'The Kid that Played Nippy', *Guardian*, 5 Sept. 1991, 25–6.
[5] S. Race, 'The Marigold Man', BBC Radio 2, 9 June 1992.

involving the harpsichord, the organ, various pianos, the prepared piano, and the synthesizer. And with the player piano, which was to have an unexpected future with Conlon Nancarrow, the instrument gained extensions into automated sound production linking it to the kind of technology which has dominated the twentieth century. This forms an ever-extending, increasingly sophisticated chain of communication through recording (78, LP, cassette, and CD), broadcasting, film, TV, video, and internet.

The 1920s was a period of rapid change, and the economic situation, as the social historian Cyril Ehrlich has demonstrated, affected music at all points.[6] There was a move away from sheet music; the demand for musicians in cinemas rose and suddenly fell with talking pictures; and the piano reached its peak as a domestic instrument and then declined.

By the First World War American sales of player pianos topped those of conventional instruments.[7] Piano rolls and recordings were reaching a wider public with a new kind of popular music disseminated through these new media, although Mayerl discovered it as a child through disc musical boxes known as penny-in-the-slot machines. This ragtime style was derived from African American elements involving syncopated rhythms and, as with jazz and rock 'n' roll later, it appealed to youth and was therefore considered subversive in some quarters. Even in the 1930s Mayerl had to deal with bigots who found something immoral in syncopation. But it was ragtime, both as a piano idiom and as popular songs, that was the catalyst for Billy Mayerl as a British performer and composer to develop his own unique style.

As with jazz later, it should never be assumed that ragtime implies triviality. Its rhythmic techniques profoundly affected Charles Ives, who had heard ragging performers in the 1890s.[8] The cakewalk style was employed in France by Erik Satie and Claude Debussy.[9] During and after the First World War Stravinsky wrote his ragtime pieces[10] and many other composers were affected by ragtime, early jazz, or dance music derivations. These included Darius Milhaud, Kurt Weill, Aaron Copland, Constant Lambert, William Walton, Michael Tippett, and many more.

At the same time the silent film industry was thriving and provided unique opportunities for an army of live musicians until the arrival of talkies brought

[6] C. Ehrlich. Many references will be made to essential information contained in *The Music Profession in Britain since the Eighteenth Century* (Clarendon Press, Oxford, 1985), and *Harmonious Alliance: A History of the Performing Right Society* (OUP, Oxford, 1989).

[7] C. Ehrlich, *The Piano: A History*, 2nd edn. (Clarendon Press, Oxford, 1990), 134.

[8] J. Kirkpatrick (ed.), *Charles E. Ives: Memos* (Calder & Boyars, London, 1973), 56–7.

[9] Erik Satie, *La Diva de l'Empire* (song, ?1904); *Le Piccadilly: Marche* (piano, 1904). Claude Debussy, *Golliwog's Cake-walk* from *Children's Corner* (piano, 1908); *The Little Nigar* (piano, 1909).

[10] Igor Stravinsky, *L'Histoire du soldat* (to be read, played, and danced, 1918); *Ragtime* (11 instruments, 1918); Piano Rag Music (1919).

serious unemployment reaching into the Depression. The constant demand for live music was the context of Mayerl's childhood and from his earliest teens, like many pianists of his generation including Shostakovitch, he grew up accompanying silent films. This type of work demanded a sure-fire technique of rapid response to events on the screen and provided contact with an audience. It was an educational experience at least as important as anything Mayerl gained in the Junior Department at Trinity College of Music, London, from 1911 to 1915.

Technology again shaped Mayerl's destiny when he became famous as the pianist with the leading British dance band to adopt the American idiom. This was the Savoy Havana which was so prominently involved in some of the first radio broadcasts from the Savoy Hotel, London, in 1923. The British Broadcasting Company (later Corporation) was set up in 1922 and gradually developed as a centralized focus for national news and culture with enormous influence. Such widespread radio exposure, especially through his solo spots, turned Mayerl into a phenomenon virtually overnight and enabled him to take off only three years later into several simultaneous careers. He composed; he toured on the Music Halls as an entertainer; he continued broadcasting; and, having helped to make his kind of syncopated pianism so fashionable, he launched the Billy Mayerl School of Music in London with branches all over the world. He was obsessed with passing on what he had learnt, which he regarded as a teachable skill. In a pioneering approach the School, anticipating later distance-learning techniques, used to send out fragile 78 records as instructional material. Mayerl was astute enough to harness all these opportunities to promote his own music.[11] In order to keep up with the demand he composed over 300 piano pieces and made over 100 song transcriptions. At the same time he was working regularly in the musical theatre, in London's West End and on tour, and supervising the School and its staff.

The prototype of the piano rag was Scott Joplin's *The Maple Leaf Rag* (1899), although the commercial song-hit was Irving Berlin's *Alexander's Ragtime Band* (1911). The next keyboard landmark in this genre was Zez Confrey's *Kitten on the Keys* (1920), sometimes described—with hindsight—as a novelty rag. Mayerl's *The Jazz Master*, although apparently sketched out much earlier, appeared in 1925 and seemed utterly contemporary, although his piano novelties remained at a consistently high artistic level throughout his career, even into his declining post-war years. He could reasonably be claimed as the Scott Joplin of novelty piano, but that description would not cover his range. If, within classical ragtime, Joplin is the Schubert, James Scott the Liszt, and Joseph Lamb the Chopin, then Mayerl contains all these

---

[11] B. Mayerl, 'High Notes in my Life of Rhythm', *Tit-bits*, 26 June 1937, 5–6.

qualities.[12] And he is equally personal in lyrical, unsyncopated styles which link him via Grieg and Delius to the English tradition of Cyril Scott, Frank Bridge, and especially John Ireland.

This book is designed to explore Mayerl and his music and the context from which it sprang. It naturally includes some discussion of the musical techniques he used to create his distinctive idiom and there are some further details in the notes to each chapter, but if this overwhelms the general reader these passages can easily be skipped. The music is what matters, and some of his finest recordings can be heard on the accompanying CD. These have been chosen to cover the range of his piano music in his own scintillating performances, rather than his work in other media, so that Mayerl can be assessed in terms of his unique contribution. Since the early 1990s many enthusiasts, linked through membership of the Midlands Gershwin Mayerl Society and the Billy Mayerl Society, have been discovering more about Mayerl's life.[13] This process will continue and, from that point of view, I hope there will always be more to add as interest in his work reaches further afield.

At the time of writing there is still only a fraction of Mayerl's output available in print, but almost all his piano music is on CD. This is his most enduring achievement—both the solos and the transcriptions in his individual style—and his career will be traced largely through this repertoire. He was a miniaturist, with unerring command of the three-minute/one-side-of-a-78-record form derived historically from the march and the piano rag. The orchestral works, few of which he scored himself, are revealingly derivative in the middle-brow, mid-century English vein represented by the stage and film composer Richard Addinsell, who wrote the *Warsaw Concerto*.

In musical comedy Mayerl was amazingly active as composer and conductor during the 1930s, working with some of the best-known stars of the day, but his work for these shows has had no independent life. In the teeth of American competition he never wrote an enduring hit song, not even in the English manner of Ivor Novello, Noel Coward, or Vivian Ellis, although Mayerl's command of harmony and form surpasses theirs in a way which reflects his European ancestry, American influences, natural musicianship, and thorough study. And his melodic charm in countless piano pieces is abundant.

[12] P. Dickinson, 'The Achievement of Ragtime: An Introductory Study with some Implications for British Research in Popular Music', *Proceedings of the Royal Musical Association*, 105 (1978–9), 63–76. This is an early British musicological approach to the subject with reference to Mayerl in this ragtime context at the end. The original paper was cut for publication. The reference in it to Mayerl playing the Grieg Concerto at 20 at the Queen's Hall is a misprint for 12 but I have not been able to discover any newspaper reports of this concert and there are no records at Trinity College of Music.

[13] The Billy Mayerl Society. Patrons Sir Richard Rodney Bennet, Eric Parkin, Susan Tomes, and Peter Jacobs. Shellwood, St Leonards Road, Thames Ditton, Surrey KT7 0RN.

British dance bands between the wars employed their own skilled arrangers to create an individual sound and reached high standards, but Mayerl's work as a bandleader was more a way of keeping in circulation and earning a living at early and later stages in his career.[14] Even his own playing in his later years, as he fought against ill health, lacked some of the effervescent sparkle of his recordings made in the 1920s and 1930s. Perhaps this was the price he paid for going to work in his early teens and never letting up on that frenetic pace. The same could be said of George Gershwin, a strong influence on Mayerl, who also started life pounding out popular tunes hour after hour and died even younger.

It is not surprising that Mayerl was affected by being born into a poor but happy family in Edwardian London and, always needing to work long hours, was unable to continue his studies at a time when it was necessary to have a private income or rich friends to survive as a composer. His obituary in *The Times* was specific about Mayerl's need to earn money:

He began studying at the Trinity College of Music when he was 7, and at the age of 12 played Grieg's Piano Concerto in the Queen's Hall. But the retirement of his father, a professional musician, brought to an end his academic studies and he went to work as a pianist in an East End cinema orchestra at a wage of 50s [£47] a week to help support his family. Within a few years—at the age of 18—he was pianist with the Savoy Havana Band at £30 [£950] a week.[15]

None of this detracts from Mayerl's unique contribution to the piano repertoire: it makes it all the more remarkable as a human story of dedication and achievement. How fortunate we are that he had a genius for writing these sharply focused, cinematic pieces and stuck to what he could do best rather than trying something more pretentious. But it is important to realize that Mayerl's work arose from his wide musical culture, not at all what might have been expected from a pianist in entertainment. At the end of his life, when he was interviewed by Roy Plomley on the BBC Radio 4 feature called *Desert Island Discs*, his selected music included works by Ravel, Stravinsky, and Milhaud as well as by English composers Quilter and Ireland and colleagues in the British light music scene.[16]

It is ironic, in view of young Billy's quarrels with the establishment at Trinity College of Music, that his piano music is now mostly the province of classically trained pianists who struggle to meet his technical demands and, by

[14] M. Hustwitt, 'Caught in a Whirlpool of Aching Sound: The Production of Dance Music in Britain in the 1920s', *Popular Music*, 3 (1983), 7–31. This excellent paper from a sociologist offers useful statistics. See also D. B. Scott, 'Incongruity and Predictability in British Dance Band Music of the 1920s and 1930s', *Musical Quarterly*, 78/2 (1992), 290–315.

[15] Obituary, *The Times*, 28 Mar. 1959. Figures in square brackets are based on the British Retail Prices Index at July 1998.

[16] See Appendix 4 for a full list of Mayerl's selected records.

comparison with Mayerl's own unedited recordings on the CD here, usually fall short. But by the early 1990s Mayerl was coming into his own in the record catalogue—the British pianist Eric Parkin alone has made ten CDs—even though, as with classical piano rags, it is still rare for his work to appear on conventional piano recital programmes. But when it does Mayerl can both move people and bring the house down, giving audiences a rare sense of discovery— or rediscovery, as their grandparents could have told them. Listeners often respond by saying that they feel better for hearing this affirmative music. It acts as a kind of therapy sorely needed as the stresses of modern life reach unparalleled severity and we are meeting the challenges of a new millenium.

I

EARLY LIFE AND ENVIRONMENT

BILLY MAYERL's paternal family origins in the old Habsburg Empire remain obscure and apparently he hardly ever talked about his background even to his friends. His younger brother, Fred, was not able to throw much light on such matters.[1] The only biographical sources are thus Mayerl's own series of articles in *Tit-bits* in 1937; hints that can be picked up from the pages of the *Billy Mayerl Club Magazine* from 1934 to August 1939; professional directories; the BBC archives; and information from people who knew him. But, as we shall see, the facts—as far as they can be ascertained—are rarely consistent. Fred Mayerl has even cast doubts on the reliability of his brother's *Tit-bits* articles. He told me he could not remember Billy writing articles and suspected a ghost-writer since they were not in his style. He thought that some parts of the articles were based on what had happened but that other parts were exaggerated to make a readable story.[2] Fred Mayerl had evidently forgotten that his brother had previously written three articles for the *Melody Maker* in 1926/7, but these were about piano technique.

At all points the encrustations of legend have to be prised away in order to trace a credible sequence of events. An example of such problems is the unsigned article about Mayerl, with photograph, which appeared in *Musical Opinion* in 1932.[3] The magazine possibly thought it was lowering its standards in writing about a popular music pianist; perhaps, like so much journalism at the time, writers were simply sloppy; maybe Mayerl was far too busy to provide details and left the magazine's enquiries to someone at the School. Whatever the reason, there were enough errors for Mrs Mayerl to scribble on her own photocopy in her characteristic light blue ink: 'Too many mistakes for me. I could write quite a bit about them: but I have no patience for these kinds of errors.'[4] The article starts promisingly: 'When Sir Henry Walford Davies

---

[1] F. Mayerl, telephone conversation with Peter Dickinson, 10 Sept. 1996.
[2] As n. 1.   [3] *Musical Opinion* (Mar. 1932), 528.
[4] Photocopy annotated by Mrs Mayerl.

was requested by his radio pupils to broadcast the names of his favourite composers, he replied, 'Bach, Beethoven, Billy Mayerl and Arnold Schoenberg.'

Davies was Britain's Master of the King's Music, the musical equivalent of the Poet Laureate. He realized the potential of gramophone and radio and started giving his influential broadcast talks about music in 1924. Like Mayerl, he reached the masses through the medium of radio as it developed, before the serious inroads from TV. Unsurprisingly neither Schoenberg nor Mayerl rate a mention in the biography of Davies by H. C. Colles, but it is good to see an establishment figure at that point recognizing Mayerl's calibre as a composer at a time when highbrow taste in England would have had equal difficulty with both him and Schoenberg.[5] The *Billy Mayerl Club Magazine* was started in January 1934 and operated as a society for syncopating pianists with Mayerl as central figure. As editor, he must have sent Walford Davies a copy since he replied: 'Thankyou for your kind letter and the little publication. I wish it a long life and a healthy life.'[6] The *Musical Opinion* article goes on with a wrong date of birth, making Mayerl ten years older; provides wrong information about his father being his only teacher; cites the Prince's Theatre as one of his silent-film jobs and states that he 'went the round of London cinemas always advancing in position', which Mrs Mayerl queries.

Some parts of the article show insight and there is a reference to the Grieg Concerto performance at London's most important concert venue of the period, the Queen's Hall, which it has not been possible to verify: 'Mayerl has never been the man to wait for opportunities: he makes them. In the year that he won the scholarship at Trinity College, he was chosen to play Grieg's Piano Concerto at a students' concert at Queen's Hall . . .'

His entry into the Junior Department of Trinity College of Music, London, was in 1911, when he was 9, and this seems more likely than other versions of the story, including one from Mayerl himself, citing the Grieg performance at the age of 6½.[7] *Musical Opinion* praised Mayerl for sometimes writing 'very seriously' and cites *Pastoral Sketches*; *Sennen Cove*; *The Legends of King Arthur*; *Pastorale Exotique*; with *Three Japanese Pictures* as a particular favourite of the composer's. It was assumed that syncopated music could not be serious. The article also contains pre-echoes of what Mayerl, in the last year of his life, told Roy Plomley on the famous BBC radio interview series called *Desert Island Discs*, when he asked him if it was a foregone conclusion that he would be a musician: 'Yes, but not a musician of the sort I turned out to be. I was supposed to be a sort of highbrow wallah.'[8]

5 H. C. Colles, *Walford Davies: A Biography* (OUP, London, 1942).

6 'From Sir Walford Davies', *Billy Mayerl Club Magazine* (hereafter *BMCM*), 1/2 (Feb. 1934), 5.

7 B. Mayerl, 'High Notes in my Life of Rhythm', *Tit-bits*, 19 June 1937, 3–4.

8 Interview with Roy Plomley on *Desert Island Discs*, BBC Home Service, 21 Apr. 1958.

Like Sullivan, who wanted his sacred music to be as popular as his comic operas, Mayerl hankered after the straight, unsyncopated idiom once novelty piano had propelled him to fame. In 1935 he recorded some classical pieces on what was billed as 'the world's largest piano', a special model of Challen: these were Rachmaninov's Prelude in C sharp minor and three Preludes by Chopin. His BBC broadcasts in 1946 included a series of six fifteen-minute recitals called *Keyboard Cavalcade*. Predictably the piece with which he was so persistently identified, *Marigold*, was the signature tune for the series, but otherwise one programme was all Grieg and another all Debussy. In the previous year he played two pieces by Cyril Scott and one by John Ireland.[9] But in 1932 *Musical Opinion* found this kind of thing distinctly odd and ends the article:

The strange case of Billy Mayerl is that he is a musician who wandered into jazz and made the most of it, commercially and artistically. We found him talking with complete and critical understanding of the works of Holst, Ireland and Bax, and in explanation played several of their pieces from memory.

Mayerl's friend, C. Corti Woodcock, noted the enormous impression that *Mars* from Holst's *The Planets* made on Mayerl and remembered an occasion—again with no details—when he astonished a group of highbrow critics by playing right through a serious piece they were discussing and which they expected him not to know at all.[10] At the turn of the century we no longer find this strange—fortunately there is some progress—and now Billy Mayerl, in middle age, would have been an obvious candidate for a first British University Chair in Popular Music. Mrs Mayerl sensed some of this: 'He was a remarkable man. He was born too early. Is that the right thing to say? He should have been born much later, because he would have been more appreciated now.'[11]

Perhaps Mrs Mayerl was reflecting their feelings from the post-war years, since she never felt her husband's music was neglected and his Performing Right Society earnings confirm this (see Appendix 3). Even in 1981 she said: 'every day I'm more and more amazed at the way he is being remembered.' But, as we shall see, in every other way Mayerl was born at exactly the right moment to take the fullest advantage of every opportunity that came his way. But, when he had time to think, he still hankered after something else. Like the influential jazz musicians J. P. Johnson and Duke Ellington, who also produced concert works divorced from the dance-floor, he wanted to be taken more seriously. Regularly, in the columns of the *BMCM*, Mayerl urged his students to explore composers outside the dance-music scene—Coates, Delius, Grieg, MacDowell, Bax, Mendelssohn. He regarded Grieg as 'one of the

---

[9] Mayerl's programmes included Scott's *Lotus Land* on 3 Dec. 1945; Ireland's *The Darkened Valley* on 26 Dec. 1945; and Falla's *Ritual Fire Dance* and Scott's *Pierrot Triste* on 31 Dec. 1945.
[10] C. C. Woodcock, 'In the Lions' Den', *BMCM*, 1/7 (July 1934), 11–13.
[11] J. Mayerl, interview with Peter Dickinson, 11 Aug. 1981.

finest composers of piano music. He understood the instrument so well, and even the moderate players can get heaps of pleasure from his music.'[12]

Mayerl practised what he preached, according to his secretary, Vesta Harrison (Mrs Vicky Matkin): 'When BM had a spare half-hour he would shut himself up in his office and just play, but not his usual syncopated style. One of his favourite composers was Delius and he had a small bust of him on his desk.'[13]

This may seem surprising since Delius wrote so little for the piano, but he had an uncanny way of creating his own atmosphere, which Mayerl must have recognized. He managed to do this himself. Fred Mayerl confirmed his brother's love of Delius when he went to see him at home in 1937 in order to try to interview him for the *BMCM*:

A glance through the collection of records made it very apparent that Billy was a lover of Delius, and quite an hour was enjoyably spent listening to the works of this British composer, with an occasional Stravinsky thrown in to give the recital a modern touch! I regret to say that *Petroushka* was somewhat overshadowed by a somewhat heated discussion on its merits.[14]

This interview took place at Marigold Lodge in fashionable Hampstead, south-west of Hampstead Heath. Several houses were given this name, but at this time it would have been 18 West Heath Close, which Fred visited, and it is still an affluent neighbourhood:

Marigold Lodge reposes in the heart of Hampstead and overlooks the Heath. The neatly clipped privet hedges in the front garden at once pleased the eye and confirmed Billy's passion for order and design. The crazy paving sparkled in the afternoon sun and the marigolds that lined the path, although not yet in bloom, promise great things in the near future. Here was an atmosphere of dignity and peace, disturbed only by the clanking of an unwilling lawn mower in the nether regions.[15]

With gardening, listening to music—Mayerl even played the oboe that day—taking the Scottie onto the Heath, discussing where the new aquarium would go, and playing cards, Fred never got his interview. So an opportunity to document the Mayerl story was lost. More can be deduced from the pages of the *BMCM*. Mayerl's own reviews show that he admired the American composers Morton Gould and Charles T. Griffes, especially his *White Peacock* (1915).[16] And in 1935 he found real innovation in the novelty piano pieces by the British-born but often American-based composer, Reginald Foresythe. He also strongly defended Foresythe, son of a British barrister and a West Indian

---

[12] 'Summertime Practice', *BMCM*, 4/42 (June 1937), 24.

[13] V. Matkin (Harrison), interview with Peter Dickinson, 11 May 1992.

[14] F. Mayerl, 'I Try to Interview my Brother', *BMCM*, 5/53 (May 1938), 3–6.

[15] Ibid.

[16] B. Mayerl, 'New Piano Music', *BMCM*, 6/65 (May 1939), 25, and *BMCM*, 6/67 (July 1939), 16–17.

mother, against racial discrimination in a *Melody Maker* review.[17] But Mayerl was being generous since Foresythe's pieces are never as inventive as his own.

How did it all start? Where did such an unusual talent as Mayerl's spring from? Information is tantalizingly limited, but the consequential British side of the story opened on 26 August 1899. This was when Joseph Mayerl (aged 28) and Elise Umbach (designated simply as a minor, actually aged 18), Billy's parents, were married 'according to the rites and ceremonies of the Church of England' at St. Pancras Parish Church, in the County of London. The residence of both parties was given as 47 Tottenham Court Road, six doors away from where Billy would be born. The bridegroom's father was cited as Anton Mayerl, which is all we know about him, and the bride's as Adam August Umbach—both described as musicians. Both Billy Mayerl's parents came to this country in their youth at a time when full lists of immigrants were not kept and they never became British citizens. This is confirmed by Mayerl's nephew, Julian Norris, who remember that they could not vote.[18]

The Umbach ancestry is less obscure than the Mayerl side of the family. The imposingly named Adam August Umbach was born in Grossenwitter (Hessen-Nassau) on 15 October 1852. His father, Willem Umbach, was a linen weaver and his mother was Anna Catherina Henkes. On 2 March 1882 he married Johanna Francisca Theodora Stockman, who was born in Amsterdam on 4 October 1861. Adam August Umbach served as a musician in the Seventh Infantry Regiment of the Dutch army. He enlisted voluntarily in 1880: six years later he obtained his first stripe and he was taken on for a further period at double his previous salary. But he decided to leave in 1887 with a certificate of good conduct. Billy's mother, Elise, had been born on 5 January 1881 at 'S-Hertogenbosch and it was on 22 July 1896 that the whole family left for England. Adam August Umbach's sister was married to Garriet Jan Ekkel, a Prussian baker, and their family had moved to England the year before.

Fortunately Billy's maternal grandfather, who died in December 1924, lived just long enough to witness his grandson's Savoy successes. Billy's father, Joseph, died in 1937 and his mother in the following year. They were both buried in common graves at Hammersmith New (now Mortlake) Cemetery as Roman Catholics.[19]

---

[17] B. Mayerl, 'The Very New Music of Reginald Foresythe', *BMCM*, 2/18 (June 1935), 3–7.

[18] J. Norris, in conversation with Peter Dickinson at Snape Maltings, 23 Aug. 1995.

[19] Mayerl's maternal grandfather, Adam August Umbach, was taken ill in Glasgow and died at the Western Infirmary there on 22 December 1924. He was intestate and left £162.1s. 8d. (£5,370). The Umbachs had been living at 85 Shaftesbury Road (now Ravenscroft Road), Hammersmith, since 1913 and she was still living there in 1930. Joseph Mayerl, Billy's father, died at West London Hospital on 21 November 1937 at the age of 66, leaving £290. 17s. 7d. [£10,870] and his mother, Elise, died at 54 Richmond Gardens, Hammersmith, on 12 February 1938 at the age of 57, leaving £302. 17s. 7d. [£11,190].

The years 1880–1905 were a peak period for immigration to London, largely from Eastern and Central Europe.[20] But nothing has been traced about the origins of Joseph Mayerl or his father Anton. At the time of writing most of the people with the name of Mayerl are living in Austria and Germany, but there are some in the USA. One of Hitler's pretexts for invading Czechoslovakia in 1938 was the presence there of Sudeten Germans who, he claimed, really belonged to the Reich. After the Second World War these Sudetendeutsche were expelled by the Czechs, including some Mayerls. It looks as if by then they were regarded as Germans and this may explain why Mayerls are hard to find in the Czech Republic. Since Billy Mayerl was the third generation of Mayerls known to be have been professional musicians, his earlier ancestry might show more. But no Mayerls have been found registered or graduating from conservatoires, universities, or technical colleges in Prague.

Before turning to evidence provided by Mayerl's living relations—he and Jill had no children—it may be worth noting the facts about his parents' three children. On 20 December 1900, Johanna Elisa, named after her maternal grandmother, was born at 15 Harrington St., in the sub-district of Regents Park, St Pancras, London, and the birth was registered on 30 January 1901. This was still the family's address in the national census conducted in March of that year, where Joseph Mayerl's place of birth is simply given as Austria, a designation which then signified the Habsburg Empire. The father's occupation for all three births was given as 'musician (violinist)'. Billy himself, as William Joseph, was born on 31 May 1902 at 53 Tottenham Court Road, in the sub-district of Tottenham Court Road, St Pancras, London, and the birth was registered on 12 July 1902. In the 1891 census there were no Mayerls at these addresses. Apart from an Italian singing teacher, there were no musicians in the street. No. 53 was occupied by a hatter and his family and No. 47 was a typical example of the kind of multi-occupancy of those days. Its eight rooms housed a baker's assistant with his wife and sister-in-law, all from Germany, as well as a police constable and a wood carver, both with their wives. The area housed servants and workers in various crafts and trades. These early numbers of Tottenham Court Road no longer exist but it would have been a ten-minute walk away from the theatre district in London's West End, where Mayerl's father must have worked. By the time Billy's younger

---

[20] I am indebted to Jerome Farrell, at the time Archivist of the London Borough of Fulham and Hammersmith, for assistance. I have also had help in carrying out various searches in the Czech Republic. These have established that there was no central register of births in the old Czechoslovakia; that no Joseph Mayerl (or Maierl) registered or graduated from the Czech or the German branches of the Charles-Ferdinand University; he was not listed in the register of Conservatoire students published for the years 1811–1911; and he was not a student at the Czech or German High Schools of Technical Studies.

brother was born the Mayerls had moved west to Hammersmith. He was named Frederick August after his maternal grandfather and was born in the Umbach's house on 2 October 1910. This was 26 Beauclere Road, Hammersmith (the Umbachs' address from 1910 to 1912) and the birth was registered on 12 November 1910. On 1 January 1911 Fred was baptized as a Roman Catholic at Holy Trinity Church in the Parish of Brook Green.[21]

I am indebted to Fred Mayerl and his wife Hilda for helpful telephone conversations on several occasions, particularly since Mr Mayerl said he objected to the current vogue for intrusive biography and felt that his—and therefore Billy's—family history was not relevant to any discussion of his music. All the same, he volunteered that they were 'quite a normal family—anything to make it interesting in Sunday paper style would have to be fabricated'.[22] Fred Mayerl told me that he understood that his father came from Prague, his mother from Amsterdam, and that they met in this country. He confirmed that his father was a violinist, who did cinema work before talkies and played at the Trocadero and in London stage orchestras. But he was 'not a soloist and not in the same league as Billy'. Joseph Mayerl had three or four brothers and Fred once saw a picture of a band with all of them in it. He remembered that his father also played in Billy's orchestras, including that for the highly successful *Over She Goes* and died from a heart attack the following year when he was going to Fred Mayerl's house to hear the recording.[23] Fred's wife, Hilda, remembers Billy's father as a 'retiring man who hardly spoke and didn't even like his wife talking to the neighbours!'[24]

Fred Mayerl remembered his grandfather, Adam August Umbach, a clarinettist in bands, as 'a man with a moustache, like most men in those days'. He used to bring foreign musicians to the house, including friends in the Concertgebouw Orchestra from Holland: to him jazz was a dirty word! Mayerl's mother, Elise, was apparently not musical, but she had to deal with plenty of musicians.[25] In those days there was no radio and Fred said that he brought the first wind-up gramophone into the house. Family recreations consisted of playing cards or chatting. Fred played the saxophone in a semi-professional way but gave up. For a time he helped at the Billy Mayerl School, conducted some interviews for the magazine, and was described as a journalist on his marriage certificate, but he pursued a career developing X-ray prototypes.[26] Billy told him he 'would be good if he practised'. The relationship between the two men was not close but, as Fred put it, charac-

---

[21] Information from the Catholic Media Office.

[22] F. Mayerl, telephone conversations with Peter Dickinson, 9 May 1992, 18 Sept. 1995.

[23] Saville Theatre, 23 Sept. 1936: recording Saville Theatre Orchestra/Mayerl, 5 Nov. 1936. See Discography.

[24] H. Mayerl, telephone conversation with Peter Dickinson, 28 Sept. 1994.

[25] As n. 22.

[26] F. Mayerl, 'I Try to Interview my Brother', *BMCM*, 4/53 (May 1938), 3–6.

teristic of an older and younger brother. The family were catholics and Elise was devout.

Fred emphasized that he was eight years younger than Billy, who was very seldom at home once he started at the Savoy. Fred remembered Billy as a good swimmer. But he had 'this sort of urge all the time to work'. They had a piano with candlesticks on either side which Billy 'used to bash for six to eight hours at a time'. He would be told: 'Get off that piano—your dinner's ready!' Fred emphasized that, though they were poor in material terms, they had a happy childhood. These family details are supplemented with those provided by Julian M. Norris, son of Billy's older sister, Johanna Elise, who died on 2 January 1968.[27] He remembers what his father told him:

If my memory serves me rightly, he spoke of my maternal grandfather [Joseph Mayerl] having played the violin in cinemas during the days of the silent film and losing work when the talkies came. Also he said that he suffered some harassment during the First World War because he was from the Austro-Hungarian Empire. My mother said her father was a refugee from Bohemia. However, I once looked in the Prague telephone directory and found no Mayerls.

Mr Norris has kindly allowed the photographs of his mother and grandmother to be reproduced (Plates 1 and 2) and has said about Billy's mother, Elise: 'According to my mother she was comely. Not only does the photograph confirm my mother's opinion but it also shows the resemblance of Billy to his mother. My wife and I both see the likeness of her nose and chin to Billy's nose and chin as he appears in the photograph on the cover of The King of Syncopation LP.'[28]

Mr Norris knew that his maternal grandmother came from Holland, but he had no idea where, although he remembered certain connections: 'Before the Second World War my mother occasionally visited 'S-Hertogenbosch. My mother also told me that her mother modelled for statuary at a railway station in the Netherlands.' He confirmed that Mayerl's sister, Johanna, did not keep in touch with either of her brothers after the war and that she felt that within the family Billy had been 'favoured at her expense'. This sibling rivalry still existed in the 1930s: one of Mayerl's secretaries remembered that his sister worked at Whipsnade Zoo and that he used to say it was 'the right place for

[27] C. Norris, letters to Peter Dickinson, 4 Dec. 1994 and 6 Feb. 1995.
[28] *The King of Syncopation: Billy Mayerl*, WRC/EMI SH.189 (1973), with notes by Irene Ashton, versatile pianist, dancer, actress, and editor who was a member of Mayerl's staff at the School. When this LP based on transfers from 78s came out, Irene Ashton generously wrote an extended letter in praise of Mayerl and gave copies to the principals of the Royal Academy of Music and the Royal College of Music—see *Billy Mayerl Circle Newsletters*, 1/5 (Spring 1975), 4–5; and 2/9 (Spring 1976), 2–4—and received courteous replies. She also tried to get Mayerl set for the Associated Board—obviously without much success.

her!' Further information about Mayerl's childhood comes from what he wrote himself and what his widow remembered.

Mrs Mayerl told me that Mayerl's grandfather, Umbach, was playing with a circus when he died suddenly in Glasgow and that 'his grandfather more or less brought him up to make him practise and do all those things'. She said that Elise Mayerl was 'a very lovely lady' but Billy 'was never much of a home person—not in those days'. When Jill (Gilda, Gil, and later mostly Jill) Mayerl first met Billy 'he was working very hard and his life was so different to theirs. They were quite poor people, as I was too, and he was leading an entirely different life at the Savoy . . . He mixed with an entirely different type of people and I think he was absorbing that life and his home-life didn't mean anything at all.'[29]

Mayerl himself has described his musical beginnings and his connection with Trinity College of Music:

I was what might be called a violinist's throw-out. My father, a teacher of the violin, had tried his best to make me a violinist. But he had failed at the very start and so he passed me on in despair to Trinity. He had taught me the notes before sending me there, and he had paid for one term's tuition. I won the rest in a series of scholarships which carried me through the College until I was fifteen years old, when I was invited to continue with a view to becoming a professor there. But I decided to make my way in music outside the walls of Trinity College.

I loved the piano. When I struggled with the fiddle—it was thrust into my hands when I was little more than four years of age—I could not connect brain and instrument. But the piano was as easy as the fiddle had been difficult.[30]

Mayerl's Trinity College career is now somewhat obscure. The College's printed lists of students show that he was registered in the academic years from 1911, when he was 9, until 1915, but there is no other information. In 1976 Mrs Mayerl wrote: 'Some years ago when I first met Mr. Cork [Cyril Cork, then Vice-Principal], he was kind enough to show me Billy's reports at the College. He must have been really clever even when he was young.'[31] These reports have not survived. Mrs Mayerl confirmed then that all Mayerl's certificates were lost when the Billy Mayerl School's records were bombed and mentioned that 'it was only quite recently that his younger brother Fred told me that he won a scholarship to his day school, was a fine swimmer and high diver, and had won prizes for running'.

Fred Mayerl thought that Billy went to the Council School at Flora Gardens in Hammersmith and then to West Kensington Central School. He

[29] J. Mayerl, interview with Peter Dickinson, 11 Aug. 1981.
[30] B. Mayerl, 'High Notes in my Life of Rhythm', *Tit-bits*, 19 June 1937, 3–14.
[31] J. Mayerl, 'The Billy Mayerl Bursary', *Billy Mayerl Circle Newsletter*, 2/11 (Autumn 1976), 6–8.

remembered him in short trousers and Eton collar.[32] Trinity College scholarships were usually announced in the *Musical Times*. The 1910 listing includes
a contemporary of Mayerl's later to become famous as a conductor. In 1932,
Mayerl said he remembered one Giovanni Barbirolli (violoncello) who was
two and a half years older than he was.[33] Barbirolli was listed again in 1911 as
Giovanni Batista Barbirolli—but no Billy Mayerl.

Trinity College was offically incorporated in 1875 and soon began to sat-
isfy the widespread demand for diplomas as a qualification for a teaching career. In 1911 the Chairman of the Board and King Edward Professor at
London University was Sir Frederick Bridge, CVO, MA, Mus.D. He was a
typical British establishment figure who had risen via the cathedral route in
spite of his reputation as a poor organist and teacher.[34] The Director of
Studies and 'School of Piano Technique' was G. E. Bambridge, FTCL,
FRAM, and the Director of Examinations was C. W. Pearce, Mus.D,
FTCL.[35] These officials presided over a rigidly conservative environment
that must have been socially as well as musically unsympathetic for young
Mayerl. The only consolation might have been that Albert Ketelby, the composer of extremely popular pieces such as *In a Monastery Garden*, was on the
piano staff.

Mayerl's own account of the climax of his Trinity career (told to Roy
Plomley on *Desert Island Discs*) came when he was a celebrity so there is naturally some exaggeration:

Syncopated jazz was born in Trinity College of Music, London, in 1915! If that is a
shock to our highbrows, then I am sorry. But there it is, and it can't be helped now!
When Dr. Pearce, the harmony teacher at that time, and the Principal of the College
heard the effort, they gave it the bird. They said it was a monstrosity that disgraced the
College, and that if I did anything like it again I would be thrown out, neck and
crop. . . . You see, at College, all I had to study was Bach, Beethoven and Mozart,
Haydn; oh, and that nasty gentleman named Clementi; but my interests in music were
very much wider than that. I loved ragtime, and I also loved the moderns. I was always
in trouble with my professor with the moderns; scores like Stravinsky, you know, I used

---

[32] F. Mayerl, telephone conversation with Peter Dickinson, 10 Sept. 1996. Records for these
schools have not survived.

[33] 'Billy Mayerl: Pianist', *Musical Opinion* (Mar. 1932), 528. See also S. Holloway, *Wiv a little
bit o' Luck* (Leslie Frewin, London, 1967), 143, where he claims that Barbirolli shared the first
half of the programme with him when he did a cello act with the Co-Optimists for a broadcast in
1925.

[34] S. Sadie (ed.), *New Grove Dictionary of Music and Musicians* (Macmillan, London, 1980).

[35] H. Rutland, *Trinity College of Music: The First Hundred Years* (Trinity College of Music,
London, 1972), 26. Dr Charles W. Pearce, whose connection with the College began in the
1880s, was made a member of the Board when he was only 26: in fact he was the youngest member. He wrote textbooks such as *Students' Counterpoint*, which went through at least eleven editions.

to sort of study—he used to say: 'Stravinsky! Dreadful music! Dreadful noises! Out-of-tune flute players!'[36]

No wonder Mayerl told his brother: 'I don't like their music and they don't like mine!'[37] All the same his scores show that he must have received an excellent grounding in academic harmony from Pearce and, according to Fred Mayerl, their father was well enough trained to help if needed. In 1952 Mayerl said about his studies at College: 'I'd spent years there studying all branches of music—theory, harmony, counterpoint and so on.'[38]

In 1981 Mrs Mayerl, who had by then generously provided some scholarship funds for the College and would later give more in her will, told me:

. . . they won't say the word at Trinity now but he was more-or-less expelled. They didn't want him any more because instead of keeping to the classical side of music he would play syncopation, which was just coming into England. So they thought 'this boy's not going to be much good—it's classical music we want' . . . So Billy left . . . and started playing gigs and he used to go all over England playing night after night.[39]

That was during the First World War, but the earliest public recognition of Mayerl's gifts was on the wall of his office at the Billy Mayerl School of Music—a 'Certificate of Merit awarded to Master W. Mayerl of Shepherds Bush for excellence in Class Four for Pianoforte Playing, British Music Exhibition, Olympia, London W, September 6th to 20th, 1913'. The adjudicator was H. A. Harding.[40]

Mayerl's piano teacher was Maude Agnes Winter, LTCL, who was in her eightieth year when she attended his funeral at Golders Green Crematorium on 31 March 1959.[41] In 1935 she visited her old pupil, now President of the Billy Mayerl School of Music, in his imposing office where Irene Ashton reported on the encounter for the *BMCM*. Although obviously somewhat fictionalized, this account is a convincing snapshot of Billy as a child. As a student in the Junior Department, he studied with Miss Winter from 1911 to 1915, had half-hour lessons twice a week at the College, and extra ones when he had a concert.

[36] B. Mayerl, interview with Roy Plomley on *Desert Island Discs*, BBC Home Service, 21 Apr. 1958. Partial tape in BBC Gramophone Library: texts as broadcast, including some deletions, at BBC Sound Archives in Caversham.

[37] F. Mayerl, telephone conversation with Peter Dickinson, 22 Mar. 1991.

[38] B. Mayerl, interview with Jean Metcalfe on *Woman's Hour*, BBC Light Programme, 27 Aug. 1952.

[39] J. Mayerl, interview with Peter Dickinson.

[40] Anon., 'They laughed when he sat down to play', *BMCM*, 1/2 (Feb. 1934), 9.

[41] Maude Agnes Winter was born on 27 January 1880 at 14 Devonshire St., Islington, daughter of Henry Richard Winter, a furrier, and Elizabeth Winter, formerly Thomas. She studied at Trinity College herself with Edmund H. Turpin, who became Warden in 1892, and G. E. Bambridge and was chorus mistress of the Opera Class until 1931. In addition to her work as a pianist she played the cello in symphony orchestras.

In 1911 she remembered him as 'a small, nine-year-old, round-faced, brown-eyed boy, dressed in a blue sailor suit'. Prophetically she urged him not to 'run away with the tempo' or he would find himself 'like a runaway car in a ditch'. He said he had been playing soldiers in a ditch, which gave him a dirty thumbnail; he liked gardening; and he had got up during the night to compose a tune. Miss Winter had to turn his attention back to the Mozart they were supposed to be studying.

In 1912 she remembered him playing a piece by Handel in public again at a 'terrific tempo': equally prophetically, the breakdown she expected never came. Miss Winter explained: 'He always had a flair for taking all his pieces and scales at a prodigious speed for a child. His parents told me—and I found out gradually—that he hated the slow routine of practising. He had an exceptionally quick-thinking brain and wanted to reach the top of the ladder, missing out the intervening rungs.'[42]

At this 1935 meeting Mayerl remembered his mother giving him tuppence (two old English pennies) for the long bus ride from Shepherds Bush to Canonbury, when he went to Miss Winter's house, and how he had to be bribed with sweets to practise. But in December 1914 Billy duly passed in Pianoforte Playing at Senior Division Honours at the Local Examination held at the London Centre. It was in the next year that establishment disapproval at Trinity catapulted him into the real world which was so clearly his *métier*. All these indicators show Mayerl as a natural musician, responding instinctively to American popular music. He was a compulsive showman, impatient to harness his skill to all available opportunities, but the Trinity training had an important role. Eric Parkin, one of the finest Mayerl pianists and a product of Trinity College himself, thought that Winter's teaching would consist of 'scales and arpeggios; the melodious studies of Cramer, Bellini and Czerny (later Mayerl mentioned Clementi); Grieg, Chopin, Schumann; and very possibly English things—Cyril Scott—and Chaminade'. Parkin said this was very similar to his own teaching at Trinity College during the Second World War.[43]

The period from Mayerl's leaving Trinity in 1915 to joining the Savoy Havana is shadowy. He told Roy Plomley that his first professional engagement was 'at a cinema in Shepherds Bush', playing every night from six to eleven.[44] In the first of his own series of articles for *Tit-bits* he says that at the age of 13, whilst still studying at Trinity, he went to the manager of his local

[42] I. Ashton, 'Twenty Years after: the President meets "Teacher" ', *BMCM*, 2/24 (Dec. 1935), 3–5 and 10. This informative article is illustrated with an excellent photograph of 'Master William Mayerl at the age of 11' in stiff white collar, bow tie and with sparkling eyes. There is also a picture of Maude Agnes Winter who told Irene Ashton he was 'one of the best pupils I ever had'.   [43] E. Parkin, letter to Peter Dickinson, 17 Aug. 1998.

[44] B. Mayerl, interview with Roy Plomley.

cinema and got the job where he was billed as the Wonder Boy Pianist.[45] This would have been in Shepherds Bush since Mayerl's parents and maternal grandparents both lived there from before the First World War until their deaths. After this Mayerl had a series of engagements at 'cinemas in the East-end and West-end of London, mostly East-end', and played for private parties.[46] He was usually required to go into the house via the servants' entrance, but there were exceptions which he particularly valued. And, as will be related later, he met Jill when they were both pianists at the Imperial Cinema, Clapham.

Mayerl's experience in cinemas as a teenager seems absolutely crucial to his whole musical make-up. Around 1916 he was paid 7s. 6d. [£15] a week and played from 6.00 p.m. to 11.00 p.m. including Sundays. He described the routines:

Most of the films in those days were about cowboys and Indians or about the American Civil War and I had a lovely bit of hurry music that fitted all films of that type—the quick bits of Beethoven's Fifth Symphony. Then I used to play 'Hearts and Flowers' whenever there was a passionate love scene! And when I was in doubt there was always the Mayerl music! After all—that was my reason for being there![47]

In silent films the figures jumped around and switched rapidly from one action to another. Music was called upon to smooth over these unreal actions, so Mayerl developed a technique of rapid response and it gave him an approach which his faster music never seems to have lost. He enjoyed it: 'You see, I could play what I liked. It didn't matter if it fitted the picture or not, I just improvised and experimented. In fact I got a lot of useful ideas which I used later in my compositions.'[48]

In 1933 Mayerl remembered one situation where he was not a success:

High on the hill (at Clapham Junction) there stands a large cinema, and it was in 1917 that an advertisement appeared in a professional paper to the effect that an 'organist, young, good musician, used to the handling of a Compton, straight and jazz' was invited to apply for the position of solo organist. This small lad, with none of the qualifications contained in the advertisement, climbed up the hill in response to the enquiry, and after recovering from the amazement that an organ had pedals, proceeded to give an audition on the full organ rendered with a natural tremolo effect caused by shaky hands! What success! £2 [£66] a week, the privilege of calling the manager by his Christian name, and the honour of reading the notice over the box office that 'Billy Mayerl, the celebrated organist, has been engaged at colossal expense' to entertain the people of Clapham Junction.

But it did not last long—only three weeks. I should never have attempted to use the

45 B. Mayerl, 'High Notes in my Life of Rhythm', *Tit-bits*, 19 June 1937, 3–4.
46 Ibid.   47 B. Mayerl, interview with Jean Metcalfe.
48 As n. 44.

pedals, certainly not until I had been there another week; you see, the day I left to crawl down that long hill, the manager went away on his holidays![49]

Mayerl told Roy Plomley that he 'messed about in dance bands', but the only surviving reference seems to be to his time with the Dutch violinist David de Groot, who led a high-class restaurant string orchestra at the Piccadilly Hotel in London from 1915–29. Mayerl told Maud Agnes Winter and Irene Ashton in 1935: 'Nobody would buy me for much in those days . . . de Groot paid me only £4 [£93 based on 1920] a week and thought I was well paid . . . I didn't . . . and solo piano work of eight hours at a stretch in picture houses was enough to break your heart and hands.'[50] But in 1918 a 17-year-old girl was paid only £1.50 [£49] a week for playing at a London suburban cinema from 4.30 to 10.30 p.m. on weekdays and 6.00 to 10.30 p.m. on Sundays—twice what Mayerl got two years before but much less than De Groot paid him. [51]

Mayerl had other problems: 'I think I may claim to have had the severest test in accompanying some years back, when I was de Groot's accompanist at the Piccadilly Hotel. If ever there was an erratic performer, it was David de Groot. He played as the mood took him.'[52] This must have been hard on Mayerl, who had such a strong sense of regular pulse. De Groot, who played a Stradivarius and had a son at an English private school, might have been a Dutch connection of the Umbachs. The following indicates his standing in 1925:

Another famous orchestra is that of De Groot's which plays in the Grill Room of the Piccadilly Hotel. De Groot, a Dutchman by birth, but naturalised as an Englishman, was one of the pioneers of restaurant music in this country, for he has been at the Piccadilly for over sixteen years, previous to which he studied in Paris, after leaving his native country. He is not at all like the traditional musician in appearance, being remarkably well-dressed and imposing, though with long, delicate hands that quickly betray his profession. He has one inveterate hatred—Jazz, a type of music which he consistently refuses to play. This is the one thing that his family in their delightful flat near Baker Street, for De Groot is married and the proud father of three children, cannot understand about him.[53]

Mayerl must have found this prejudice against American idioms confusing since it came from all sides—his father, Trinity College, and now from his employer. But it was his dexterity in self-taught syncopated piano styles that was soon to lift

---

[49] B. Mayerl, 'Syncopation and the Cinema Organ', *Cinema Organ Herald* (June–July 1933), 151.

[50] I. Ashton, 'Twenty Years after: The President meets "Teacher"', *BMCM*, 2/24 (Dec. 1935), 3–5 and 10.

[51] C. Ehrlich, *The Music Profession in Britain since the Eighteenth Century* (Clarendon Press, Oxford, 1985), 196.

[52] B. Mayerl, 'This Month's Lesson', *BMCM*, 2/3 (Mar. 1935), 23.

[53] Part 38, 'Music for All', *Popular Radio Favourites* (1925), 47–8.

him out of this context. He never learnt that from Trinity College but his compositions always show a good grounding in classical harmony, with—remarkably—not a single faulty progression. Then, after two frantic inter-war decades, Mayerl came down to earth again in the more conventional world as leader of the band at the Grosvenor House Hotel, Piccadilly, during the Second World War.

2

FROM SOUTHAMPTON TO THE SAVOY

THE 1920s was a boom period for live music largely thanks to the demands of cinemas throughout the country—until talkies came in 1927. Publishers of sheet music were at the centre of commercial activity, many of them located in Denmark Street, off Shaftesbury Avenue in the West End, which became known as London's Tin Pan Alley. Mayerl's friend Leslie Osborne, started work there in 1922 and in the following year took a job at the publishing firm Wests Ltd., where the managing director was Geoffrey Clayton, Mayerl's future business partner in the Billy Mayerl School. Through Clayton, Osborne met Mayerl in 1923 and his reminiscences may be as close as we can get to a reliable account of how Mayerl came to join the Savoy Havana Band. Osborne said it was at the Polygon Hotel in Southampton where a meeting took place which profoundly affected British popular music, although other sources differ.[1] As a result the unique mood of the 1920s was captured in some of the most popular piano-playing and piano music of the period—the syncopated novelties of Billy Mayerl. The Polygon Hotel itself now has no records to confirm Mayerl's presence but it was another of those coincidences putting him in exactly the right place at the right time.[2] These provided the formula for success

[1] L. Osborne, interview with Peter Dickinson, 11 Aug. 1981 at Hove. Osborne also named the Polygon Hotel in the fifth programme of a BBC Radio 2 series, produced by Ann Mann, called *Life is Nothing without Music*. The full series, with transmission dates, was: (1) 'The Publishers' (7 Apr. 1981); (2) 'The Songs' (14 Apr. 1981); (3) 'The Songwriters' (21 Apr. 1981); (4) 'The Bandleaders (I)' (28 Apr. 1981); (5) 'The Bandleaders (II)' (5 May 1981); (6) 'The Artists' (12 May 1981). *Rhythm* (Oct. 1929) announced Billy Mayerl's New Locarno Orchestra for the Locarno Dance Hall at Streatham Hill, London. The eleven-piece band was to be led by Osborne, who is described as playing piano, sax, clarinet, and drums apart from his prowess as an arranger. The opening night cabaret consisted of Mayerl, Gwen Farrar, and Ivy Tresmand. When West's went into liquidation in 1924, Osborne joined Francis, Day & Hunter. During the war he was Progress Manager in an aircraft factory, and afterwards joined Keith Prowse.

[2] Letter to Peter Dickinson from Sue Pestridge of the Polygon Hotel, 1 Nov. 1994, followed by a telephone call on 7 Aug. 1996 in which she confirmed that the Polygon was rebuilt in 1937, although there had been a hotel of that name on the site for some 200 years. In 'England's Gershwin was discovered in Southampton', *Hampshire* (Apr. 1992), 40–1, John Edgar Mann

and—in terms of his music—it was also the success of a sharply defined formula for short snappy pieces. The story of Mayerl's meeting with Bert Ralton has been told countless times but is worth investigating. Each version is slightly different and consequently provides both illumination and confusion. This is what Mayerl himself said in a BBC live broadcast on 13 April 1937 called 'Anniversary of Dance Music at the Savoy Hotel'.[3] The compère was John Watt:

BM: The Savoy Havana Band was formed by Bert Ralton in 1920. He arrived from America with the band but without a pianist—he'd gone sick or let him down or something. I was at the time playing in a hotel in Southampton at £7 a week—£7 a week, John! [£162]

JW: Big money!

BM: It was in those days. Well, one day a rather American-looking bloke came in and he sat down near the orchestra and he seemed very attentive towards me. After a bit of time he said, 'Are you American?' I said, 'No, thank Heaven!' or words to that effect. Well he said, 'I've just arrived from America and I've formed a new band at the Savoy Hotel, London. I like your playing—you seem to be the only one with any idea of American technique in this country—would you like to come along and how much do you want?'

In those days my young brain worked quickly. It doesn't now, of course! Well I said, 'I'm getting £7 [£162] a week.' I thought to myself, 'Dare I ask for eight or nine or....Yes, I think I'll ask for nine.' Well I said, 'Mr Ralton, I'll take it at nine' and, do you know, before I'd finished the words he interrupted me and said, 'You want nineteen: well, I'll pay you twenty!' [£464] Jolly decent, I thought. Still, I was going to ask nine, so I promptly fainted and when they gave me the brandy, or whatever, I came round and found that I was the only Englishman in the band. And we were the first band to go on the Halls, long before Carroll Gibbons or these other assassins ever came near the place.

Significantly, Ralton was looking for—and admired—what he called Mayerl's American technique. The series of four articles by Mayerl for *Tit-bits* were the only time he wrote about himself at such length. On 28 June 1937, just over two months after that BBC broadcast, Mayerl appeared in print with a different slant on his meeting with Ralton:

During the war, being too young to enlist, I offered my services as an entertainer for the troops—and one experience that befell me then was responsible for my being launched on my professional career as an entertainer. I was being flown in a seaplane to play for officers and men of the then Royal Flying Corps at Calshot.

states that Mayerl was discovered by Ralton when he was playing in the South Western Hotel. He provided absolutely no evidence for this assertion, so it looks as though Osborne, who first met Mayerl very near the time, is more reliable.

3 Available as a cassette, *Savoy Memories 1937*, Neovox Sound Archive 901, serial No. 39171.

It was a most distressing trip; my suitcase containing my dress suit and my music fell overboard and sank for ever to the bottom of the Solent—and I felt so ill after the journey that I decided to rest at Southampton before returning to London.

I stayed at a well-known hotel there, and when I heard that they needed a pianist for the band I offered my services to the manager.

While I was playing, Bert Ralton, the leader of the band—which was destined to become famous as the Savoy Havana—parked himself near my piano.

'You play nippy, kid', he said during an interval.

'Glad you like it', I told him.

'Say', he added, 'I've come over here to form a band. How would you like to join me?'

'Depends', I said, on my guard. After all, he was a total stranger to me. But I was destined to prove him a fine man and a great musician. He told me about the band he was forming, explained that his pianist had fallen ill just before they left America, and offered me £20 [£460] a week and a share in all the proceeds from playing away from the Savoy Hotel . . . A fortnight after meeting Bert Ralton I was playing in the Savoy Havana Band. Bert was a great fellow, a musician to his finger-tips, and well-deserving the title of 'Kreisler of the saxophone'. It was a pleasure to work under him. We were a happy family and we helped to make broadcasting history . . . Four of the happiest years of my career were spent at the Savoy under Bert Ralton. I loved the life—the colour, the gaiety, the evidence of luxury and beauty all about me as I played.[4]

Further versions of Ralton's discovery of Mayerl appear in the *Keith Prowse Courier* as 1920 and, in 1939, the *Radio Times* put it at 1919.[5] Much later, when he was interviewed for Roy Plomley's *Desert Island Discs* on BBC Radio in 1958, Mayerl referred to landing a job at the Savoy in the Savoy Havana Band in 'about 1921'.[6] There is an unsigned biographical note in *The Jazz Master: A Collection of Famous Piano Solos by Billy Mayerl from the Golden Age of Jazz* (Sam Fox/Keith Prowse, 1972), which has been the only music in print for over

---

[4] See also B. Mayerl, 'Syncopating through Life', *Popular Music and Film Song Weekly*, 1/9 (Dec. 1937) for a condensed version of the same story: 'Although too young to enlist during the war, I did all I could in the way of entertaining the troops, and, returning from one of these missions in Calshot, I put up at an hotel in Southampton, where the manager gave me a job. By a lucky chance the late Bert Ralton, who had just landed in Southampton from New York, was in the same hotel. Apparently he required a pianist and, hearing me play, asked me to go to the Savoy with him.' And for further embroidery see. K. Harley, 'Men who made British Dance Music', *BMCM*, 5/56 (Aug. 1938), 3–4.

Rhythm (Sept. 1934) recalled the 'good old days at the Savoy' when first Van Phillips and then Mayerl and Newton emulated the Hotel's patrons by turning up for evening work in top hats. This 'added to the prestige and decorum of the band' but was 'more for a joke than anything else'.

[5] See *Keith Prowse Courier*, December 1925, which has Mayerl joining the Savoy Havana Band in 1920, and 'Billy Mayerl: Personal Facts about a Popular Broadcaster', *Radio Times*, 19 May 1939, which puts it back to 1919.

[6] Interview with Roy Plomley on *Desert Island Discs*, BBC Home Service, 21 Apr. 1958.

thirty years. Mrs Mayerl used to give a copy of this note to anyone interested and it contains still further glosses but well after the event.[7]

The second version of this story, the one in *Tit-bits*, suggests that an odd coincidence of circumstances brought Mayerl to Southampton in the first place. He seems naturally to have gravitated towards the comfortable environment of a major hotel there, even though he was probably only 19, indicating how soon he would become attached to the fashionable world of the Savoy, a milieu very different from that of his own family background. The broadcast version reveals some bantering anti-American feeling, which is not surprising considering the American dominance of popular music and jazz and the unions' fear of what were called 'aliens' stealing British jobs. But the situation put Mayerl in an odd position since his brand of pianism had American origins and so did his syncopated novelties. In the musical theatre, like many an English composer before Andrew Lloyd Webber, he must often have felt suffocated by the competition from Broadway.

Information from the Savoy Hotel archives does not settle the date of Mayerl's meeting with Ralton, but it does date the start of the New York Havana Band. By 1919 the Hotel was using Wilfred (Bill) de Mornys to organize its dance music, working under contract with the Hotel's own Entertainments Office.[8] There was a tradition of employing American musicians and it was on

---

[7] 'About 1920 he secured a job in an orchestra at an hotel in Southampton and was playing there when the late Bert Ralton arrived by liner in Southampton. Unable to get to London that night, Ralton stayed the night at the same hotel. Bert Ralton had been engaged by the Savoy Hotel, London, to appear with his band, but at the last moment before leaving America, his pianist had been prevented from travelling owing to an attack of jaundice, and Ralton was in urgent need of a pianist to appear at the Savoy. Listening to the band, which included Mayerl, whilst having dinner, he offered Billy the job which he immediately accepted. The band opened at the Savoy and at the end of the first week of the engagement Billy was handed his pay packet. Opening it, he found it contained £30 (in 1920?) and he promptly took it back to Ralton and told him that there must be some mistake. Ralton very anxiously asked him if he wasn't satisfied because, if he wasn't, it could be increased a little. Billy said far from it, but when he had been discussing terms he had thought that Bert had said £13 and not £30!' This note was probably written by Leslie Osborne, since the salary figures quoted agree with what he told me later. Osborne told me that he, and not Johnny Pearson who merely signed it, wrote the foreword to *The Jazz Master: A Collection of Famous Piano Solos from the Golden Age of Jazz*. Note that even in 1972 confusions about Mayerl and jazz were allowed to persist.

[8] Information from the Savoy Hotel Archive, and also from Nick Dellow, provides this background: Armand Vescey, the Hungarian-American, led an orchestra from 1910 and Murray's Savoy Quartet, led by Joe Wilbur, was apparently started in 1915. It was also known as the Savoy Quartet, recording under that name from 1915 and was augmented two years later to become the Savoy Dance Orchestra. The Quartet was a ragtime group which originally consisted of banjo-vocal-director, banjo, piano, and drums. Maurice Singer and his Orchestra, managed by Joe Wilbur, started in January 1920 and Sherbo's Orchestra, a five-piece group, played for foyer tea dances and evenings from October to the following January. In February 1921 the Savoy Dance Orchestra, which De Mornys had formed in October 1920, was reorganized and replaced Sherbo's Orchestra. From 5–31 July an American student group, the Princeton University Band, was in residence.

27 September 1921 that Bert Ralton and his New York Havana Band started playing in the Hotel's Main Ballrooom and in the Foyer for tea dances. By December 1921 the New York Havana Band was also known as the Savoy Havana Band, but the *Midland Telegraph*, on 29 March 1922, was still referring to the New York Havana Band and records continued to be made under this name well into 1923. The bands recorded under various titles—the New York Havana, *c.*November 1921–*c.*July 1923; the Havana Band, *c.*July 1923 but at least one release in September after Ralton had taken the original band to Australia; Savoy Havana Band at the Savoy Hotel, London, *c.*August to October 1923; Savoy Havana Band, 7 November 1923 onwards; and Savoy Orpheans (also as Albany Dance Orchestra and the Romane Orchestra), November 1923 onwards. According to Brian Rust, Mayerl replaced John Firman in the Savoy Havana recordings by July 1922, was in the Havana Band and the Savoy Havana from 1923 until he was replaced by Donald Thorne in May 1926.[9]

The archives at the Savoy state that Mayerl was officially the pianist with the Savoy Havana from as late as May 1922, when he replaced John Firman, and Mayerl officially left in January 1926. Bert Firman, John's brother, has confirmed to John Archer that his brother was actually the pianist in the early days of the Savoy Havana and he is credited on records.[10] All this qualifies Mayerl's hazy recollection of 1920 in the 1937 broadcast, John Watt's reference to the start of the Savoy Havana as 1920, and countless confusions in the other sources. So, since Mayerl was not on the books as the official pianist in the initial New York Havana days, his arrival was probably in early 1922 and it could not have been before 1921. The period from early 1922 to January 1926, when Mayerl definitely left, would have given him the four complete years at the Savoy which he mentioned in *Tit-bits* with such relish. And by 1922 he was already collaborating with Ralton since two songs appeared with Ralton as lyricist ('Dearie if you knew' and 'Longing for you'), and another one in 1923 ('Some day in Cambay'), all published by Boosey.

The year 1922 is also the most likely for the legendary first meeting between Mayerl and Ralton, since James Lincoln Collier's sources have confirmed that Ralton finally left Art Hickman's band in 1921 and we know he started at the Savoy in September.[11] But Mayerl can hardly have been entertaining troops 'during the war' (1914–18) if the Ralton meeting was as late as 1921 or 1922. A prophetic touch is that Ralton apparently described Mayerl's playing as 'nippy'— aptly enough—thus pre-echoing the title of his 1930 musical of the same name.

[9] B. Rust and S. Forbes, *British Dance Bands on Record 1911–1945* (General Gramophone Publications, London, 1989).

[10] M. Harth (ed.), *Lightning Fingers: Billy Mayerl the Man and his Music* (Paradise Press, London, 1995), 7–10.

[11] J. L. Collier, *Benny Goodman and the Swing Era* (Oxford University Press, New York, 1989).

Ralton himself gave some details of his career in an article he wrote for the *Melody Maker* but he also fails to settle the date of his initial contact with Mayerl and confuses matters with the reasons he gives for his trip to England. He was born in Minnesota, educated in Chicago and California, and joined Art Hickman's Band in San Francisco in 1918. This ten-piece group, featuring saxophone and banjo, created a sensation when it moved to New York to play at the Biltmore Hotel Roof. But Ralton says he left in 1919 for a short season in Havana, Cuba, where he organized a band of his own, but he may have returned to Hickman afterwards.

Ralton then accounts for his presence in London:

The 'wanderlust' came upon me (I'm afraid I shall never settle down), and I decided to make a world tour, London being the first port of call. I set out with two original members of my band for companions, a letter of introduction to Columbia's London Manager, who I was told would show me round, and no idea of doing any work—my sole object being to see the world and pick up new ideas on music. However, 'Man proposes, and (in this case) Columbia disposes'. On my arrival here I was asked to form a band for the purpose of recording and was introduced to the management of the Savoy with a view to starting a modern dance band for that famous hotel as well. Perhaps you remember the result. With six instrumentalists the Savoy Havana Band was inaugurated, finally becoming ten strong. It wasn't an easy job. There were few English musicians at the time whom jazz had finally reached, and I had to select those whom I considered would be capable of handling music of this type purely on their straight musical abilities. All I can say is they picked it up wonderfully quickly and all still in this country are today at the top of the ladder. Thanks to the way all the English boys worked, the Havana Band became most popular and was the very first syncopated orchestra, since the Original Dixieland Band appeared here in 1917, to appear on the music halls, obtaining a most enthusiastic reception at the Coliseum, London, at the end of 1921.[12]

How does this fit with Mayerl's various accounts? It may finally be worth going back to Mayerl's publisher friend, Leslie Osborne, and quoting verbatim what he told me in 1981:

Bill was playing at the Polygon Hotel in Southampton and Bert Ralton, who was running a band called the New York Havana (was asked by) the Manager of the Savoy to come over here and form a band—and of course they were cashing in on the name of the New York Havana, but they called it the Savoy Havana. Now the pianist developed jaundice and Bert Ralton arrived over here without a pianist. He stayed the night, after having come off the ship, at the Polygon Hotel and went down to dinner and the pianist

---

[12] B. Ralton, 'The Original Havana Band: Its Inception and Some Experiences with it', *Melody Maker* (Feb. 1926), 29–32. But see John Archer's different diagnosis in Harth, *Lightning Fingers*, 9. He cites the début of the New York (Savoy) Havana at the Coliseum as 13 March 1922, not 1921, and has seen a photograph of the band at that occasion with a pianist 'looking suspiciously like Billy Mayerl'.

sitting there was Billy Mayerl. Now Billy Mayerl was getting £6 [£190] a week. Bert Ralton heard him, went over to the piano and he said: 'Would you like to come and have a chat with me?' To cut a long story short, Bert offered him the job at the Savoy.... That's how he joined Bert Ralton, but there's a very funny story which is perfectly true I do assure you. Bill, when he got his first pay envelope at the end of the first week, got £30 [£950]. Don't forget he'd been getting £6. So he went to Bert Ralton and said: 'Oh, Mr. Ralton, I think there's some mistake here'. Ralton said: 'Why, what's the matter?' He said: 'I've got £30 in my envelope!' And Bert Ralton said to him in broad American: 'Why, aren't you satisfied?' Bill said: 'Yes, but it's wrong—I thought you said £13!' And he actually got £30 a week from £6 a week and that is a true story! Bill dined out on that for years![13]

We may never get nearer to the facts than this, bearing in mind that Osborne met Mayerl a year or less after the Ralton meeting. Why would Mayerl bother to invent the Southampton location? The financial dealings between Mayerl and Ralton vary between accounts but the implications of such a sudden rise are clear enough and show the earning power of dance-band musicians at the time. Osborne, nearly sixty years later, even remembered the name of the hotel and Ralton could well have been there again after his first arrival in England. Southampton, in the days of the great ocean liners, was a major centre and Ralton could have been meeting friends from the USA.

In 1923 Ralton had some disagreements with the Savoy Hotel and left, taking some of the Original Havana Band on a continental tour and they then spent more than a year in Australia and New Zealand. When he returned to Britain after more than two years away he was billed in Edinburgh as 'The Great Bert Ralton and His Havana Band listened to by 20,000,000 people'. The Savoy objected to this and brought an injunction for breach of copyright, later withdrawn. The ill-fated South African tour, which resulted in Ralton's accidental death, then followed.

But two years earlier Ralton had worked with Gershwin in New York. When Gershwin was in London for the opening of *The Rainbow* at the Empire Theatre on 3 April 1923, he stayed at the Savoy Hotel where he would have heard Mayerl and must have met him. Gershwin wrote to his brother, Ira:

Last night we went to see Jean Bedini's *You'd be surprised*, a revue. It's a fast show with many scenes from burlesque and music by Melville Morris. I wonder what he wrote as all I heard were popular American songs. George Robey, a famous comedian, is in the show and I think he is a fine artist. He puts over a lyric song as good as anyone I've seen. The hit of the show is an orchestra, the Savoy Orchestra. And who do you suppose is the leader? Bert Ralton the sax player who recorded my Mexican Dance with me. [The song 'Tomale (I'm hot for you)' from *The Perfect Fool*, George M. Cohan Theatre, 7 November 1921] He's got a great band and is a hit over here.[14]

[13]   L. Osborne, interview with Peter Dickinson.
[14]   E. Jablonski and L. D. Stewart, *The Gershwin Years* (Robson Books, London, 1974), 82.

This announcement shows a typical programme given by the Savoy Havana Band at the Coliseum on 2 October 1922:

W. de Mornys presents
SAVOY HAVANA BAND
Leader—B. L. Ralton

The Premier Saxophonist
The World's Greatest Exponents of Syncopated Music

Prelude	Rachmaninoff
'The Sheik'	Oriental Fox-trot
'Hawaian Hula'	Dance
Symphonic Syncopation	
Banjo—D.Wallace	Piano—Billy Mayerl
'Longing for You'	Ralton/Mayerl
'Allah's Holiday'	
Soprano sax—B.Ralton	
American Southern Airs	Medley

or various selections from their repertoire

'The Sheik of Araby' was the major hit by the American team of Harry B. Smith, Ted Snyder, and Francis Wheeler, and other titles show the fashion for things exotic. An announcement in the *Hotel Review* of October 1921 confirms, from an American source, the amazingly lavish terms under which players were apparently engaged and refers to Ralton's first season. It was claimed that $300, then £80 [£2,000], a week was needed to attract the very best players over from America. In a magazine such as the *Hotel Review* there could well have been an element of showing off by the Savoy to impress people in the trade. If the band was that expensive, no wonder it was so good. Even allowing for this, the £30 for Mayerl was far from generous in this context—no wonder Ralton upped it from £13—and one hopes he soon got much more.[15]

In the following year De Mornys was contracted by the Savoy Hotel on 3 July 1922 on much lower figures—'to supply two first-class bands (including the present Savoy Havana Band comprising nine musicians under Ralton) at a total weekly cost of £487.10.0 [£15,400] from October 1 to December 31 with an option to renew either or both for a further three months from January 1,

[15] *Hotel Review*, Oct. 1921, 260–1.
MODERN DANCE MUSICIANS
Mr. de Mornys, enterprising musical director of the Savoy Hotel . . . discloses fees for players. $300 (£80 [£2,049]) a week for top players and $1900 (£506 [£13,000])–$1500 (£400[£10,250]) for a good, but not tip-top band. Dance musicians are now getting fees comparable to music-hall artistes. The primary attraction at the Savoy Hotel will be the Havana Band for the winter season, led by Ralton. Bert Ralton plays six instruments—the soprano sax; tenor sax; oboe; clarinet; sarrusophone; and he is an expert whistler.

1923'. A further contractual letter of 14 November 1922 refers to a ten-piece Savoy Havana and implies that if Ralton left and took more than two players with him an agreement would be needed.

However, by 1925 success had bred success and remuneration—or perhaps rumours—had followed suit. The *Stirling Observer* claimed that some players in the Savoy Orpheans, which Mayerl had joined for the Easter tour, 'get £120 [£3,900] a week' and on average £100 [£3,300].[16] This was remarkable pay, even for celebrities. The top levels offered by the powerful bandleader Bert Ambrose in the 1930s, after talkies and into the Depression, were around £70–£80 [£2,800–£3,200] but much lower fees were maintained during the Second World War.[17]

On 3 October 1923 the Savoy Orpheans became the new band formed under the leadership of Debroy Somers, an ex-army band-master who had originally come to the Savoy as an arranger for the Savoy Havana Band. In 1937 Somers remembered that at the start only two players were British but three and a half years later only two were American. Billy Mayerl's first record-ing with the Savoy Havana seems to have been in July 1922 in a line-up con-sisting of Bert Ralton (clarinet, soprano and alto sax, and oboe/leader); Bill Marcus (trombone); Frank Kilduff (alto, tenor, baritone sax); William Wagner (soprano and tenor sax); Ramon Newton (violin/vocal); Billy Mayerl (piano); Dave Wallace (banjo); and McCabe (drums).[18] For the First Concert of Syncopated Music at the Queen's Hall on 3 January 1925 the programme listed the Savoy Havana as: saxophone (Rudy Vallee); sousaphone (Jim Bellamy); banjo (David Thomas); trumpet (Harry Thompson); trombone (Bernard Tipping); piano (Billy Mayerl); drums, harp, timpani (Ronnie Gubertini); with violin-leader (Ramon Newton).

At the same time as Debroy Somers started the Savoy Orpheans on 3 October 1923 Bert Ralton left. We have noted his subsequent travels, but he was accidentally shot on safari in January 1927, thus ending the short but bril-liant career of a man to whom Mayerl owed so much.[19] The *Melody Maker* pro-vided some touching detail, recalling that Ralton 'died bravely playing the

---

[16] 'The World's Most Popular Band', *Stirling Observer*, 8 Jan. 1925.

[17] L. Osborne, *Life is Nothing without Music*, BBC Radio 2, programme (4), 'The Bandleaders: I'.

[18] Rust and Forbes, *British Dance Bands on Record 1911–1945*.

[19] *The Cape Argus* 17 Jan. 1927

TRAGIC DEATH OF BERT RALTON
ACCIDENTALLY SHOT WHILST HUNTING
FULL CHARGE FROM GUN AT CLOSE RANGE

[From Our Own Correspondent]
Salisbury, Monday.
Bert Ralton, leader of the well-known Havana Band, which has been touring South Africa

ukelele and singing to his attendants whilst waiting to be borne to hospital'.[20]

Before considering the music played by the Savoy Bands and the unique opportunity they gave to Billy Mayerl, we need to turn to the new developments in broadcasting which enabled the bands to reach such a vast new public.

In the 1937 BBC broadcast, 'Anniversary of Dance Music at the Savoy Hotel', John Watt recalled how it started.[21] On the programme Mayerl had just played *Kitten on the Keys* (1921) by Zez Confrey. This piece is as crucial to the new novelty idiom as Scott Joplin's *Maple Leaf Rag* was to classic ragtime in 1899. Most unusually for Mayerl, judging by his remarkable 78 records made in the days when editing was not possible, this was a hasty and rather inaccurate performance. This could partly have been because Mayerl had just referred in a good-natured way to the fact that when the American pianist Carroll Gibbons, arrived at the Savoy, stealing all his thunder, he became jealous. Mayerl then said he thought he could play *Kitten on the Keys* faster and with fewer wrong notes—and was obviously hoping to prove it! Watt took up the threads:

It was about the time of *Kitten on the Keys* that broadcasting started. Jeffries [L. Stanton Jeffries] and Eckersley [Captain P. Eckersley] of the BBC called at the Savoy one day and asked Bert Ralton if it was possible to record—on records that was—the big drum. It wasn't. It was the old days of horn recording when the band even had to use a sort of permanent wedge in the piano pedal. And early experiments of broadcasting were made from the Ballroom at the Savoy to the Mirror Room with the Savoy Havana Band. The total distance was about 100 yards and the fact that anything was heard at the other end was considered to be, and probably was, a miracle . . . Nobody took much notice of these tests or took broadcasting very seriously and it wasn't until 13 April 1923, that the Savoy Havana Band was on the air for the first time.

The first programme contained *Kitten on the Keys* and the band's virtual signature tune, 'Three o'clock in the morning', one of Whiteman's biggest hits. Broadcasting was such a novelty that *The Times* reported, on 29 January 1923:

DANCING TO MUSIC BY WIRELESS
NEW EXPERIMENTS AT PUNCH AND JUDY BALL
There will be one feature of the Punch and Judy Ball in aid of the British Drama League

---

and Rhodesia, has died in hospital here as the result of an accident whilst out shooting on a farm in the Hunyani district yesterday afternoon.

A shot-gun was accidentally fired by a companion, and the whole charge entered Mr, Ralton's body near the right thigh-bone at close range.

The thigh-bone was shattered. An ambulance from Salisbury was sent out and conveyed the injured man to the local hospital, where he died today.

Mr. Ralton's band had just completed a week's engagement at the Palace Theatre, Salisbury. The band left today for Umtali under Mr. Barton, who deputises for Mr. Ralton.

[20] 'The Tragedy of Bert Ralton', *Melody Maker* (Feb. 1927), 127. See also B. Oakley, 'Bert Ralton's Death', *Melody Maker* (April 1927), 345.

[21] Cassette, *Savoy Memories*, Neovox Sound Archive 901.

which is being held at the Savoy Hotel on Thursday evening which will distinguish it from the many other costume balls held during recent years.

With the advent of broadcasting the dance music supplied by this agency has been eagerly utilised for dances in private houses, but so far as one knows, such music has not yet been utilised at a big costume ball. Arrangements have been made, however, with the British Broadcasting Company to transmit a number of dance tunes on Thursday evening and they will be included in the earlier part of the programme of the Punch and Judy Ball, which begins at 10 o'clock. The Marconi Company are installing special apparatus in the Savoy Hotel for the purpose.

The Savoy was one of the smartest places in London to be seen dancing between courses at dinner or after the theatre in an atmosphere of effortless luxury. The hotel had been opened in 1889, extended in 1904 and 1912, and was the first hotel in London to have private bathrooms. But the high life that Mayerl enjoyed there had its own dramas. On 10 July 1923 he was close to a tragedy when the band played on in the tradition of the musicians on the *Titanic*:

Suddenly in a corridor outside a revolver snapped. Its metallic crack broke across the melody. Some of the dancers heard it and stopped in their tracks, throwing the others out of step as they swerved to avoid collision. Although the dancing for that number terminated abruptly, we of the band could not stop playing. We carried on as if nothing had happened—but wondering all the time what had happened when we saw some couples near the door hurry out into the corridor.[22]

As *The Times* confirmed on July 23, Marie Marguerite Fahmy was charged with the murder of her husband, the Egyptian Prince Ali Kamel Bey, by shooting him at their suite at the Savoy Hotel. She was acquitted because of his cruelties and allowed to go back home. Mayerl knew her well by sight and remembered her as 'a woman of wonderful poise and dignity, well able to hide from others the depth of her suffering'.

On 7 December 1923, *The Times* reported that there were 500,000 holders of radio licences and that two million people heard the election result—the three-cornered contest which brought Ramsey MacDonald to power with a Labour government supported by the Liberals. By 1939 there would be nine million licences bringing radio to 73 per cent of homes in Britain.[23]

Leslie Osborne has described the Savoy bands as the 'crème de la crème of dance music in society, which hadn't been heard by the man in the street' until the advent of radio.[24] In 1990 Dr Richard Head remembered what it was like listening in:

[22] B. Mayerl, 'We played on as a Prince Lay Dying', *Tit-bits*, 26 June 1937, 5–6.

[23] C. Ehrlich, *The Music Profession in Britain since the Eighteenth Century* (Clarendon Press, Oxford, 1985), 212.

[24] L. Osborne, *Life is Nothing without Music*, BBC Radio 2, programme (4).

When I was nine, I used to listen to the Savoy Havana on 2LO with a crystal set wearing earphones that had hard ebonite earpieces which hurt after a few minutes, so that one was always moving them to a more comfortable place. Billy Mayerl used to play the piano alone without any rhythmic backing, so that one only heard the piano and the sliding of the dancers' feet on the floor. It was amazing to hear all the complicated breaks and embellishments played in really strict rhythm so effortlessly. In the interval after the music stopped you heard laughter, snatches of conversation, and the tinkling of cutlery, and then a few slow very attractive bars which I can still play by ear—I am ninety per cent sure it was Billy.[25]

The connection between the BBC and the Savoy seems to have arisen because the BBC headquarters was nearby in Savoy Hill and many employees found the hotel congenial. Some idea of the hectic working life of a musician in these bands and the response they elicited in London can be gained from the *Midland Telegraph*, 20 March 1922:

THE NEW YORK HAVANA BAND

It would be difficult to imagine London nowadays without the New York Havana Band—which goes to show how very much brighter the metropolis already is. This remarkable troup of musicians demonstrates how really fascinating ragtime can be. 'It is a jazz band without the noise' according to one young dance enthusiast, and the way in which the performers make something smooth, pleasing and artistic out of syncopated music commands our admiration. The band, I think, is about the hardest worked in the country. It starts at 10.00 in the morning, 'recording' for a famous gramophone company. At 2.30 it rushes round to the Coliseum to take part in the afternoon programme. At 6.30 its work at the Savoy Hotel commences; at 8.15 it is back at the Coliseum and thence it returns to the Savoy Ballroom, where it plays as long as the dancing lasts—usually until well past midnight.

This hectic schedule was confirmed by Mrs Mayerl fifty years after their marriage in 1923:

During the first two years of our marriage Billy was with the Savoy Havana Band at the Savoy Hotel and I had to learn that punctuality meant a great deal to him. Billy earned the nickname of 'On-the-nail-Mayerl'. He was such a stickler for time and everything had to be ready for the occasion—meals included and evening clothes laid out and so on. He would rush in after a tea-dance, change, eat a small meal and rush out again. It was all go-go-go. His work would finish usually at 2 a.m. but very often he was offered a private party which meant good money but also meant he might not be home before 6 a.m. It was very hard work indeed, especially as in-between he was broadcasting and composing.

I often used to say to him, 'Why do you want to work so hard? We don't need all this money. You will ruin your health.' He answered, 'It is easier to get to the top of the tree than to stay there.' Then I just had to keep quiet![26]

---

[25] Communication with Peter Dickinson.
[26] J. Mayerl, interview with Peter Dickinson, 11 Aug. 1981.

The Savoy worked its musicians hard for their high wages and took the choice of repertoire seriously, too. In 1923 a team of six men at the Savoy examined 13,000 dance tunes in six months. A popular song used to stay in currency for about three years, but this changed to only three months.[27]

One of the reasons for the accelerated time-scale was broadcasting. The Savoy bands started with a virtual monopoly, on the radio several times a week and, as a result of reaching a mass audience for the first time in history, a hit could be created in days. Getting on the air was overtaking the traditional mechanisms of publishers employing pluggers to market songs as sheet music, and performers getting royalties for using them. This indicates the importance of radio at a time when sheet music sales would halve between 1925 and 1933 and gramophone royalties would also slump under its impact.[28] The development of 78 recordings continued alongside radio and a landmark came with the introduction of electrical recordings in 1925, replacing the older acoustic recordings where piano reproduction was particularly poor. Mayerl was on the spot for that too:

Some of my most amusing experiences were when making gramophone recordings with the Savoy Havana Band. It was in the days of the old acoustic recording, before the electrical process, and all the players had to be huddled together on to each others' elbows in order to get unified reception by the ancient 'mike'. When Ralton whispered, 'Solo, Billy', the rest of the band would duck low to allow the sound waves of my piano to pass over their bent bodies to the horn.

They looked a queer kettle of fish, all hunched up and hugging their instruments while I hammered on the piano. And always the piano came out on the record as a feeble little tinkle!

The coming of the electrical system of recording ended this comedy business, and I like to recall that I was the first pianist in England to record by this system. On that occasion I played for one side of the record *The Jazz Master* and for the other side *The Jazz Mistress*.[29]

Mayerl recorded four of his virtuoso *Pianolettes* on two 78s for HMV in October 1925: *All-of-a-Twist/Eskimo Shivers* and *The Jazz Master/The Jazz Mistress*. Technical limitations meant that one side of a ten-inch 78 was limited to about three minutes but a twelve-inch one could take four minutes. This was a constant problem with extended classical works until the microgroove LP arrived in 1948 but it was ideal for Mayerl's short pieces and significantly affected the development of classical jazz. Before the use of microphones and electric playback the pianola was a more faithful medium for piano music. In the early 1920s Mayerl made about thirty rolls for Echo, including two of his

[27] *Mail*, 13 Sept. 1923.

[28] Anon (foreword by Sir Edward German), *Radio and the Composer: The Economics of Modern Music* (Ivor Nicholson & Watson, London, 1935), 19.

[29] B. Mayerl. 'We Played on as a Prince Lay Dying', *Tit-bits*, 26 June 1937, 5–6.

Gee Paul songs, 'Just keep on dancing' (April 1924) and 'Tell me in the moon-light'. In 1925 he also made a Duo-Art piano roll of *Eskimo Shivers*, which has appeared to great advantage in a modern transfer.[30]

These massively influential twentieth-century media of radio and record-ing provided unique opportunities for Mayerl as performer and composer and instinctively he used them to the full.[31] Very soon he would discover the vast potential of teaching applications too.

[30] Duo-Art 0708 transferred to CD on *Conifer Happy Days* CDHD 205. Information sup-plied by Robin Cherry.

[31] C. Ehrlich, *The Music Profession in Britain since the Eighteenth Century*, 186 *et seq*. See also M. Hustwitt, 'The Production of Dance Music in Britain in the 1920s', *Popular Music*, 3 (Cambridge, 1983), 7–31.

3

London, Marriage, and Jazz Confusions

Leslie Osborne, whose reminiscences I have already drawn upon, first met Mayerl, whom he always referred to as Bill, in 1923. Osborne was 18 and sometimes deputized for Mayerl at the Savoy. The publishing firm he worked for, West's, had brought out the Mayerl-Gee Paul song, 'I loved, I lost, but what do I care', of which there were three band recordings in 1925. Osborne has provided a vivid picture of the professional life of a song-plugger.[1] It was non-stop: he was at his desk all day and out going the rounds of cafés, hotels, music-halls, and theatres in the evenings. All these establishments, as well as the cinemas, employed musicians. Oxford Street, from the top floor of Selfridges to the Lyons Corner Houses below, was dominated by live not canned music. The *thé dansant* was all the rage: a hotel without a band would have been considered a curiosity.

Billy Mayerl entered this scene just as it was being transformed from a live performance and sheet-music economy to one based on mechanical media and performing rights. Everything was given greater immediacy by broadcasting and increasingly rapid cultural colonization by the USA.

The mechanisms of promotion included what was known as plug money. By 1920 a singer could get 3 guineas [£75] from the publisher for giving a dozen performances of a song. Big stars, such as Clara Butt, might also get a royalty of 16.6 per cent on the price of each copy of the sheet music, which often had the performer's picture on the cover. According to Osborne, the composer-publisher-promoter Horatio Nicholls, commercially active under his real name of Lawrence Wright, paid Talbot O'Farrell the astronomical sum of £2,000 [£80,400] a year to perform his songs. Such deals, which were often controversial, were struck by publishers and added to the income of performers and bandleaders. Publishers were also involved in concert promo-

---

[1] L. Osborne, *Life is Nothing without Music*, BBC Radio 2, Programme (I): 'The Publishers'.

tion—the Boosey Ballad Concerts at the Queen's Hall were given before large audiences and secured valuable newspaper coverage as a result.

The whole issue of plugging became serious in 1929. The Performing Right Society (the British equivalent of ASCAP and BMI in the USA) had deplored it, and in 1929 the BBC tried to control matters by refusing to broadcast the titles of tunes played. This aroused so much opposition that it was soon abandoned but it was never possible to prevent plugging.[2]

Top bandleaders, such as Bert Ambrose, earning an incredible £10,000 [£402,000] a year plus plug money, were strong personalities and the superstars of their day. They attracted high society—the Prince of Wales, later a pupil of Mayerl's, might have been encouraged to attend a function if Ambrose's band was playing. Ambrose, who operated at the Embassy Club in Bond Street and the Mayfair Hotel in the years between the wars, used only the best players and arrangers.

Some bandleaders, such as Henry Hall with his Salvation Army background, apparently never took plug money. Neither did Mayerl, although he found other ways of putting himself forward early in his career, as he recalled in 1937:

Through my broadcasting with the Savoy Havana Band every night on the wireless, I was inundated with requests from publishers to get their products on the air. They offered me 50% of the royalties if I could get their songs played by the Band when I was broadcasting. I am glad now, upon looking back, that I never accepted a single offer of 50% of royalties on songs or compositions merely for getting them put on to the air. What I did, however, was to take full advantage of the publicity I was getting to produce as much of my own work as I could. I wrote as many as it was humanly possible to do, and those which met the approval of Bert Ralton, our leader, were played by the Band. In this way my own compositions became widely known.[3]

Actually there were not many of Mayerl's own compositions in print until the last of his four Savoy years, 1925. As we have noted, he published two songs in 1922 to lyrics by Ralton; two in 1923, one with Ralton's lyrics; six songs in 1924, all but one with lyrics by Gee Paul; fifteen songs in 1925, again all but one with Gee Paul, and the piano solos, *Six Pianolettes*, those superb vehicles for Mayerl's own dazzling virtuosity all better known individually under their own names—*The Jazz Master*; *The Jazz Mistress*; *Eskimo Shivers*; *All-of-a-Twist*; *Virginia Creeper*; and *Jazzaristrix*.

Those works will be considered later, but it is now necessary to expand on Mayerl's domestic life, where he was as fortunate in his happy marriage to Jill Bernini as in the other aspects of his early career. He takes up the story

[2] C. Ehrlich, *Harmonious Alliance: A History of the Performing Right Society* (OUP, Oxford, 1989), 212.
[3] B. Mayerl, 'We Played on as a Prince Lay Dying', *Tit-bits*, 26 June 1937, 5–6.

himself, in 1937, at the point where Bert Ralton gave him the job of pianist with the Savoy Havana:

I jumped at his offer. First, it seemed rich with promise for the future; and, second, it would make me rich enough to marry the girl I had been head over ears in love with since, it seemed to me, the very beginning of Time!

Her name was Jill Bernini. I had met her first when I was the boy pianist at the Imperial Cinema, Clapham. There were two orchestras there, and she was the pianist in the other one.

It was a shock to me when I learnt that she was engaged to the drummer in her orchestra. And it was a shock to her when I told her that, notwithstanding that fact, she was going to marry me! I persisted, my mind was made up, and finally to my intense joy Jill said 'No!' to the drummer and 'Yes!' to me. My romance still lives. We are sweethearts to this day.[4]

On 11 August 1981 I went to see Mrs Mayerl at her flat in Hove, to interview her for a BBC Radio 3 documentary about Billy Mayerl. A small woman, with blue eyes and wearing spectacles, she talked for over an hour with quiet dignity and confidence of their life together. She well understood the quality of her husband's work and was pleased to find renewed interest in later generations. So it was particularly distressing for me to have to tell her later that the BBC was not going to be able to go ahead with the programme because some tapes had been lost. She took it very calmly and sent me a note in June 1983 saying it was 'just one of those things' and went on to say: 'I am more than amazed and gratified at the amount of music played by the BBC and plus records sold, I cannot complain.'[5] She enclosed a photograph of Mayerl at the keyboard and wrote on the back: 'To Peter Dickinson with many thanks for trying so hard on a project that was not to be, but it was nice meeting you. Gilda Mayerl.' Fortunately it was possible for the BBC to make amends, but not until fifteen years later, twelve years after Mrs Mayerl had died.[6]

Mayerl's widow must have been reasonably comfortable financially since, when he died on 25 March 1959, his estate was valued at £20,329 [£265,700] and his Performing Right Society income for that year was £900 [£11,800]. This showed a drop since it had been over £1,000 [£13,000] in the previous four years. When Mrs Mayerl died on 21 August 1984 her estate came to £63,434 [£115,900] and the PRS income in that year was over £2,500 [£4,600]. (See Appendix 3 for Mayerl's PRS earnings from 1927 to 1998.) Before she died she made donations to cover bursaries for students at Trinity College of

---

4 B. Mayerl, 'We Played on as a Prince Lay Dying', *Tit-bits*, 26 June 1937.

5 J. Mayerl, letter to Peter Dickinson, 7 June 1983.

6 P. Dickinson, *Billy Mayerl: A Formula for Success*, BBC Radio 3, 11 Feb. 1996 (repeated 24 Aug.), devised and presented by Peter Dickinson, produced by Derek Drescher with technical assistance from Robin Cherry.

Music and her will added £10,000 [£18,300] to these trusts. She left to the Members' Fund of the Performing Right Society 'all copyright and interest in copyright and all royalties' as a gift 'in commemoration of the late Billy Mayerl'. Smaller bequests included £5,000 [£9,100] each to the Musicians Benevolent Fund and the British Heart Foundation and £2,000 [£3,700] each to the Jazz Centre Society and the Royal National Institute for the Blind.

In her interview with me Mrs Mayerl talked about the second crucial meeting in her husband's life:

He was a pianist in a cinema and I was too. And that was how we met. Then, soon after, he started at the Savoy and of course gradually he went on. He was always very ambitious: I wasn't at all. I didn't like all this publicity. But I couldn't get away from it. So I had to learn, you know, to mix and do the right things and try and say the right things. And then, of course, we just went on from there.[7]

Mayerl's wife was Italian by birth and came to England as a child of about 7, speaking no English but young enough to have lost any trace of an accent in later life. She was born in Minori, a picturesque town of lemon groves and Roman remains, on the rocky Amalfi coast south of Pompei. Her name was Ermenegilda Bernini, daughter of Isidoro Bernini and Lucia de Lucia, of Via Dietro le Chiesa. Bernini was a tailor, as Reginald Leopold remembered with some satisfaction much later, since he had been recommended to him by the players at the Savoy as someone who could make really fine suits.[8] Her birth certificate states that Jill was born on 23 March 1896 but these details do not tally with her last British passport where her date of birth was given as 27 March 1898, making her two years younger. She must have been sensitive about her age and the fact that, when they were married, she was 27 and he was 20. Even in her 1981 interview with me she charmingly disguised the age gap, hesitating when I—not realizing that she had known him since his Wonder Boy Pianist days—asked her if he was famous when she first met him. She said she was about 18, then added, 'We were about 18'. She went on: 'He was a man very much older than his years. He was very mature when I met him—of course because he had been out in the world since he was 14 and I hadn't'.[9]

His maturity came of necessity and she seems to have accepted philosophically his superiority as a pianist:

Billy thought I was the worst pianist that ever was! He always used to wonder why I ever earned a living! But as I was very young and was only a girl—a girl among lots of

[7] J. Mayerl, interview with Peter Dickinson, 11 Aug. 1981.
[8] R. Leopold, interview with Peter Dickinson on 11 Nov. 1994 at Saltdean, East Sussex.
[9] According to a copy of her birth certificate obtained from Minori on 5 August 1958, Ermenegilda Bernini was born at 6.30 in the afternoon of 23 March 1896, and the birth was registered the following day. Her last British passport was issued in London on 10 September 1959 and renewed on 1 September 1964, valid until 10 September 1969.

men—it was quite all right. He taught me a little bit how to play the piano and we made a few records but, frankly, after we got married I didn't want to do any more.[10]

On 4 April 1923 formal notification was made to the Registrar of the District of Hammersmith, in the County of London, by William Joseph Mayerl that a marriage was intended to be had by licence between him and Ermenegilda Bernini. Like his brother and his sister, Billy was married not in church but at a Register Office. The wedding took place on 19 April 1923. William Joseph Mayerl gave his occupation as pianist and gave his parents' address as 54 Richmond Gardens, Shepherds Bush, which stayed in the family until his mother's death the year after his father in 1938.

Jill left her occupation blank and gave her own address as 8 Cromwell Grove, Shepherds Bush. Her father was then living at 29 Gibson St., Islington. The profession of Jill's father, Isidoro Bernini, was shown as 'Tailor (journeyman)' but the witnesses were Mayerl's father and his maternal grandfather.

Billy and Jill Mayerl moved house every year or two. The saxophonist Van Phillips told me that he joined the Savoy Havana Band in September 1925, but it may have been sooner because he was recording with them in 1923, and confirmed that both he and the Mayerls lived in the same road.[11] A printed party invitation from Billy and Jill confirms this—it was for their second wedding anniversary on 19 April 1925—and they were living at 30 Catherine St., Buckingham Gate, London SW1.[12] In August 1924, when he sailed to New York with Geoffrey Clayton, Mayerl gave his address as 4 Roland Gardens and when he made a simple will, leaving everything to Jill, on 20 February 1929, they were living at a house called Jazzaristrix in Cranbourne Gardens, Golders Green in North London. After this, as we shall see, their houses were usually called Marigold Lodge, presumably because the sales of *Marigold* (1927) had

---

[10] J. Mayerl, Interview with Peter Dickinson. Billy and Jill Mayerl recorded the duet versions of *Ace of Spades* and *Marigold* on Columbia FB 1161 in 1935.

[11] V. Phillips, interview with Peter Dickinson, 8 Nov. 1982.

[12]   THE CATHERINE THEATRE OF (DECIDED) VARIETY
COMING SHORTLY !!!
BILLY AND GIL MAYERL
KNOCKABOUT COMEDIANS
Request your presence at their
ANNIVERSARY BINGE
when they present the Screaming Farce
BUNG HO!
All Drinking, All Eating, All Yelling, All Talking (at once)
in several unsteady reels
DON'T STOP TO DRESS
Just put on your hat and draw up at
30 Catherine St., Buckingham Gate, S.W.1.

rapidly overtaken those of the earlier *Pianolette No. 6* otherwise known as *Jazzaristrix* (1925).[13]

Mayerl used the term 'jazz' in connection with his own work, but later regretted it. Even a cursory examination of the British and American popular music scenes between the wars shows how indiscriminately the word was applied at that time. Anything syncopated was given this label, whereas actually popular song and dance music were steeped in the commercialized forms of ragtime rhythms. These enhanced the rhythmic life of popular music and real skill went into dance-band arrangement and the selection of players in order to create an individual sound profile for each group. Purism about such matters is futile. Jazz, like ragtime before it, is formed from an interaction between black and white, folk and commercial, improvised and notated. Ultimately it hardly matters whether the stimulus for jazz-influenced concert works by composers such as Milhaud, Walton, Copland, Lambert, Weill, Stravinsky, Bernstein, and many more came from 'the real thing', if that can ever be disentangled, or via popularized derivations. The achievement in a notated score is there. It is as absurd to object to composers drawing on African American practices as it would be to carp at the use of dance music such as the sarabande, gavotte, jig, or waltz in the notated music of earlier centuries. In fact, a sharply etched Joplin rag or a novelty piano piece by Mayerl is more admirable than many a sprawling improvisation, especially after the restrictions of the three-minute 78 record were lifted through LP and CD.

Two major American imports affected the British scene in the years before and during Mayerl's time at the Savoy and provided a context for his own further development—the Original Dixieland Jazz Band and Paul Whiteman. What they, Gershwin, and Mayerl, were all doing was to make the musical practices of African Americans more acceptable to white audiences. They broke the ice, moving towards the pluralistic musical society which developed through the rest of the twentieth century. This was not their primary aim but, once the novelty had worn off, it became clear that Gershwin's work for both theatre and concert hall would be enduring on its own terms. This was the context for early Mayerl too.

The first of the American imports was the ODJB (Nick LaRocca, leader and cornet; Larry Shields, clarinet; Eddie Edwards/Emil Christian, trombone; Tony Sbabaro, drums; Henry Ragas/J. Russell Robinson, piano). All white, they came from New Orleans via Chicago to New York and created a sensation when they played at the fashionable Reisenweber's Restaurant there

---

[13] Mayerl's addresses were given in *Who's Who in the Theatre*: 9th edn. (1939)—Marigold Lodge, West Heath Close, Hampstead, NW3; 10th and 11th edns. (1950, 1952)—Marigold Lodge, 2 Telegraph Hill, Hampstead, NW3; 12th edn. (1957)—407A Edgware Rd., W2.

in January 1917, some four years after the word 'jazz' had apparently been used in print for the first time—a date which is constantly being put further and further back.[14] In the same year the ODJB were the first jazz band to make records. John Chilton, in the *New Grove Dictionary of Jazz*, considered that this gave them 'a degree of eminence that was out of proportion to their musical skills',[15] but a balanced appraisal of the ODJB came from Gunther Schuller in his authoritative study of early jazz, where he cited the 'novelty of the music, its unprecedented exuberance and unabashed vulgarity'.[16] Although it was claimed that they could not read music, their limited improvisation now seems stilted alongside comparable Black groups. But they had an enormous influence through their recordings, caught the mood of a new youth culture at a crucial moment towards the end of the First World War and helped to raise the status of jazz in a way that no Black group could have done at that time. Their impact and star quality paved the way for a British tour in 1919.

The ODJB confidently billed themselves as 'Creators of Jazz' much as Ben Harney a generation before had spuriously described himself as the 'Originator of Ragtime', and—closer to home—*Tit-bits*, in its 1937 series, announced Billy Mayerl as 'Master of Jazz' and/or 'Inventor of Syncopated Jazz'. The ODJB tour started badly at the London Hippodrome on 7 April 1919 when the leading star of *Joy Bells*, George Robey whom Gershwin would later admire, refused to have their 'jungle music' in the show. This is a term that Mayerl himself was capable of using. [17] The ODJB then retreated to night clubs until they were asked to open the Hammersmith Palais de Danse on 29 November along with Billy Arnold's Novelty Jazz Band. The latter title captures the comic routines that went with such performances at this stage, often to excess. But David Boulton identified a particularly British tradition affecting the ODJB here and therefore other novelty developments on and off stage: 'The Original Dixielanders borrowed their novelty antics from the British jazz bands preceding them. They fell into line with current public taste, but they did not, in the first place, create it.'[18]

But a characteristic of Dixieland, especially in the war-weary dance-crazy Jazz Age, was humour. Leonard Bernstein understood this when he wrote much later, in an epoch when he had helped to make it respectable for an internationally famous conductor and composer to be deeply involved in jazz and the musical theatre:

[14] J. L. Collier, *The Reception of Jazz in America: A New View* (Institute for Studies in American Music, Brooklyn, New York, 1988), 6.

[15] B. Kernfeld, *New Grove Dictionary of Jazz* (Macmillan, London, 1988).

[16] G. Schuller, *Early Jazz: its Roots and Musical Development* (Oxford University Press, New York, 1968), 176.

[17] M. Worlock, interview with Peter Dickinson, 30 Sept. 1995.

[18] D. Boulton, *Jazz in Britain* (Jazz Book Club, London, 1959), 38.

I love jazz because it is an original kind of emotional expression, in that it is never wholly sad or wholly happy . . . I also love it for its humour . . . It 'fools around' with notes, so to speak, and has fun with them. It is therefore an entertainment in its truest sense. But I find I have to defend jazz to those who say it is low-class. As a matter of fact, all music has low-class origins, since it comes from folk music, which is necessarily earthy.[19]

Or as Philip Larkin, whom Bernstein read in the last year of his life as his favourite modern poet, said about his enthusiasm for jazz as a teenager in the 1930s: 'For us jazz became part of the private joke of existence, rather than a public expertise.'[20] The humour Bernstein observed stems from minstrel shows, cakewalks, and ragtime, with its irreverent swung versions of classics, and there is an element of the comic stunt in Billy Mayerl's vivid initial impact as performer and composer of vehicles for his own publicly displayed virtuosity. His star turns included playing two pianos at once. When he was filmed for *Pathé News* as Billy Mayerl and his Claviers with three other keyboard players, they all played *Bats in the Belfry*. The film shows Mayerl seated between two pianos with keyboards facing each other. During the performance Mayerl starts on one piano, then switches to play facing the audience with one hand on each piano, then, just in case that seemed easy, he swivels round and plays the two keyboards with his back to the audience. The Scottish pianist, composer, and arranger, Clarence Falkener saw this stunt at the Edinburgh Royal Theatre in 1944 and paid tribute to Mayerl's 'exactness: he never fumbled and he never looked at the keys'.[21]

It was Billy Arnold's band at the Hammersmith Palais in 1919 which fascinated Darius Milhaud, an initiation into jazz which he later followed up in New York's Harlem before writing his masterpiece in a jazz-influenced idiom, *La Création du Monde* (1923).[22] This made him one of the first European composers to respond to the full colour of instrumental jazz, as opposed to the ragtime sheet music which Stravinsky said had inspired him.[23] As the turmoil created by the ODJB's visit to London in 1919 subsided, it became obvious that 'hot' jazz was on the way out in England even by 1921, with a few exceptions, notably the Filipino pianist and bandleader, Fred Elizalde, who came via the USA to study at Cambridge in 1925 and brought a remarkable galaxy of American jazzmen to the Savoy when he directed, not without controversy, Fred Elizalde and his Savoy Hotel Music and the Savoy Orpheans from 1927 to 1929.

On 6 January 1923 the *Evening News*, with a reference to Thomas Moore's song 'The Harp that once through Tara's Halls' (1807), reported:

[19] L. Bernstein, *The Joy of Music* (Weidenfeld & Nicolson, London, 1960), 97.
[20] P. Larkin, *All What Jazz* (Faber, London, 1970), 4.
[21] C. Falkener, interview with Robin Cherry and John Watson, 23 Mar. 1996.
[22] D. Milhaud, *Notes without Music* (Dobson, London, 1952), 101.
[23] I. Stravinsky, *An Autobiography* (Norton, New York, 1962), 78.

THE HARP THAT NOW—SOFTER DANCE MUSIC REPLACING THE DISCORDANT JAZZ

Mr. De Mornys, Dance Band Manager of the Savoy Hotel: 'It is certainly a sign of the times. The softer music is responsible for better dancing. The crashing blare of orchestras used to conceal both the inefficiency of the musicians and the shuffling of the dancers . . . Our orchestras are daily becoming softer. Jazz in England is dead'.

And again in the *Evening News*, 25 January 1923: 'The "jazz" is certainly going out of the jazz bands.'

In the following month this change of fashion was confirmed, and back-dated to 1921, by the *Star*, 10 February 1923:

DANCE MUSIC NOW OF THE SOFTEST

'Jazz music is as dead as short skirts. No first-class orchestra has played jazz for eighteen months', reported an official of the Savoy Hotel. The Savoy Havana was described as 'the finest syncopated orchestra in the world', however there was 'no jazz in London amongst first-class orchestras. Jazz might be very fine in America but the British public do not want it'.

But there was still a problem with terminology. It may be worth taking soundings about this issue a year or two later when the Queen's Hall concerts were taking place in 1925. Debroy Somers felt he needed to put the record straight in a variety of newspaper appearances and even offered a silly story about how jazz came to be named:

WHAT JAZZ IS

Mr. Debroy Somers, conductor of the Savoy Orpheans, wishes 'to protest most strongly against the now almost universal use of the epithet "jazz" to describe what is really syncopated music. The two are entirely different. Jazz music is essentially erratic; it gets the weirdest effects by breaking all the rules. As far as I can elicit, the word came from a little town in the Southern States of America, where the toughs used to shout "Chas! Chas!" for a negro minstrel Charles by name. Charles became "jazz" and the name stuck to the "music" which took New York by storm at the time of the Armistice. But when folk cooled down "jazz" properly so termed expired. Is it not then grotesque that a self-respecting syncopated orchestra should inherit this wretched epithet? A syncopated band may behave in an eccentric fashion; it does at least pay attention to the rules of music in its execution and its playing'.[24]

The issue grated on with Tetrazzini saying jazz was not music[25] and J. B. Priestley inexplicably dismissing Paul Whiteman's band without even going to their last concert early in 1926.[26] The conductor-composer-pianist Sir

---

[24] D. Somers, *Huddersfield Examiner*, 5 Oct. 1925; *Morning Post*, 8 Oct. 1925; *Islington Gazette*, 8 Oct. 1925; *Paisley Daily Express*, 8 Oct. 1925. These are just a few examples of Somers's press coverage on this issue.   [25] *Morning Post*, 30 Dec. 1925.
[26] *Saturday Review*, 1 May 1925.

Hamilton Harty made a fool of himself, which was surprising, since he played the solo piano part splendidly in Lambert's *The Rio Grande* only two years later. So de Mornys swung back into the attack trying to eliminate jazz from the map altogether:

NON-EXISTENT JAZZ
NAME OF LONG-DEAD MUSIC MISAPPLIED

Mr. W. De Mornys, the musical director of the Savoy Hotel, made a vigorous reply to Sir Hamilton Harty's denunciation of jazz music.

Speaking at the Conference of the National Union of Organists, Sir Hamilton described jazz as the curse of music, and said it was 'sensual, noisy and incredibly stupid', the grotesqueness of which resulted from a treatment of instruments 'which ought to result in three months' hard labour for the performer'.

'Sir Hamilton Harty', observed William de Mornys, 'makes the mistake which is very common among English people of calling dance music jazz'.

'As a matter of fact, jazz has not been heard in this country for at least six or seven years. There is no such thing as jazz nowadays. I have just returned from a seven-weeks' tour in America, and even there, the home of jazz, you cannot hear it . . . The public knows what it wants perfectly well'.[27]

Further letters followed with confused and perplexing headings such as 'Non-existent jazz';[28] 'Sour grapes and syncopation';[29] and 'Why call it Jazz?'[30] All the time the public was waiting for the new messiah, now in the wings and symbolically named—Paul Whiteman. The item in the *Star* in 1923 that found jazz as dead as short skirts also referred to the fact that Whiteman had been engaged to bring 'real jazz', but this anticipates events.

One result of the publicity surrounding the ODJB in England was to bring something more complex than ragtime to the attention of the serious musical profession. Opinions were given, some of which make fascinating reading now. One came from one of the last representatives of the great Austro-German musical tradition which was coming under threat from the encroachments of African American musical practices affecting all kinds of Western music. Richard Strauss was interviewed on the subject and his pronouncements appeared in both the *Evening Star* and the *Birmingham Gazette* on 14 January 1922. He started by saying that he had a high opinion of standards of American musical life after his tour there and went on, after his interviewer had mentioned jazz:

'No, no, that is not music', he said with a significant shrug. 'It is not even founded on genuine folk music, as some of its admirers claim. A programme of jazz would be an eminently suitable concert for the Palace of King Attila [ruler of the Huns in the fifth century]. In a word, I have a better opinion of the negroes than jazz would suggest if it

[27] *Daily Graphic*, 2 Sept. 1926.   [28] *Yorkshire Evening News*, 2 Sept. 1926.
[29] *Morning Advertiser*, 4 Sept. 1926.   [30] *Daily News*, 4 Sept. 1926.

were to be seriously accepted as a national idiom. The original melodies from which jazz is derived are sublime, but jazz—'. Dr. Strauss shook his head as if in great pain![31]

Strauss was conspicuously less generous to the achievements and potential of the African American than Anton Dvořák had been a generation earlier. Did he mean spirituals as the 'original melodies'? But the battle for jazz to be taken seriously was not over even in America—some would say especially in America. In 1929 the influential critic, Paul Rosenfeld, could write with alarming certainty: 'American Music is not jazz. Jazz is not music. Jazz remains a striking indigenous product, a small, sounding, folk-chaos, counterpart of other national developments.'[32]

No wonder, with so many confusions stemming from the sound of syncopation, that the public in the 'silly twenties' lost its bearings, if indeed it cared. But Scott Joplin knew the problem and in the preface to his *School of Ragtime* (1908) defended himself in language which is still sometimes needed now to justify the idiom of Billy Mayerl: 'Syncopations are no indication of light or trashy music, and to shy bricks at "hateful ragtime" no longer passes for musical culture.' What a dignified way of putting a case that has had to be made for most of the rest of the twentieth century. The instructive comparison between Mayerl and Joplin will be drawn again later. Terminology remained an intractable problem. But the term 'jazz' came to signify something basic which was repellent to some and yet mesmerically alluring—like Josephine Baker's titillating dance routines in the *Revue Nègre* and the *Folies-Bergère* in Paris in 1925.[33] The situation was symbolized by John B. Soutar's painting called *The Breakdown*, exhibited at the Royal Academy in London the following year. The picture showed a grinning, black saxophonist sitting on a bed playing while a white woman is dancing naked. The *Melody Maker* objected to the image and suggested the picture should be burnt—but the magazine still reproduced it.[34] Llewelyn C. Lloyd astutely summed up the situation:

The picture is, of course, a protest against the widespread influence in Western countries of primitive rhythms in music and dancing, which we broadly designate jazz. It expresses very powerfully a point of view . . . shared by a great many people. But, whether we like it or not, whether we see in jazz a sinister influence working for the downfall of civilisation as we know it, or an important source of fresh inspiration in art, we cannot deny that it has gripped the minds of what are usually called the civilised peoples of the world and that it has come to stay.[35]

[31] *Evening Star* and the *Birmingham Gazette*, 14 Jan. 1922.
[32] P. Rosenfeld, 'An Hour with American Music', *Musical Impressions* (Allen & Unwin, London, 1970), 221.
[33] P. Rose, *Jazz Cleopatra: Josephine Baker in her Time* (Chatto & Windus, London, 1990).
[34] *Melody Maker* (June 1926), 1.
[35] L. C. Lloyd, 'Jazz and the Modern Spirit', *Monthly Musical Record* (1 Nov. 1926).

4

SYNCOPATION AT THE QUEEN'S HALL

BY the 1920s the gap between mass-produced popular culture and so-called serious music had widened and there was scope for trying to bring the two sides together again. A landmark in New York City was the recital by the Canadian-born soprano, Eva Gautier, at the Aeolian Hall on 1 November 1923. In this programme, described as a 'Recital of Ancient and Modern Music for Voice', Gautier followed some Bartok and Hindemith with a group of American songs accompanied by Gershwin himself, appearing specially for this item. It was his concert début and he was a sensation, especially with his own songs. On 22 May 1925 Gautier gave a similar recital at London's Aeolian Hall, called 'From Java to Jazz', again with Gershwin accompanying the American group, a month before his broadcast of *Rhapsody in Blue* from the Savoy. The *Era* caught the mood and emphasized the move towards unifying the musical scene, which still had a long way to go:

Frankly, the audience liked a collection of American popular songs with the inimitable George Gershwin at the piano best of all—and they were quite right. Eva Gautier sang them admirably, and Gershwin's playing (particularly of his own 'Swanee' and 'Stairway to Paradise') was a sheer delight . . . She introduced us to a conception of the unity of all music quite new in our concert halls.[1]

The second American invasion affecting the British popular music scene between the wars came from Paul Whiteman. Unlike the members of the ODJB, he was classically trained and had played the viola in symphony orchestras at Denver, Colorado, where he was born, and San Francisco. He conducted a forty-piece band in the US Navy, then formed a dance orchestra in Santa Barbara, California, before turning towards what he called 'symphonized syncopation' later to be known as symphonic jazz. Meanwhile, in 1920, his record of 'Whispering' and 'Japanese Sandman', arranged by Ferde Grofé, apparently

---

[1] *Era*, 30 May 1925, 7. For Gautier's complete programme, see C. Schwartz, *Gershwin: His Life and Music* (Bobbs-Merrill, Indianapolis, 1973), 75.

sold over a million, but Whiteman had his eye on the serious musical establishment too.

In April 1923 Whiteman's Orchestra (two trumpets doubling flugel-horns; two trombones; two horns; flute; various saxophones, oboes and clarinets; two violins; two double-basses doubling on tuba; banjo; piano; drums) appeared in *Brighter London* at the Hippodrome in London. Whiteman enjoyed the kind of success which resulted in his being lionized by high society including Edward, Prince of Wales. Whiteman found him 'a fine dancer as well as a good drummer who occasionally sat in with the band'.[2] Like other members of the royal family, the Prince idolized Fred and Adèle Astaire.[3] Whiteman was ambitious, so on 12 February 1924, he took the Aeolian Hall in New York City for a concert billed as:

Paul Whiteman and his Palais Royal Orchestra
will offer an Experiment in Modern Music
Assisted by Zez Confrey and George Gershwin

New typically American Compositions by Victor Herbert, Irving Berlin and George Gershwin will be played for the first time.

The concert will always be remembered as the launch for Gershwin's *Rhapsody in Blue* (scored by Ferde Grofé), with the composer at the piano, but it also contained a group of novelty piano pieces, including *Kitten on the Keys*, played by Zez Confrey. David Jasen, in the preface to his collection of ninety Confrey piano solos, identifies the common currency shared between novelty composer-performers like Confrey and the pianists in both jazz and dance bands:

By this time Confrey had made a lasting contribution to those jazz and dance bands where, because of the popularity of his novelty rags, every band pianist was employing those runs and breaks that Zez had invented as part of his compositions (and within his piano roll arrangements). Zez's influence was all-pervasive during the twenties.[4]

It is interesting to compare Confrey's position in America with that of Mayerl in England. Even if Confrey did not exactly 'invent' those runs and breaks, he certainly made his own style widely known. Mayerl's debt to Confrey's novelty pianism will later be documented, but the scale, range, and consistent quality of the former's output will not suffer from the comparison.

The jazz historian, Marshall Stearns, rated Whiteman's 'Experiment in Modern Music' a success in both commercial and jazz terms. He lost money on it, but by this time he had plenty to lose:

[2] E. Jablonski, *Gershwin: A Biography* (Simon & Schuster, London, 1988), 62.
[3] T. Satchell, *Astaire: The Biography* (Hutchinson, London, 1987), 57 *et seq.*
[4] R. S. Schiff (ed.), *Zez Confrey: Ragtime, Novelty, and Jazz Piano Solos* (Belwyn Mills, New York, 1982).

Whiteman advanced the cause of jazz immeasurably. After the concert, jazz bands—good and bad—had an easier time finding jobs, and the evolution within the music was speeded up. Whiteman's own tendency was towards adopting European concert devices and blending them with jazz. The result was striking, easily intelligible and profitable.[5]

We can turn again to Gunther Schuller for as balanced a view of Whiteman as he took of the ODJB:

Whiteman was a sociological phenomenon responding to a particular need in the society of his time, the 1920s . . . On purely musical terms, however, the Whiteman Orchestra achieved much that was admirable, and there is no question that it was admired (and envied) by many musicians both black and white. For it was an orchestra which was overflowing with excellent musicians and virtuoso instrumentalists . . . Many of their performances are fascinating musical period pieces, at least as significant in their way as many a mediocre jazz performance which happens to possess the proper pedigree.[6]

Most of that applies to the Mayerl of the 1920s, in terms of social relevance, virtuosity, musicianship, and period charm too. But we are primarily concerned with the impact this concert had on London where the Savoy Bands made a comparable assault on the highbrow public with what was launched as an educational programme and sited at the Queen's Hall, London's most illustrious venue for classical music. In all there were five of these concerts at the Queen's Hall in 1925. David Boulton has described Bert Ralton as 'the ambassador of the Whiteman gospel' in Britain,[7] but by the time the Savoy Bands played at the Queen's Hall in 1925 Ralton had, of course, left although Mayerl was still in the Savoy Havana for the rest of that year.

The programme book was an eight-page coloured production containing a fulsome apologia. It cost one shilling, which Fred Mayerl, Billy's younger brother, remembers was a lot of money for a 14-year-old at that time.[8]

The unsigned portions of a kind of populist manifesto printed in the programme have much in common with the mood of the 1990s. They might even have come from a policy document of the new radio station, Classic FM, based on market forces and outlining accessibility criteria. But this aesthetic position, with its paean to syncopation, relates rather precisely to the appeal of Mayerl himself—it was his context too—and the details are worth examining before considering the reception of these concerts:

THE FIRST CONCERT OF SYNCOPATED MUSIC
THE SAVOY-ORPHEANS (Aumented Symphony Orchestra)

5   M. Stearns, *The Story of Jazz* (Mentor Books, New York, 1964), 121.
6   G. Schuller, *Early Jazz: Its Roots and Musical Development* (OUP, New York, 1968), 192.
7   D. Boulton, *Jazz in Britain* (Jazz Book Club, London, 1959), 44.
8   F. Mayerl, telephone conversation with Peter Dickinson, 22 Mar. 1991.

THE SAVOY-HAVANA BAND & THE BOSTON ORCHESTRA
By special permission of the Savoy Hotel
Queen's Hall
SATURDAY, JANUARY 3, at 8.15 p.m.[9]

And in the programme book:

MUST DULLNESS BE THE HALL-MARK OF ALL THINGS WORTH WHILE?

The arts which produce dullness and boredom are fake and bogus. Their sole accomplishment is a thinning of the mental corpuscles in a refined manner. Art is not art unless it carries a lively anticipation of delights—communicates ecstasy.

The great arts are begun in strength and happiness! Thus are begun and thus progress the brisk and gay arts, than which there is none more brilliant and brisk than syncopation and its new child, Symphonised-Syncopation—the spirit of happiness and music, the fullest expression of the joy there is in living—in life itself.

Among the Patrons and Patronesses:

Arnold Bennett	Freida Hempel	Dame Nellie Melba
Feodor Chaliapin	Augustus John	Sir William Orpen
Serge Diaghileff	Fritz Kreisler	Sir Landon Ronald
Amelita Galli-Curci	Robert Lynd	Leopold Stokowski
Jascha Heifetz	Senatore G. Marconi	Luisa Tetrazini

Mr. George Bernard Shaw said that he 'never patronises anything, and it would be of no use if he did, as people can read lists of Patrons without paying'.

This programme (for further detail see Appendix 1) sets the tone of the event as an assertive panegyric on syncopation. The list of patrons is distinctly fashionable, although Percy Scholes pointed out that they were not all there.[10] Impressario Sergei Diaghilev of the Ballets Russes always stayed at the Savoy Hotel and so did his leading dancers such as Tamara Karsavina and Lydia Lopukhova. The stars of international opera were represented by Fyodor Chaliapin, who even sent the Savoy Orpheans a tune which they arranged and played in the concert; Amelita Galli-Curci; Dame Nellie Melba, whose farewell performance would be at Covent Garden in the following year; Luisa Tetrazzini; and Frieda Hempel. Literature was represented by journalist Robert Lynd and the novelist Arnold Bennett, who considered, in 1923, that the Savoy Orpheans 'played bad music well'.[11] But he might have been converted later since ten years before that he had been unusually enlightened about ragtime in *The Times*: 'Ragtime is absolutely characteristic of its inventors—from nowhere but the United States could such music have sprung . . . Here for those who have ears to hear are the seeds from which a national art

---

[9] Personnel as listed in the programme are given in Appendix 1.
[10] *Observer*, 4 Jan. 1925.
[11] R. Pearsall, *Popular Music of the Twenties* (David & Charles, London, 1976), 77.

may ultimately spring.'[12] And after rebuking Americans for being too rooted in European sophistication rather than their own indigenous creations Bennett concluded with an assertion of market forces, so familiar in the 1990s, and well understood by Billy Mayerl in more than one of his capacities: 'Genuine art flourishes best in the atmosphere of genuine public demand.'[13]

Violinists were represented amongst the patrons by Fritz Kreisler and Jascha Heifetz; conductors by Landon Ronald and Leopold Stokowski; but there was only Augustus John for the visual arts and Guglielmo Marconi himself, whose invention had brought about the celebrity of these Savoy performers. But what would these patrons have made of this assertion in the programme? 'Only a small percentage of the people who support the "arty" arts really enjoy them . . . At many concerts, most opera, some classic dances and nearly all pageants, the spectators are suffering, and burning incense before the altar of the "arty" arts.'

On a longer time-scale this argument is phoney, which would not stop it emerging again, but Mayerl would have understood. He used to tell his brother, Fred, that 'people like to buy the things they like and don't want it all pushed down their throats'.[14] Further, when Mayerl met a reporter known as 'The Cavalier' on *Popular Music and Film Song Weekly* in 1937, he horrified his interviewer's mother 'with his devastating criticisms of Beethoven, Mozart and Wagner'.[15] The list of players for the Queen's Hall concert included Rudy Vallee, who really was the American singer and pre-Bing Crosby mass idol in his pre-college days, following service in the US Army. Herbert 'Rudy' Vallee, alto sax, replaced D. Smith in the Savoy Havana in September 1924: the much loved Carroll Gibbons came over with him and De Mornys gave him the job as pianist with the Boston Orchestra and soon after as second pianist with the Savoy Orpheans.

The programme was designed to be historical and educational in showing how ragtime and jazz developed into what was now being rather grandly called 'Syncopated Music of Today and Tomorrow'. Unfortunately it is not possible to tell exactly which pieces were played in some items. The programme notes now seem simple-minded and can be expected to make any student of jazz froth at the mouth. They may have been written by Norman Long, who used to present some of the Savoy Orpheans programmes. He worked in concert party and variety, was an early broadcaster, and specialized

[12] *The Times*, 8 Feb. 1913.

[13] When I sent this remark of Arnold Bennett's to Michael Bukht, then Programme Controller of Classic FM, he wrote: 'Many thanks for your letter and marvellous quote—I will use it often!' Letter to me of 16 Jan. 1995.

[14] F. Mayerl, telephone conversation with Peter Dickinson, 9 May 1997.

[15] H. Hall (ed.), *Popular Music and Film Song Weekly*, 1/3, 13 Nov. 1937, 14.

in songs and stories at the piano. Part of the Queen's Hall programme is re-produced in Appendix 1 as a document of the period, warts and all, which captures something of the mood of London at the height of the so-called jazz craze in 1925.[16]

A page of the programme I have not quoted is headed, '—and statistics prove it'. Details are provided only for the Savoy Orpheans, launched on 3 October 1923. Apparently 110,000 miles were covered in Europe and America in order to audition players for the all-star band; 7,800 pieces were tested to obtain the orchestra's original repertoire of 200 tunes; and more than three million records of this band had been sold in the previous ten months with three of their standards selling more than a million copies of sheet music each. The further claim that 'more people have heard and danced to the Savoy Orpheans than to any other group of musicians in any period of time or history' seems quite likely. And on 13 March 1924 it was the Savoy Orpheans who took part in the first 'organised attempt to broadcast a complete concert from Europe to all-America'. That was a success too.

It is amusing to see London's establishment paper, *The Times*, on 5 January 1925, grudgingly reporting the first of the five concerts given by the Savoy Bands at the Queen's Hall during that year:

A MUSICAL NOVELTY
JAZZ CONCERT AT THE QUEEN'S HALL

An innovation in musical entertainment was made on Saturday night at the Queen's Hall, usually the home of classical music, when a full programme of 'symphonised syncopation' was given by the Savoy Orpheans and associated orchestras. The Hall was filled in every part, and for two hours the bands held the attention of the audience with a series of numbers, in the main simply dance music, based on a syncopated form of rhythm. There was some reason to doubt whether this class of music, designed as it is to capture the dancer rather than the listener, would not tire a concert-hall audience, but if enthusiasm can be regarded as any criterion there would seem to be a place for this form of melody played with an arbitrary rhythm. Judged by its own standard the concert was certainly a success.

Leigh Henry, editor of a short-lived avant-garde magazine called *Fanfare*, was more enthusiastic in the *Chesterian* in February 1925:

Jazz in the concert-hall, to which the British lead was given last season at a British Music Society evening, 'A Synopsis of Syncopation', reached its culmination in the concert of the Savoy Orpheans at Queen's Hall, which demonstrated that jazz, on its own plane, can be a definite art-form, an epitome of what Cocteau terms 'the folk music of today'. Many dreary symphonic works would benefit by being imbued with such virile and amusing rhythms and such tuneful force. [17]

---

[16] Further details of the programme are also given in Appendix 1.
[17] L. Henry, *Chesterian*, 6/44 (Jan.–Feb. 1925), 128–9.

The *Gramophone*, two years after it had been launched, responded quickly and positively on 10 January 1925:

It is perfectly safe to say that never before last Saturday has the Queen's Hall witnessed such a sense of sheer cheeriness as when the Savoy Orpheans gave their first public concert. It provided one prolonged thrill . . . To me these Savoyards make a particular appeal because of their masterly, almost unique efficiency. Just how they have achieved this efficiency I know not, unless through the endless labour of genius.[18]

The *Morning Post* also praised ensemble, at the expense of the London orchestras of the period, which were paralysed by poor funding and the deputy system:

The Savoy Orpheans have a certainty of attack which makes in comparison the most famous symphony orchestra seem like a collection of amateurs. And it is not difficult to understand how an age, which suffers from habitual violence to its ears, should have succumbed to the exaggerated emphasis of syncopated music, just as the romantic Europe of a century ago fell a victim to the lilts of the waltz or the latter half of the eighteenth century to the sedate minuet.[19]

There was a similar programme for the second concert on 24 January described by *The Times* as 'in the nature of a demonstration' of the evolution of dance music and as such was 'most admirably drawn up and brilliantly executed'.[20]

But the anonymous writer goes on to castigate the style of performance in what must have been Billy Mayerl's solo (see Appendix 1) although it is unfortunately not clear what else he played:

Alexander's Ragtime Band, the point of departure, was a simple case of syncopation in which a strong accent was retarded to the second quaver of the bar. Imagine, then, the outrage to the mind when this happy memory of pre-war festivities (who could forget *Alexander* who danced to him in 1911 or lay off Phyllis Court wall during Regatta Week in 1912?) was played at twice its old speed, and with accents peppered onto every beat on which they would not go! Too much super-syncopation has destroyed the memory of what ragtime was. Too much accentuation—on every quaver and several semi-quavers of a bar of common time—is monotonous. The formula is too rigid; the rhythm is that of the mechanical road-breaker in Oxford Street; this music is dull.

---

[18] *Gramophone*, 10 Jan. 1925. The issues raised by the Queen's Hall concerts prompted several subsequent items in the *Gramophone*. In the issue of Sept. 1926 (145–6), Jack Hylton argued for a British touch rather than the American approach to syncopation. He had found that American dance-band arrangements were not popular in England. There was extensive further discussion based on correspondence and supportive comments from Basil Maine in an article, 'Symphonic Syncopation', in the issue of Dec. 1926, 302–5.

[19] *Morning Post*, 7 Jan. 1925.   [20] 'The Savoy Orpheans', *The Times*, 26 Jan. 1925.

Obviously the Mayerl pace was too much for him. The *Telegraph* described the bands as 'efficiency raised to its highest power'[21] but, as with ragtime a generation before, there was a kind of moral squeamishness in some responses. Dance music was still being tarred with the same brush as hot jazz: it was said to be unhealthy. A typical reaction came from the Australian poet and critic, W. J. Turner in the *New Statesman*: 'I conclude that those who feed exclusively or even mainly upon jazz music will find themselves sooner or later in a deplorable mental state.'[22]

Since the promoters of symphonized syncopation were claiming to rescue straight music from dullness, it is not surprising that some critics turned the tables on them. Tolerance of repetition varies according to culture. A regular beat has emerged from African tribal music into jazz; the use of ostinato has grown in twentieth-century music, with the relaxation of functional harmony; and repetition to engender trance-like states, often reflecting the use of drugs, is a feature of rock from the 1960s onwards. Minimalism, as a multicultural development in Western music in reaction to mainstream modernism, continues the process. Like so many other cultural and technological patterns affecting this century, the first major impact came in the 1920s.

The writer, broadcaster, and pioneer of musical appreciation Percy Scholes, realized what the programme was trying to do but found similar limitations. When he refers to 'eight years ago' he may have been thinking of the ODJB in 1919 rather than the Murray Club Jazz Band, which was the first British group to use such a title in 1917:

A determined attempt was made last night to legitimise Jazz, to throw over it the cloak of respectability. It was brought away from the dance floor to the concert platform . . . The rhythms, novel as they sounded eight years ago, do not seem to have developed a great deal in complexity. The greatest rhythmic interest was perhaps found in some clever piano solos by Mr. Mayerl, but the interest was quickly dissipated by that accursed habit of over-repetition, which, as already suggested, seems to be an inevitable feature of the genre, and which however much in place in the ballroom, becomes less so when transferred to the concert hall . . . The technical equipment of many of the players was, of course, consummate.[23]

Scholes went on to refer enviously to the line of smart cars not at the front of the Queen's Hall but outside the orchestra door.

Mayerl's formula of strain patterns and phrase repetitions in his compositions comes directly, as we shall see, from the piano rag and popular marches and dances before that. The way in which Stravinsky's British publisher advertised his *Ragtime for Eleven Instruments* (1919) in their house journal, the

---

[21] *Telegraph*, 22 Jan. 1925.   [22] W. J. Turner, *New Statesman*, 10 Jan. 1925.
[23] P. A. Scholes, *Observer*, 4 Jan. 1925.

Chesterian, made it all seem topical enough, but still assumed that raw ragtime, like sewerage, required treatment:

The modern predilection for the chamber orchestra and for syncopated music have jointly found their ideal interpretation in this work of Stravinsky's, which has already been performed with immense success in most of the world's musical capitals. Stravinsky here takes the elements of the jazz band and turns them, with his extraordinary sureness of touch, into artistic values.[24]

Jazz was faced with the same problem of identity when the first live performance in London of Constant Lambert's *The Rio Grande* on 13 December 1929 was received with headlines such as: 'Sudden Fame for Young Composer—Queen's Hall in a Frenzy—Jazz changed into Music of Genius.'[25] But, like *Rhapsody in Blue*, it was a more lasting triumph for symphonized syncopation than anything in the 1925 concerts by the Savoy Bands. It was admired even by Elgar who wrote to Lambert: 'May I take this opportunity to say how much I have enjoyed your *Rio Grande* and how highly I think of it.'[26]

The third Queen's Hall concert in 1925 was on 10 March. The patrons were the same; the personnel was the same—except that W. Huntington replaced Gubertini as percussion in the Savoy Havana and R. Purseglove replaced Motylinski in the violins of the Savoy Orpheans who now used two percussionists with Alec Ure added to Gubertini. But this programme was different, with more emphasis on a kind of nostalgia on a longer time-scale back into the nineteenth century.[27] In the programme notes, probably by Norman Long, the difficulties of playing syncopation seem calculatedly exaggerated, but if Stephen Foster was being played straight, authentically, this cannot fail to have been impressive. The Savoy Bands' connections with Horatio Nicholls—alias Lawrence Wright, the publisher, promoter, and founder of the *Melody Maker*—were maintained with 'Sahara' in the first of the Queen's Hall concerts, and now 'Shanghai', both of which the Savoy Havana had recorded. This third programme also cost one shilling, but it did not contain the same heavy propaganda for symphonized syncopation as the first one and it provided photographs of all three Savoy groups. But public enthusiasm was showing signs of declining. The music critic of *The Times* was hostile but confused:

The truth is that the whole claim that this so-called 'syncopated music' can be listened to as concert music is a pose. One can extract entertainment from the perfectly executed 'stunts' of the curiously constituted orchestra, but it goes no further, because the

---

[24] *Chesterian*, 6/45 (March–April 1925), 165.

[25] R. Shead, *Constant Lambert* (Simon Publications, London, 1973), 82.

[26] J. Northrop Moore (ed.), *Elgar and his Publishers: Letters of a Creative Life* (Clarendon Press, Oxford, 1987), 882.   [27] See Appendix 1 for details.

whole is based, not on rhythm, syncopated or otherwise, but on a trite formula of time which cannot expand into a style . . . [28]

Another report, much longer and not from a music reporter, appeared on 18 March. It was more good-natured about the enterprise, slightly guilty about enjoying the evening, and uncannily anticipated the late twentieth-century scene where music of all kinds became so readily available through mechanical media of increasing sophistication:

BARBARIANS
THE SAVOY BANDS
SOME SOURCES OF PLEASURE

. . . this week I find myself submerged among the musical barbarians. Who are the musical barbarians? They are the vast crowd to whom music is amongst the ancillary, if not the merely mechanical, arts. They dance to it, or 'listen in' to it, with a head-piece over their ears . . . or extract it with needles and a whirring disc, from the gramophone. 'Absolute' music—a violin sonata of Brahms or a Beethoven quartet—is to them the abomination of desolation spoken of in the book of the Prophet . . .

A certain elegance! That, I fancy, is the chief source of my pleasure, the elegance with which these Savoy bands play music in itself far from elegant and often verging on the vulgar. Even when they descend to the intentionally cacophonous they do it with a style and grace of their own. No one will deny that they are at their best in foxtrot music, and some of us think they would be wiser to stick to it. Its rhythm is as monotonous as the ticking of a clock, and the superimposed melodies are apt to be cloying; but when I hear it played with the daintiness and perfect finish of the Savoy bands, I feel that it has a real value among the excitements and exhilarations of life. Their typical instrument is the saxophone, a terror in unwary hands and the butt of the comic press; but if any honest musician, after hearing Mr. Jacobs of the Boston Orchestra play his solo, can ever pooh-pooh the saxophone again, I'll eat my hat. A.R.W. [29]

The *Gramophone* found the third concert 'as great a success as the others'; and felt that 'Carroll Gibbons carried off the honours at the piano . . . though Messrs. Gibbons and Mayerl, as before, were wonderful in their duets'.[30] This time Mayerl played no solos. The music critic of the *Daily Telegraph*, Robin H. Legge, was more sympathetic than most of his colleagues. In a favourable review of the first concert [31] which does not mention Mayerl, he regretted the absence of Gershwin's *Rhapsody in Blue* since he regarded it as 'an outstanding example (at present) of the meeting of the ancient and the modern both in form (more or less) and in matter'. Then in his Saturday column, *World of Music*, on 24 October, he announced the fourth of the Queen's Hall concerts on 28 October but added disappointing news about Gershwin:

[28] 'Syncopated Rhythm: Savoy Orpheans at the Queen's Hall', *The Times*, 11 Mar. 1925.
[29] 'Barbarians, The Savoy Bands, Some Sources of Pleasure', *The Times*, 18 Mar. 1925.
[30] *Gramophone*, April 1925.
[31] R. H. Legge, 'Syncopation in Excelsis', *Daily Telegraph*, 5 Jan. 1925.

Inspired by the success which has attended their previous efforts, the Savoy Orpheans are giving a concert of the music they play so superbly in the Queen's Hall next Wednesday. It is interesting to hear that several days ago upwards of 75% of the seats had already been sold! The feature of the programme is Gershwin's *Rhapsody in Blue* of which some months ago we heard a good deal, but never the music, for so far it has not yet been performed in public. Unfortunately the composer himself, who was to have played it, now finds himself unable to reach London from New York in time to take part in the performance. But there are several accomplished pianists in the honourable company of the Orpheans . . .

Indeed there were but it is quite complicated to prove exactly who played what from written evidence in these early British performances of *Rhapsody in Blue*. The attempt to do so can even make matters worse. And, inexplicably after what he said, Legge does not appear to have reviewed it. There was ample coverage in the *Daily Telegraph* of the première of Holst's Choral Symphony and a revival of Stravinsky's *Petrushka* in the same week but it is astonishing that the main dailies and Sundays were silent about the first live performance of *Rhapsody in Blue*, when the earlier Queen's Hall concerts had attracted so much excitement.[32]

But first we must go back a bit. On 15 June 1925, from the Savoy Hotel, the BBC broadcast a programme called 'Syncopated Symphonic Music' with the Savoy Orpheans Augmented Symphonic Orchestra, conducted by Debroy Somers, and the Savoy Havana, conducted by Raymon Newton. This included the first performance in Great Britain of *Rhapsody in Blue* with the composer at the piano. This is confirmed in the BBC archives[33] and also by an item in the *Sphere* with a picture of Gershwin and a prophetic pointer towards *Porgy and Bess*:

The American Composer Whose 'Dignified Jazz' has been Broadcasted in England

Mr. George Gershwin, the well-known American songwriter who composes 'dignified jazz', is now in England for the broadcasting of his Rhapsody in Blue by the Savoy Orpheans. Mr. Gershwin played the piano part. This Rhapsody indicates the possibilities of jazz, and he has been urged to compose an entire opera in the jazz musical idiom.[34]

The *Westminster Gazette* felt that the *Rhapsody* 'commanded attention and stood repetition', and would 'find a place in musical history'.[35] Much more detail and some intelligent deductions came from the *Liverpool Post*:

---

[32] The situation is extraordinary. There were no reviews of the 28 Oct. Queen's Hall concert in the *Daily Telegraph, The Times, Sunday Times, Observer, Evening News, Daily News, Morning Advertiser*, and, of course, the concerts were ignored by the serious magazines like *Musical Times, Musical Opinion* and *Monthly Musical Record*.

[33] BBC Programme Records, Vol. I, 1922–6.   [34] *Sphere*, 27 June 1925.

[35] *Westminster Gazette*, 16 June 1925.

The Evolution of Jazz

Many musical notabilities, who might otherwise have been at the opera last night, were gathered by invitation at the Savoy Hotel to hear the first performance of George Gershwin's now famous *Rhapsody in Blue*. I saw there many well-known pianists—Moiseiwitch, Myra Hess, Marcelle Meyer—and among other musicians, Mme. Poldowski and Eugene Goossens. The band was that of the Savoy Orpheans, with the composer at the piano. The movement of which this work is an early fruit proposes to deal with jazz as Chopin dealt with the mazurka or Mozart with the minuet. It is, however, only a beginning. So long as it keeps to an improved quality of jazz it is full of interest, but when Gershwin falls back on what a purist might call 'the legitimate', the quality is immediately let down and even the date set back by some years.

So far as anything may be taken as proven, this shows that the jazz movement must either master all the resources of modern music or restrict itself to those of its own making. No midway path will lead anywhere. Gershwin probably realises that much from this experience, and the Concerto which Walter Damrosch has commissioned from him for the New York Symphony Orchestra will show how the style is to develop.[36]

The *Daily News* also reported on the occasion as the 'first performance in London' of the *Rhapsody in Blue* at the ballroom of the Savoy Hotel with the composer and the Savoy Orpheans[37]—a work previously known through Paul Whiteman's recording made the year before.[38]

Apart from the broadcast audience, a concert at London's most exclusive hotel was hardly a public occasion. So some interest attaches to the next hearing of *Rhapsody in Blue* in London. In view of the fact that Legge, in his column in the *Daily Telegraph* four days before the concert on 28 October, had said that Gershwin would not be able to play, the following reports are surprising. First, the *Star*:

Gershwin's Rhapsody in Blue at Queen's Hall

Under Mr. Debroy Somers the Savoy Orpheans gave a concert at the Queen's Hall last night, which was darkened—as though it were Bayreuth—while coloured lights played on the muslin curtains which formed the background to the platform . . .

Gershwin's *Rhapsody in Blue* was played, for the first time in public, by the composer. If all jazz music were of the same quality one would not regard its prevalence with such uneasiness . . .[39]

And the *Daily News* also claimed Gershwin's presence:

Savoy Orpheans

The augmented symphonic orchestra and the Savoy star soloists gave another of their popular concerts at the Queen's Hall last night, with darkened hall and coloured light

36 *Liverpool Post*, 16 June 1925.   37 *Daily News*, 16 June 1925.
38 Paul Whiteman and his Concert Orchestra, 10 June 1924, released on Vic. 55225, HMV C1171, 30173–2, and 30174–1.
39 'Gershwin's *Rhapsody in Blue* in the Queen's Hall', *Star*, 29 Oct. 1925.

effects. The chief item in the programme was the *Rhapsody in Blue* played by its composer Mr. Gershwin of which I have said several times that it is the only piece of jazz
which deserves serious consideration and is very like Liszt.[40]

The item is signed A.K. and, as with earlier reviews, confirms that these
Queen's Hall concerts, long before competition from films and TV, were ex-
perimenting with new ways of presenting live music in the concert hall. The
dimmed lights might have made it difficult to see who played what or to read
the programme but it is surprising how careless reviewers at this period were
about including performers' names. Perhaps they were not even there?
Newspapers which did report on the concert infuriatingly failed to mention
even the soloist. For example, the *Daily Mail*:

RHAPSODY IN BLUE

The Savoy Orpheans last night at Queen's Hall gave a highly rhythmical concert of
symphonic music to a delighted audience. The most amusing thing was Mr. George
Gershwin's *Rhapsody in Blue*, a fierce and very comical burlesque of a piano concerto. It
is the work of a musician and a wit.[41]

The *Dundee Courier* seemed to have a hot line to Gershwin himself when it announced the October concert in advance:

ENRICHED BY MUSIC

Mr. George Gershwin, whose *Rhapsody in Blue* is to be played by the Savoy Orpheans
at their next concert at Queen's Hall, London, on October 28, is one of the young men
whom music has made rich. It is musical comedy rather than the *Rhapsody* that is
mainly responsible for this. The *Rhapsody* is so difficult that few can master it
sufficiently for public performance. Mr. Gershwin says that its difficulty lies in the fact
that he has used the piano more as an instrument of percussion than melody. To get
these effects one has to develop a technique contrary to a good many piano playing
principles. Mr. Gershwin finds the *Rhapsody* easy because he has written it for his own
technique.[42]

Before reaching a verdict on the 28 October concert we can note that the
fifth Queen's Hall concert took place on 9 December, by which time there was
even less press interest. The identity of the soloist this time was clear, at least
to the *Manchester Guardian*:

At the close of the concert George Gershwin's *Rhapsody in Blue* was played with Billy
Thorburn in the difficult piano part. This work, the most interesting product of jazz
so far, is written in the form of a concerto and is full of effects which, though they fail
to blend into one single impression, are new and arresting in themselves . . .[43]

---

[40] *Daily News*, 29 Oct. 1925. [41] 'Rhapsody in Blue', *Daily Mail*, 29 Oct. 1925.
[42] 'Enriched by Music', *Dundee Courier*, 22 Oct. 1925.
[43] *Manchester Guardian*, 10 Dec. 1925.

How does this confusing press comment about the Queen's Hall concert of 28 October referring to Gershwin himself as a performer fit with what came from Mayerl or his agents?

The *Keith Prowse Courier* for December 1925, just over a month after the October 28 concert stated:

At the Savoy Orpheans' Concert held at the Queen's Hall on October 28, 1925, Mr. Mayerl rendered from memory, in marvellous style, Gershwin's *Rhapsody in Blue* . . . Mr. Mayerl was the first pianist in this country to play this celebrated composition in public, and it is admitted that he did it full justice and interpreted the composer's ideas in masterly fashion, his execution being nothing short of marvellous. [44]

And, from Mayerl himself, in the *BMCM* ten years later where he discusses the approach to the final grandioso:[45]

Light treatment is again necessary until the contrary motion progression leading up to the grandioso. This progression should be started piano and each chord should be played with plenty of hand weight. A slight rall. may be included, although this is not specified [it is in the Warner score]; but I did this when I played it at the first performance in England at the Queen's Hall in 1925, and the composer was sitting in front: he commented upon what he thought was an excellent effect.[46]

In 1973 Irene Ashton, who met Mayerl a few years later than the Queen's Hall concerts, supported this:

Billy gave the first public performance in Great Britain of Gershwin's *Rhapsody in Blue*, again at the Queen's Hall. He was a great personal friend of George Gershwin who, during the rehearsals before this performance discussed with Billy his own ideas of the interpretation of the work.[47]

The only person I have reached who was actually there was the composer's brother, Fred, who as an impressionable schoolboy queued up at the Queen's Hall to go to the concert. He told me that Mayerl's performance was one of his earliest recollections of the Queen's Hall and he was quite definite that on the first occasion *Rhapsody in Blue* was played by Mayerl—and Fred used to have a

44   Quoted in the Biographical Note to the *Billy Mayerl Book of Breaks*, 'published by arrangement with the Billy Mayerl School of Modern Syncopation, who own all rights in all educational work from the pen of Billy Mayerl'. This note refers to Billy playing the Grieg Piano Concerto at the Queen's Hall at the age of 6½; writing his *Eastern Suite* [presumably *Egyptian Suite*] at the age of 12; and joining the Savoy Havana in 1920. The note also states that 'in performing the classics of the great composers his execution and technique are just as wonderful as when he is rendering the popular syncopated music'.

45   G. Gershwin, *Rhapsody in Blue*, 1924, 1942 WB Music Corp., New York. Mayerl is referring to figure 39, although he is obviously not using the Warner Brothers miniature score available now.

46   B. Mayerl, 'Some Practising Hints for the Rhapsody in Blue', *BMCM*, 2/17 (May 1935), 27–8.

47   I. Ashton, sleeve-notes for *The King of Syncopation*, EMI WRC SH.189.

photo of Billy and Gershwin together—then it was played next by Billy Thorburn.[48]

Fred Mayerl interviewed a series of professional musicians for the *BMCM* which included Debroy Somers. Almost eleven years after the Queen's Hall concert, which was conducted by Somers, Fred commented:

I remember seeing him conduct the Savoy Band in a concert of dance music given at the Queen's Hall, London, in 1925. The triumph of the evening was the performance of Gershwin's *Rhapsody in Blue*. This was the first public performance of the work to be given in this country, and at the piano was Billy Mayerl.[49]

In 1996 Fred Mayerl remembered that his brother had told him he was going to play *Rhapsody in Blue* long before the October concert took place. Further, Fred confirmed that Gershwin certainly was not there—he was not introduced, not on stage, and did not take a bow after Mayerl's performance. A decisive factor is that Gershwin was not in England in October 1925. He sailed from Southampton on 24 June on the *Majestic* and on his return was working flat out to finish three works for December performances in New York—the Piano Concerto in F, *Tip-toes*, and the operetta *Song of the Flame*—and the second half of October was fully occupied with orchestrating the Concerto which was completed by 10 November.[50] So what did Mayerl mean when he said that he had played the Rhapsody with Gershwin 'sitting in front'? As we have seen, the press have been no help in sorting this out, but Fred Mayerl, who was there, has helped to confirm the only acceptable solution—Billy Mayerl did play it on 28 October and Billy Thorburn on 9 December.

What follows from all this is that we can regard the *Daily Telegraph* announcement as correct whereas the other lesser papers were probably using common syndicated material about the concert which had simply not been brought up to date. Since Gershwin was not there on 28 October Mayerl may have played *Rhapsody in Blue* for Gershwin when he was in England that summer. Ten years later, living at such high pressure, he may have fused memories of two separate occasions—or he may have been claiming to know Gershwin better than he did. Mayerl's first secretary, Mrs McInerney, could not recall Gershwin visiting the Billy Mayerl School when he was in London, although Louis Armstrong apparently did.[51] Mayerl's performance of *Rhapsody in Blue* would certainly have been authentic in style since he had heard Gershwin play it, had met him, and was in total sympathy with his aims.

Another revealing connection between the Savoy Bands and a major composer concerns William Walton, as his biographer Michael Kennedy reports.

---

[48] F. Mayerl, telephone conversation with Peter Dickinson, 10 Sept. 1996.
[49] 'A Famous Savoyard: Debroy Somers', *BMCM*, 3/7 (July 1936), 3–5.
[50] Jablonski, *Gershwin*, 101.
[51] E. A. McInerney (Hooper), Interview with Peter Dickinson, 11 May 1992.

Around 1923 Walton apparently worked with the Savoy Orpheans but they never played anything 'except at rehearsals . . . They were more occupied with the current "hits" to bother very much about my somewhat clumsy efforts . . . I wasn't quick enough really to be of any use. I used to be allowed a free tea. Quite a help in those days.'[52]

And again:

Walton was introduced to Debroy Somers by Richmond Temple, a director of the hotel. Invited to make arrangements of foxtrots for them, Walton spent a year in fruit-less endeavours. His interest in jazz had led him to improvise tunes on two pianos with Angus Morrison, but he never committed any to paper. However, in 1923 he com-pleted a large-scale project, a Fantasia Concertante for two pianos, jazz band, and or-chestra. 'I have to see what can be done with my concerto for these Savoy people', he wrote to his mother from 2 Carlyle Square (Osbert Sitwell's house in Chelsea) on 4 May 1925, 'though I am afraid there is only a remote chance of anything satisfactory coming out of it'.

According to his close friend, Constant Lambert:

Walton suddenly abandoned the jazz style in a fit of disgust, rightly realising that the virtues of ragtime, its pungent timbres and intriguing syncopation, are more than handicapped by the deadly monotony of the four-square phrases, the inevitable har-monic clichés stolen from Debussy and Delius, the trite nostalgia of the whole atmos-phere.[53]

That fits with Lambert's later strictures about *Rhapsody in Blue* in *Music Ho!*[54]—although by then Lambert himself had written both *Rio Grande* and his Piano Concerto in the symphonic jazz tradition—but William de Mornys, in a letter to Stewart Craggs, goes further and explains the immediate climate in which Mayerl's Queen's Hall performance of 28 October took place. It looks as if the claims for symphonized syncopation, at least with dance bands in-volved, had simply been pushed too hard: 'He (Gershwin) gave a "first" of the *Rhapsody in Blue*. At the Savoy it had a snob success. On the concert platform at the Queen's Hall, it had no success and worse on the provincial tours. There was no interest then in that type of music and I feared for the Fantasia.'[55] Others confirmed the change of mood. W. B. Parkin, in the *Sound Wave*, wrote:

The *Rhapsody in Blue* forged by the genius of Gershwin was a sure and unmistakable token that the crest of the wave of this particular 'new' music had been reached. It was

52   M. Kennedy, *Portrait of Walton* (OUP, Oxford, 1990), 33.
53   Ibid. 39.
54   C. Lambert, *Music Ho!: A Study of Music in Decline* (Faber & Faber, London, 1934), 223. (Penguin edn. (Harmondsworth, 1948), 162–3.)
55   Kennedy, *Portrait of Walton*, 39.

itself a glorious compendium of all the up-to-date achievements of foxtrot music and the distilled essence in symphonic form of modern dance-o-mania and saxophobia.[56]

So Walton's answer to *Rhapsody in Blue*, the most enduring monument in the genre, was thus lost for ever. It might just have been as successful as England's answer to Schoenberg's *Pierrot Lunaire* launched on 24 January 1922 but revised and added to through the decade—*Façade*.

The Savoy Orpheans' 1926 tour was announced in the *Radio Times* with the following dates—Brighton, 1 and 2 January; Leeds, 4 January; Bradford, 5 January; Liverpool, 6 and 7 January; Manchester, 8 and 9 January; and visits to BBC stations.[57] This gives an idea of the pace of their schedule: Mayerl took part in the Easter tour even though his regular contract had ceased.[58] Since they aimed to be up to date in every way they were travelling by air, 'weather permitting'. It was good for publicity and further headlines followed when the Orpheans actually broadcast from the air: 'THE FLYING SAXOPHONES'; 'AIR-SICK SAXOPHONE'; and 'SYNCOPATING THE AIR'.[59] The Orpheans, with the two last Queen's Hall concerts still to come, were using this publicity to elevate—even literally—the status of symphonized syncopation, which Bill de Mornys in October 1926 brashly referred to as having 're-placed jazz three years ago'.[60] Their stunt was imitated by Jack Hylton's band broadcasting 'Me and Jane in a Plane' by Leslie and Gilbert from the air over Blackpool in 1927. The *Radio Times* declared: 'The Orpheans will endeavour to establish their claim that syncopated music such as Gershwin's *Rhapsody in Blue* deserves to be accepted as a serious contribution to art.'[61]

On more than one level Mayerl and Gershwin had much in common. They were both of central European extraction. Both composer-pianists grew up in the ragtime era and matured in the 1920s. They were both affected by the symphonized syncopation movement, coupling the swung idiom with the rhetorical gestures of the romantic piano concerto. Mayerl played the Grieg concerto as a child—the work obviously left an indelible impression—and Gershwin incorporated romantic cadenzas into *Rhapsody in Blue* which are blatantly juxtaposed with the band scoring of Whiteman's arranger, Ferde Grofé. Constant Lambert found *Rhapsody in Blue* a 'singularly inept albeit popular piece . . . neither good jazz nor good Liszt, and in no sense of the word a good concerto'.[62]

---

[56] W. B. Parkin. 'The Fox-trot and its Music', *Sound Wave*, Mar. 1925, 206–8.
[57] 'Savoy Orpheans to Tour', *Radio Times*, 16 Oct. 1925.
[58] 'Billy Mayerl', *Sound Wave*, 26 June, 163.
[59] 'The Flying Saxophones', *Daily News*, 23 Oct. 1925; 'Air-sick Saxophone', *Daily Mail*, 10 Nov. 1925; 'Syncopating the Air', *Daily Chronicle*, 10 Nov. 1925.
[60] 'New Dance Music', *Glasgow Bulletin*, 1 Oct. 1926.
[61] 'Savoy Orpheans to Tour', *Radio Times*, 16 Oct. 1925.
[62] Lambert, *Music Ho!*, 223.

Lambert's criticism has dated in that *Rhapsody in Blue* has triumphantly lived on and such criticisms may have missed the point—certainly if applied to Gershwin's next landmark, the Piano Concerto (1925), where conventional academic strictures about weak form have had to be adapted to recognize a typical late twentieth-century technique involving 'style-modulation'.[63] Mayerl, too, did not score all his own orchestral works, such as *Sennen Cove*, and the way in which he employed conventional passage-work for the piano in his larger pieces was a weakness probably encouraged by *Rhapsody in Blue*. In the orchestral field Gershwin came out on top. But on his own ground Mayerl was just as successful, as scrutiny of his works will now show. Unfortunately there is no record of what Gershwin thought of Mayerl, or whether they met in New York in 1924, but we do know how Mayerl reacted to Gershwin's sudden death in 1937, since Irene Ashton was there:

I can still remember the day when Billy came into the distinguished Steinway Hall premises where he had his School of Music. Madge Howard was teaching in her studio, Geoffrey Clayton was at the central desk, a few feet from my desk, when I heard these slow weary steps climbing the outer staircase. Billy entered through the School's swing door wearing the then fashionable camel hair coat and his soft felt hat slightly back. Mr. Clayton and I looked at him with alarm for we had discussed the sudden early death of George Gershwin. News in the 1930s does not travel as fast as it does today. Looking directly at Mr. Clayton he said in a choked voice: 'George has gone!' And, as he walked slowly through the central office to his studio he called out to his two secretaries, his brother Fred and another young girl: 'Please don't disturb me. Cancel all my appointments'. He was now alone for well over an hour and we were all shattered knowing that our boss was an enormous admirer of Gershwin and his unique music. Many telephone calls went through saying that Mr. Mayerl could not deal with current business and lessons. When Billy did leave the School that sad morning he had, in my opinion, been weeping copiously.[64]

[63] P. Dickinson, *Style-Modulation as a Compositional Technique* (Goldsmiths College, London, 1996). Based on 'Style-Modulation, an Approach to Stylistic Pluralism', *Musical Times* (April 1989), 208–11.

[64] I. Ashton, 'My Memories of Billy Mayerl and Gershwin', *Billy Mayerl Circle Newsletter*, 3/17 (Summer 1978), 4–6.

5

THE MUSIC OF THE SAVOY YEARS

A PICTURE is now emerging of Mayerl as a product of influences from American popular music with a remarkable piano technique evolved from ragtime, novelty, and early jazz. His piano-playing survives as transfers from old 78 recordings, as on the CD with this book, but the core of his work lies in his compositions, especially the solo piano music. In looking at all these, it becomes clear that Mayerl's music was not just a question of American influences. The razzle-dazzle of 1920s novelty piano is only one element which was soon found alongside distinctly English qualities in his solo music from concert platform to salon.

Early works are always revealing in the light of a composer's future development and, since no unpublished juvenilia has emerged, the canon starts with Mayerl's *Egyptian Suite*. It was published by an obscure firm rather improbably named the Renaissance Music, Art and General Publishing Co., of 36 Cromwell House, High Holborn, London WC1. The cover sports a sailing boat on a lake with pyramids in the distance and informs us that the Suite 'may be performed as a pianoforte solo in public without fee or licence, but orchestral performances must be from the score which is on hire from the publishers'. The composer is specified as William Mayerl and he had signed the copy I have seen with 'Best Wishes: W. Mayerl'. The ownership is indicated as Copyright 1919 William Mayerl. Was Mayerl such a businessman, even at the age of 17, that he retained his own copyrights? He never did this again, although he often made or authorized orchestral versions of his piano works.

The Suite consists of three movements—*Souvenir* (Moderato)—*Song of the Desert* (Andante)—*Patrol of the Camels* (Allegro). The use of tonic pedals and major ninth chords confirms that Grieg was his 'favourite composer', but there are original touches in the harmony especially at cadences.[1] This acute

---

[1] B. Mayerl, 'High Notes in my Life of Rhythm', *Tit-bits*, 19 June 1937. The Grieg inheritance was particularly useful when highly successful commercial composers, such as Albert A. Ketelby, wanted to create an exotic effect for films with bare fifths and pedal-points. Not so much in his salon evergreen, *In a Monastery Garden* (1915), but travelogues like *In a Persian Market* (1920) and *In a Chinese Temple Garden* (1923), both written after Mayerl's *Egyptian Suite*.

harmonic ear is particularly individual in the second movement—as focused as anything Mayerl ever wrote (Ex. 1).

The gapped scale of Bflat minor with a sharpened fourth creates an exotic atmosphere; there are attractive arcs of melody; and the harmony is distinctly original for a 17-year-old. The cadences at the end of phrases drop onto a tonic chord with added second at the end of the second and third four-bar phrases and this harmony ends the piece poignantly. There are even suggestions of what we shall soon identify as popular music's barbershop chord. This is not popular music but is part of a suite which is an unusual first opus.

Grieg is again the model for the third movement—specifically the folk-like bass patterns—and, as in the first piece, there is plenty of repetition in more technically demanding textures which would make a good show in performance. Finally, even at this stage knowing the drill for cyclic form, Mayerl brings back into the last movement three bars of the Andante followed by five bars of the opening Moderato before the *Patrol's* final fling.

Ex. 1. Mayerl, *Song of the Desert* from *Egyptian Suite* (1919)

As it happens, there is a work by Cyril Scott, known as the English Debussy, called *Egypt: An Album of Five Impressions*, which was published in 1913 and could well have formed a model. Scott was particularly adept at writing short pieces which define a mood, and Mayerl would have noticed his almost constant employment of impressionist chords. Mayerl played Scott in some of his later radio broadcasts and this influence seems to have been just as strong as the more obvious ones of Debussy and Ravel.

The lack of response to his *Egyptian Suite* had a profound effect on the composer. In 1937 Mayerl told his own story, showing that he must have written a lot more music at this period:

During this time I must have been London's most prolific composer and the world's leading optimist. I told myself that I must be a commercial composer, and not one who wrote music for art's sake. I worked hard at my creations and eventually produced a little *Eastern Suite* in three movements, and a song which I called 'Longing'. It might never have been published had I not taken it to a fellow-student of Trinity who had turned publisher. His name was Cecil Dudley, and his business was called the Renaissance Music, Art and General Publishing Company, High Holborn.

My composition came out at 4*s*. [£5.40] a copy. Some people must have bought it for I drew 3*s*. 6*d*. [£4.70] in royalties. Keith Prowse, then as now, exhibited all the latest music in their Bond Street window, changing their window dressing every Monday. But there was never a hint of my *Eastern Suite* being in existence. Finally I went inside and asked about it. But they had never heard of it. I came to the conclusion that sales must be stimulated.

For days I tramped the entire round of West-end and suburban music shops asking for a copy of the *Eastern Suite* and boosting its merits in ecstatic terms. Alas, nobody had ever heard of it. My sales-stimulation plan was, like my *Suite*, a failure.

I started on dance tunes and songs and hawked them round publishers, but they were never the required 'type of stuff'. I took to studying types—classical solos, novelty numbers, comedy songs, ballads, drawing-room music—and then set to supply the entire market with the right 'type of stuff', trying to be a musical Einstein-cum-Charlie Chaplin-cum-G. K.Chesterton-cum-Bernard Shaw-cum-P. G.Wodehouse all rolled into one. What ambition! What optimism!

My music-case bulged with 'types'. As soon as a publisher murmured 'not our type', I thrust the next example before him. And I'll swear no living composer ever hawked more of his own compositions than I did during my cinema-playing years, when I was still in my 'teens.[2]

Particularly noticeable is that Mayerl presumed that his *Egyptian Suite*—he had even forgotten the title twenty years later—was a failure just because it never reached the public. It satisfied no demand. So he concluded, 'I must be a commercial composer'. He did not have long to wait. In 1924 four of his songs with lyricist Gee Paul were British hits; so were two of the *Pianolettes* in

---

[2] B. Mayerl, 'High Notes in my Life of Rhythm', *Tit-bits*, 19 June 1937.

1925, *The Jazz Master* and *The Jazz Mistress*; and 1927 listed *Hollyhock* and (no surprises here) *Marigold*.[3] In an interview on *Woman's Hour* for the BBC Home Service in 1952 Mayerl himself explained what made the difference:

I was on the air three or four times a week, gradually introducing new pieces I had written, and the music publishers began to sit up and take notice. Compositions which had been rejected came out in print, and I became known as the inventor of new rhythmic noises—very nice to listen to but rather difficult to play! Cross hands and black notes— almost playing in between the cracks![4]

Mayerl's first British hit song was 'Did Tosti raise his bowler hat? (When he said "Goodbye")', from the revue, *Punchbowl*, which ran for over 500 performances. This bouncy tune was recorded by the original performers, Norah Blaney and Gwen Farrar with piano, and by Ramon Newton with the Savoy Havana.[5] In both performances it makes an impact in spite of the song's roundabout title and complicated scenario which now needs explaining.

Sir Paolo Tosti was the Italian ballad-composer and singing teacher who settled in London in 1880, the year he published his popular ballad 'Addio'— there were twenty-three versions on CD in 1998. He was appointed singing teacher to the royal family and was knighted by King Edward VII in 1908, returning to Italy four years later. Tosti said goodbye in more than one sense— leaving England and writing his song about the end of summer called 'Goodbye'.

Mayerl's song, 'Did Tosti raise his bowler hat', is basically in the ragtime tradition complete with barbershop chords on the flat sixth of the scale, as a way of harmonizing the blue minor third, in both verse and chorus (Ex. 2).

This tactic goes back to *The Maple Leaf Rag*, quite apart from its history in classical and romantic music. But it was the American Lewis F. Muir, who came to London with the American Ragtime Octette in 1912, who made the process overt in his song called 'Play that barbershop chord' (1910). The chord appears four times in the first four bars of the verse (a dominant seventh on F in relation to tonic A minor) and the chorus contains stretches of two bars of this harmony (A flat in relation to tonic C). This relationship is behind the first three notes of Rachmaninov's famous Prelude in C sharp minor, Op. 3 (1892), which was

3 *Sixty Years of British Hits 1907–66* (The Songwriters Guild of Great Britain, 1968).
4 B. Mayerl, interviewed by Jean Metcalfe as Guest of the Week on *Woman's Hour*, BBC Light Programme, 27 Aug. 1952.
5 'Did Tosti raise his bowler hat (When he said "Goodbye")?' Savoy Havana Band Bb-6215–1. See B. Rust and S. Forbes, *British Dance Bands on Record 1911–1945* (General Gramophone Publications, London, 1989), 865. There were two other band recordings of this song in 1925: Percival Mackey's Band and the Marlborough Dance Orchestra. The British jazz musician and writer, Spike Hughes, in *Opening Bars* (Pilot Press, London, 1946), 307–8 and 323, reveals that he possessed recordings of Mayerl's 'Did Tosti' and refers to *Virginia Creeper*, but he never even mentions the name of the composer.

Ex. 2. Mayerl, Song (Gee Paul), 'Did Tosti raise his bowler hat?' (1924), Refrain

so - la to - pee or a vel - our, ___ A fire-man's hel - met would have look'd ab-

- surd: ___ So some-how I'm quite cer - tain that it

must have been a bow - ler hat that Tos - ti raised when Tos - ti said 'Good-

- bye'. ___ Did - bye. ___

very popular and was frequently swung, as in George L. Cobb's *Russian Rag* (1918). The first three bars of the introduction to Jelly Roll Morton's *Jelly Roll Blues* (copyright 1915) turn out to be based on this harmonic relationship. Mayerl used this procedure consistently throughout his career—so often that it is not always worth mentioning.

The use of breaks at the end of the chorus of Mayerl's 'Did Tosti', where the voice is on its own with dry chords for punctuation, is a routine of both ragtime and jazz combos. It works splendidly, especially in the Savoy Havana recording where Ramon Newton sings one chorus. Their tempo is minim 120, but the Blaney–Farrar performance is slightly slower. The Gee Paul text is witty too:

> Stocks and shares don't worry me, nor the income tax
> I don't care where flies in winter go:
> I don't mind if ladies' gowns haven't any backs,
> But there's one thing that I'd like to know.
>
> REFRAIN
> Did Tosti raise his bowler hat when he said 'Goodbye'?
> (See Ex. 2)

In the same year 'I'll take you to Kew' from the show *London Revue* seems pretty routine. 'Just a little love', described on the sheet music which appeared in *Popular Music Weekly* as 'The Savoy Havana Band's Great Song Fox Trot Success', is a flapper song with the barbershop chord again in the chorus to emphasize the words 'nervous and terribly shy'. But 'Love's Lottery' from *Charlot's Revue* is in a different league—the chorus, 'Any time, any place, anywhere', could have a controlled intensity somewhere between Kurt Weill and Cole Porter with the right singer.

Popular songs come to life with a particular performer and arrangement: the sheet music is, of course, only the start and there is far more leeway than with the art song. We shall return to the question of the status of popular songs which have never been or have not remained popular. But Mayerl's piano pieces are in a different category. The notation is enough just as it stands. The problem is to find performers who can play such dazzlers as *The Jazz Master* anywhere near as well as Mayerl himself, as he realized.

The foxtrot tempo of 'Did Tosti raise his bowler hat' is applied to most of Mayerl's solos in his own performances. That breathless 1920s pace is part of the music. But first it is necessary to try to establish when Mayerl achieved this style and where he got it from. This is his own account in 1937:

Unknown to the authorities at Trinity College, and to my father, I had made a habit of visiting a place called Gayland in Shepherd's Bush and spending all the money I could raise on the penny-in-the-slot machines which squawked American ragtime tunes like *Robert E. Lee* and *Alexander's Ragtime Band*. They had a thrill and a liveliness which fascinated me. I never wanted anything so much in my young life as to be able to infuse my weekly College composition with some of that 'go' and quick rhythm.

Actually, an excess of classical highbrow music rushed me towards syncopated jazz. My first syncopated tune was a part of my life. After the horror of its reception by my tutors I cherished it secretly through the years and in 1923 I presented it to the world, dressed up in all the finery and elegance at my command, as *The Jazz Master*.

It was the first English syncopated jazz composition for the piano, quite different from the honky-tonk of the American ragtimes. Over 150,000 people bought copies of it. I say 'bought' advisedly, for I can't say they were playing it. They couldn't! For at first there was only one man in all England capable of playing it—and that was the young composer, myself! That, I consider, was the foundation-stone of my career. Since *The Jazz Master* I have taught 30,000 people in Europe, the Dominions, and other countries what is now known as 'the Mayerl style of syncopation'.[6]

As we shall see, *The Jazz Master* was not 'quite different from' American extensions of ragtime into novelty piano but it can be regarded as the 'foundation-stone of his career'. Mayerl told his Trinity College piano teacher, Maud Agnes Winter, in 1935: 'I was always writing queer rag-time tunes. No, I never told anyone about them—I used to keep them all hidden away.'[7] The medium through which he absorbed these tunes must have been the polyphon, a disc musical box often found in London pubs. It was invented in the 1880s and after the turn of the century an automatic disc-changing device was added, all activated when the penny went into the slot. The songs he mentions with such relish made a tremendous impact, which could not be acknowledged in family circles or at College. He had to operate in a kind of underground movement.

'Waiting for the Robert E. Lee' (1912) by Lewis F. Muir was one of the biggest hits in the second generation of ragtime songs, a regular feature in the repertoire of the Original American Ragtime Octette. This was the period dominated by 'Alexander's Ragtime Band' (1911) by Irving Berlin, the second song Mayerl cites. The verse of both songs decorates the third degree of the scale—the first three bars even use the same notes before Berlin goes down and Muir up. Berlin continues with obsessive decoration of the third degree above tonic and subdominant chords in his chorus, but then he goes in for comic quotation—the bugle call and Stephen Foster's 'Old Folks at Home', 1851. Mayerl, too, followed this pattern of putting witty quotes into his pieces.

---

[6] B. Mayerl, interview with Jean Metcalfe. Mayerl's claim to have written the first English syncopated jazz composition for the piano may need qualification as more work from this period emerges. A curiosity is the solitary rag written by Max Darewski, younger brother of Hermann, called *Monkey Blues* (apparently written in 1918) and played with real panache on *Early Piano Ragtime 1913–1930*, compiled by David A. Jasen on Folkways Records RFB 33, New York 1977. Stanley C. Holt is another British figure who produced pre-Mayerl novelties.

[7] I. Ashton, 'Twenty Years After', *BMCM*, 2/12 (Dec. 1934), 3–5, 10.

Muir's layout is exceptionally spacious harmonically, like the nineteenth-century evangelical hymns where it would be easy for anyone to pick up the bass-line by ear. The whole chorus is based on tonic and dominant with tonic for the first four bars, dominant for the next eight, tonic for the next four, with the whole sixteen-bar pattern repeated. This is a rousing chorus with a real charge from the initial syncopation onto the sixth above the tonic (a tactic from Viennese waltzes) and good contrast with its long notes. Both Berlin and Muir have choruses in the subdominant, the tradition inherited from marches and rags. In 1898 Sousa explained that in his childhood in Washington he noticed that bands often finished marches with the trio, in the subdominant, rather than going back to the beginning as the da capo indication implied. Consequently Sousa felt that if that was how marches were going to be played he might as well write them that way in the first place.[8] The influential *Creole Belles* by J. Bodewalt Lampe, recorded nine times before 1908, is a well-known example. This tradition remained valid for Mayerl: five of the six *Pianolettes* and *Marigold* follow it, even if he himself did not always end his performances with the trio.

But the differences between the two songs are the most striking. As is often pointed out, Berlin's sheet music actually contains no syncopations, although its dotted rhythms invite some and the tune's catchiness has helped to turn it into a standard.[9] The same is true of 'Waiting for the Robert E. Lee', a song about cotton workers waiting for their cargo ship, whereas Berlin's song, like Muir's 'Play that barbershop chord', is celebrating the music itself or its performers.

If Mayerl is precise in saying that he wanted to put this 'go and vigour' into his compositions for Trinity College then he must be referring to 1914/15, his last recorded year as a student there. So he absorbed ragtime formulas through popular song derivations in his early teens in a fundamental, ineradicable way. The vast majority of his pieces are in rag form, including *Marigold* (CD ⑪ and ⑫) and a much later piece like *Look Lively*.

It still seems surprising that Mayerl said he 'cherished *The Jazz Master* (CD ①) secretly through the years' and kept such things 'hidden away' until 1923. It is extraordinary that he waited to publish when he was so anxious to get into print. By this time Mayerl had witnessed *Kitten on the Keys* become a sensational hit, cast as the prototype of the novelty idiom when it was recorded by the composer (at least three times) and published in 1921. Taking the published sequence to be *Kitten on the Keys* (1921) and *The Jazz Master* (1925), we are bound to look at internal evidence to see how Mayerl responded to early

---

[8] E. Berlin, *Ragtime: A Musical and Cultural History* (University of California Press, Berkeley, 1980), 100–1.

[9] C. Hamm, 'Alexander and his Band', *American Music*, 14/1 (Spring 1996), 65–102.

Confrey. There has been no traffic back across the Atlantic where Mayerl's longer-term failure to penetrate the American market is confirmed by what Ronald Riddle wrote inaccurately in 1985: 'In England the genre was promoted by Billy Mayerl, who published a dozen of what he called Syncopated Impressions.'[10]

Zez (Edward Elzear) Confrey was born in Peru, Illinois, in 1895. As a pianist he was something of a prodigy, played on the Chicago River steamboats when at LaSalle-Peru High School and then had a classical training at the Chicago Musical College, which introduced him to Debussy and Ravel. He became associated with the new style of novelty piano, making piano rolls, starting with *My Pet*—unusually in a minor key—as early as 1918. Then it was the appearance of Confrey's first five pieces as sheet music in 1921 that established the novelty genre. They came out in this order—*My Pet*; *Kitten on the Keys*; *You Tell 'em, Ivories*; *Poor Buttermilk*; *Greenwich Witch*—and *Coaxing the Piano* the next year.

Landmarks in some of these Confrey pieces are worth observing from Mayerl's point of view. *Kitten* has an introduction in right-hand parallel fourths ending with two bars of till-ready. This type of filling in, known as vamping, was common in music-hall turns when the soloist's entry was being anticipated; it is found in the sheetmusic of popular songs but is rare in piano rags; the A strain employs what is called secondary ragtime or three-over-four rhythmic figures in the right hand, decorating the third degree in the manner of *Alexander's Ragtime Band* but going as far back as Joplin's *The Easy Winners* (1901); similar secondary ragtime figures are extended through three octaves in the trio. *You Tell 'em, Ivories* has relaxed melodic fourths in the right hand, in a similar mood to *Marigold* and in the same key. The trio of *Coaxing the Piano* has an eight-bar introduction based on a long chromatic descent in the left hand with the right outlining the French sixth chord. Mayerl would often use chromatic descents for his introductions, as in *Marigold* and *Mignonette*. Then comes Confrey's sixteen-bar trio proper, which is repeated (Ex. 3).

Similarities to Mayerl now seem too close for coincidence since Confrey's right-hand figuration uses the same notes as the A strain of *The Jazz Master*, but Mayerl is far more inventive (Ex. 4 and CD ☐1).

Confrey's trio is not a particularly striking conclusion to *Coaxing the Piano*—he has made his pieces easier since *Kitten* in any case. Mayerl, on the other hand, quickens up the Confrey model and uses it in his own way, even more difficult than *Kitten*. In *The Jazz Master* bar 1 of the A strain echoes

[10] R. Riddle, 'Novelty Piano Music', *Ragtime, its History, Composers and Music* (Macmillan, London, 1985), 285–93.

Ex. 3. Zez Confrey, *Coaxing the Piano* (1922)

the Confrey figure up an octave in the manner of James Scott's rags; the last F in the right hand, bar 2 of this strain, should be natural (corrected here) and is played that way by Mayerl; the second-time bar at the end of the A strain and its later repeat sports the barbershop chord. This opening is vintage Mayerl. It may have been bonded in Confrey but it is still Mayerl's challenge to the world—and to future generations of pianists. The stomping left-hand figure at the start of the B strain recalls the till-ready in *Kitten* and there is a tendency in many pieces for Mayerl to follow the fashion for employing a dominant chord with raised fifth, which Confrey does not do at cadences.

Ex. 4. Mayerl, *The Jazz Master* (1925)

After years of silent film accompaniment, Mayerl had countless syncopated routines up his sleeve, but perhaps he needed the stimulus of Confrey before he could put them into final form, 'dressed up in all the finery and elegance at my command'. He also admitted:

It was at this time [1925]—encouraged by my wife, who had faith in it—that I went ahead with my idea of a new jazz composition and produced my syncopated solo, *The Jazz Master*. It sold so well that, with a royalty of only 3*d.* a copy, I quickly realised my first £1,000 [£32,800] on it. [80,000 copies, if any such figures can be trusted, bringing a considerable sum.][11]

This may explain things—Mayerl delayed to gain confidence, perhaps surprisingly, and waited for the right moment when he had absorbed Confrey and other influences such as Roy Bargy, whose novelty solos were also in print by 1921.[12] Mayerl also had to wait for a publisher. This immediate ancestry is no detraction from Mayerl's achievement: even Gershwin acknowledged his debt to a host of pianists and mentioned Mike Bernard, Les Copeland, Melville Ellis, Luckey Roberts, Zez Confrey, Victor Arden, and Phil Oman.[13]

Gershwin also provides a complicating factor in this whole discussion of chronology. His *Novelette in Fourths* came out on a piano roll as early as 1919, predating *Kitten on the Keys*. In the key of E flat, like *You Tell 'em Ivories* and *Marigold* and its imitators, the *Novelette* anticipates many of the stylistic features we have been discussing. But it was not published until 1925 and then only as a violin and piano piece called *Short Story*, arranged by the violinist Samuel Dushkin.[14] It came from a manuscript notebook of pieces that Gershwin called his *Novelettes* and he dismissed them as 'not worth bringing out'.[15] Since the *Novelette in Fourths* was not printed in the original piano version until 1993 it has often escaped notice. The *Novelette* displays novelty features to be found later in *Marigold*. The melody is doubled in fourths immediately; the dominant has raised fifths; the melodic syncopations and their accompaniments produce a 3+3+2 rhythm; and there are excursions to the barbershop chord. All this comes in the first strain of a piece in rag form. The *Novelette* is an unexpected landmark in novelty

[11]   B. Mayerl, 'We Played on as a Prince Lay Dying', *Tit-bits*, 26 June 1937.
[12]   It is unfortunate that Bargy has been submerged by Confrey, since his dozen piano novelties have real character and show all the tricks of the trade. *Knice and Knifty* (1922) has right-hand fourths, 3+3+2 rhythms, and repetitive figures. *Rufenreddy* has witty repeated minor-second breaks. Bargy played and recorded them himself and it is easy to imagine Mayerl doing so.
[13]   G. Gershwin, Preface to *Gershwin at the Keyboard: 18 Song Hits, arranged by the Composer* (Chappell, 1932).
[14]   *Gershwin plays Gershwin: The Piano Rolls*, Elektra Nonesuch 7559–79287–2 (1993).
[15]   E. Jablonski, *Gershwin: A Biography* (Simon & Schuster, London, 1988), 94.

piano, re-emerging so late, but it seems unlikely that it could have had any effect on Mayerl.

Gershwin's teenage contribution to the piano rag came earlier still, in 1916, when he made piano rolls of *Rialto Ripples (A Rag)*, his joint composition with Walter Donaldson, another highly successful composer of popular songs. Its one-bar principal motif is repeated obsessively—twice in the four-bar introduction and three times in each of the first four-bar phrases of strain A. This type of repetition, allied to a breathless pace, is a feature of Mayerl's numbers. The trio contains two bars taken from strain B, has three appearances of an extra flourish in small notes, and a right-hand break. Following the lead of *Twelfth Street Rag* (1914) by Euday Bowman, *Rialto Ripples* has the driving force of Tin Pan Alley behind it, made the more formidable by the rare minor key. Given Gershwin's exhibitionist style of performance, it is not unreasonable to regard *Rialto Ripples* as an early novelty piano piece in rag form, showing Gershwin, like Mayerl, responding to the tempo of the times, but it never made the impact of *The Jazz Master*.

Any pre-history of Mayerl influences needs to mention some important sources of rhythmic ideas common to Gershwin, Confrey, and Mayerl. In particular the secondary ragtime or rhythmic three-over-four found in the most popular rag of all, *Twelfth Street Rag* (1914) by Euday Bowman, which Mayerl must also have heard in those penny-in-the-slot machines at Shepherds Bush. In sheet music this rhythmic technique goes back to the first two strains of Joplin's *The Maple Leaf Rag* (1899), where it does not start on the downbeat: Bowman does and uses this tactic to devastating effect. However, in gentler mood, the A strain of Joplin's *Original Rags* (1899) begins on a downbeat and creates the 3+3+2 rhythm often found in Mayerl.[16] Other precursors of Bowman are the final strain of Percy Wenrich's *Peaches and Cream* (1905) and C. L. Johnson's *Dill Pickles* (1906).[17]

In 1934 Mayerl called this Latin-American rhythm a rumba, which he defined as having the same 3+3+2 rhythm as the Charleston but with all the intervening notes filled in and no rests.[18] The Charleston was at the height of its

---

[16] B. Mayerl, 'This Month's Lesson', *BMCM*, 1/12 (Dec. 1934), 32, 12.

[17] F. J. Gills, 'Hot Rhythm in Piano Ragtime'; J. E. Hasse, 'Ragtime from the Top'; and other chapters in J. E. Hasse (ed.), *Ragtime: Its History, Composers and Music*.

[18] As n. 16. For his students, in *The Billy Mayerl Special Tutor Course in Modern Syncopation* (undated), Mayerl describes this cross-rhythm effect as 'the 3/4 foxtrot metre' and says that it is 'the foundation of at least 50% of breaks and embellishments that will occur in the correct rendering of a syncopated tune'. The simple version is in Confrey's 'Stumbling' (1922) but the Gershwins' 'Fascinating Rhythm' from *Lady, Be Good!* (1924) goes much further with a 7/8 fragment against 4/4 which does not come to heel until bar 4. In 'Jazz Structure and Influence', in *Modern Music* (Jan.–Feb. 1927), 9–14, Aaron Copland observed that this type of cross-rhythm 'typified the jazz age with its independent rhythms spread over more than one measure'.

fame when Mayerl wrote the *Pianolettes* in 1925–6. So much so that its rhythm infiltrates the opening of the first movement of both Gershwin's Piano Concerto (1925) and the second movement of Copland's Piano Concerto (1926).

Mayerl's rhythmic tricks, allied with speed, helped to dazzle his audiences and are an essential feature of his style. Almost every strain has something slightly dislocating happening with comic effect, a musical equivalent of the silent Charlie Chaplin films. For example, all six *Pianolettes* are in quadruple time and Mayerl has a habit of breaking disconcertingly into waltz tempo, usually momentarily. In *The Jazz Master* (CD ① 0′ 35″) strain B has its first two bars effectively in 3/4; strain C of *The Jazz Mistress* (CD ② 1′ 27″ and 1′ 42″) has a brief example of this where Mayerl plays an internal melodic scrap not in the score; the A strain of *Eskimo Shivers* (CD ③ 0′ 10″) goes off the rails with five waltz oom-pahs in the left hand before it starts to recover; this tactic is very obvious in the C strain of *Virginia Creeper* (CD ⑤ 1′ 38″) when there is nothing else going on; and there is a particularly disrupting example in *Loose Elbows* during the A strain (CD ⑦ 0′ 15″ and 0′ 24″).

Then there are the cross rhythms based on smaller units of, usually, 3+3+2 as well as patches of 3/8. Examples of 3+3+2 include the introduction of *The Jazz Mistress* (CD ②), where it is also developed in strain B (0′ 35″); there are many examples in *All-of-a-Twist* (CD ④), most obviously in the right-hand break of the A strain (0′ 17″) but this is preceded by 3/4 and 3/8 passages. When the left hand rhythm section ceases and these effects are unaccompanied, as in both strains A and B, the effect is as 'weird and intoxicating' as Joplin said he wanted his ragtime to be.[19] Exactly the same thing happens in the trio of Confrey's *Kitten on the Keys*, and *Stumbling* is based on the conflict between 4/4 and 3/4.[20] In Mayerl these errant cross-rhythms, over a strong beat, usually come to heel inside two bars and conform or stop to take stock. There is a longer one lasting four bars in the second half of the introduction to *Antiquary* (CD ① 0′ 04″). This is four runs of 3/4 against the 4/4 context rounded up with the perfect cadence: as usual the passage recurs but, as with a successful conjuror, the trick still works. In strain 2 of *Sleepy Piano* (CD ⑩ 1′ 10″) the blue right-hand tenths are enhanced by the 3/4 cross-rhythm. The mini-cadenza in strain A of *Marigold* is another example which will be referred to later.

These *Pianolettes* are a set of transcendental studies in the novelty idiom where the authentic impact comes from the speed. They are also of their time in that, in between the rhythmic stunts, there are fascinating scraps of melody

---

[19] Scott Joplin, 'School of Ragtime', *Collected Piano Works* (New York Public Library, 1971), 284.

[20] Note Alan Feinberg's stunning performance of *Kitten on the Keys*, ending an American anthology called *Fascinatin' Rhythm*, on Argo 444 457-2 (1992). And see Eteri Andjaparidze, the pianist from the republic of Georgia, on a fine all-Confrey CD on Marco Polo 8.223826 (1999).

like nostalgic echoes of popular songs of the day—a feature of the piano music of Erik Satie and Francis Poulenc too. In later life Mrs Mayerl still took justifiable pleasure in the fact that nobody else could play them like Mayerl himself, with his effortless, weightless delivery.[21] The *Pianolettes* make a brilliant set, although they have never been republished as such, with a greater technical range than Confrey, who soon turned away from pyrotechnics to something much blander, as his collected piano works shows. Confrey's essential role for Mayerl was that of catalyst at a crucial stage to his eventually more extensive and varied output. But there are further points of comparison to which we shall return. As early as 1926 Confrey wrote his *Fantasy (Classical)*, indicating the frame of reference in the title itself, and followed it with what he called a jazz arrangement of the same piece. This parallels Mayerl's transcriptions but lacks his kind of individuality. By the end of the 1920s Confrey was writing unsyncopated pieces such as waltzes and concert studies.

All six Mayerl pieces are listed on the original sheet music covers as *Billy Mayerl Pianolettes* and his picture is captioned with 'Solo Pianist to the Savoy Havana Band'. They are worth looking at in some detail simply as performances since they show Mayerl at the height of his powers and give some idea why his playing created such a sensation.

Mayerl plays all six at around the same speed, ranging from *The Jazz Mistress* at ♩ = 120 and *Virginia Creeper* about ♩ = 136. There are no tempo markings on the sheet music, apart from a hopeful 'moderato' attached to *Eskimo Shivers*. There is not much dynamic range in the recordings, but more in the transfer from a piano roll of *Eskimo Shivers*.[22] The overwhelming impression is of speed and accuracy in unedited recordings and the sheer stamina of delivery. This must have been true of Mayerl's live performances surrounded by the excitement of a circus stunt. Comedians such as the Cheeky Chappie (Max Miller) also gave this kind of impression: 'When he was on stage he generated a sense of danger—you thought this is somebody who is dicing, gambling, and is going to get away with it.'[23] Mayerl was accustomed to playing from memory so that some details in the sheet music naturally got ironed out or varied. He rarely misjudged one of the demanding left-hand jumps but if he did he almost invariably managed to leave it out rather than play a wrong note.

Everything Mayerl said about left-hand emphasis in his 1926 *Melody Maker* articles, and in all his teaching, is evident in his approach. The basis is a rock-solid left-hand rhythm section, in the tradition of ragtime and stride piano. Classically trained pianists rarely appreciate this and they sometimes go further

[21] J. Mayerl, interview with Peter Dickinson, 11 Aug. 1981.
[22] *Marigold: Billy Mayerl's Music*, on Conifer CDHD 205
[23] J. Fisher, *Funny Way to be a Hero* (Frederick Muller, London, 1973), 83.

by indulging in unsuitable rubato. The debate about correct style for Mayerl could be carried on as it was for Joplin in the early 1970s, with Joshua Rifkin ex-emplifying the purists and others feeling the need to amplify the sheet music. In Mayerl performances we have seen Katia and Marielle Labèque amplify *Honky-Tonk* for their riotous two-piano version, as Mayerl did himself for the duet version of *Marigold* (CD ⑫). But what few pianists have yet been able to do in the mid-twenties virtuoso pieces is to deliver them as effortlessly at speed as he did. One of the clues is a light touch—Mayerl did put 'lightly' as the only marking on *The Jazz Mistress* and *Jack-in-the-Box*—and another is a piano with a light action. This was a characteristic of the Challens that Mayerl liked to play and they also had a slightly thin tone.

Another clue to Mayerl's astonishing virtuosity is that he was at the key-board for long hours in adolescence. As he was growing up physically the lo-cation of the keys must have been built into his responses so that he could operate with the skilled precision of a fine string player trained from child-hood. However, there were times when he overdid it:

I was fulfilling an engagement at the house of the late Mr. Norman O'Neill, when my left arm suddenly dropped dead at my side, as useless and lifeless as a piece of putty. It scared me, and it also embarrassed me, for the guests were left standing in the middle of a dance. The hostess hurried towards me and I assured her that it would be all right in a few moments. But it didn't come right for three months.[24]

After that the left arm recovered but the right one became affected for some months. The condition was diagnosed at the time as moving neuritis, might now be regarded as repetitive strain injury, and Mayerl recovered completely. He was so shocked by the experience that he undertook never to play for ex-cessive periods again, admitting that he had not kept his promise.

Ironically the layout of Mayerl's keyboard writing feels more natural when played at high speed, the very thing that amateurs would never have had the courage to risk however much they proved that they wanted to try by buying copies of the music.

Mayerl is again described as 'Solo Pianist with the Savoy Havana Band' on the sheet music covers of the four *Piano Exaggerations—Loose Elbows*; *Antiquary*; *Jack-in-the-Box*; and *Sleepy Piano*, four more examples of vintage early Mayerl, which develop the Mayerl mannerisms at their freshest and most resourceful. This time the pieces are numbered in the order of publication with the first three appearing together and the last one later.[25]

---

[24] B. Mayerl, 'We Played on as a Prince Lay Dying', *Tit-bits*, 26 June 1937. Norman O'Neill was one of the most successful composers and conductors of incidental music for the theatre in London. He was a friend of Delius and may well have discussed his music with Mayerl.

[25] *Piano Exaggerations—Loose Elbows* (KP 3013); *Antiquary* (KP 3014); *Jack-in-the-Box* (KP 3015); *Sleepy Piano* (KP 3075).

Loose Elbows (CD ⑦) starts in G and ends with a trio in A flat. Like the next two in the set, it has an eight-bar introduction: this one is placed over consecutive $^6_4$ chords in the left hand and in the fifth bar the dotted 3+3+2 rhythm, which does need the loose elbows, is introduced. The A strain of *Loose Elbows* lands on a prominent blue note in its second bar, a figure which is not repeated when the twelve-bar section comes back as the strain's second half. After the B strain (0′ 28″)(another double one but based on sixteen bars) the introduction and A strain recur, followed by a transition ingeniously related to the introduction's $^6_4$ chords, now whole-tone rather than chromatic, but leading to a C strain (1′ 28″) as trio, with a catchy second half. Mayerl's own performance at about ♩ = 138 does not finish here but goes back to the beginning, stopping short of the trio.

Antiquary (CD ⑧), named after Mayerl's favourite whisky, according to Mrs Mayerl, makes a feature of dotted rhythms rather than syncopation. It too lacks a tempo indication in the printed score, but Mayerl's own performance is again at about ♩ = 138, which is stunning for such a difficult piece and makes it sound close to the jazz piano of J. P. Johnson. When Mayerl repeats strain A, characterized by its right-hand dotted rhythms over a regular bass, he goes back to the eight-bar introduction where the barbershop chord relationship is the basis of most of it.[26] The double B strain (starting at 0′ 36″) plays rhythmic games of the kind we have observed in the *Pianolettes*; the A returns; and then there is an elegant A major C strain (1′ 15″) with the introduction coming back at the end in the major. But Mayerl himself is unstoppable and cannot resist playing both the A and B strains again.

Jack-in-the-Box (CD ⑨), marked 'Lightly', starts repetitively but already in the A strain there are melodies, first ingeniously picked out in the passage-work and then overt, and the C strain (1′ 29″) in sub-dominant D flat has a lovely nostalgic tenor melody, in an unusual left-hand thumb layout, alternating with swung breaks. Mayerl himself, at a similar tempo to the first two pieces, does not repeat strain A this time and stops at the end. Two years later Confrey published a piece called *Jack in the Box*. It is much easier to play, but the square four-bar phrases, feebly repeated, and limited textures show how Mayerl developed from Confrey's early initiatives but Confrey himself did not.

The title of the fourth piece in the set, *Sleepy Piano* (CD ⑩), might suggest some relaxation of pace, if anyone can imagine any piano Mayerl played as sleepy, and there are further new features in a style that is moving closer to *Marigold*. *Sleepy Piano* is more melodic, marked 'Slow Fox-trot tempo', but Mayerl himself still recorded it at almost the same speed as the others. It is perfectly proportioned with every strain at the highest level. The six-bar introduction, coming down

[26] Note how the descending bass of the introduction *Antiquary* is augmented at the start of strain A (unusually only 12 bars) but then the harmony goes not to the barbershop F (minor sixth up) again but to its opposite D flat (minor sixth down).

from highish register, prefigures the pentatonic melody of strain A (double), which sets it in right-hand octaves. Then there is a delightful secondary melody in parallel thirds, as a perfect foil, plus some accordion chording to finish the strain. Like the B strain of *Marigold*, this B strain (1′ 06″) starts with right-hand trills and continues with—for Mayerl—an unusual focus on jazz piano effects such as split notes, right-hand blue tenths, breaks, and *tremolandi*. The transition to the D flat strain C is marked *pp* and consists almost entirely of dominant major ninth chords over a chromatic bass (1′ 47″). Dr Richard Head, the seasoned Mayerl connoisseur, considers this nostalgic final strain to be 'the real Mayerl magic'—he is right and this applies to the whole of *Sleepy Piano*.[27] Mayerl himself cut the repeats of strains A and C and there is nothing sentimental about his recording. His rhythm is precise, in dance-band tradition, his touch light and the texture is dry, never over-pedalled.

All this shows Mayerl expanding his range as a composer at the start of his career at the same time as he took on new responsibilities as an entertainer and as head of the Billy Mayerl School.

At the height of his Savoy years, about to launch off on his own, he was a sensation. His sheer speed captured the public imagination and, since there was nothing like it in England, it called for documentation in the most up-to-date medium that 1925 could offer. Under the heading 'JAZZER' FILMED, Mayerl told the *Daily Herald*:

About 25,000 copies of this volume [*The Jazz Master*] have been sold and although the printed music does not contain anything like the amount of 'stuff' I put into the playing of it, there are not 25,000 people who can play it as it is written.

But they will persist in having a go, and the idea of taking a slow-motion picture is to get the actual fingering into a film and, in that way, record the music as it is really played.[28]

Mayerl was trying to consolidate his monopoly before going freelance. Firstly he implied that his own pyrotechnics added to the printed page, which does not always fit the facts, and, secondly, that the way he himself played was the authentic version. Thus, to get the full experience you need him or his recordings, which was good for business when the score and the record had been out only a few months. The story was hot news for the rest of the year as is indicated by the number of papers which covered it after the *Daily Herald* piece on 28 October.[29]

[27] R. Head, letter to Peter Dickinson. On tapes which H. Nichols made for the Billy Mayerl Circle, he recalled that Mayerl used to come on stage dressed in a nightcap and carrying a candle to perform *Sleepy Piano*.   [28] *Daily Herald*, 28 Oct. 1925.
[29] Press cuttings from the Savoy archives include—*Daily Graphic*, 29 Oct. 1925; *Glasgow Bulletin*, 30 Oct. 1925 (with photo); *Sydenham Gazette*, 4 Nov. 1925 (describing him as a 'popular radio performer'); *Hinckley Times*, 21 Nov. 1925 ('Famous Jazz Pianist', with photo); *Eve-and-Everybody's Film Review* (same period, with photo but no date); *Daily News*, 11 Dec. 1925.

It was an item in the *Daily Graphic* which brought in the caption of 'lightning fingers':

SLOW MOTION FILM OF LIGHTNING PIANIST

[photo of Billy Mayerl being filmed]

Mr. Billy Mayerl, the pianist of the Savoy Havana Band, being filmed by a slow-motion camera in order that the script writers may be able to record his compositions accurately. Previously his lightning fingers baffled them.[30]

All this was excellent publicity at a time when Mayerl was about to leave the Savoy to start his new ventures. The *Era* provided a variation on this caption:

SAVOY PIANIST'S NEW ROLE

Billy Mayerl, the pianist for the Savoy Havana Band, is appearing at the Coliseum on April 19. Known familiarly as the pianist with the 'twinkling fingers', he will feature a number of syncopated piano solos of his own composition. It is an interesting fact that every member of this famous band is distinguishing himself in some individual way.[31]

An item in the *Sound Wave* in June 1926 showed that Mayerl went on appearing with the Savoy bands after he had officially left in January and confirmed his role with *Rhapsody in Blue*. We also learn something about his method of composition and more about his attitude to the term 'jazz':

His wonderful solo playing at the now historic Savoy concerts held at Queen's Hall and others in important provincial cities, was considered to be the best of its kind ever heard in this country, a special test being the marvellously skilful render of Gershwin's *Rhapsody in Blue*—a classic of syncopation—the first time it was publicly performed in England. He is accompanying the Savoy Orpheans on an Eastern tour, as solo pianist, performing at Glasgow, Edinburgh and Newcastle-on-Tyne . . .

He composes on paper and revises several times with great care before trying over on the piano, and is not content until he has the work perfect.

The word 'jazz' does not appeal to Mr. Mayerl as descriptive of his compositions—he prefers the term 'syncopation'.[32]

The reception of this tour in Edinburgh showed that syncopation still had some hurdles to vault in the puritannical Scotland of 1926. It was another example of what we have already observed as a fear of primitive urges even though, in the Savoy Orpheans, there was not a Black person in sight. In 1936 Debroy Somers told Fred Mayerl that a Scotsman travelled all the way from Aberdeen to hear the band under the impression that all the players were Black.[33]

---

[30] *Daily Graphic*, 29 Oct. 1925. [31] *Era*, 7 Apr. 1926.
[32] *Sound Wave*, June 1926, 163.
[33] F. Mayerl, 'A Famous Savoyard: Debroy Somers', interview with Somers, *BMCM*, 3/7 (July 1936), 4.

JAZZ ON GOOD FRIDAY

Protest against a Savoy Band Concert, Edinburgh
Meeting of Members of the Board of Edinburgh Royal Infirmary confronted with
protest. The Rev. Canon Gordon said that the performance of jazz music on Good
Friday was an outrage in the capital of a Christian country.[34]

All the same the Infirmary did not refuse a present of a cabinet gramophone
and letters of support for the Savoy Orpheans followed.

The year 1926 was crucial for the music business in London. The princi-
ple of payment for the right to perform copyright music was controversial at
first and took some years to establish. A major group of popular music publishers left the Performing Right Society in 1919 but returned in 1926.
Mayerl himself became a member then and so did Gustav Holst (see
Appendix 3). The new media of broadcasting and enhanced recording quality caused patterns to shift away from sheet music and domestic performance.
This was the period when Mayerl's fame was still rocketing—he became a
spectator sport—and he benefited from another lucky coincidence.
Lawrence Wright launched a new magazine, the *Melody Maker*, in January
1926—exactly the right moment to promote Mayerl in all his capacities. In its
first number the magazine announced that he was leaving the Savoy and
starting his School of Syncopation. In April there was a report on his
Birmingham Hippodrome appearance where he got top billing. His act
lasted fifteen minutes, included popular songs as well as his own pieces, his
two-pianos-at-once stunt, and finished with requests—where it was said that
he was never caught out since he had the advantage of a photographic memory. Just in case the public became sceptical about his ability to handle all
these demands, the *Melody Maker* reporter confirmed that he would still be
able to attend daily to the School business.[35]

In the June issue a report on his week at the London Coliseum from 17 May
found him 'at the height of his fame' and 'displaying an astounding perfection
of technique'.[36] His début with the singer-cellist-comedienne, Gwen Farrar,
was announced for July. By the October issue Mayerl's photo prominently
adorned the front cover as a prelude to three articles from him in November
and December 1926 and January 1927. Readers were warned in no uncertain
terms that 'no modern pianist who desires to emulate Billy Mayerl's own unrivalled technique should miss so splendid a feature'.[37] As if all this was not
more than enough, the November issue launched the Billy Mayerl Salon
Syncopators, with Ron Gray as pianist-leader, described as 'supplied and

---

[34] *Daily Express*, 6 Apr. 1926.
[35] 'Billy Mayerl on the Halls', *Melody Maker* (Apr. 1926), 25.
[36] 'Billy Mayerl Stops the Show', *Melody Maker* (June 1926), 21.
[37] 'Billy Mayerl to Write for the *Melody Maker*', *Melody Maker* (Oct. 1926), 10.

trained by Billy Mayerl', and Billy Mayerl's Vocalion Dance Band, which recorded some fifty titles as Billy Mayerl and his 'Vocalion' Orchestra, appeared with him at the Queen's Hall.

The three articles themselves are a preview of the techniques Mayerl was starting to use at the School in its teaching materials and through the instructional sections of the Billy Mayerl Club Magazine, which we shall consider later. All three emphasize the pre-eminent role of the left hand with the first two entitled: 'That Left Hand! Or the Secret of Syncopation on the Piano'. Even the last one is called: 'That Left Hand! And how it should be assisted by the Right'.

Mayerl was included amongst the stars wishing readers a Happy Christmas in the December issue and he must have been delighted with the opportunities provided by a new magazine for a multi-pronged attack on the soft target of his avid public. So must his business partner, Geoffrey Clayton, whose facetious articles are sprinkled around these issues too. The Mayerl monopoly at this stage created a fantastic start for what was already being heralded as the Rolls Royce of Correspondence Courses.[38] And he was even developing a career in London's musical theatre as well.

---

[38] Advertisement in the *Melody Maker* (July 1926), 6.

6

MAYERL ON STAGE

AFTER the First World War London retained its position as a centre for musical comedy but American influences were gaining ground.[1] Pre-war British works followed the traditions of comic opera in distant historical settings, but American developments emphasized dancing choruses, hit songs, and syncopation. Initially the Americans were able to continue to produce popular music and market it without the demands of war and after the American entry in April 1917 there was enhanced British enthusiasm for the American way of life—and some resentment at such prosperity. Major American figures such as Kern, Gershwin, Rodgers, and Porter wrote musicals specially for London, offering sharp competition to the leading British exponents, Noel Coward and Ivor Novello. Music-hall in England developed in the mid-nineteenth century as free entertainment in taverns and signified a mixed collection of acts or stunts designed to appeal to a working-class audience. It was also known as variety and had much in common with the French *café-concert* and American vaudeville. After the First World War variety became big business and celebrities played to large audiences in purpose-built theatres in London and throughout the country. In 1920 there were some seventy halls in the capital and over 600 outside. Powerful managers, knighted for their services, such as Sir Edward Moss and Sir Oswald Stoll, operated circuits for tours based on family entertainment. This is what Mayerl meant by 'going on the Halls' and in the *Performer* of 27 May 1926 he was described as 'the world's greatest pianist from the Savoy Havana Band': under the management of Will Goldstone, he was advertised as 'now booking vaudeville'. The revue was yet another format—it took on American influence in pre-war shows such as *Hello, Ragtime!* (1913)—and it was maintained by leading promoters such as C. B. Cochran and André Charlot. Categories and terminology overlapped

---

[1] W. Macqueen-Pope, *Night of Gladness* (Hutchinson, London, 1956), 245: 'The decline of the British musical play and the virtual death of musical comedy were brought about by the invasion of syncopated music—jazz, if that is preferred, and then by the First World War.'

and there was a flexible interchange between them. For all these forms of entertainment the early 1920s was a boom period but the development of the cinema and radio, combined with widespread unemployment, made inroads into live audiences in the 1930s until the war created a revival.

Mayerl's entries in *Who's Who in the Theatre* list his first engagement as in variety in 1920. In terms of hard facts, this is a shadowy period. His first London theatrical engagement is given there as in the revue *You'd be Surprised*, Covent Garden Theatre, 27 January 1923, with the Savoy Havana. Before this Mayerl had appeared at the Coliseum—with what was billed as the Savoy New York Havana Band—on 5 and 12 June 1922 and with the Savoy Havana on 25 September and 2 October. In all these programmes his name was wrongly spelt as W. Mayrle. The Mayerl–Ralton song, 'Longing for you', was played on 2 October. As we have seen, Gershwin reported on *You'd be Surprised* to his brother Ira.[2] This show was described in the *Stage* with a derivation from the fashionable jazz word as 'A Jazzaganza in two acts and 15 surprises', music by Melville Morris and William K. Wells, who also wrote the book.[3] George Robey featured as an American policeman in a Central Park episode. 'The Savoy Havana Band have a special scene—interrupted by Pyjama Blues sung by Ethel Rosevere—and cause much enthusiasm with their rendering of foxtrots etc. played in their own individual manner.' The cast also included star dancers such as Lydia Lopukhova, Léonide Massine, and Ninette de Valois. A piece by Darius Milhaud was used for a Mexican Dance. One can see how Milhaud's early 1920s style would have appealed to Mayerl—for his *Desert Island Discs* on BBC Radio 4 in 1958 he chose *Sumare* from *Saudades do Brasil* in the violin and piano version.[4]

Another revue, *The Punch Bowl* (1924), featured Norah Blaney and Gwen Farrar, playing her cello like a banjo, and contained some of Mayerl's earliest successes. His song, 'Did Tosti raise his bowler hat', was a British hit and so was another song contribution, 'Georgie-Porgie', which involved the full chorus. Mayerl said he recorded it with Paul Whiteman's Band when he was in the USA during 1924 for what he called 'a business holiday to create an interest in Mayerl jazz'—on 16 August he left with Geoffrey Clayton on the *Aquitania*, a magnificent vessel with four funnels. Whiteman did not record 'Georgie-Porgie' until 1928, without Mayerl, but he recorded 'Southern Rose' shortly after Mayerl left New York. This comes off well and is a strong number with verse and chorus equally memorable.[5] However, it was 'Georgie-Porgie' that Mayerl said he played when put on the spot by his rich

  [2] See ch. 2, n. 14.   [3] *Stage*, 1 Feb. 1923, 16.

  [4] D. Milhaud, *Saudades do Brasil: Suite de Danses*, Op. 67, Book 2, No. IX (1920–1), Schott, London. See Appendix 4 for a complete list of Mayerl's choices.

  [5] B. Mayerl, 'They Gave me "the Bird" in Birkenhead', *Tit-bits*, 3 July 1937, 24–5. The recording of 'Georgie-Porgie' was not made until 17 June 1928, but Whiteman did record 'Southern Rose' on 17 Nov. 1924 (rejected) and 7 May 1925–31416–6: Vic 19694, HMV

American host, the canned-beef magnate Klaus, who placed a $100 bet on Mayerl being able to play two pianos at once.[6] Mayerl, apparently admitting that he had never done it before, nevertheless succeeded. His host won his bet and the episode must have given Mayerl the idea for one of his best remembered stunts. Looking back in 1937 Mayerl claimed that 'Georgie' became 'the work finder for almost every chorus girl in London, and a round dozen of those who used it for their audition piece have since risen to stardom, including Gilly Flower, Polly Ward, Doris Patson, Eileen Peel and Doris Bransgrove'.[7] Gilly Flower was in the Co-Optimists, then sang in most of the Lupino-Cliff musical comedies with music by Mayerl and is on the recordings; Polly Ward recorded in other shows.[8]

For *The London Revue* (1925) Mayerl's contribution included the following songs, which were all published—'Down our Way', 'Everyone oughter love someone', 'Hullo London', 'I'll take you to Kew', 'Somehow, someday, somebody', 'Take off a little bit of this', and 'Those Men-in-blue Blues'. There was also the usual kind of published piano selection, a medley of songs from the show.

Leslie Osborne has explained that once a bandleader had made his name on the BBC, he went on the Halls to make money. Billy Mayerl obviously managed to do the same in spite of the changing climate for live entertainment. Having made a shrewd estimate of his prospects, he came back from the Savoy one day and told his wife he had resigned. She was surprised and said much later that he told her he was 'bored and wanted to try something different. He did not want to be an orchestral pianist all his life.'[9]

Mayerl made a good story out of his début on the halls at the Argyll Theatre, Birkenhead, Cheshire, so it must have made an impression. He delivered some of his usual fireworks and was devastated to receive no applause whatsoever: 'Trembling violently, I managed to say I would attempt something never before done on stage—I would play two pianos at once. And a voice bawled out from the gallery: "Play two pianos at once! You can't bloody well play *one* at once let alone a couple!" '[10] Backstage, in tears, Mayerl was advised by the manager that everything would be all right if he played old chestnuts like Nevin's *The Rosary*

B2089. See 'Paul Whiteman: A Discography', *Recorded Sound*, 27 (July 1967), 219–28. This is the song published by West's in 1923 and described on the sheet music as 'written and composed by Billy Mayerl and Charles Horn'. It was popular enough to achieve five band recordings in England, including the Savoy Havana, and was given new lyrics for separate American publication by L. Feist in 1924. The lyric is not by Gee Paul, as stated in Rust and Forbes, *British Dance Bands*. On his handwritten PRS notification forms Mayerl described 'Southern Rose' as 'a big hit in USA'.

6 Klaus is not listed in *Who was Who in America* at this period.
7 Mayerl, 'They Gave me "the Bird" in Birkenhead'.
8 R. Seeley and R. Bunnett (eds.), *London Musical Shows on Record 1889–1989* (General Gramophone Publications, London, 1989).
9 J. Mayerl, 'Venture into Variety', *Billy Mayerl Circle Journal*, 3/16 (Spring 1978), 6–9.
10 B. Mayerl, 'They gave me "the Bird" in Birkenhead', *Tit-bits*, 3 July 1937, 24–5.

(1898), the *Poet and Peasant Overture* (1846) by Suppé, and *The Maiden's Prayer* (1856) by the Polish amateur composer, Thekla Badarzewska. Mayerl was learning about provincial audiences unreached by his fame at the Savoy.

Mrs Mayerl did not remember how Mayerl and Gwen Farrar got together, although they were both in *Punchbowl*, but she recalled the successful duo that Farrar had with Norah Blaney from the First World War until Blaney's retirement (but not permanent) in 1932. The song, 'Mabel's Pigtail', 'composed and sung by Norah Blaney' was published in 1915, adorned with her picture on the cover. She took a year off later in 1924 to get married and Mayerl and Farrar started their partnership after this with increasing activity from 1926 to 1929.[11] The Blaney–Farrar partnership was high profile. When asked why he used them in his spectacular reviews, Charlot said: 'I have the best of both worlds—Norah fills the stalls with all the young men and Gwen has all the lesbians in London to see her!'[12]

Compared with Mayerl, the actress, singer, and cellist Gwen Farrar came from a completely different background. Her father was Sir George Herbert Farrar, who gained the DSO in the South African War, was knighted in 1902, and made a baronet in 1911. With six daughters he was left with no heir. He was Chairman of the East Rand Proprietary Mines and had a farm outside Johannesburg. His English country house was Chicheley Hall, Newport Pagnell, Buckinghamshire, which Gwen gave as her country address, and his predictable recreations were given in *Who's Who* as 'hunting, shooting, racing and croquet'. Gwen herself was an 'expert horsewoman, having gained more than thirty cups and prizes at horse shows'.

Like Norah Blaney, Farrar had a professional training at the Royal Academy of Music in London, where she gained the LRAM and three gold medals. But she was a temperamental 1920s girl of independent means and things did not always go smoothly. Blaney remembered some background:

Gwen was at school at Heathfield, Ascot—where all the grand girls go—and she ran away on the top of a Harrods van and went to stay with an aunt in London. Lady Farrar said [to the famous tenor Gervase Elwes who was going to France to entertain troops]: 'Oh, Gervase, do take Gwen—I can't do anything with her!' So Gwen played the cello—she played very well—and I was the comic relief, because I sang silly songs at the piano. We had no rehearsal or anything—I sang my silly little songs, and Gwen didn't know them, so she stood up at the piano and pulled faces at me! And I don't know why, but the soldiers loved it.

We worked the Palladium, the Victoria Palace, and the Coliseum . . . only the West

---

[11]   John Watson has kindly let me see details of what he has compiled from *Performer*, *Encore*, and *Sunday Referee*. Of those Variety dates recorded in these sources Farrar and Mayerl had eight weeks in 1926; nine in 1927; fourteen in 1928; eighteen in 1929; and just three in 1930.

[12]   R. Wilmut, *Kindly Leave the Stage: The Story of Variety 1919–1960* (Methuen, London, 1985), 70.

End—we were awful snobs. Gwen didn't want to go on tour—it was top or nothing! So we were always top of the bill or she wouldn't go.[13]

Mrs Mayerl revealed how the partnership ended. The crunch came with the song 'Masculine Women, and Feminine Men', which was on Farrar's first recording with Mayerl in 1926 and was also recorded by Ramon Newton with the Savoy Havana on 26 February 1926.[14] The sexual orientations being so openly satirized in this song by the Italian-American composer James V. Monaco with saucy lyric by Edgar Leslie have become only too familiar since. The song observes the difficulty of telling the difference between men and women merely by their clothes; apparently sister is 'learning to shave' whereas brother 'just loves his permanent wave'; it is hard to tell 'who's who and what's what'; and knickers and trousers are 'baggy and wide' so that 'nobody knows what's walking inside'.

That may have been a bit *risqué* in England when it was published in 1923, emphasized by the fact that Gwen herself sang in a tenor register and was distinctly a tomboy. Mayerl himself seems to have been nervous about it for the Coliseum. Sir Oswald Stoll, the most famous of all music-hall proprietors who built the Coliseum in 1904, heard them rehearsing it at band-call. He was renowned for vetting every act himself and this time he asked for a substitute.[15] Farrar refused, threatened to walk off if she couldn't sing it, and actually did so with her cello in front of a full house. It was generally thought she was unwell, until she was spotted at the Kit-Kat Club with her friends afterwards and the press pounced. Such temperament brought their act to an end and Mayerl then concentrated on his solo turns.[16] Surprisingly, Farrar's *Who's Who in the Theatre* (1936) entry makes no mention of her work with Mayerl

[13] Ibid.,23. According to John Watson, Farrar and Mayerl seem to have played only in London in 1926 and 1927 but in the next two years they were on tour for four weeks each year and visited Liverpool near the end of their partnership in 1930.

[14] 'Masculine Women and Feminine Men' (Leslie/Monaco), Gwen Farrar and Billy Mayerl on Vocalion X9887 M 017–2, transferred to CD on Flapper/Pavilion Past CD 9708; Ramon Newton and the Savoy Havana on HMV B5027, transferred to LP on WRC/EMI SH 165/6.

[15] R. Hudd, *Music Hall* (Eyre-Methuen, London, 1976). See also J. Mayerl, 'Venture into Variety'.

[16] H. R. Schleman, *Rhythm on Record: A Complete Survey and Register of all the Principal Recorded Dance Music from 1906–1936* (*Melody Maker*, London, 1936), lists Mayerl's stage partners after Gwen Farrar as Billie Hill and Lena Chisholm. John Watson confirms that Mayerl appeared with Marjorie Lotinga for at least seven weeks from 1930 to 1932 and that his act with Hill and Chisholm was a threesome for at least five weeks in the 1932/3 season. But Mayerl's partnership with Farrar was longer, they made records, and it attracted far more attention. Songs were often published as 'featured by' the pair: three examples from different publishers, none conspicuously successful; a photograph of them at a piano each adorned the covers of 'It won't be long now' (1926) by Howard Johnson and Irving Bibo and 'It must be love' (1928) by Clifford Seyler and Billy Milton; another photograph of Farrar singing and Mayerl playing appears on the cover of 'Chilly Billy Wung Lung' (1927) by Raymond Wallace and Buddy Rose.

and, judging by reports at the time and since, her act with Blaney was better known.

Eddie Banfield witnessed a slice of variety life:

One vivid memory I must recall. It was when Billy was partnering Gwen Farrar on the Halls. At the end of their act I went 'round the back' of Victoria Palace to see them. They were doubling at another theatre and I was invited to travel with them in Miss Farrar's car, a Stutz open tourer. They rushed from the stage door, Miss Farrar 'flung' her cello—in its case luckily—into the back of the car and proceeded to drive the vehicle. Did I say 'drive'? I have never before or since experienced such a car ride. But we arrived safely and they proceded on stage just in the nick of time and gave a wonderful performance.[17]

Beverley Nichols summed up society's view of Gwen Farrar:

The disapproval of the music of the period was extended to some of its performers, in particular to a young lady with straight black hair, horn-rimmed glasses, and square shoulders, who was called Gwen Farrar. Really, said the dowagers, there was no excuse for Gwen; after all she was a lady; she was quite rich, she had a delicious panelled house in Chelsea, and she played the cello more than passably. The trouble was that she also insisted on singing, which was the gravest mistake, since her voice was only a semitone higher than dear Mr. Chaliapin's. Moreover she insisted on singing in public, on the music-hall stage, with that young Nora Blaney at the piano. True, they drew the town, but somehow when one remembered Gwen's dear father, who was a near millionaire, it all seemed a great pity.[18]

Both Mayerl and Farrar were involved initially in one of the most notorious theatrical miscalculations of the period: *Whitebirds*, at His Majesty's Theatre in 1927. Mayerl told the story himself:

It was Gwen Farrar who made me take up singing, when she suggested one night after I had appeared at the Coliseum that we might usefully link up as a double turn. During the four years we toured together I grew to regard her as a real, sporting pal.

We shared an extraordinary experience in the production of *Whitebirds*, the spectacular revue that had such a short run at His Majesty's Theatre in the summer of 1927 and cost Everard Gates round about £40,000 [£1,375,000]. Gwen's advice to Gates, which I backed up, was to make a start with a small, intimate revue which would risk not more than £5,000 [£172,000] and might make a lot of money.

At first he accepted our advice. I made a start on the music, and Gwen did some sketches, and some of her friends helped to write songs and prepare scenes. And then

[17] E. Banfield, *Billy Mayerl Circle Newsletter*, 3/17 (Summer 1978), 9.
[18] B. Nichols, *The Sweet and Twenties* (Quality Book Club, London, 1958), 190–1. In the *Daily Mail*, 29 Oct. 1925, Blaney and Farrar were announced as going to the USA 'to rehearse their parts for *Down South*, a new Florenz Ziegfeld musical comedy. It will be their first visit . . . they are even taking "It ain't gonna rain no mo' " to the country of its birth.' 'It ain't gonna rain no mo" (1923), based on a country dance tune, was by Wendell Woods Hall, who apparently sold over two millions copies of his own singer/ukelele recording in the first year.

Gates dropped a bombshell with the news that he had engaged Lew Leslie, of *Blackbirds* fame, to produce the show. Gwen and I had to take a back-seat, and Leslie engaged a galaxy of international stars, including José Collins, Maisie Gay, Betty Chester, Maurice Chevalier, George Gee, Lucien Herval, Chick Farr, Anton Dolin, Phyllis Bedells, and a special turn imported from America. The chorus numbered sixty and the orchestra fifty. Imagine the salary bill!

Rehearsals were changed from daytime to midnight, coaches were engaged to take the chorus girls home, and Lyons were called in to provide refreshments during the night. Everything was done regardless of cost. What a change from our small, intimate revue!

Our part in the show ended when the producer tried to separate Gwen and me; I had to appear half-dressed and Gwen, in an individual role, in brown cotton tights, had to give an imitation of Florence Mills. We both objected strongly.

It looked as if we would be compelled to do what the management dictated—until Gwen's solicitor found a phrase in the contract which made us an 'inseparable' turn. The separation idea was dropped, and we were paid off with a cheque for £400 [£13,000]![19]

No wonder Mayerl was pleased with this outcome. His contribution as a singer, accounted for here, enhanced his versatility. In a song like 'Old-Fashioned Girls', Mayerl's light tenor is more musical than Farrar's gruff flapper personification of the modern girl, which fits the scenario.[20]

Florence Mills was the Black singer launched on Broadway in *Shuffle Along* (1921) who captivated London in *Dover Street to Dixie* (1924) and, of course, *Blackbirds* (1926), both shows which caught fashionable taste and profoundly inspired Constant Lambert.[21] The *Stage* reported on a moribund dinosaur intended as a follow-up:

HIS MAJESTY'S: WHITEBIRDS

On Tuesday, May 31, 1927, Mr. Lew Leslie produced here a revue in 29 scenes or items, the music and lyrics by George W. Meyer, the orchestral arrangements by Will Vodery, the scenery by John Bull and the entire production staged and conceived by Lew Leslie. Whatever may or may not have occurred behind the scenes to postpone the production more than once of this ornate but stupendously dull and overloaded

[19] B. Mayerl, 'They Gave me "the Bird" in Birkenhead', *Tit-bits*, 3 July 1937, 24–5.
[20] Gwen Farrar and Billy Mayerl in 'Old-Fashioned Girls' on Columbia 5186.
[21] C. B. Cochran, *The Secrets of a Showman* (Heinemann, London, 1925), 415: 'She sang a plaintive song about the dreamy hills of Tennessee. She controlled the emotions of the audience as only a true artist can. There was a heart-throb in her bird-like voice that brought a lump to the throat. Then her eyes would flash. Her thin, little arms and legs became animated with a dancing delirium. It was all natural art . . . and the audience applauded as any audience applauds an artist in whom it detects genius. That night, and every night she appeared at the London Pavilion, Florence Mills received an ovation every time she came on stage—before every song she sang. That is a tribute . . . I have never known to be offered to any other artist.' But see also S. Hughes, *Opening Bars* (Pilot Press, London, 1946), 305–9. He saw *Blackbirds* several times and comments in detail but found Mills too refined.

revue, it was quite evident that it had not yet reached proper shipshape production order by Tuesday evening.[22]

Apparently the first half did not finish until nearly 10.30 on Tuesday and the final curtain fell at 12.20. The gallery, understandably, was restless. There were only a few bouquets from the press: 'Mr. Edward Lowery does well, as do Miss Farrar and Billy Mayerl.'

Included was a burlesque of the recent *Blackbirds*, but the reviewer for the *Stage* had to conclude that *Whitebirds* was 'totally unworthy of a house with such fine artistic traditions as His Majesty's'. Billy Milton, who took part, gave an insider's view of things with slightly different timings:

White Birds started twenty minutes late on opening night. The delay was caused by Lew Leslie who had dropped one of his diamond dress-studs. He went berserk and held the curtain until it was found. By 11.00 that night we had just finished the first half of the revue and were shuddering at the thought of the second half because there had been no proper run-through. Standing in the prompt corner, Leslie tried frantically to rearrange the running order. This resulted in chaos. For example, the orchestra played a dance number when it should have been a sketch and the chorus girls started to dress for a scene which, unbeknown to them, had been cut. When the finale mercifully arrived the whole company was incorrectly dressed. Nobody had any idea of what was happening. It would have been laughable if it hadn't been so tragic. Such a waste of great talent and good money![23]

All the same, Billy Mayerl's song 'What'you going to do', with lyric by singer-entertainer-composer Leslie Sarony, was published in 1927 as 'The Whitebirds Revue Song Sensation' with a picture of Mayerl and Farrar on the cover. He is sitting down with one hand on each of two keyboards: she, Eton cropped and arms akimbo, is standing behind him in her customary white shirt and black waistcoat. The *News of the World* cartoons of *Whitebirds* showed Mayerl and Farrar with him sitting at the piano and singing and her standing in the crook of the piano in a short skirt very different from the regalia of José Collins, in old-world manteau and crinoline, near the end of her career.

The song—'What'you going to do when the other bird flies away from you?'—is coy about finding a new lover, but charming. Mayerl catches the mood precisely. Characteristic features include the barbershop chord for the blue note in the chorus and he even doubles the catchy melody in the perfect fourths of novelty piano. Another song of the same year, 'Doing it all for England' with lyric by Kenneth Western (half of the Western Brothers cabaret act), is labelled 'as sung by Gwen Farrar and Billy Mayerl' reflecting the joint nature of their turn. This is a type of patter song with roots in Gilbert and Sullivan.

---

[22] 'His Majesty's: Whitebirds', *Stage*, 2 June 1927.
[23] B. Milton, *Milton's Paradise Mislaid* (Jupiter Books, London, 1976), 21.

Arthur Bliss, Master of the Queen's Music from 1953, who had previously written a one-step actually called *Bliss* for a *Punch and Judy Ball* at the Savoy Hotel, contributed *The Rout Trot* to *Whitebirds*—another indication that serious composers were interested in what went on in the commercial, or in this case non-commercial, side of the profession.[24] *Shake your Feet*, at the London Hippodrome, 20 July, 1927 was the next landmark. The *Stage* reported:

On Wednesday, July 20, 1927, Laddie Cliff presented here a revue, book by Greatrex Newman, Clifford Grey and Noel Scott; music by George Gershwin, Fred Astaire, Carroll Gibbons, Jack Strachey, H. Morley Acres and H. B. Hedley; lyrics by Desmond Carter and James Dyrenforth: book produced by Felix Edwardes; dances and ensembles by Max Rivers.

The show was found too long at its Liverpool opening: 'Others conspicuous in a varied entertainment were Gwen Farrar and Billy Mayerl. Gwen Farrar's "Nashville Nightingale" number is nothing out of the common; but she does well in a combined piano, cello and singing turn, together with Billy Mayerl, the latter concerned in another for five pianos.'

Mayerl composed nothing for *Shake your Feet* but he told Roy Plomley that he 'played juvenile lead' and danced.[25] The programme shows that Mayerl and Farrar were included in the company of nine dancers in the second item; they had a spot on their own in Part 2; but the piece for five pianos looks like *The Doll Dance* by the American Nacio Herb Brown. The American copyright date is 1924 and it was published in England by Keith Prowse about two years later, when it became an early Brown hit with at least seventeen British band recordings mostly made in 1927, including one by the Savoy Orpheans and one by Billy Milton and Billy Mayerl. *The Doll Dance* has several novelty characteristics later to be found in Mayerl, including the usual melodies doubled in fourths and the repetitive use of catchy phrases. But the programme for *Shake your Feet* does not mention the Grieg concerto, which Mayerl said he played. It would certainly have been simply a medley and might have been put in as an encore without announcement. This could explain why, seven years later, Mayerl remembered how furious he was when an antagonistic theatre critic he disliked reported on it as by Schumann.[26]

In 1976 Billy Milton wrote to H. Nichols, who ran the Billy Mayerl Circle:

I was very fond of Billy and Jill and often visited their home. I shared a dressing room with him during the run of *Shake your Feet*. Billy brought me luck by asking me to deputise for him at a charity concert. I went so well with my songs at the piano that Laddie Cliff who was in the audience at the time asked me if I would like to replace

---

[24] *Star*, 27 Jan. 1923.
[25] B. Mayerl, interview with Roy Plomley on *Desert Island Discs*, BBC Home Service, 21 Apr. 1958.
[26] B. Mayerl, 'From the President's Chair', *BMCM*, 1/5 (May, 1934), 2.

Melville Gideon in the Co-Optimists which he was to present under another name at the Prince of Wales Theatre. (*Bow-wows* it was finally called.) . . . So all in all, he is alive in my memory and professionally as far as I was concerned. He was a wonderful musician, and to me, a wonderful friend.[27]

All this experience in the theatre was building up towards Mayerl's first full score, *Nippy* (1930), where he was ready to contribute to British musical comedy of the 1930s. In other ways, too, Mayerl was becoming more obviously part of the British tradition of Ivor Novello, Noel Gay, or Vivian Ellis rather than the Americans who gave them all such competition. But Mayerl was active in more dimensions than any of them and by the time *Nippy* reached the stage he was famous as the composer of a short, catchy piano piece called *Marigold*.

[27] B. Milton, letter to H. Nichols in the *Billy Mayerl Circle Newsletter*, 2/11 (Autumn 1976), 3. Apparently Nichols expected to find several references to Billy Mayerl in Milton's book, but—as so often in such cases—there was only one. In 1928 Billy Milton's song with Clifford Seyler, 'It must be love' was published by Francis, Day & Hunter as 'featured by Gwen Farrar & Billy Mayerl' with a picture of them at a piano each on the cover.

7

THE MUSIC AROUND *MARIGOLD*

SCOTT JOPLIN became identified with *The Maple Leaf Rag* and Zez Confrey with *Kitten on the Keys*. The Mayerl work in this succession of piano pieces in rag form should be *The Jazz Master* but in fact he was haunted instead by *Marigold* written three years later. It employs the same rag formulae as the other pieces but was originally what Mayerl himself called 'a slow tune' which he regarded as a new development. Later on he tore it to shreds in a travesty of this description, almost as if he needed to avenge its disproportionate popularity. It is worth looking at Mayerl's works leading up to *Marigold* to see how it arose and as a way of accounting for its position.

The year 1925 saw the publication of the *Pianolettes* and 1926 the *Piano Exaggerations*. At first it looks as if no works before the *Egyptian Suite* and no unpublished manuscripts have survived and that dates of publication are the nearest we can get to a chronology. But as we know, once Mayerl was launched with the Savoy he was in demand and, as he said, 'sold many of the compositions I couldn't get publishers to look at in my earlier days when I went begging their favours'.[1] As it happens, somebody attached widely varying opus numbers to just nineteen works published between 1927 and 1931. This list covers only a fraction of Mayerl's overall published output, but these numbers may provide some hints about the actual order of composition and give some idea of Mayerl's development during this limited period. Here they are by year of publication, although there were also many pieces without numbers published in the same period:

1927	Marigold	Op. 78 (CD ⑪ and ⑫)
	Chop-sticks	Op. 79 (CD ⑰)
	Hollyhock: a Syncopated Impression	Op. 80 (CD ⑯)
1928	Pastoral Sketches	Op. 56
	3 Miniatures in Syncopation	Op. 76

---

[1] B. Mayerl, 'We Played on as a Prince Lay Dying', *Tit-bits*, 26 June 1937, 5–6.

	Robots: a Syncopated Impression	Op. 81
	Honky-Tonk: a Rhythmical Absurdity	Op. 82 (CD 18)
1929	A Lily Pond: Idyll	Op. 12
	Three Contrasts	Op. 24
	Sennen Cove: Poem for orchestra	Op. 53
	Legends of King Arthur: Six Impressions	Op. 64
	Wisteria: a Syncopated Impression	Op. 83
	Jasmine: a Syncopated Impression	Op. 84
1930	6 Studies in Syncopation: Book 3	Op. 55
	3 Dances in Syncopation	Op. 73
	3 Japanese Pictures	Op. 25
1931	Oriental: a Syncopated Impression	Op. 21
	6 Studies in Syncopation: Book 1	Op. 55
	6 Studies in Syncopation: Book 2	Op. 55

It is difficult to see much logic in this partial allocation of opus numbers. Perhaps someone at Keith Prowse tried to set up a numerical scheme around the time of *Marigold*, Op. 78, but gave up after Op. 84. The situation confirms the interest publishers took in his early works after he became famous. So Op. 12 for *A Lily Pond* could put it well back from the publication date of 1929, possibly soon after the *Egyptian Suite* around 1920 (Ex. 5).

A Lily Pond is a neatly crafted salon piece in ternary form with real melodic charm linked to Grieg. It has the innocence of an early work and is in E major, a key that Mayerl hardly ever used for a solo piece again. There is a charming naked nymph playing a pipe on the cover of the sheet music. Every move works pianistically in the later nineteenth-century salon tradition and the textures build well to the central climax which occurs twice.[2] The Grieg connection relates to the rhetoric of his Piano Concerto (1883) which has affected some of Mayerl's more serious pieces, sometimes in the same key; there is even a pre-echo of parallel perfect fourths later on; and a five-bar coda which expands delightfully after much literal repetition.

Oriental, as Op. 21 with the other numbers now missing, looks like the next available piano work. Although it was not published until 1931 when it was given the title of Syncopated Impression, its date of composition can be put well back into the 1920s. With the indication 'Slowly (well marked)', the opening melody is mostly modal G minor. As usual the form is the strain pattern of marches and rags. After an introduction there is a till-ready and the main section of strain A features Mayerl's cross-hand technique. (See *Hop-o'-my-Thumb* later and several transcriptions.) The loud, amplified repeat of strain A gives the

---

[2] *A Lily Pond* was orchestrated by Fred Adlington and sounds well in the recording by the Slovak Radio Symphony Orchestra/Gary Carpenter on *British Light Music: Billy Mayerl*, Marco Polo 8.223514 (1994).

Ex. 5. Mayerl, *A Lily Pond* (1929)

ceremonial flavour in a spacious piano layout and there is little syncopation—
just one dislocating bar (Ex. 6).

Strain B consists of an altered setting of the strain A melody in single notes
(some blue notes later), accompanied by parallel sixths (as in *Wistaria*). The descending chromatic progressions in *Oriental* sound like Delius but also go back
to Grieg (the Ballade, Op. 24)—compare these with the end of *Marigold*. Strain
C, marked *grandioso*, is rhetorical and has some off-beat repeated notes, a Mayerl
fingerprint, notably in *Bats in the Belfry* later. The last strain echoes and varies
earlier elements and ends with a subtle *pp* reminiscence of the *grandioso* music
from strain C. *Oriental* is a polished piece with a strong atmosphere, especially if
played at a slow processional pace.

Ex. 6. Mayerl, *Oriental* (1931)

The *Three Contrasts*, Op. 24, are next in opus order. The first one, *Ladybird*, uses parallel fourths under the melody; the succeeding *Pastoral* is in the same placid G major as the first of the *Pastoral Sketches*; and the last piece, *Fiddle Dance*, is one of several instrumental imitations with a clear reference to Grieg's folk idioms in the middle section. The set is dedicated 'To my Friend Corti'—this is Corti Woodcock, who worked in advertising, was chairman of the English Table Tennis Association, and admired Mrs Mayerl.[3] As an early triptych the *Three Contrasts* are more like a rehearsal for what was to come. The much more original *Three Japanese Pictures*, Op. 25, follow immediately.

3 'Bridge that Gap', *Billy Mayerl Circle Newsletter*, 1/3 (Autumn 1974), 10.

In the outer movements Mayerl is still thinking in piano rag strain patterns of sixteen bars, but the effect is different. He has moved on harmonically from Grieg. No. 1, *Almond Blossom*, is close to the piano style of John Ireland in its English lyricism—specifically *Amberley Wild Brooks* in the same key—but there is a middle section where the main theme is developed in the tonic minor leading to a climax on a chain of bitonal discords; No. 2, *A Temple in Kyoto*, is atmospheric in the manner of Cyril Scott rather than Debussy, although Mayerl admired both; in No. 3, *The Cherry Dance*, the toccata textures draw on Ravel. A new factor common to all three pieces is the use of bitonality, smoothly assimilated but overt in a piece like *Beetle in the Bottle* later. These more adventurous moments, reflecting Mayerl's admiration for Stravinsky, occur in all three Japanese pieces. The setting of C against F sharp is also found in *Merlin the Wizard*, in *The Legends of King Arthur*, and creates an evocative sound-world for *A Temple in Kyoto* (Ex. 7).

As a set, *Three Japanese Pictures* is as focused as the concentrated Japanese poems called haiku, and Mayerl told *Musical Opinion* in 1932 that it was a particular favourite of his, but he never recorded it. This triptych indicates

Ex. 7. Mayerl, *A Temple in Kyoto* from *Three Japanese Pictures* (1930)

directions Mayerl might have taken if he had not been compelled to recognize, as Leslie Osborne put it, that there was 'more money in frills and furbe-
lows'.[4] Or, as he put himself in the last of his *Tit-bits* articles: 'I own quite
frankly that I am a commercial composer . . . I am not rich enough to become a "good" composer.'[5]

In economic terms these are relative categories. Mayerl never earned as
much from performing rights as a 'good' composer such as Gustav Holst,
whom he much admired, and nowhere near what could be earned by a really
commercial composer such as Albert Ketelby, composer of *In a Monastery
Garden* (1915). In 1955, quite a good year for Mayerl who earned £1,025 4 s.
[£15,100] from performing rights (see Appendix 3), Ketelby earned three
times as much but Holst, the serious classical composer, almost double that.[6]
All the same, Mayerl remained committed to writing what he regarded as
serious pieces from time to time and obviously attached importance to them.
We shall see later what this meant in terms of style.

He was equally committed to the whole question of teaching, with the
School launched in 1926, and he wrote pieces specially for students at various
stages. The importance of the three volumes each entitled *Six Studies in
Syncopation*, Op. 55, should not be overlooked. The opus number of 55 suggests a composition date near to 1927 even though the *Studies* were not in print
then. The three books have the same publisher's number even though Book III
was published first in 1930 and the other two in 1931.[7] They are a counterpart
in syncopated piano-playing to the six books of Bartok's *Mikrokosmos*, rewarding as pieces to play and not mere exercises. No. 14 is particularly interesting
since it starts with an early example in Mayerl's work of right-hand chords
built out of two perfect fourths, and the left hand has the anticipatory tenth
which had become such a Mayerl fingerprint. All these tricks were susceptible
to teaching from elementary levels onwards. Mayerl never recorded these
studies, but Eric Parkin has brought their qualities to light on CD.[8]

The orchestral piece, *Sennen Cove*, Op. 58, also orchestrated by Fred
Aldington, is often regarded as the primary example of Mayerl's work on a
larger scale. He recorded it, cut to fit two sides of a 78, with the Court

[4] L. Osborne, interview with Peter Dickinson, 11 Aug. 1981.

[5] B. Mayerl, 'My Piano Fell into the Band', *Tit-bits*, 10 July 1937, 20–1.

[6] C. Ehrlich, *Harmonious Alliance: A History of the Performing Right Society* (OUP, Oxford
1989), 164.

[7] B. Mayerl, *Six Studies in Syncopation, Books I–III* (Keith Prowse, 1930–1). See *Postman's
Knock: Billy Mayerl Selection for the Piano* for most of these studies. Eric Parkin on Shellwood
SWCD9 (1998).

[8] E. Parkin, *The Billy Mayerl Piano Transcriptions*, vols. 1–3 on Priory PRCD 466, 467, and
468 (1993). Also further transcriptions included on *Puppets* and *Scallywag* (which also includes
five of the Studies) on Priory PRCD 544 and 565 (1995) and more on *Robots* on Shellwood
SWCD 3 (1997) and *Postman's Knock* (see n. 7 above).

Symphony Orchestra in 1929: there is a piano solo version, dedicated 'To my friend Raymund Langley', but with its *tremolando* effects it feels very much like a transcription.⁹ Claims made for Mayerl as a serious composer rather than just a purveyor of brilliant novelties are often based on *Sennen Cove*, named after a bay in Cornwall near Land's End where he and Jill had a holiday, so its musical language merits some consideration. The orchestral sound at the beginning is impressionist—a term Mayerl used about his own music—and falls somewhere between Debussy's *La Mer* (1905) and Bax's *Tintagel* (1919).¹⁰ The rhythmic groupings at the start are ingenious (Ex. 8). This soft opening acts as an introduction to the Vivace by way of some striking chords over a pedal-point. The Vivace itself is a kind of dance, winding down to slower material with a good tune in A major blown up to *grandioso* before returning to the Vivace and a fulsome ending. The context here, as emerges later, is the light music of Eric Coates and there seems no reason why *Sennen Cove* should not make its mark in this field. The connection between Coates and Mayerl emerges in *The Man about Town* from Coates's Suite *The Three Men* (1935)— some of the syncopated passages could almost be Mayerl, especially with the bits of melody doubled in fourths. Coates had been impressed by the best dance bands, especially when Jack Hylton performed his Orchestral Phantasy, *The Selfish Giant* (1925), based on a short story by Oscar Wilde. This was arranged by conductor-composer Leighton Lucas for twenty-five players and given at the Royal Albert Hall on 20 February 1926, following a run-through at the Kit-Kat Club. Coates said: 'I am overwhelmed by Mr. Hylton's performance, which was such that my ideas on music may become revolutionised . . . all of us may be forced to modify many of our ideas.'¹¹ Much later he felt that 'this style of playing has had the effect of raising the standard of orchestral technique in general, particularly in the brass, woodwind and percussion sections of even our symphony orchestras'.¹² This remark came at a time when the rhythmic acumen and ensemble of the Savoy Bands had been much admired at the Queen's Hall concerts and standards in British symphony orchestras were at an all-time low.¹³ As we shall see later, when the Light Music Society was formed in April 1957, Coates was President and Mayerl was Vice-Chairman and took on the editorship of the *Light Music Magazine*.¹⁴

⁹ B. Mayerl, *Sennen Cove*, Court Symphony Orchestra/Mayerl on Columbia, 16 Nov. 1928. See Discography.

¹⁰ B. Mayerl, interview for Radiotjanst, Sweden, 18 Nov. 1937.

¹¹ 'Syncopation and Dance Band News', *Melody Maker* (Mar. 1926), 11.

¹² E. Coates, *Suite in Four Movements* (Heinemann, London, 1953), 203.

¹³ C. Ehrlich. *The Music Profession in Britain since the Eighteenth Century* (Clarendon Press, Oxford 1985), 207.

¹⁴ *Light Music Magazine* was issued by the Light Music Society, founded in April 1957. The whole enterprise represented an ideal that Mayerl found increasingly congenial in his later years—the cause of light music—but the Society languished through lack of support.

Ex. 8. Mayerl, *Sennen Cove* (1929)

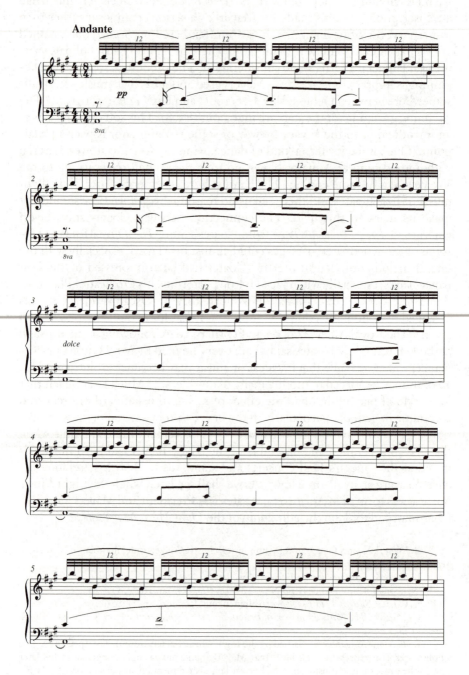

The comparison with Coates recurs, since *Pastoral Sketches*, Op. 56, is only two opus numbers before *Sennen Cove* and has many of the same light-music characteristics, especially in the orchestral version made by Arthur Wood, composer of *Barwick Green Maypole*, used for generations as the signature-tune for *The Archers*, the long-running popular radio serial on the BBC Home Service/Radio 4. It seems ironic that the recording of Mayerl's orchestral works made by the Slovak Radio Symphony Orchestra in 1992 (released in 1994) took place at Bratislava, which is probably not far from where the Mayerls originated, but the modern players sound uncomfortable in this idiom.[15] In No. 2, when the first theme recurs at the climax, the intensity is comparable to Ireland's *Chelsea Reach* (1917) in the same key, and the recurring arpeggio flourishes (dominants with raised fifth) are exactly the same as those in the C strain of *Marigold*.

The *Pastoral Sketches*, Op. 56, was the first of only three publications taken by Boosey & Co., apart from Mayerl's first two published popular songs in 1923/4. The others were *A Lily Pond*, Op. 12, and *Sennen Cove*, Op. 58. One might guess the date of the *Pastoral Sketches* as around the time of the Mayerls' marriage, although they knew each other much earlier. All these pieces, where Boosey seems to have taken on a group of Mayerl's 'serious' work ranging from Op. 12 to Op. 58, are very much in the affable diatonic English tradition of Edward German and Roger Quilter, as well as Coates.

The same is largely true of *The Legends of King Arthur*, Op. 64, although this six-movement suite for piano is more ambitious. Eight of these opus numbers later, it is dedicated 'to my friend Geoffrey Clayton', managing director of West's who published two Mayerl songs in 1924, and was, of course, Mayerl's entrepreneurial partner in the School, started in 1926. If plans for the School were hatched when Mayerl and Clayton went to America in 1924, that might suggest a date of composition at this time. However—just to confuse matters—Mrs Mayerl told me: 'He'd composed when he was 17, I think, *Knights of the Round Table* or *King Arthur's Knights*, which I think is still selling nowadays . . . He started composing then.'[16] So *The Legends* could be as early as 1919—in spite of the fact that the score of *Six Studies in Syncopation: Book II*, published in 1931, advertises *The Legends* as 'A new Suite by Billy Mayerl' when it had been in print for two years and could have been composed more than ten years before that.

The unsyncopated style of *The Legends* does suggest an earlier date. It is harmonically much less adventurous than either the *Three Japanese Pictures* or the *Pianolettes* but the writing, as usual, is grateful to play. The rhetorical qualities of the opening *Prelude* recall some of the piano sagas of Edward MacDowell,

---

[15] B. Mayerl, *Pastoral Sketches*, Slovak Radio Symphony Orchestra/Gary Carpenter on *British Light Music: Billy Mayerl*, Marco Polo 8.223514 (1994).

[16] J. Mayerl, interview with Peter Dickinson, 11 Aug. 1981.

but *Merlin the Wizard* opens bitonally, like the second of the *Japanese Pictures*. *The Sword Excalibur* goes back to Grieg but *The Lady of the Lake*—thirty-two bars of identical patterns in even notes—makes a mystical effect. Guinevere is depicted in a type of jig, but *The Passing of Arthur* conveys genuine tragedy. The opening Siciliano gives way to quotes from *Merlin* and the central climax comes with a quote from *Prelude*—the same cyclic approach as in the last movement of Mayerl's early *Egyptian Suite*, again suggesting the two works might be near contemporaries.

Those oddly attached opus numbers may have provided some clues to Mayerl's stylistic development, however limited this seems. The *Three Dances in Syncopation*, Op. 73, and the *Three Miniatures in Syncopation*, Op. 76, can now be put before *Marigold*, Op. 78. They show Mayerl moving to a more catchy type of melody, something he must have been aiming for in his songs, and fewer pyrotechnics compared with the *Pianolettes*.

In the *Three Dances* this trend is noticeable in the first one, *English Dance*, at a gentle pace—and with a possible reference to Gershwin's *Rhapsody in Blue* at the end. No. 2, the *Cricket Dance*, has breathless syncopations (anticipating *Bats in the Belfry*) but No. 3, *Harmonica Dance*, is a clever mouth-organ imitation. The same Yale Blues tempo is used for No. 2, *The Muffin Man*, of *Three Miniatures in Syncopation*. Its opening piece, *Cobweb*, is another suave A major melody, doubled in fourths, and the finale is another helter-skelter.

This is the immediate context for *Marigold* (CD ⑪ and ⑫), which now falls into place stylistically and chronologically, and can be looked at in detail. It was published in 1927 and recorded by Mayerl in the following year with *Hollyhock* (CD ⑭) on the other side: Mayerl and his wife recorded the duet version of *Marigold* in 1934 coupled with *Ace of Spades* on the other side.[17] *Marigold* was the first of a series of pieces, often with floral titles, in a genre which Mayerl claimed he established, using the subtitle *A Syncopated Impression* for the first time. These pieces were less virtuoso than the *Pianolettes*, less outrageous than the *Exaggerations*.

Marigold (Ex. 9) continues to use the formulae Mayerl inherited from the piano rag: Introduction–A–B–A–C–C. The four-bar introduction starts on the barbershop chord, looks as if the harmony drops down the whole-tone scale, but this is actually the chromatic descent tactic taken from the B♮ down to F as dominant of the dominant of E flat. This is spelt out in the lower part of the piano duet version published in 1934, where there are a number of extra details. The first three bars are thus exact falling sequences, anticipating the triplets of the main theme although, in performance terms, the time-signature might just as well have been 12/8.

---

[17] B. Mayerl, *Marigold/Hollyhock*, on Columbia, 7 Oct. 1927. Mr and Mrs Billy Mayerl (duet), *Marigold/Ace of Spades*, on Columbia, 31 Aug. 1934. See Discography.

Ex. 9. Mayerl, *Marigold* (1927)

The opening phrase of strain A is the catchiest figure in the whole piece—the hook, in popular song parlance. It is supported by the widely used chord pattern of I–VI–II–V which Mayerl would come back to in some of his last pieces in the 1950s. This pattern is also the harmonic basis of the opening of strain C (CD ⑪ 1′ 26″; CD ⑫ 1′ 51″). The initially pentatonic melody is not consistently doubled in fourths. There are some concessions to the prevailing harmony and ease of playing. Bar 7 of this strain is easier with thirds for its first half than fourths would have been. The break in fourths in the next bar must have spelt disaster for countless amateurs.

Mayerl's colleague, William Davies, confirms this. He found it very difficult to finger this passage academically and was trying to play it in a BBC Maida Vale Studio one day when Mayerl himself walked in:

He said, 'You're making a bit of a pig's ear of that aren't you?', in the friendliest of manners.

'Well', I said, 'it's an impossible cadenza!'

'No way', he said. 'How are you fingering it?' So I showed him.

'Ah yes', he said, 'perhaps that's the way you were taught at the Royal College. My style is to cheat—you do this and you do that.' He sat down and played it and I thought, 'What a fool I am: it sticks out like a sore thumb!' It was so obvious when it was shown. This was the man: this was Billy, because he was so helpful. Anybody who genuinely wanted to know he would go out of his way to help. Nothing was too much trouble.[18]

Mayerl had dealt with the fingering issue much earlier in the *BMCM* in 1935:

During my recent visit to Manchester several members present expressed their wish that I should finger the break appearing on bar 8 of the first subject of *Marigold*, and while I do not insist that this is the only fingering, I think greater speed and more accurate phrasing will be possible if this is used.

Ex. 10. Mayerl's suggested fingering for *Marigold* (BMCM, May 1935).

---

[18] W. Davies, interview with Ann Stanger, 17 Sept. 1982. In a letter to me of 4 Sept. 1998 Davies said: 'I had been taught never to put one's thumb on black notes and, of course, without doing this (in *Marigold* and a number of his other compositions) I was finding it virtually impossible.'

I have included some accent markings, together with the correct sense of phrasing. These are very important, and attention to them will greatly facilitate a smooth working.
B.M.[19]

These accents confirm that Mayerl wanted to hear the underlying duple cross-rhythm of the kind already discussed from the *Pianolettes* onwards but he talks about 'greater speed' in a piece marked 'slowly and lightly'.

Strain B (CD ⑪ 0′ 34″; CD ⑫ 0′ 58″) opens with a dance-band slide figure (three bars of rising sequences, not quite exact) later developed into a *tremolando*, that stand-by of the silent cinema pianist, which Mayerl himself (on record) extended into a fourth bar, and had used earlier in the C strain of *Eskimo Shivers* (CD ③ 1′ 15″) and *Sleepy Piano* (CD ⑩ 1′ 06″). The tremolo is not in the duet version at all (CD ⑫). The cadence point at the end of both strains is as formal as in any classical rag.

Strain A is repeated, but with enriching variations in the duet version where the melody is set in the tenor with some chromatic filling-in. There are new chords in the duet (a chromatically rising sequence of dominant major ninths at bar 8), placed rhythmically so as to confirm the implied duple contradiction of the original mini-cadenza. Finally strain C (repeated) (CD ⑪ 1′ 26″; CD ⑫ 1′ 51″) is in the subdominant key to end the piece, in the march and rag tradition. The two rising arpeggios are based on a whole-tone chord but the break midway is more difficult to play and it again confirms the duple cross-rhythm. The second-time ending (CD ⑪ 2′ 15″; CD ⑫ 2′ 38″) harks back to the introduction with its descending chromatic series of dominant sevenths and it winds down gracefully onto an added sixth chord. The final chord of the duet version includes an added second as well, and there is a counter-melody from the start of this strain.

Marigold, originally more dainty than flashy, was first recorded by Mayerl in 1927 at his standard tempo of about ♩ = 132, but when he opened a medley with it in 1939 he had moved up to 164, making it quite a show piece. So Mayerl was the opposite of Joplin, who wanted his rags played slowly, but in 1937 he was still thinking of *Marigold* as something different:

As a change from the quick and flashy stuff of my *The Jazz Master* and *The Jazz Mistress*, I wrote a slow tune, again the first of its kind in the country. This was *Marigold*, musically one of the best things I've done. It has brought me in over £5,000 [£186,900] and still makes money every year. I have named my Hampstead house after it.[20]

---

[19] B. Mayerl, 'Correct Fingering for the Fourth Break in the First Subject of Marigold', *BMCM*, 2/17 (May 1935), 32. See also 'This Month's Lesson', *BMCM*, 1/6 (June 1934), 20–4, for detailed comments about duet-writing including *Marigold*.

[20] B. Mayerl, 'We Played on as a Prince Lay Dying', *Tit-bits*, 26 June 1937.

No wonder Mayerl found it difficult to separate *Marigold* from its commercial success but he did say he regarded it as 'musically one of the best things I've done', a view he contradicts later. Unfortunately sales figures for individual items for these years, which would be so revealing as an indicator of taste, are no longer available.[21]

We have noticed the connection between Confrey and Mayerl in *Marigold* but the genre goes further back. *Marigold* has clear American predecessors in *Nola* (1915) by Felix Arndt and even *Narcissus* (from *Water Scenes Suite*, Op. 13, 1891) by Ethelbert Nevin. Notice how there are comparable right-hand breaks in the first section of *Narcissus*. The role of that salon classic, Dvořák's *Humoresque*, Op. 101 No. 7 (1894), should not be forgotten. Especially the use of dotted rhythms of a kind which are an essential feature of so much Mayerl, including *Marigold*. On *Desert Island Discs* Roy Plomley asked Mayerl about his perennial favourite:

BM: Ah, good old Marigold—yes.
RP: How many copies of Marigold have you sold?
BM: Oh, well over a million now I should think. It's my bread, my butter and my jam![22]

Mrs Mayerl used exactly the same description in 1981.[23]

In 1973 Irene Ashton referred to the genesis of this piece with some rather different sales figures:

In the early days of his marriage to Jill Bernini the décor of their home was blue and gold. The piece *Marigold* was written on the floor—a favourite place—and on that particular day a big blue bowl of marigolds was stood on a table. These flowers were the inspiration. However he never imagined that this composition would be the success it was but Keith Prowse, who published it in 1927, sold over 150,000 copies in twenty years. The present day sales are possibly 200,000.

It was said that to recognise the sale of over a million copies of the sheet music and/or recordings the publisher, Keith Prowse/EMI, commissioned a handsome oil painting, about two feet square, of a vase of marigolds from Jan van Gort.[24]

To put this achievement in perspective we should note that *Kitten on the Keys* apparently sold a million copies in its first year, if any of these figures can be trusted.

I discussed *Marigold* mania with Mrs Mayerl in 1981:

PD: Did he mind being the composer of *Marigold* with such an emphasis on that piece?
JM: Well, at the time we needed the money very badly! Because we hadn't got very

---

[21]   See Appendix 3.
[22]   B. Mayerl, interview with Roy Plomley, 21 Apr. 1958.
[23]   J. Mayerl, interview with Peter Dickinson, 11 Aug. 1981.
[24]   I. Ashton, Sleeve-notes for *The King of Syncopation: Billy Mayerl*, LP WRC/EMI SH 189 (1973).

much. We hadn't been married very long. We were living quite nicely, better than I'd ever known about. So it was wonderful.[25]

I came back to *Marigold* later when she told me that audiences always asked for it as an encore:

PD: Which he played fast?
JM: Too fast, sometimes. Much too fast. It wasn't supposed to be fast at all. When he first wrote it, it was sort-of with a jaunty air, lightly. He used to race it. I'd say, 'much too fast—don't play it like that! It's awful!' He'd say, 'I'm fed up with it!' He was—it had gone on and on.
PD: So he turned it into a snappy number?
JM: Which I think spoils it really.[25]

Marigold's versatility is such that it can function effectively either way. But on one occasion Mayerl was put in the position of having to defend *Marigold*. Irene Ashton represented Billy Mayerl and his teaching methods at the Woman's Fair, Olympia, 1938:

We were on the first floor set in the careers section and opposite the Constance Spry stand with all their exquisite flowers and plants. Billy was always loaded with bouquets, as fast as he played one of his flower compositions. (Because of the layout of the stands it was not usually possible to see who was playing.) One day an extremely irate woman came up to Billy, who had just played *Marigold* as a special request. He had left the piano and was standing. She stormed up and shouted: 'I want you to ask that girl to stop playing that awful *Marigold*!' Billy bowed, white with anger: 'Madam, I am selling *Marigold* because I wrote it and everyone here asks for it. What do you sell?'[26]

We have already noted Mayerl's immediate sources in Confrey. Melodic parallel fourths in the same key as *Marigold* appear in *You Tell 'em Ivories* (1921), although they are much less of a feature. As we have also noticed, the device can be traced further back in Gershwin's 1919 piano roll of his *Novelette in Fourths*.[27] Mayerl urged fourths onto his students claiming that 'with the right backing and used with discretion, they become *the* most effective embellishment in modern syncopated piano playing'. He put in a plea for extra practice.[28] The American ragtime authorities, David A. Jasen and Trebor Jay Tichenor, confirm what we have recognized as Mayerl's debt to Confrey: 'While his Novelty rags were called "Syncopated Impressions" and were patterned after Zez Confrey's enormous successes, Mayerl developed his own

[25] J. Mayerl, interview with Peter Dickinson.
[26] I. Ashton, 'My Memories of Billy Mayerl and Gershwin', *Billy Mayerl Newsletter*, 3/17 (Summer 1978), 4–6.
[27] See Ch. 5: also *Gershwin plays Gershwin: the Piano Rolls*, Elektra Nonesuch 7559–79287–2, 1993 and E. Jablonski, *Gershwin: A Biography* (Simon & Schuster, London, 1988), 94.
[28] B. Mayerl, *The Billy Mayerl Special Tutor Course of Modern Syncopation for the Piano* (undated, probably 1931), 40.

original phrases, harmonies and rhythmical devices, as well as rich and beauti-ful melodies. He was probably the finest pianist of all.'[29]

It is good to find this American recognition of Mayerl's panache as a per-former as well as his melodic gifts, which ought to feature in his songs, but we must first look at some other piano pieces that immediately follow *Marigold*. They are all called *Syncopated Impressions*, and, in their different ways, add to Mayerl's resources. *Chop-sticks*, Op. 79 (CD ⒔), marked 'Moderato', is based on the anonymous brief quick waltz that anybody could play on the black notes of the piano. It is witty and subtle, not least in John Hart's cover design which picks up the Far Eastern connection with a cross-legged figure eating with chop-sticks out of a bowl, joss sticks burning in front of a statue of the Buddha. *Chop-sticks* has a twelve-bar introduction which opens with an imposing fanfare based on parallel chords of the dominant eleventh (or, in more detail, chords containing the dominant seventh, major ninth, and sharp eleventh): Lambert's *The Rio Grande*, premièred the following year, reaches this chord for the climax just before the piano cadenza. This is the kind of harmony Duke Ellington was supposed to have got from Delius but cannot have done, since he was unaware of his music. It is an extension of the Debussy and Ravel chords Confrey used into something Mayerl found in Delius and Scott. The fanfares opening *Chop-sticks* are interspersed with cheeky breaks in the whole-tone scale, but the tune itself is pentatonic. The C strain (0′ 53″) has a repeated-note figure with blue notes and the final A strain, after another quirky whole-tone break, gets tired of itself and flourishes down to a *pianissimo* ending. Although the piece is marked 'Moderato', Mayerl's own performance, after the introduction, settles down to the foxtrot tempo of the *Pianolettes* and the *Exaggerations*.

Hollyhock, Op. 80, (CD ⒕) is very closely knit with every detail integrated. It is marked lightly, but Mayerl himself takes it at his usual speed and very dry. The left-hand chords under the main theme last for about one beat instead of the marked three. At first the main motif, appearing five times in the first twelve bars, seems twitchily repetitive, but there is contrast to come—another repeated-note figure with blue notes in strain B (0′ 34″) and, after the repeat of the A strain, a subdominant C strain (1′ 17″) to finish which includes (surely) a left-hand reference (1′ 21″) to the till-ready in Confrey's *Kitten on the Keys*.

Robots, Op. 81, with another cover by John Hart looking like something out of science fiction, is laid out for high speed and even marked vivace. In view of Mayerl's own rapid pace when his tempo markings were moderate, the prospect is frightening but he made no recording. There are new gambits here, such as the off-beat left-hand chords over a tonic pedal in the opening; comic banter with till-ready figures; and the piece is through-composed,

[29] D. A. Jasen and T. J. Tichenor, *Rags and Ragtime: A Musical History* (Seabury Press, New York, 1987), 94.

hardly modulating, with less reliance on the strain structure of the piano rag. In the final section there is a right-hand break of chords built from two perfect fourths in a disruptive 3+2+3 cross-rhythm.

Honky-Tonk, Op. 82, is appropriately called *A Rhythmical Absurdity* since it is a brilliant take-off of various jazz piano mannerisms (CD ⑮). Mayerl himself puts an extra minim beat into the opening three bars (slightly less in later appearances) making them 6/4 and not 4/4. He starts at a relaxed pace of about ♩ = 112 but quickens up as he goes along into a splendid performance. This piece again adds to his resources. He may have known the boogie-woogie classic by Meade Lux Lewis—*Honky Tonk Train Blues* written in 1927 and recorded that year. But the only obvious connection here is the title, which meant a dance hall, although Mayerl had his own use for this term in a 1934 article entitled 'You've got to have Rhythm!': 'Without rhythm you can't phrase music properly. 'Honky-tonks' play the notes one after another and are content. They don't seem to realise that music is written in *groups* of notes which must be *treated* as groups if the dance tune is to come over properly.'[30] And his last word was to urge 'hard work, hours of practice, and a determination never to have the label Honky-tonk pinned to you'. But Mayerl's response to African American piano idioms had been established well before *Honky Tonk Train Blues*, probably through J. P. Johnson, whose piano rolls had been available from 1917 and recordings, such as *Carolina Shout*, from 1921. An important difference between Mayerl and these stride pianists is that Johnson, like Jelly Roll Morton, never stuck to his sheet music and things were different every time.

Early in the first strain of *Honky-Tonk* there is a prominent blue note and then there are some curious cross-references of a kind that would not have happened in earlier Mayerl. Strain B (1' 42″) starts afresh, with its own right-hand breaks, then quotes strain A followed by the introduction used as a transition into strain C (1' 04″), which has another blue-note figure separated by six appearances of a bass break marked 'hammer'. Then what arrives as a strain D (1' 37″) simply alternates one new phrase with a modification of the main strain C phrase. A double strain A to finish is followed by the introduction again, dying away to *ppp*.

The last of these opus numbers, *Wistaria*, Op.88, and *Jasmine*, Op. 89, use the new term syncopated impression and have floral titles. They hardly break new ground but the introduction to *Wistaria* clearly echoes Gershwin's 'Clap yo' Hands' (*Oh Kay!* 1926) and the A strain makes a more extended melody out of it, accompanied by left-hand parallel sixths of the sort found in Gershwin's own piano transcription of this song. Mayerl's own recording cuts the introduction after strain B but adds it again at the end. *Jasmine*, dedicated to Jill

---

30 B. Mayerl 'You've got to have Rhythm', *Popular Music and Dancing Weekly*, 1/2 (Oct. 1934), 20.

Mayerl and marked 'slowly', is charming, with the melody of the first bar of the introduction largely in the whole-tone scale, which is evocative this time rather than comic. This is beautifully extended to finish the piece with an uncertain ending on the dominant with raised fifth. Mayerl himself plays *Jasmine* at his slightly slower foxtrot tempo and, with a supple right hand, manages to make a relaxed effect in characteristic swinging rhythm. Strain A, with a lovely rising phrase in dotted rhythm, has a tendency for the left-hand accompaniment, as in *Robots* and later in No. 4 of *Four Aces*, to strike a major ninth instead of a doubled tonic or dominant.

One of Mayerl's finest triptychs was published in the same year as *Marigold*—this is his *Puppets Suite* consisting of *Golliwog*, *Judy*, and *Punch*. *Golliwog* (CD ⒃) is marked 'Umoristico, giocoso', and is a reminder that the clue to Mayerl is often comedy of the kind found in knock-about farce or Punch and Judy shows. The sheet music shows the three figures suspended from their strings. Strain A of *Golliwog* has a catchy tune related to the one in *Hollyhock*, which was published later, but more extended. There are some fine cadenzas in the *Rhapsody in Blue* vein used as transitions and, when we get to strain C (1′ 12″), Mayerl himself creates a counter-melody out of the left-hand tenths with the upper note taken legato. *Judy* (CD ⒄) is marked 'Blues tempo' and is certainly a relation of *Marigold* in the same key of E flat major. The initially pentatonic melody of strain A is doubled in fourths; there are similar two-part right-hand breaks; excursions into the barbershop chord; and a similar dainty atmosphere pervades. Strain B (0′ 55″) is dominated by repeated notes with blue inflections, including slides of the kind associated with jazz singers or brass players. The strain A melody of *Judy* is catchy but not as developed as *Marigold* for which it feels like a rehearsal, even though in the context of the Suite *Judy* is at Mayerl's highest level. His own performance of *Punch* (CD ⒅) is dazzling and its final strain C (1′ 35″) contains adventurous chords with added minor seconds—the rest becomes so ferocious that Mayerl himself has to end loudly and not at all *ppp* as in the score. Unusually neither the first nor the last movement of this suite ends in the key in which it began.

Consideration of Mayerl's solos since *Marigold* establishes that he was still exploring and mapping out his pianistic territory. The atmosphere created by 1920s Mayerl is unique, either in terms of rhythmic tricks and perfectly calculated pianistic effects or sheer melodic flow. The few available opus numbers suggest that the pieces were written in the sequence taken here and they show Mayerl at the peak of his form. For him the 1920s was a wonderful decade. His later developments rarely expand this territory significantly: at their best they consolidate the high standard he had reached in these miniatures. Anyway, Mayerl was far too busy fulfilling the simultaneous demands of the West End, the Music Halls, broadcasting, recording, and the School to concern himself with much more than the very tangible public demand for him in all his capacities.

8

THE SONG-WRITER

THE character Pedrolino in traditional Italian *commedia dell' arte* seems to have given rise to Pierrot in French mime during the mid-nineteenth century. By the 1890s pierrot troupes of actors, singers, and dancers in fancy costumes were a regular feature of entertainment at British holiday resorts. Soon after Mayerl's partnership with Gwen Farrar ended dramatically in 1930 he spent over a year with the Co-Optimists, the pierrot-style concert party dressed in purple and gold with ruffles and skull-caps, which brought this tradition to London's West End.[1] The Co-Optimists were launched by the monocled comedian and astute promoter David Burnaby, encouraged by Leslie Henson, with Archibald de Bear, Laddie Cliff, and Clifford Whiteley as backers in 1921. They started with a capital of £900 [£23,000] and by the time William Pollock, Theatre Correspondent of *The Daily Mail*, was assessing their progress five years later there was a gross turnover of more than £300,000 [£7,685,000].[2] They opened at the Royalty Theatre on 27 June 1921 and went on for 500 performances. The Duke of Connaught sent a message after a performance: 'What I like about you is that you all look so happy.' So they contributed to what would now be called the 'feel-good' factor and were very funny, much needed in the immediate post-war years.[3]

The group broke up in 1927 but set off again at the Vaudeville in July 1929 and operated as the Co-Optimists of 1930 the following year, which was when Mayerl joined. The compère was David Burnaby and the original team

---

[1] H. R. Schleman's *Rhythm on Record* (London, 1936), lists Mayerl's stage partners after Farrar as Billie Hill and Lena Chisholm but there was also reference to his pupil Marjorie Lotinga, billed as a 'syncopated actress' in the *BMCM*, 3/29 (May 1936), 5.

[2] A. Sterne and A. de Bear, *The Comic History of the Co-Optimists* (H. Jenkins, London, 1926), 114–17. See also S. Holloway, *Wiv a little bit o' Luck* (Leslie Frewin, London, 1967), for plenty of detail about the Co-Optimists. No mention of Mayerl here, nor of their Australian trip together: just one sentence about Mayerl giving good parties on p. 224. In 1929 Robert Graves's autobiography, *Goodbye to all that*, appeared. In the following year Harry S. Pepper's song with the same title was published as 'broadcast and recorded by Melville Gideon': there were four band recordings that year.   [3] Sterne and De Bear, *Comic History*, 123.

as photographed in June 1921 consisted of Betty Chester, Phyllis Monkman, Elsa Macfarlane, Babs Valerie, Stanley Holloway, Melville Gideon, Laddie Cliff, Gilbert Childs, and H. B. Hedley. Gideon wrote most of the songs and he and Headley played the pianos. But there were changes and by 1926 Anita Elson, Doris Bentley, Austin Melford, Cicely James, and Wolseley Charles were replacements, and Phyllis Monkman, Laddie Cliff, Elsa Macfarlane, H. B. Hedley, Babs Valerie, and Hermione Baddeley were being described as ex-co-optimists. Or, in the ubiquitous punning style of the times:

SOME EX CO-OPTIMISTS

'Tis better to have Co-Opped and 'Opt it, than never to have Co-Opped at all.
DAVID CO-OPPERFIELD[4]

The Co-Optimists included a number of Mayerl's friends and colleagues at the start of substantial careers in show business. Some of the most influential were the comic dialect actor-singer Stanley Holloway, with whom Mayerl and his wife went to Australia and New Zealand in 1949; Laddie Cliff, who acted in, produced, or managed many of the shows Mayerl worked with; and Archibald de Bear, who was the producer of *The Punchbowl*. Many of the men were members of the Savage Club, as were Mayerl and his regular lyricist, Frank Eyton. Other musician members Mayerl would have met there were Sir Landon Ronald, Benno Moiseiwitsch and, in the popular scene, Jack Byfield and Max Jaffa.[5] David Burnaby had a personal role during the period when Mayerl was working with the Co-Optimists and was obviously under enormous stress with a hectic performing career plus the responsibilities of the Mayerl School. As Mayerl explained: 'I then joined up with the Co-Optimists, but I was ill most of the fourteen months I was with them. I had my first real nervous breakdown at that time, which caused me to sprint all the way to the post-office with a telegram to my wife which intimated: "I am dying. You must come at once!" '[6]

Mayerl goes on to say that one visit to a friend of Burnaby's who ran, in the blunt terminology of the times, a Mental Home in Sheffield put him right and 'with my wife's help I managed to get back to that joyous don't-care-a-darn feeling that is a sign of first-class health'.

[4] Stern and De Bear, *Comic History*, 85.

[5] Mayerl was nominated for membership of the Savage Club on 4 June 1930 and elected on 2 October that year. His proposer was Arthur Wood and his seconders were Morris Harvey and Billy Leonard. There were eight signatures in the supporters column, most of them hard to decipher. When Mayerl was informed of his successful nomination he wrote from 30 Catherine Street, London SW1 on 30 Aug. 1930, saying that he was pleased to have been elected but could not visit the club for the next three months since he would be on tour. Letter to Peter Dickinson from Peter D. Bond, Archivist of the Savage Club, 21 Mar. 1995. See also M. Jaffa, *A Life on the Fiddle* (Hodder & Stoughton, London 1991), for Savage Club connections.

[6] B. Mayerl, 'My Piano Fell into the Band', *Tit-bits*, 10 July 1937, 20–1.

In 1930 Keith Prowse published the *Co-Optimists New Song Album*, six tailor-made songs by Mayerl with lyrics by Frank Eyton.[7] There are few recordings of Mayerl's songs so their effectiveness or their potential can only be judged by the printed page or by comments from those who heard them in context. The style of the Co-Optimists can be judged from their earlier recordings and Mayerl's contributions fitted into the format set by Gideon, but seem more polished. The first song, 'Brush the cobwebs from your feet', has Mayerl mannerisms of the period including the barbershop chord early and late in the syncopated chorus and the 3+3+2 cross rhythm in the seventh and eighth bars of the piano accompaniment.

'Sky Lady', where the singer dreams of his up-to-date girl, who is an air pilot, was apparently sung by Mayerl himself and could have been very touching. 'Baby, maybe it's you' was for one of the original stars, Phyllis Monkman, who was Laddie Cliff's second wife, and 'Oi gave 'er a nod, oi gave 'er a wink' was, of course, a dialect song for Stanley Holloway. The last two are waltz songs for Sylvia Cecil and Elaine Roslyn—'The road to Fairyland' and 'My love flew in through the window', with the punch line 'when my husband came in through the door!' That scenario shows that times were changing by 1930. Musically the song is in the tradition of Charles K. Harris's 1892 hit, 'After the ball was over', where a romance is stifled because the man catches his girl kissing another man who much later turns out to have been only her brother, but the Eyton scenario reflects the calculated naughtiness of the 1920s.

All these songs are old-fashioned for 1930, which may have been necessary to fit the brief for the Co-Optimists. The waltz songs in particular have a somewhat flowery English approach like Noel Coward at the same period—'I'll see you again' from *Bitter Sweet* (1929) or 'Someday I'll find you' from *Private Lives* (1930)—but Mayerl lacks a strong idea to open the chorus and sustain repetition. All of these songs pall against the massive appeal of classics like Berlin's 'All alone' (1924) which Norah Blaney sang in *The Punch Bowl* in the year it appeared and the sheet music of the British edition is adorned with her photograph.

The reasons for the success of 'All alone' compared with Mayerl's waltz songs are tangibly in the notes, but one could also say that the English frame of reference is still stylized middle class and would remain so—the women singers in the Co-Optimists sounded posh—whereas the American constituency is much wider and increasingly international. Berlin's chorus opens with a simple step-wise idea—the memorable hook in popular music terms—which is repeated. The rhythmic figure, which builds towards a climax, is used ten times and the implied harmony moves slowly, although the sheet music doubles the melody, Puccini-style, without a bass until the fifth phrase.

---

7 F. Eyton, 'Concerning the Lyre', *BMCM*, 1/3 (Mar. 1934), 3–4.

Mayerl's waltzes come from nineteenth-century types but Berlin is slower and, of course, sadness—the lonely girl hoping for a telephone call—always has a deeper resonance.

That may not have been a fair comparison, but Mayerl was well aware of the latest American developments in other ways, as we have seen in the 1920s piano works. His songs have understandable echoes of the major figures whose worth he recognized, as Mrs Mayerl confirmed: 'He always admired Cole Porter, Gershwin. All those people he thought were marvellous. He said, "These will never die"—and of course they haven't.'[8]

So, as we have seen, Mayerl recognized American achievement in piano idioms and took this as his point of departure. But in songs, he was too close to his English roots and his collaborators in the theatre to break out of that mould. Their territory was between the old-fashioned operetta of Sigmund Romberg and the American musicals of Gershwin and Rodgers and Hart, at a time when the BBC, fighting a losing battle, was trying to discourage American accents.

There are signs of homage too. One of Mayerl's songs for *Silver Wings* (1930), 'Indispensable you' (marked 'Yale Blue Tempo' like No. 2 of *Three Miniatures in Syncopation* and No. 3 of *Three Dances in Syncopation* and characterized by its blue notes and stomping bass), is related to Kern's 'Can't help lovin' dat man of mine' (*Showboat*, 1927) or, earlier, Gershwin's 'Kickin' the Clouds away' (*Tell Me More*, 1925). The Co-Optimists' shows helped to cement the popularity in England of another of Berlin's waltzes, 'Always' (1925) which Melville Gideon sang in the shows and recorded in 1926, and—such was their range—Betty Chester made a hit with John Ireland's 'Sea Fever' (1913, published after various rejections in 1915).[9] Mayerl included this song in his *Desert Island Discs* choice in 1958.[10] The poem is by the British Poet Laureate, John Masefield, and the Co-Optimists said they resisted the temptation to add a chorus to it in the manner of the moment:

> I want to go back—
> I want to go back—
> I want to go back to the sea:
> Where the whales are,
> And the gales are,
> And the blown spume waits for me.

[8] J. Mayerl, interview with Peter Dickinson, 11 Aug, 1981.

[9] J. Longmire, *John Ireland: Portrait of a Friend* (John Baker, London, 1966), 50. Kenneth Wright, who later dealt with Mayerl's bookings in the Programme Department of the BBC, recalled that 'Sea Fever' became so popular that listeners voted it 'the most popular of all British songs' in about 1924. The recording that Mayerl chose for his *Desert Island Discs* was by Frederick Harvey (baritone) with orchestra/Philip Green on HMV B.10233.

[10] B. Mayerl, interview with Roy Plomley, 21 Apr. 1958.

But they persisted with an orgy of punning jokes about Betty Chester's alleged fever.[11]

The lyricist to the Co-Optimists at the time when Mayerl arrived was Frank Eyton, Mayerl's regular partner. He and Arthur Wimperis provided the lyrics for *Nippy* which, with twelve numbers and opening and closing music, was Mayerl's first full-length show, setting his pattern for the rest of the decade.

The *Sketch* previewed the production as very much a show-piece for one of the leading ladies of the period, Binnie Hale.[12] In February 1930 she had finished over a year as Jill Kemp in *Mr Cinders* composed by Vivian Ellis and Richard Myers, which ran for 529 performances.[13] Peter Gammond, in the *Oxford Companion to Popular Music*, regarded Ellis's shows as in an 'Eton-accented musical-comedy style that made the British musical such a domestic affair'. *Nippy* cannot have been very different in this respect.

Nippy, the new musical comedy featuring Miss Binnie Hale and Mr. Clifford Mollison, has had a most successful try-out in the provinces, and is due to arrive in London on 30 October at the Prince Edward Theatre. The story—as the title indicates—opens in the Corner House, where Nippy, the waitresss, serves. Bob, the rich young man, falls in love with her, and she loses her job on his account. The next act has a garage setting, and introduces Nippy as helping her mother run the business. She is persuaded to give up her high-born lover, and sets off for Hollywood, with stardom as her goal: so in the last act we meet her transformed into the Complete Cinema Star, and matters speed up to a happy ending. The musical numbers include 'The Toy Town Party', sung by Miss Binnie Hale; and there is plenty of comedy, dancing, and first-rate fooling, as well as gorgeous production.[14]

The Corner House referred to was one in the popular chain of cafés run by Lyons, a British institution. The first teashop was opened at 213 Piccadilly, London, in 1894, the first Corner House in 1908, and they became centres of informal social life. By 1910 there were 98 of them in London, at their peak there were 250 across the country, but the last one closed in the 1970s. The Coventry Street Corner House in London was an example of the ubiquity of live music. There were four floors and each floor had two orchestras.

---

[11] Sterne and De Bear, *Comic History*, 49. It looks as if the Co-Optimists were introduced to the Ireland song by a piano pupil of his, Charles Markes, who accompanied 'Sea Fever' and also played Ireland's *The Island Spell*. However, when Markes told his teacher that he would be appearing on the Halls, Ireland was horrified and a misunderstanding ruined their friendship for some years. See M. V. Searle, *John Ireland: The Man and his Music* (Midas Books, Tunbridge Wells, 1979), 55.

[12] *Sketch*, 29 Oct. 1930. See also Holloway, *Wiv a little bit o' Luck*, 168–9: 'Binne was a girl who could make me laugh; such timing with a satirical sketch, a great sense of the ridiculous and also for tugging at your heart with a lightly poignant song.'

[13] V. Ellis and R. Myers, *Mr Cinders*. In 1929 Billy Mayerl recorded a two-part selection on Columbia WA 5336 8487–2 and WA 8488–1.   [14] *Sketch*, 29 Oct. 1930.

Waitresses were known as a nippies because the service was fast. The *Sketch* also provided photographs of Nippy on a motor bike and with her agent. The caption below reads: ' "NIPPY"–TO BE HALE-D AT THE PRINCE EDWARD THE-ATRE!'

The Times set the context by defining the parameters of public appeal in ways that apply equally to popular music and noted that *Nippy* was resisting American cultural imperialism:

We hardly look for originality in musical comedy. The purveyors of entertainment of this sort believe rather in continuity—the continuity of that which has lately proved its worth elsewhere. But a piece that in these days is unashamedly English at least deserves to be unusual. In humour, sentiment, and setting *Nippy* is English, and in the last half an hour when some hard American jokes are hurled about the stage there is mockery in the air. Indeed we may go further and declare that *Nippy* has originality, for it has Miss Binnie Hale, and there is nobody quite like her on the stage today.[15]

Another critic thought some of the plot was boring and trite but found compensations and, interestingly at this stage, placed Mayerl's music in an in-between territory:

The dialogue was of better quality than usual, because the ensemble was bright with joy and vivacity, because the scenery was most attractive, and because the music of Mr. Billy Mayerl has a peculiar flavour, something between jazz and the melodists, with some numbers of originality, although he borrows often from his well-known pre-serves.[16]

And another panegyric to Binnie Hale: 'She is a genius, a little goddess of mirth and grace and ubiquitous dynamic force. She acts with her body, her heart, her soul, her gyrating arms, aye, with her legs and feet—legs that would make Mistinguett's green with envy.'

Mistinguett was the French singer and actress famous in Paris at the Moulin Rouge, the *Folies-Bergère*, and later Hollywood. The appeal of female legs for so many generations has tended to be overlooked in the full-frontal-ism of more recent times.

The *Observer* critic started, 'Miss Binnie Hale is delightful. She prompts lyrical praises such as, on rare occasions, theatrical historians of the past were wont to sing of their particular favourites.' And finished prophetically: 'Thanks to Miss Binnie Hale no less than to her colleagues, this large theatre should be filled for many weeks to come.'[17] No mention of the music, with Debroy Somers and his Band, and the show closed on 14 February 1931 after a decent run of 137 performances.

---

15 *The Times*, 31 Oct. 1930.
16 J.T.G., unidentified cutting dated 12 Nov. 1930 in the Savoy Archives.
17 H.H. in the *Observer*, 2 Nov. 1930.

Binnie Hale's recording shows plenty of zip for her cheerful and catchy rhythmic song 'Nippy', and her duet 'Two of everything' flirts with a *double entendre*. The music treats it all deadpan and seems aware of Gershwin's 'S'Wonderful' from *Funny Face* (1927).[18] But 'A couple of fine old schools', which turn out to be Eton College and Borstal Prison, is hilarious in the old-fashioned manner of British public (private) schools and obviously made a wide enough impact to prompt a debate at the Union of Oxford University 'That Borstal and Eton are a couple of fine old schools'. This was the same debating society which would vote against fighting for King and country when Hitler was looming on the European scene in 1933. 'I feel so safe with you', with its sensuous added sixths in the chorus, is a poised melody which could accumulate intensity in the right performance. The Piano Selection from *Nippy* was made by Guy Jones—so was the one for *The Millionaire Kid*, but not *Sporting Love*, which Mayerl made himself.

In June 1937 Mayerl reflected on show business:

Working for the theare is a great gamble—believe me! I was paid £500 [£17,400] advance royalties for my music for the musical comedy *So long, Letty*. Yet the publisher lost on the deal. And the music was written with some care, too. My music for another show, *Nippy*, was written with more dash and eagerness and caught the public ear right away. The most successful number, 'Borstal and Eton', was dashed off on the back of a menu card in a cocktail bar in Edinburgh.

Clifford Mollison and Arthur Riscoe, who played the 'Varsity man and the cockney, wanted a comedy number and we were discussing it. Suddenly Frank Eyton said: 'What about this?

> Borstal and Eton,
> They cannot be beaten,
> A couple of fine old schools.'

In ten minutes I wrote the music while Eyton completed the words. The song was the hit of the show, which brought me over £4,000 [£146,000].[19]

The Millionaire Kid, where Mayerl wrote all the music except one song, was far less successful than *Nippy*. It was billed as 'A new musical play in two acts and four scenes by Noel Scott': Eyton wrote the lyrics and it opened at the Gaiety Theatre on 20 May 1931, ran for 87 performances, then toured and

---

[18] B. Mayerl, *Nippy*. Recordings of selections include Billy Mayerl on Columbia DB 288 WA 10739–3 and WA 10740–4; Patricia Rossborough on Parlophone R 791 WE 3741–2 and WE 3743–2 (CD transfer on *Patricia Rossborough: The Queen of Syncopation*, Shellwood SWCD 10, 1998); original cast selections with orchestra under Debroy Somers on Columbia DB 349, 350, and 351; and Debroy Somers Band with Dan Donovan on Columbia DX 167.

[19] B. Mayerl, 'We Played on as a Prince Lay Dying', *Tit-bits*, 26 June 1937, 5–6. See also details of the Oxford Union debate announced in the *Daily Express* in 'What others think about us', *BMCM*, 1/3 (Mar. 1934), 30. Eyton sometimes wrote the tunes too—see the feebly conventional 'Make your heart a trap to catch the sunshine', 1926.

returned to the Prince Edward Theatre for a month, ending on 16 January 1931. Presented and produced by Laddie Cliff, it featured old-fashioned dances, and the tunes are not distinctive. 'Life is meant for love' is a type of Ivor Novello waltz: 'Thank you most sincerely' neatly escapes Gershwin's 'Looking for a boy' (*Tip-toes*, 1925), which is its starting-point. All the same there was a recorded medley with the New Mayfair Orchestra under Ray Noble and Mayerl recorded the Piano Selection on 8 May 1931.[20]

By 1934 things were different. *Sporting Love*, billed as 'a Musical Horse Play', was written by Stanley Lupino as a vehicle for himself and Laddie Cliff in an all-star context. The *Daily Telegraph* hailed him—'Stanley Lupino in great form' and admitted that 'without him the show would hardly exist'.[21] *Sporting Love* was a hit amongst British musicals. Mayerl was more heavily involved than ever since he wrote the music and was also musical director, planning to conduct the entire run. It opened at the Gaiety Theatre on 31 March 1934 and closed on 26 January 1935, lasting for 302 performances plus tours. Thanks to a column called 'Our President's Activities' in the *Billy Mayerl Club Magazine*, which had started in January 1934, we can trace Mayerl's schedule, which was horrendous even for a young man of 31. At the same time as rehearsing *Sporting Love* Mayerl was taking part in a film, *Without You*, where he played the part of a composer whose songs were so bad that he was upstaged by one written by the piano tuner! A typical day was itemized in the second issue of the *BMCM*:

6 am Try to get up and fight your way through the fog in order to be on location at 8 am.

8 am Arrive on location and mess about the place for a couple of hours. Try and make the film till about six o'clock in the evening, with a five-minute pause for lunch—if you are lucky!

8 pm Having got back to town, start rehearsing the musical comedy again.

2 am Think about getting something to eat.

3 am Think about going to bed.

3.5 am Decide that as you have to get up so early it is not worth going to bed.

6 am Repeat the mixture as before.[22]

[20] B. Mayerl, *The Millionaire Kid*, selections with the New Mayfair Orchestra/Gibbons on HMV C 2231: Piano Selection by Billy Mayerl on Columbia DB 517C 11578 and 11579 recorded on 8 May 1931. Apparently Mayerl was telephoned on one day, recorded the next, and inside a week the record was on sale. See 'Quick Work', *BMCM*, 1/5 (May 1934) 4.

[21] *Daily Telegraph*, 2 Apr. 1934.

[22] 'Our President's Activities', *BMCM*, 1/2 (Feb. 1934), 28. See also ibid., 1/4 (Apr. 1934), 28, for a picture of him in the film. Apart from the major shows where Mayerl wrote all or most of the music, he and Eyton contributed to *Darling, I Love You!* (Gaiety, 1930); *My Sister and I* (Shaftesbury, 1931); and a one-off benefit called *The Green Room Rag-Picker's Revue* (Drury Lane, 1933). They were entirely responsible for *Taking the Count: or the Infernal Waltz* (Shaftesbury, 1932, Mayerl directing); and he also directed *Spring Tide* by Billam and Goldsmith (Duchess, 1936). See J. P. Wearing, *The London Stage: 1930–39: A Calendar of Plays and Players* (Scarecrow Press, Methuen, NJ, 1990).

The out-of-town opening of *Sporting Love* was at the Alhambra Theatre, Glasgow, on 22 January 1934. When interviewed in the first number of the *BMCM* Mayerl explained that he was going to conduct the orchestra:

'Well, why not? I have done most things in my life, and it has always been my ambition to conduct a really fine orchestra, especially in my own music'. He said he would play the piano 'as and when I feel the need for some solo work; and it will be great fun inventing new embellishments and figurations while the orchestra is playing'.[23]

To cope with his other responsibilities, Mayerl took his secretary with him and came back to London every weekend for personal lessons and recording. The pressure mounted in proportion to the success of *Sporting Love* as it ran right through 1934, which meant Mayerl had to cancel outside engagements. An independent tour of *Sporting Love* was launched at Brighton on 14 July 1934 with some forty weeks planned.[24] But—not for the first time—Mayerl himself was overdoing things and had an attack of shingles.[25] George Windeatt took over *Sporting Love* at the Gaiety with only one rehearsal and Mayerl went to the seaside, but he soon admitted: 'I don't like a life of leisure, and after nine days I headed the car back to London shingles or no shingles—and believe me they still tickle!'[26]

These details about Mayerl's manic schedule have been worth uncovering since they show the conditions under which he had to operate. Another fine novelty pianist, Raie da Costa, had the same sort of pressures up to her untimely death: 'My life has been one ceaseless rush from engagement to engagement. I have played somewhere for somebody every single day, on the variety halls, recording, official entertaining—until I almost begin to eat, sleep and drink syncopation.'[27] But Mayerl was no longer just a pianist. He was committed to the musical theatre and, as the songs for *Sporting Love* showed, assessing these demands more accurately:

A lot of what they said a hundred years ago is still applicable today, perhaps more so in the simpler popular tunes than in the bigger works; this is because the man in the street has no musical knowledge whatsoever, and what little ear for music he possesses can only absorb the easier modulations and simple harmonic constructions. Therefore we all write down when attempting to cater for the masses, and to a much greater degree do we follow out the laws laid down for us by the old school, frightened lest any deviation from this should be over the heads of the few remaining people to whom we hope to sell a copy![28]

---

[23] 'Our President's Activities', *BMCM*, 1/1 (Jan. 1934), 28.

[24] Ibid., 1/8 (Aug. 1934), 30.

[25] G. Clayton, 'All Work and no Play: An Apology to Members', *BMCM*, 1/6 (June 1934), 25.

[26] B. Mayerl, 'From the President's Chair', *BMCM*, 1/7 (July 1934), 2.

[27] J. Watson, CD booklet to *Raie da Costa: The Parlophone Girl*, on Shellwood SWCD 8 (1998).

[28] B. Mayerl, 'This Month's Lesson', *BMCM*, 1/7 (July 1934), 24.

Mayerl benefited from his association with this sparkling comedy, although he said 'a year of the same thing every night is as good as a feast . . . we are all very tired of it'.[29]

As usual his music was regarded merely as a contributory element: the *Daily Telegraph* called it 'bright, and there is not too much of it'. Stanley Lupino himself did well out it—he signed a lavish £20,000 [£819,000] a year film contract starting after *Sporting Love*, which was filmed by Hammer, but as a play without the music.[30] The 200th London performance was celebrated with the show being described as 'funnier than ever', with new lines introduced, and it seemed set to run for another 200 performances.[31]

Of Mayerl's tunes, the British authority on the musical theatre, Kurt Ganzel, finds the rather routine duet 'Have a heart' 'perhaps the most effective'.[32] Of the others 'You're the reason why' is too close, again, to Gershwin's 'Someone to watch over me' (*Oh, Kay!* 1926); the chorus of 'Who asked you?' has a strong opening phrase and a cumulative rhythm; 'I ought not to' is a viable Viennese waltz, better than those Mayerl wrote for the Co-Optimists; and 'Those in favour' is a snappy syncopated number with some 3+2+3 cross rhythms to spice it up in the manner of Mayerl's 1920s piano novelties.

Mayerl's next complete show was *Twenty to One*, billed as 'the funniest sporting farce ever staged', written and produced by L. Arthur Rose with lyrics by Eyton. With Lupino Lane as actor-manager, it opened at the London Coliseum on 12 November 1935 and closed on 28 May 1936 after 383 performances. This was another substantial success with a wartime revival at the Victoria Palace from 10 February 1942 to 5 December 1943?—a further 408 performances. Mayerl recorded the Piano Selection on 7 December 1935[33] and the *Daily Telegraph* said the usual things about his lively and tuneful music.[34] The duet 'How d'you like your eggs fried' stayed in the show after revisions and has a jaunty light touch.

In these years Mayerl was associated with musical comedies which ran longer than most of their British—and American—competitors. There were greater British hits, such as Noel Coward's *Bitter Sweet* (1929) which ran for 697 performances and Noel Gay's legendary *Me and my Girl* which clocked up 1,646 performances between 1937 and 1940. But in spite of his association with such successes Mayerl invariably got less than his share of the credit, at least in print. The public went to such shows to see the latest from household names in musical comedy.

---

[29] Mayerl, 'From the President's Chair', *BMCM*, 2/14 (Feb. 1935), 2.
[30] *Daily Telegraph*, 3 Apr. 1934.
[31] G. W. Bishop, *Daily Telegraph*, 5 Sept. 1934.
[32] K. Ganzel, *The British Musical Theatre*, ii. 401.
[33] See Discography.
[34] *Daily Telegraph*, item by G.W.B.—no date.

Over She Goes, another highly successful Stanley Lupino–Laddie Cliff comedy, followed: it opened at the Saville Theatre on 23 September 1936 and closed on 22 May 1937 after 248 performances, slightly less than Ivor Novello's *Careless Rapture* with 295, and was made into a film by the Associated British Picture Corporation in the same year. Mayerl was using Harry Perritt as an orchestrator, discussing matters with him at the Savage Club. But only a few days later he died, and consequently Mayerl had to get George Windeatt to take over[35] Mayerl conducted *Over She Goes* himself and, since it was a success, had to cancel engagements again to cope with eight performances a week.[36] He recorded the Piano Selection himself[37] and told Roy Plomley that *Over She Goes* was his favourite show: 'I wrote the music, I conducted the orchestra and Laddie allowed me to have a corner of financial interest in it—it was a big success, as you know.'[38] The show also contained Richard Murdoch, early in his career, as a police sergeant.

The catchy title song used in the film as an opening and closing number is not by Mayerl but by Michael Carr and Jimmy Kennedy. Of the six separately published Mayerl numbers 'I breathe on windows' has rising figures and a sustained mood almost worthy of Kern; 'Mine's a hopeless case', which was not in the film, is simply routine, but there were five band recordings of 'I breathe on windows' and both Henry Hall and Arthur Salisbury put 'Mine's a hopeless case' on the other side.[39] Mayerl recorded a selection with the Saville Theatre Orchestra, conducting himself, on 5 November 1936;[40] 'Side by side' is the kind of snappy number which obviously caused Mayerl's show tunes to be described as bright and tinkling; 'Yes! No!', not in the film, was a near hit in Lupino's performance but it is now hard to see why; and Mayerl's own title song, 'Over she goes', tempts providence as Carter and Eyton's pedestrian lyric shows:

> Writing songs is easy,
> Take it from one who knows;
> Be sure the words are breezy,
> And OVER SHE GOES!

[35] B. Mayerl, 'From the President's Chair, *BMCM*, 3/33 (Sept. 1936), 2.

[36] Ibid., 3/34 (Oct. 1936), 2.

[37] B. Mayerl, *Over She Goes*, 30 Mar. 1937. See Discography.

[38] B. Mayerl, interview with Roy Plomley on *Desert Island Discs*, BBC Home Service, 21 Apr. 1958.

[39] B. Mayerl, *Over She Goes*, 'I breathe on Windows', the BBC Dance Orchestra/Hall CA-15957–1 Col. FB 1528; Casani Club Orchestra/Kunz F-2057–1 Rex 8917; Joe Loss and his Orchestra OEA-4072–1 HMV BD-5123; Arthur Salisbury and his Savoy Hotel Orchestra TB-2494-1 Dec. F-6123.

[40] B. Mayerl, *Over She Goes*, Saville Theatre Orchestra/Mayerl, 5 Nov. 1936. See Discography.

Cruelly enough it was not that easy for Mayerl, but in the middle to late 1930s he was getting nearer—and certainly trying, as he explained in 1935:

Honeymoon for Three, the first film to be made by Gaiety Productions Ltd., 'took the floor' at the Ealing Studios on May 10. The music for the film, which I have written, is going to be exploited to the utmost degree. Special quartets of singers and solo vocalists have been engaged to do a few bars here and there, and the orchestral arrangements are under the direction of Percival Mackey, who is conducting with an augmented orchestra of thirty. The three important numbers are 'Make Hey while the Moon shines', 'I'll build a Fence around you', and 'Why not, Madame?'. Judging by the preliminary shots I saw when last at the Studio, I feel that the latter two numbers are likely candidates for the 'hit' stakes.[41]

Mayerl was right. 'Make Hey!' has a strong pentatonic opening motif—compare it with Gershwin's 'I got rhythm' (*Girl Crazy*, 1930)—and a syncopated backing. The result is well above the normal snappy number required of musical comedy composers. 'I'll build a fence' is delicate and touching, with its dotted rhythm and smooth modulations neatly placed. There is a lot of tonic F major, and the G♯ at the end of the middle eight is not a blue note but simply a conventional raised fifth. A kind of English innocence also pervades 'Why not, Madame?'. But Eyton's lyrics are, as usual, basic even if they have moved away from the kind of moon–June banalities satirized by Ira Gershwin in 'Blah, Blah, Blah' (*Delicious*, 1931) and, incidentally, long before by Charles Ives in 'Romanzo di Central Park' (1900). And, to be fair, Eyton was one of three lyric writers involved in 'Body and Soul' by the versatile American John W. Green. This song was one of the Golden 100 Tin Pan Alley Songs 1918–35 cited by *Variety Magazine*.[42] And Eyton helped to create three British hits with Noel Gay in 1940 and their partnership continued.

In 1936 Mayerl wrote three songs for the film *Cheer Up*, and the music credits also include Val Guest and Noel Gay, with arrangements by Percival Mackey, who conducted his own orchestra. Lyrics were by Eyton, Stanley Lupino, and Desmond Carter and the director was Leo Mittler. The whole thing was an elaborate comic vehicle centred on Lupino, as a penniless playwright, and the lovely Sally Gray, an actress looking for her chance on stage. Both 'Apart from business' and 'There's a star in the sky' are turned into sumptuous song-and-dance routines of real visual appeal providing exactly what the film required. In real life Sally Gray found her chance when she married into the aristocracy as the third wife of Lord Oranmore and Browne in 1953.

There was usually a transcription of a popular song in each issue of the

41 B. Mayerl, 'From the President' Chair', *BMCM*, 2/18 (June 1935), 2.
42 C. Hamm, *Yesterdays: Popular Song in America* (Norton, New York, 1979), 489.

BMCM. For May 1936 Mayerl chose his own 'There's a star in the sky' for detailed discussion and called it:

'a melodious number. In the film it is sung in various different ways, but the style in each case is similar. The verse should be taken ad lib.—I have marked it 'Molto moderato', so here you may use your own judgement. The rallentando in the middle of bar 8 is essential: this will 'pull you up' in time to set a definite pace in the Chorus which is to come. Note the tenuto markings on the two chords prior to the chorus; these are rather important.[43]

Mayerl goes on with more details about how to play the transcription of this song, which seems only to have been recorded by Harry Saville and his Orchestra until Eric Parkin's revelatory series of the piano transcriptions.[44] This is strange since the chorus is a perfect example of what Mayerl could now do as a song-writer (see Exx. 11 and 12).

The verse is casual and light-weight, setting the scene. Again its decorations are conventional auxiliary notes and not blue. But the lead into the chorus is the first original stroke as Mayerl's tenuto marks in the piano transcription indicate. In the song version, these are two augmented triads over the dominant C: in the transcription they become four-note chords in the whole-tone scale. Mayerl loved Debussy and Ravel and it is likely that this lead-in came via Ravel's *Valses nobles et sentimentales* (1911), No. VII, bars 17 and 18 after the pause. Note that Ravel's eighth waltz quotes from earlier movements, a tactic adopted by Mayerl in his early *Egyptian Suite*, *The Legends of King Arthur*, and the vivid extra number of the *Four Aces Suite* called *The Joker*.

Further, on the French side, the major seventh chord under the first bar of the chorus—at that time still not all that common in popular song—may have come from Debussy's *La plus que lente* (1910). Mayerl, so immaculately schooled, actually resolves it twice but this figure, always associated with the triplet, builds successfully to the climax at bar 28. The dominant seventh under the first arch of melody at bar 3 may seem weak at first, but it fits, and the major ninth chords on 'say' at bar 7 and at bar 28 show Mayerl being slightly more adventurous harmonically. A possible model is Berlin's classic, 'How deep is the ocean?' (*Face the Music*, 1932), which has the same triplet rhythm, even the same dominant sevenths more conventionally treated, and Steve Race has pointed out that Vincent Youman's 'Time on my hands' (1930)

---

[43] B. Mayerl, 'Analysis of the Transcription', *BMCM*, 3/29 (May 1936), 22.

[44] B. Mayerl, 'There's a star in the sky', Harry Saville and his Orchestra, CE-7680-1 Par. F-519; included in Vol. II of *The Billy Mayerl Piano Transcriptions*, Vols. I–III, Eric Parkin on Priory PRCD 466–8. See Peter Dickinson's reviews in *Gramophone*: Vol. I (Jan. 1995), 78; Vol. II (May 1995), 83; and Vol. III (July 1995), 86—also Editor's Choice. See also *Critics Choice* (Dec. 1995), 44.

Ex. 11. Mayerl, Song (Frank Eyton), 'There's a star in the sky' (1936), Refrain.

Ex. 12. Mayerl, piano transcription, 'There's a star in the sky' (*BMCM* May 1936)

has an identical first phrase. [45] But nobody would have cared in a performance like Sally Gray's on the screen and harmonic niceties are irrelevant to the larger public, which is affected by the memorabilty of the tune. Perhaps Mayerl felt fewer restrictions when composing for a film like this, whereas the staged comedies had to fit the massive public success courted by the all-star cast, producers, and backers.

The piano transcription of 'There's a star' repays detailed study. Particular fingerprints are the anticipatory quaver beats and the setting is an example of how Mayerl treats a melody slowly before swinging it in his inimitable, faster rhythmic style. He did this in a few piano pieces at the same period—*Willow Moss* (*Aquarium Suite* No. 1, 1937); *The Song of the Fir Tree* (1938); and *Harp of the Winds* (1939). [46] 'There's a star in the sky' was one of some twenty Mayerl songs and transcriptions published by the Victoria Music Publishing Company between 1933 and 1936. In the *BMCM* for July 1936 there was a special notification:

Mr. Jimmy Green, general manager of the Victoria Music Publishing Co., was so impressed with the commercial possibilities of the recent Magazine transcription, 'There's a Star in the Sky', that he has asked us if he may publish it. Although it is our policy for all the transcriptions which appear in the magazine to be for the exclusive use of members, in response to the very generous co-operation he has given us in overcoming the copyright restrictions attached to many numbers we have used in the past, we were very pleased to give him this permission. [47]

Copyright difficulties would explain why Mayerl was able to publish so few arrangements of songs by the major American song-writers.

Mayerl's career in the West End had flourished since *Nippy* in 1930, but things were changing. *Crazy Days*, the next Lupino comedy, was put on at the Shaftesbury Theatre, 14 September 1937, and closed on 20 November after only 78 performances. But a more sombre shadow was cast over everything when Laddie Cliff, acting and managing as usual, was taken ill a few days before the opening night and died only two weeks after the show closed. The *BMCM* described Cliff as 'one of our President's best friends and for many years his associate in variety and musical shows'. [48] Mayerl lost one of his best allies. Cliff was a prodigy who started his career at the age of 6 and toured Australia and America in his teens. In June 1920—and this would not have been lost on Mayerl—Cliff made a big hit with Gershwin's 'Swanee' (*Sinbad*, 1919) in *Jig-Saw* at the Hippodrome, very soon after Al Jolson had added the song to *Sinbad*

45 S. Race, letter to Peter Dickinson, 26 Aug. 1996.

46 P. Dickinson, *Style-Modulation as a Compositional Technique* (Goldsmiths College, London, 1996). Includes discussion of Mayerl's *Song of the Fir Tree*.

47 Transcription of 'There's a star in the sky', *BMCM*, 3/29 (May 1936), 18.

48 'In the News: Laddie Cliff', *BMCM*, 4/37 (Jan. 1937), 5.

in New York and recorded it (8 January 1920) and Gershwin had made the piano rolls.[49] Nobody lost any time and 'Swanee', apparently written in less than an hour, launched Gershwin. When he came to England in 1923 even the customs officer at Southampton recognized him as 'the composer of *Swanee*'.[50] Cliff's role in Mayerl's career in the musical theatre had been crucial and he was now well into his stride: some of the songs for *Crazy Days* show new developments. Most of the reviews said some of the usual things about him—'Billy Mayerl's music is lively'[51]—but one went further, coupling the music with the latest discovery of the American dancer, Gloria Day: 'Indeed her dancing and Mr. Mayerl's gay and pretty tunes are the best things of the evening.'[52] Other reviewers considered that she rescued the show.

Lyrics this time were a joint effort by Eyton and Desmond Carter. 'Do' is an excellent snappy number with a driving, syncopated verse that goes straight through into the chorus. There is notably more harmonic originality, with the odd blue note and pounding added sixth chords in the verse and a set of oom-pah parallel triads going down and then back up the whole-tone scale that might have come from Vaughan Williams. 'You're not too bad yourself' has another rhythmic verse, complete with blue notes and Cole Porter syncopations, leading to a verse, catchy at first but handicapped by clichéd diminished sevenths. A real musical discovery is 'Love was born', with an obvious lyric based on the usual trappings:

> A night in June
> Some stars—a moon—
> And LOVE WAS BORN
> Out of the sky.

The core of the song is the sustained refrain, marked 'Moderato (in strict time)': the melody starts by decorating the fifth degree of the scale and the harmony moves slowly over pedal-points. Everything is beautifully shaped and smooth and the song now seems to have more potential than in Fred Conyngham's recording, although this was under the composer's baton.[53] 'Stranger in a cup of tea' is elegant but slender, approaching the sophistication of Coward.

Mayerl recorded these last two songs with his Shaftesbury Theatre Orchestra, the Piano Selection on his own, and approved of the *Crazy*

---

[49] G. Gershwin, 'Swanee', piano rolls on Melodee 3707 and Duo Art 1649 (Feb. 1920) now on CD as *Gershwin plays Gershwin: The Piano Rolls*, Elektra Nonesuch 7559–79287–2.

[50] E. Jablonski, *Gershwin: A Biography* (Simon & Schuster, London, 1988), 54.

[51] *Daily Telegraph*, 15 Sept. 1937.

[52] Unidentified cutting, 19 Sept. 1937, in Savoy Archives.

[53] B. Mayerl, 'Love was born', Shaftesbury Theatre Orchestra/Mayerl, 9 Sept. 1939. See Discography .

Days Souvenir Album issued by the publisher, the Cinephonic Music Company.[54]

Three weeks after *Crazy Days* closed, Noel Gay's *Me and my Girl* took over and, with its song-and-dance mania around 'The Lambeth Walk', became an institution.[55] The year 1939 was dominated in the musical theatre by *Me and my Girl*, joined by Novello's *The Dancing Years*, but all under the threat of war.

In spite of his unrivalled virtuosity as a soloist, Mayerl was always interested in playing with other pianists. In 1938 he launched Billy Mayerl and His Claviers, Challens of special design, which went on tour at the Theatre Royal, Norwich, from 4 April.[56] His partners were Dorothy Carless, George Myddleton, and Marian Turner, an unusual group, all of whom had a future. At the time Myddleton broke his ankle, which turned the Liverpool performances into a trio, but he came back into the Mayerl story years later when, after her husband's death, Mrs Mayerl got to know him but decided not to marry him.[57] Dorothy Carless became much better known as a singer. She had recorded with Ray Noble in 1934 and from 1940 had a long association with the fashionable band-leader, Geraldo, before emigrating to the USA. In her hey-day, and very impressive too, she recorded with Mayerl—Kennedy/Carr's 'Mayfair merry-go-round' and the 1938 Carmichael/Loesser song, 'Heart and soul'. Mayerl's solos in both songs are absolutely vintage.[58] Another interesting connection from this period is that Marian Turner later became the jazz musician Marian McPartland, wife for a time of the American jazz trumpeter Jimmy McPartland, who recalled her own entry into this side of the profession in the *New Yorker* in 1973. The disapproval of her London conservatoire, the Guildhall School of Music and Drama, shows that not much had changed since Mayerl got into trouble at Trinity College twenty-five years earlier, but it is revealing to see what sort of American pianists she compared Mayerl with in order to introduce him to a 1973 American readership who would have no idea who he was:

I was playing a sort of cocktail piano outside of the classroom, and once, when my piano professor at the Guildhall, a solemn white-haired man named Orlando Morgan, heard me, he said: 'Don't let me catch you playing that rubbish again!' Well, he never got the chance. One day I sneaked over to the West End, where Billy Mayerl had a studio. He played a lot on the BBC, and he was like Frankie Carle or Eddie Duchin. I played 'Where are you?' [1937 song by Hollywood composer Jimmy McHugh] for

---

54 B. Mayerl, 'From the President's Chair', *BMCM*, 4/45 (Sept. 1937), 2.

55 Mayerl made a transcription of Gay's 'The Lambeth Walk' for the *BMCM*, 5/54 (June 1938), 18–21.

56 'In the News: The Claviers on Tour', *BMCM*, 5/52 (Apr. 1938), 7. See also: J. Archer, 'The Challen Multitone Piano Orchestra', *Billy Mayerl Society Magazine*, No. 2, 16–17.

57 S. Frankel, in ibid., No. 6, 5–9.

58 B. Mayerl and D. Carless, 25 Oct. 1938. See Discography.

him, and a little later he asked me to join a piano quartet he was putting together—
Billy Mayerl and his Claviers. I was twenty [actually just 19], and I was tremendously
excited. The family were horrified, but I said I'd go back to the Guildhall when the tour
was over. My father charged up to London to see 'this Billy Mayerl'. He didn't want
any daughter of his being preyed on, and he wanted to know what I'd be paid—ten
pounds a week it turned out. So my parents agreed. The quartet included Billy and
George Myddleton and Dorothy Carless and myself. She and I were outfitted in glamorous gowns, and we played music-hall stuff. We played variety theatres—a week in
each town. We lived in rented digs in somebody's house. If it was 'all in', it included
food. Some of the places were great, and they'd even bring you up a cup of tea in the
morning . . . The tour with Billy lasted almost a year, and then I joined Carroll Levis's
Discoveries, a vaudeville show.[59]

McPartland's comparisons, Carle and Duchin, were pianists known for
their lightly swinging style as well as bandleaders and composers. Carle was
known as 'the Golden Touch' and his major hit, his equivalent of *Marigold*, was
Sunrise Serenade (1938). Marked 'very slow', this is an attractive, memorable
piece with a bluesy minor-key main theme, simpler breaks than those in
Marigold, and a comic chordal refrain that ends all strains. As with most of
Mayerl, the form is that of the piano rag. Duchin, who was quite a matinée-
idol pianist, was prominent in broadcasts and films from the 1930s. A biographical film was made five years after his death with Tyrone Power playing
Duchin—showbiz canonization of a kind Mayerl could never have achieved.

Billy Mayerl and his Claviers recorded four sides for Columbia on 1 April
1938. These consisted of 'The Toy Trumpet' a 1937 song by Raymond Scott
with a compilation called *Clavierhapsody* on the other side, which delves into
history with the Minuet by Boccherini, 'Bunch of roses' by Ruperto Chapi di
Lorente, and a Hungarian *Czardas* by Monti. The other 78 contained a medley of Mayerl classics: *Sweet William, Green Tulips, Marigold, Chop-sticks, Ace of
Spades, Ace of Diamonds, Bats in the Belfry.*[60]

Marian Turner, like Dorothy Carless, went on to entertain troops during
the war and, as Marian McPartland, had a remarkable jazz career as performer,
writer, and broadcaster but, in 1980, she toured the USA playing Grieg's Piano
Concerto—another connection with Mayerl perhaps.[61]

Virtually Mayerl's last throw was *Runaway Love*, described as a musical play by
Barry Lupino and Frank Eyton. This time it was presented by Billy Mayerl
Enterprises Ltd. and Mayerl drew on his experience with an ensemble of pianos.
The show was launched at the King's Theatre, Southsea, on 31 July 1939 and ran
in London at the Saville Theatre from 3 November 1939 until 30 March 1940.
The *Evening Standard* reported: 'It is all very light and nonsensical . . . but Billy

59 W. Balliett, 'Profile of Marian McPartland', *New Yorker*, 20 Jan. 1973.
60 Billy Mayerl and his Claviers, 1 Apr. 1938. See Discography.
61 B. Kernfeld, *The New Grove Dictionary of Jazz* (Macmillan, London, 1988).

Mayerl, supported by a battery of four girl pianists and four pianos, rattles out some lively tunes on a new electric piano capable of almost any combination of electric noises.'[62]

Another reporter displayed all the suspicion which has generally greeted new electronic developments until the all-conquering synthesizer:

The principal attraction here is the supplanting of the ordinary theatre-orchestra by something called a Multitone, which some will doubtless regard as a musical instrument. It is a contraption in which a kind of cinema organ presides over four other instrumentalists of the piano-cum-mouth-organ persuasion, the whole being linked together by a system of harmonious plumbing. The resultant melody, whose timbre is of the celeste-cum-glockenspiel order, spreads over one's consciousness like molasses spilt upon plush.[63]

For a long time Mayerl had been associated with Challen pianos: he liked their light touch which helped to make his own rapid figurations seem effortless. When he gained publicity for playing 'the largest piano in the world' at the British Industries Fair in 1935, this nine-foot monster was a Challen. The firm was established in London in 1804, gained a reputation as a supplier of reliable instruments in the medium price range, and was proud of the fact that its instruments—along with those of Bösendorfer and Steinway—were selected by the BBC, after thorough tests in 1936. Two years later, even when the market for pianos had been falling for some years, Challen aimed for social status appeal, using advertisements with phrases like: 'Beautify your home with a piano—the Challen.' Grands cost 69 guineas (£2,680) and the small upright 49 guineas (£1,900). These fashionable miniatures, suited to modern living conditions, did something to rescue piano sales and the Multi-Tone was an example with extras. The new instrument was proudly advertised in the April 1938 *BMCM*:

CHALLEN
NEW MULTI-TONE PIANO
SENSATION OF B.I.F.
Graciously inspected by
H.M. THE QUEEN
THE LORD MAYOR OF LONDON
etc. etc. etc.
ALREADY INSTALLED FOR
The B.B.C.
The Royal Academy of Music
Sir Walford Davies
(Master of the King's Musick)
AND

[62] D. Baker, *Evening Standard*, 4 Nov. 1939.
[63] Unidentified cutting, 3 Nov. 1939, in Savoy Archives.

The Billy Mayerl New
Multi-Tone Piano Orchestra
Full particulars from -
CHALLEN'S PIANOS LTD
13 & 14 HANOVER STREET, REGENT STREET, W.I.[64]

Mayerl directed an ensemble of five keyboards for *Runaway Love:* he played the Multi-Tone piano and the other modified Challen instruments were played by four girls. One of them was Irene Ashton who, in 1976, would write to the principals of the London conservatoires urging them to recognize the work of Billy Mayerl.[65] In a handwritten c.v. with absolutely no dates, Ashton described herself as 'Pianist, Dancer, Actress'.[66] The daughter and granddaughter of clergymen, she was amazingly versatile, gaining diplomas from the Royal Academy of Music and the Royal Academy of Dancing. Her piano teacher at the Academy was Claude Pollard. She first met Mayerl when she was dancing in shows with his music, became a pupil, then edited the *BMCM* from 1934 to 1935, played and toured in the theatre and worked in films and broadcasting. In about 1968 she wrote about *Runaway Love*:

In 1939–40 I appeared at the Saville Theatre in a show called *Runaway Love*, with music composed and played by Billy Mayerl and three other pianists. We played nine songs for singing and dancing in this play, every chorus transposed and arranged differently in a new key and the whole score memorised. The evening that Sir Malcolm Sargent and his wife came—they sat behind me, the orchestra rails being removed and with the whole ensemble being raised and on show—he said to Billy afterwards at the end of the play:

'I have not heard such delicacy of scoring and rhythm from four pianos and a Novachord, placed at such a distance from each other before, not only memorised entirely for the whole show but without a baton!'

He then turned to we four girls and said:

'I don't know how you all remember not to come in, as you do to come in!'

The following day the night watchman told us that Sir Malcolm Sargent and Billy Mayerl were talking for over two hours in his theatre dressing-room.[67]

By 1940 the war was dominating everything and *Runaway Love* was the end of Mayerl's career in the musical theatre, where his orchestra of pianos was a shrewd and economical move. The sound of the Multi-Tone piano is close to electronic organs of the period, or even the Ondes Martenot, and it functioned as the only sustained ingredient in an overall context of piano tone.

---

[64] Advertisement inside front cover, *BMCM*, 5/52 (Apr. 1938).

[65] I. Ashton, 'A Tale of Two Presents', *Billy Mayerl Circle Newsletter*, 1/5 (Spring, 1975), 4, 5, and 8. And: 'A Third Present', ibid., 2/9 (Spring 1976), 2–4.

[66] I. Ashton, incomplete handwritten letter found in Mrs Mayerl's papers probably written to the Associated Board of the Royal Schools of Music in 1967.

[67] Ibid.

Mayerl had an instinct about future developments as an amusing article by Geoffrey Clayton indicated.[68] The programme at the Saville, for which there was no charge, carried the warning DON'T FORGET TO BRING YOUR GAS MASK. Even the lovers in the song 'Nice to know'—Eyton lyrics again—were drably making the best of things in wartime:

> VERSE: I don't exaggerate or overstate
> As so many men do.
> I won't call you an angel,
> For that wouldn't be true;
> I couldn't say you're divine,
> Or that your eyes like stars shine,
> But if you want a truthful man's opinion of you
> CHORUS: YOU'RE NICE TO KNOW.

The three-beat lead-in to the chorus follows established patterns such as Kern's 'They didn't believe me' (1914), or Gershwin's 'Our love is here to stay' (*Goldwyn Follies*, 1938), and Mayerl's song written jointly with Horatio Nicholls in 1942, 'Please order your last drinks!'. At 'dainty and charming' in the chorus there is a Mayerl cross-rhythm which can be read as 3+2+3 crotchets, echoing the 1920s.

That was just about Mayerl's last popular song too. Leslie Osborne summed up his position and mentions further suggestions he made:

LO: As a song-writer, I am sorry but Bill was—to my way of thinking—very [spoken with some hesitation] ordinary. He used to come to me sometimes and he'd say to me: 'Why is it these chaps—"When the Poppies bloom again" [1936 British hit by Towers, Morrow, and Petosi], "Sally" [1931 hit by Leon, Towers, and Haines, sung by Gracie Fields], and so on—they write hit songs and I write songs and nothing happens?' I said to him, on one occasion: 'The trouble is, Bill, you are too well educated musically to write anything like "Sally" or "Now is the hour" [another song associated with Gracie Fields and later Bing Crosby]. You couldn't write down enough, low enough, to write that kind of—well, all right, call it trash!' Money-making trash, granted, but still trash. I mean, Harry Leon, who wrote 'Sally' could only play in the key of D and he always played cross-handed with his hands the wrong way up! Michael Carr, who wrote 'South of the Border', 'Dinner for one please James', 'Home Town' [British hits in 1939, 1935, and 1935] and dozens of others, could only play in the key of G and then he had to get somebody else to take it down for him. But Bill, when he wrote a song, got frightfully complicated. In other words, to write 100% popular songs, Bill couldn't lower himself enough to get into the idiom. He couldn't have written 'When the Poppies bloom again' as long as he lived. Now you might say, in that case how do you compare him with a man like Jerome Kern or Cole Porter? Even then I don't think that Bill had got it. I really don't. Because if he had've got it he'd have hit the jackpot at least once anyway. But Bill never wrote a hit song.

---

[68] G. Clayton, 'Klayton on the Klaviers', *BMCM*, 4/59 (Nov. 1938), 11.

PD: But Cole Porter and Gershwin were musically very well educated.

LO: Exactly. But most of his lyrics were written by Frank Eyton. I think really that Bill would have done a lot better if he'd had another lyric-writer. But he was very loyal. Frank Eyton and he had written together and he was not the sort of person to say: 'Oh, I'll go somewhere else'.

After I joined Keith Prowse in 1945, where Bill was a contracted writer, I had seven years and it was like a reunion. I said to him: 'Why don't you get off this pop kick and try and write some ballads?' Which he did. Some of those ballads did extraordinarily well and I think I got two of those ballads recorded by [Richard] Tauber.[69]

After the War Mayerl did write five concert songs which Keith Prowse published between 1946 and 1950, the first four with insipid texts by Howard Alexander. The last song is dedicated to the extremely popular Australian bass-baritone, Peter Dawson, whose prodigious recording and performing activities were extended through a variety of pseudonyms. Even by 1925 Dawson was said to have made 'more than 3,000 recordings, claimed to be the most ever sung by one individual'.[70] Mayerl's song for him was 'The Portsmouth Road', to a poem in the manner of Masefield by Ralph Howard which, complete with modal touches, might have come from a composer of the English folk-song school like Peter Warlock. Richard Tauber, the famous Austrian tenor who settled in England in 1938, did record Mayerl's song, 'Resting', in about the last year of his life. Tauber was still able to bring all his Viennese operetta charm to Mayerl's suave and expertly harmonized melody. The only concession Tauber made was to bring the last note down a fourth instead of staying up on the held note. The promotional copy simply said 'For Jill' but the trade edition was labelled 'recorded and sung by Richard Tauber'. Another of these platform songs, 'Those Precious Things', came to life in a different era—the early 1960s—when the winsome Julie Andrews recorded it, heavily arranged by Irwin Kostal.[71]

The versatile American musician and activist in musical politics, Van Phillips, provided another view about Mayerl's songs. Phillips was brought to London in September 1925 by Carroll Gibbons to play in the Savoy Havana Band, no doubt lured by the lavish salaries. He scored a British hit in 1926 with 'The two of us' and knew Mayerl in those early Savoy days, although they overlapped in the bands for only a few months. In 1982 I asked him why he thought the songs had not survived:

There's a very good reason for that! I'm surprised you even ask. Of course, Billy's songs were not memorable: he was not a Noel Coward, he was not a Gershwin. As a matter

---

[69] L. Osborne, interview with Peter Dickinson, 11 Aug. 1981.

[70] Unsigned, 'Gramophone Notes', *The Times*, 21 Dec. 1925.

[71] B. Mayerl, 'These Precious Things', arranged by Irwin Kostal, sung by Julie Andrews in 'The Lass with the Delicate Air' on RCA Mono RD-27061 (LPM-1403)70 (1962).

of fact *Marigold* has got the most feeble melody you ever thought of. If you take it apart and get rid of all the fireworks—those lovely, delicate filigree things that Oscar Peterson does today without even stopping to think. You know, those double stops rattling up and down the piano. Billy could do that marvellously. He had a wonderful technique. But, of course, he never wrote a good tune, a memorable tune.[72]

We have not mentioned the most successful song with which Mayerl was associated, an early experience which might have given him a sharper grasp of what was required. This was 'Show me the way to go home'. Mayerl explained how it got written:

Four of us were joining in a merry sing-song in a flat over a livestock shop in Tottenham Court Road . . . I was playing, and before we knew what was happening we had slipped into a simple sixteen-bar chant with only four changes of harmony in it—really an old Canadian lumber-jack tune. We each took a hand in supplying the words. First one uttered a line, then another, then another, and so on until it was complete.

The song was published. It was broadcast by the Savoy Havana Band. And it took the country by storm. Everyone seemed to be singing 'Show me the way to go home' before we had time to look round. Over a million copies have been sold [some sources quote two million in the first year], and altogether that song must have made £10,000 [£374,000].[73]

But not for Mayerl. As so often with popular music, there is another side to the story. Nearer the time Ramon Newton told the *Morning Post* in 1926 that he wrote it: 'one evening after dinner and finished it before going to bed'.[74] The song was published under the pseudonym of Irving King, which looks like a cunning fusion of Irving Berlin and one of the popular Kings, possibly Robert A. King. Newton said he wrote it, Mayerl said he had a role in producing it, but Performing Right Society earnings have been paid to Jimmy Campbell, Reg Connelly, and one Ivor King, a pseudonym for the band-leader Hal Swain. Campbell and Connelly started their firm with this song and never looked back. 'Show me the way to go home' was publicized as 'the great singing fox-trot'; 'the sensational broadcast success'; and 'sung with immense success by Ella Shields'. It was a standard for the Savoy Havana and twenty years later was still alive with the American close-harmony group, the Andrews Sisters.

But Mayerl did not follow this lead: his songs are in the position of not having achieved or maintained popularity. What has happened to classics by Gershwin, Kern, Berlin, Porter, the Beatles, and more is that they have entered the repertoire of great twentieth-century melodies. They have become established enough to be regarded as the property of the entire musical community rather

---

[72] V. Phillips, interview with Peter Dickinson, 30 Sept. 1982. See also his obituary in *The Times*, 21 Dec. 1992.

[73] B. Mayerl, 'We Played on as a Prince Lay Dying', *Tit-bits*, 26 June 1937, 5–6.

[74] Unsigned, 'In Support of Jazz', *Morning Post*, 3 Feb. 1926.

than just a limited category such as art music, pop, jazz, or light music. The conservationists are usually in the serious music camp, so it is they who have made scholarly editions of Berlin's songs, Joplin's rags, and have transcribed Jelly Roll Morton's piano solos.[75] It is to be hoped that someday Mayerl's Collected Piano Works will join them.

His transcriptions of popular songs, very few of which he recorded, were most successfully resurrected by Eric Parkin—they also provide a slant on his own songs, some of which he transcribed.[76] But the songs themselves, so much a part of the frothy, ephemeral 1930s British shows they served, are left with millions of others in limbo.[77] Mayerl's good friend and colleague, Leslie Osborne and a more detached, even caustic observer like Van Phillips are in general agreement that that is where they belong, but—noting the quality of Mayerl's other work—it may not be the end of the story.

[75] C. Hamm (ed.), *Irving Berlin: Early Songs, Vols. I–III* (Music of the United States of America, A-R Editions, Madison, Wis., 1994); V. B. Lawrence (ed.), *Scott Joplin: Collected Piano Works* (New York Public Library, 1971); J. Dapogny (ed.), *Ferdinand 'Jelly Roll' Morton: The Collected Piano Music* (Smithsonian Institution Press, Washington, 1982).

[76] *The Billy Mayerl Piano Transcriptions, Vols. I–III*, Eric Parkin on Priory PRCD 466–8. For further transcriptions played by Parkin see also *Puppets: A Tribute to Billy Mayerl* on Priory PRCD 544; *Scallywag: A Further Tribute to Billy Mayerl* on Priory PRCD 565; and *Robots: Impressions for the Piano* on Shellwood SWCD 3. For arrangements of Mayerl's songs mostly made by Alex Hassan see *Rediscoveries*, Vol. I and II on Shellwood SWCD 1 and SWCD 6.

[77] But there were revivals of the Mayerl musicals through amateur societies, as Philip Scowcroft has pointed out in the *Midland Gershwin Mayerl Society Magazine*, 35 (June 1996), 8; and 40 (June 1997), 9. *Over She Goes* was put on by Doncaster Amateur Operatic Society from 3–8 Feb., 1947, and *Sporting Love* from 23–8 Feb., 1948.

1. Mayerl's mother, Elise (Umbach) d. 1881-1938

2. Mayerl's sister, Johanna Elisa 1901-1968

3. Mayerl's brother, Frederick August 1910 -

4. Billy Mayerl 1902-1959

5. Mayerl's wife, Jill
(Ermenegilda Bernini)
1896-1984

6. With Gwen Farrar (1899-1944)

7. At the Piano with *Marigold*

8. Billy Mayerl's Salon Syncopators led by Ron Gray, seated

9. Making the transcription of 'Everything's been done before' (*BMCM* Feb. 1936)

10. In later life at the BBC

11. At the piano

12. Mayerl and friends entertaining the troops

13. With Laddie Cliff for the centenary of the billiards firm Buroughs and Watts

14. Mayerl in lights for Noel Gay's *Love Laughs!* (1935)

15. On the links with comedian Reg Purdell

16. Mayerl at the microphone

9

THE BILLY MAYERL SCHOOL

THE 1920s was a prosperous period for professional musicians. In 1924 cinemas employed half the membership of the Musicians' Union and this approached 80 per cent of paid employment by 1928, just as everything was changing with talking pictures.[1] The *Melody Maker* was started by composer-publisher-promoter Lawrence Wright (Horatio Nicholls) in January 1926 in a context of national industrial unrest leading to the General Strike in May. The frantic enjoyment at all costs of the Bright Young Things was against a background of great poverty for lower-paid workers, including many of those who had recently fought for their country. But entertainment was booming and The *Melody Maker* soon established itself for the rest of the century as the principal British journal for popular music and dance. It also covered jazz, notably in contributions by Fred Elizalde early on and in the columns by Spike Hughes from 1930. In its second issue, the magazine carried two significant announcements:

BILLY MAYERL LEAVES THE SAVOY

Billy Mayerl, the famous young English pianist, who for so long has been such a favourite at the Savoy Hotel, having been with the Savoy Havana Band since its inception [*sic*], has found it necessary to give up his orchestral work. He intends to devote his attention to recording, broadcasting, the halls and, in particular, teaching. The Billy Mayerl School of Modern Syncopation for the Piano will be ready to open any day now, and correspondence courses have been arranged.

Three separate courses will be inaugurated. Grade 1 for young amateurs, Grade 2 for amateurs and the less experienced professionals, and Grade 3 for advanced professionals. We have been privileged to peruse these courses and can only say we consider them indispensable to all pianists, whether amateur or advanced professionals. The whole subject is treated most lucidly and thoroughly, and fills a long-felt want which even the best musicians cannot afford to miss.

---

[1] C. Ehrlich, *The Music Profession in Britain since the Eighteenth Century* (Clarendon Press, Oxford 1985), 194–9.

This was the text of the advertisement a few pages earlier:

SYNCOPATED PIANO PLAYING CAN BE TAUGHT!
THE BILLY MAYERL COURSE OF MODERN SYNCOPATION FOR THE PIANO

is easy—interesting—quick, up-to-the-minute
Not merely a list of 'breaks' which you
may (or may not!) want, but everything
about syncopated piano playing: how you
can use your own ideas—not simply copy other people's.
Gives all Billy Mayerl's own embellishments, and explains
how. Covers the whole field, including the all-
important left hand. No knowledge of harmony needed.
Enrol today! For full particulars
and Special Professional Offer, write:
THE BILLY MAYERL SCHOOL
Temporary Address: 46, Hallswell Road, London N.W.11

The address given was Geoffrey Clayton's house and by the March number of the *Melody Maker* the headquarters had become 29 Oxford St. Readers were also told that the response to the first advertisement had been so overwhelming that the School threatened to cease advertising altogether. This did not happen, but the tone of the adverts just became more ebullient. By the June issue:

SYNCOPATION!

Real tuition in dance-piano work
By Billy Mayerl—your guarantee
By post—your spare time
By instalments—your convenience
By results—your satisfaction
Hundreds of delighted pupils. Special offers to the profession *if* they enclose card.

In the first issue of the *BMCM*, January 1934, there was an article entitled 'The Pair who started Something', which recalled the old days of 1926. The author was shown simply as 'One who knows them'. It could have been Leslie Osborne since he met Mayerl 'just after he had joined up at the Savoy Hotel' and he would have known Geoffrey Clayton since they both worked for the same music publisher, West's.[2] Osborne also fancied himself 'as a song-writer in those days' and was to contribute regularly to the *BMCM*. However,

---

[2] L. Osborne, interview with Peter Dickinson, 11 Aug. 1981. But see L. Osborne, 'Notes from our President', *Billy Mayerl Circle Newsletter*, 1/1 (Spring 1974), where he says he 'first met Bill in late 1923 when working for the publisher West's Ltd.'. This was over a year after Mayerl started officially with the Savoy in May 1922. In 1926 West's published 'Lov'-lov'-lovin' you!' by Edgar Stanley and Ronnie Munro as 'featured and recorded by Billy Mayerl and his Orchestra'. This song is a very rare example where Rust and Forbes's *British Dance Bands on Record 1911–1945* does not provide the names of the creators.

Osborne used to call his friend and colleague Bill and not Billy, as in the article, but that usage might have been edited out to avoid confusion in the magazine.

The article in the *BMCM* refers to the visit that Mayerl and Clayton made to America when they left Southampton on the *Aquitania* on 16 August 1924.[3] Twelve years later, reviewing Mayerl's record called *Savoy Havana Memories* for the *BMCM*, Clayton said that he and Mayerl heard Gershwin's 'I'll build a stairway to paradise' in the show called *Scandals* 'one sweltering night in New York played by the one and only Paul Whiteman'. But this cannot have been on his visit with Mayerl in 1924 since the song was not in the *Scandals* that year. In fact Clayton had already been to New York on his own, sailing from Southampton on the *America* on 17 August 1922. So it must have been then that he heard Gershwin's 'I'll build a stairway to paradise', which was featured in the 1922 edition of the *Scandals*. Clayton was a novelist and it would be surprising if some of his experiences had not found their way into his fiction. His second novel, *What Price Gloria?* (1936) does involve the music business. Most of the characters are stereotypes but the situations they get into are much funnier than Clayton's dated and silly columns in the *BMCM* might suggest. Sure enough the hero goes to New York in search of Gloria, and Clayton describes how they had dinner to Don Blackman's Orchestra and then went to George White's *Scandals*, but, tantalizingly, there are no details. All the same this is close to what Mayerl must have seen of New York in 1924 and how he and Clayton may have responded:

The summer evening lingered, as summer evenings are prone to do, and it was not until he came out of the theatre that he had his first glimpse of Broadway by night. Hugh contemplated the spectacle and blinked as he did so; somehow it was on a much larger scale than anything he had imagined. The blaze of light, coupled with every known kind of noise, at first dazzled and confused him. It was clear that twice as much was taking place as went on during the less romantic hours of daylight. As far as Hugh could make out, all the shops seemed open still, and an endless procession of pedestrian-hunting automobiles snapped hungrily at him as they flashed by.

The entire population of Manhattan, it would appear, was in the habit of taking its evening stroll between Times Square and Fiftieth Street, most of them shouting at the top of their voices as they passed leisurely on their way . . . like about ten Piccadilly Circuses and half-a-dozen Oxford Streets rolled into one.[4]

Apparently Clayton suggested the American trip, described as Mayerl's first holiday for four years. Over seventy years later Mayerl's younger brother, Fred, remembered him preparing for the visit. He had a new suit, which was light, shiny, and double-breasted and he was there for a fortnight. Mayerl had

---

[3] G. Clayton, 'Looking back', *BMCM*, 1/10 (Oct. 1934), 28. Passenger lists held at the Public Record Office, Kew, provided these actual dates.

[4] G. Clayton, *Blame it on Betty* (1936), 89 (see n. 20).

his wallet stolen on arrival, which left him with no money so he had to go to the British Embassy. He said he would never go to America again and he never did.[5]

To quote the anonymous author again, who is the closest to an eye-witness that we shall ever get:

It was on the boat when returning to England that they conceived the idea of conducting a School of Modern Syncopation for the Pianoforte, and both thought so much of it that Mayerl decided to throw up the Savoy and Clayton his publishing business at West's. You can imagine them writing their first *Course of Instruction*; it was a very long and tedious job, but all the methods that had been discussed for so long at last began to take shape on paper. The *Course*, its examples and exercises, the literature describing it, all at last were completed.[6]

This type of correspondence course was not unique. Postal teaching for degrees and diplomas developed in England from the 1880s and became popular by the 1920s. Mayerl and Clayton must have come across examples in America and in a 1925 issue of *Popular Radio Favourites*, containing an advertisement for all six of Mayerl's *Pianolettes*, there was a feeble, wordy quarter-page statement from a Mr H. Becker headed 'I have Taught Thousands to Play the Piano brilliantly and read readily at Sight'.[7]

When he was in America Mayerl met the radio and vaudeville pianist, Lee Sims. They must have found plenty of common ground. Like Mayerl, Sims started life as a pianist for silent films; he was one of the first Americans to publish piano transcriptions of popular songs; and around 1926 he set up his own Music School in the Lyon and Healy Building, Chicago. But unlike Mayerl he was an improvising player.[8]

Mayerl and Clayton tried the course out on six student friends and took criticism, advertised as above; printed their course materials, and found offices. They enrolled their first student, Eric Adams, who later worked for a major publisher, and at first 'Billy Mayerl packed the lessons and kept the books while Geoffrey Clayton typed the correspondence and looked after the executive side'.[9] Trading under the name of Modern Postal Tuition Ltd., the

---

5   F. Mayerl, telephone conversation with Peter Dickinson, 22 Sept. 1996.

6   One who knows them, 'The Pair who started Something', *BMCM*, 1/1 (Jan. 1934), 3–5.

7   *Popular Radio Favourites Part 38, Music for All* [1925], opp. p. 75.

8   E. Cornwall, 'Lee Sims: One of America's favourite Sons', *BMCM*, 2/14 (Feb. 1935), 12–13; Earle Cornwall, reporting from the USA, said that Sims had a massive following, but nobody was making transcriptions like Mayerl's and there was nothing like the Billy Mayerl Club over there.

9   E. A. McInerney (Hooper), letter to Alan Rusbridger, 16 Sept. 1991. Edmund A. Stanbrook has kindly provided some details about Modern Postal Tuition Ltd., which was incorporated on 2 June 1928 with a nominal capital of £5,000 [£173,800] in £1 shares. Mayerl and Clayton had 1,000 shares each and there were twelve other shareholders, including one of the School's teachers Howard Redley and the pianist-conductor George Windeatt.

School developed its own technique of giving lessons by post. The idea caught on and within months the first secretary was appointed, Eve Hooper (Mrs E. A. McInerney), and another one, Vesta Harrison (Mrs Vicky Matkin), in 1927. In 1991 Mrs McInerny remembered:

I started with him and Geoffrey Clayton when they opened an office on the sixth floor of No. 29 Oxford Street, opposite Frascati's; then it was great fun, with Billy Mayerl sending out for ice-creams when it got hot in the summer, and he was very happy to lick stamps and count the growing number of enquiries we had and literature to send out . . .

One of my jobs was to answer the queries from our students in the Progress Sheets which had to be completed before receiving the next part of the Course, and later I was kept very busy working all hours when BM decided to take over an agency for small bands—very often a whole crowd would march in wanting contracts made out and signed for each one—just around 6 o'clock, getting home time! . . . It was even worse when we started publishing our magazine; often just before D Day BM was called away and even abroad when he was on stage work. Had it not been for Geoffrey Clayton we could never have coped. . . . He was the one who started it all with BM, organised everything and was really the oil in the works! At that time BM was so very busy performing, playing, on stage and composing, but he did manage to get into the office sometime each day, if only for a short time, if he was not away.

Later on, we moved ourselves to superior premises on the first floor of Steinway Hall, and as our offices were at the back facing St. George's, Hanover Square, we were able to watch many society weddings. We also had to increase our staff further. After a year or so, Geoffrey Clayton became interested in starting his own music publishing business—the Maurice Music Co., if I remember correctly [The Peter Maurice Music Co. Ltd., 21 Denmark St., London WC2] . . . and Ron Gray came to our rescue, and he was able to work full time . . . Ron Gray was a pianist, too. We also had a lady teacher on the staff called Madge Howard, who gave lessons in syncopation on the premises. She and I made a record—not for sale outside but for the *Course*—of the *Marigold* duet.[10]

The materials the school provided for its students included a thirty-one-page booklet called *Lightning Fingers: An Interesting and Explanatory Talk on the Billy Mayerl School of Modern Syncopation for the Piano*. This explains the philosophy of the School, its founder and its personalities and ends with six pages of tributes from satisfied students. The document is a very clever piece of marketing, showing how precisely Clayton and Mayerl knew their constituency, analysed it, and went straight for it. The Introduction starts persuasively:

'I would give anything to be able to play like that!' How often, after reluctantly putting down the head 'phones, turning off the gramophone, or returning from a dance, have you said this to yourself? And, perhaps, not only to yourself but to your friends. How they crowded round the piano, marvelling at the ingenuity and intricacies of the dance

[10] E. A. McInerney (Hooper), interview with Peter Dickinson, 11 May 1992.

tune, so simple if only the truth were known! How envious they would be if you could play dance music in the way it should be played—how they would crowd round you![11]

The scene is set to elaborate the case for syncopation as the key to social success but it was more than that. In 1928 Noel Coward's 'Dance, little lady' in *This Year of Grace* runs: 'Though you're only seventeen, | Far too much of life you've seen, | Syncopated child . . .' Syncopation was part of the psychology of the 1920s and in 1929 there was even a film with this title. But the case being made for syncopated pianism was in unique circumstances. It was Mayerl himself who was the role model, having made his name with the first broadcasts in a way that would not otherwise have been possible. Another inducement, at a time when live musicians were in all hotels, restaurants, and cinemas, was aimed at professional and semi-professional players. If they could be up to date in terms of syncopated playing, their work would be more attractive, they could earn more, and more easily get a job. Or, as *Lightning Fingers* bluntly stated: 'And, don't forget, that unless you can syncopate, it is more than likely that they won't want to hear you play at all. Today you have got to do it.'[12]

This was no idle boast at the height of the silent cinema boom. The *Daily News* revealed that a dance-music pianist could earn £1,000 to £1,500 [£33,000 to £49,000] a year even in provincial centres, and the writer complained that the musical world was upside down.[13] In various newspapers Mayerl's colleague from the Savoy, the conductor Debroy Somers, claimed: 'any boy or girl should be able to earn £500–£1,500 [£16,000–£49,000] a year out of dance music, but it has yet to be developed here, as it has been in America, in a businesslike way.'[14] Mayerl and Clayton were planning to put that right for pianists, and Somers himself founded the Debroy Somers School of Dancing, at 86 Baker St., London W.[15]

Lightning Fingers explains that Mayerl was 'inundated with letters asking him to give lessons in his own individual style of syncopation' as a result of his broadcasts. Since 'he alone is competent to teach his own creations' and he

---

[11] *Lightning Fingers*, various editions, undated—not to be confused with the book of the same title (Paradise Press, 1995). Eve McInerney's copy, inscribed by Clayton, Gray, and Mayerl, looks like the first edition. Mayerl wrote two articles for *Cinema Organ Herald*. The second one (June–July 1933, 151) was accompanied by an advertisement for the Billy Mayerl School, now boasting an Organists' Section: 'Your audiences demand that you should give them syncopated music during your interludes. No cinema organist of today can hope to keep his position if he renders his popular numbers in the old style.' Some idea of what might have been meant can be heard on the 78 called *Organola* with pianist Jimmy Leach and organist Harry Farmer, Columbia FB 2684—a far cry from Fats Waller on the organ and much slower than Mayerl!

[12] *Lightning Fingers*, introduction.

[13] 'The Music that Pays Best', *Daily News*, 31 Oct. 1925.

[14] D. Somers, 'Big Salary Prospects for Dance Music', *Daily News*, 26 Apr. 1926; *Glasgow Citizen*, 20 May 1926.   [15] *Dancing Times*, Sept. 1925.

could never cope personally with the numbers of students involved, the School's system of teaching through postal study was devised. There were advantages claimed for this method:

1. It could take place at home at a time to suit the student.
2. The instructional material sent out enabled the student to go over things at any time.
3. It was much cheaper than personal lessons.

It was claimed that, 'in the first year of the School's existence, over one thousand professional students' enrolled, many as a result of recommendation.

The whole approach—what would later be called distance learning—anticipated the techniques employed by the Open University in Britain from the 1960s. It was a development of earlier correspondence courses but now supporting records were sent out, in spite of the fragility of 78s. Student progress was monitored by a series of forms used in a type of 'self-assessment' demanded by quality-control procedures in British higher education in the 1990s.

For example, in the course called 'Advanced Instruction in the Modern Rhythm Styles of Pianoforte Playing' the student had to sign a form to confirm that he/she had carefully studied the last lesson. Specific questions were then asked:

Have you been able to put the instructions to practical use in your work?
Are you satisfied with the progress you have made as a result of our tuition?
Please note here and overleaf any special difficulties or points of information for Mr. Mayerl's reply and advice.

The individual lessons were thorough. Lesson III of the standard course consisted of fourteen pages, printed on one side of high-quality paper, and twenty-six music examples. It also provided a twelve-page booklet of Exercises. At the end of each lesson the Progress Sheet, with eleven separate questions to be answered, had to be filled in and returned to the School. The scheme was for a minimum of half an hour's practice a day in order to complete the course in three months. If more than three months elapsed between one lesson and the next, it was presumed that the student had given up and would have to enrol again—and pay a further fee. Leslie Osborne once asked Mayerl how much piano anybody could learn for four guineas (£4.20 [£140]) and was given the reply: 'Four guineas' worth!'[16]

In order to impress potential students, Mayerl obtained testimonials from well-known practitioners. Confrey had done the same in 1923 when he published *Zez Confrey's Modern Course in Novelty Piano Playing* and

---

[16] L. Osborne, interview with Peter Dickinson, 11 Aug. 1981.

printed advertisements containing the endorsements of 'World Famous Pianists' such as Victor Arden and Phil Oman, both of whom were mentioned by Gershwin as having influenced his piano style. The first edition of Mayerl's *Lightning Fingers* contained recommendations from Miss Tony Farrell—reassuring ladies that they did not need big hands to syncopate—Horatio Nicholls (alias Lawrence Wright), H. B. Hedley of the Co-Optimists, the late Bert Ralton (since he died in January 1927, this edition of *Lightning Fingers* must have gone into print in 1926), and Debroy Somers. A later edition of eleven pages repeated Somers's tribute with more endorsements from Carroll Gibbons, Paul Whiteman, Doris Arnold, Henry Hall, and Jack Hylton. Both editions contained photographs of these stars. This later edition, also undated but with a photograph of Mayerl as an older man, emanated from the Billy Mayerl International Schools of Music which claimed to have taught 43,000 students. But by 1939 Mayerl used lower figures and told the *Radio Times* that the School had 'a staff of about 117 and branches all over the world. We have taught over 30,000 people, of whom 5,000 have become professionals.'[17] *Lightning Fingers* refers prominently to the Personal Demonstration Records. These were published in a boxed set of four 78s with a black binding with a round photo of Mayerl on the front and no other information on the covers.[18] Mayerl's voice, in didactic mode sounding like a slightly fruity radio announcer of the period, emerges clearly throughout.

Mayerl's colleague, Van Phillips, realized the role Geoffrey Clayton played:

He had a very astute friend who was what you would call today an entrepreneur. The sort of guy who could see the possibilities in some plan or idea . . . and go away and turn it into a small business enterprise. And he did this with Billy. He'd been after Billy for a long time to get in on this correspondence course but Billy couldn't believe that anyone would take it seriously, that you could learn to play the piano by post! But when I saw the first lesson I realised that they couldn't miss. Because it was Billy's name. Sally, Mary and Jane all the way from Scotland to Bristol would think: 'Well, if we can get these lessons from Billy it must be a good thing!' . . . The correspondence course was a great success and they made a lot of money.[19]

It cannot have been as easy as Van Phillips implied more than fifty years later. The School must have been sustained by Mayerl's own reputation in a declining market—and sheer hard work. Mrs McInerney's diaries show exactly how busy they were. The entry for 9 January 1929 reads 'absolutely mobbed by enquiries' and on the following day 'worse than ever in the office—180 enquiries

---

[17] 'Personal Facts about a Popular Broadcasting Pianist', *Radio Times*, 19 May 1939.
[18] The Billy Mayerl International School of Music Personal Demonstration Course in Modern Syncopation for the Pianoforte. Eight sides 'electrically recorded by Marconi Co's process'.   [19] V. Phillips, interview with Peter Dickinson, 30 Sept. 1982.

and heaps of post'. On both these evenings she could not leave the office until 8.30 and, in those days, there was no overtime.

Geoffrey Clayton is described in the first edition of *Lightning Fingers* as 'a public [private] school and 'varsity man' who, 'besides being a musician himself, personally took down the *Course* from Mr. Mayerl and in conjunction with him arranged it for postal instruction'. Apart from his music publishing connections, Clayton wrote four novels, dedicating his second one, *Blame it on Betty* (1936) to Billy Mayerl as 'my registered reader' and the third one, *Rally round Rosalind* (1937), to Laddie Cliff 'who ought to know better but, thank goodness, does not'. These novels—long out of print—are absolutely of their period, more skilled than Clayton's columns in the *BMCM* would lead one to expect. The characters, situations, and dialogue emerge from the stereotyped world portrayed by P. G. Wodehouse and Noel Coward, but there are direct connections between Clayton's fiction and the world in which he and Mayerl operated. In *What Price Gloria!* the Hon. Hubert Wynne plays syncopated piano and is joined by Jack Manning on drums. Manning leaves the city and lands a job in music publishing for which, we are told, the qualifications are smart contacts and the ability to survive without sleeping. Like Mayerl and Clayton, Gloria sails on the *Aquitania* and she stays at the Savoy. They all get into implausible and amusing predicaments.

Favourable reviews reflected the need for diversion in the final years of the 1930s. Peter Belloc in the *Daily Sketch* found *Blame it on Betty* to be 'fooling of the most exquisite and delicate kind'; the *Birmingham Gazette* found *Rally round Rosalind* to be 'Geoffrey Clayton at his most hilarious'; and the *Saturday Review* called it 'one of the most amusing books I have read for a long time'. Mayerl gave his own view in the *BMCM*:

Now I am not a bookworm; very much to the contrary, in fact. The only reading relaxation I get is between London and the big towns in the provinces, and then my taste in literature leans towards the lowest type of 'blood and thunder' sold for 9d. [£1.57] on the bookstalls. But I read *What Price Gloria!*—in fact I read it again; and to say that each chapter contains a hundred laughs is no exaggeration. Naturally, I was interested. It is all about our profession—the crazy profession (some people call it the musical profession). It has a strong and original plot that constantly reminds some of us of the world we live in and the man-in-the-street of the world he would like to live in.[20]

---

[20] B. Mayerl, 'In the News', *BMCM*, 3/28 (Apr. 1936), 5. The first three novels were advertised in the *BMCM*—*What Price Gloria* in May and June 1936—already claimed as the 3rd impression—and both *Gloria* and *Blame it on Betty* in Aug. 1936 and *Rally round Rosalind* in Aug. 1937. There was a further item about *Blame it on Betty*, with a photograph of Clayton, in Dec. 1936, 7.

Rhythm (November 1932) announced that Clayton was moving from his post as Managing Director of the Billy Mayerl School to be General Manager of the Peter Maurice Music Co. Ltd. although he would retain his seat on the Board of the School and kept many official connections.

Clayton was even more versatile. The year 1936 was his sixth as an umpire at Wimbledon in charge at Centre Court. Out of a pool of eighty umpires at that time only twenty were allocated to Centre Court, so Clayton clearly knew what he was doing.[21] When they had a staff outing on 25 September 1931 the two secretaries, Madge Howard, Mayerl, and Clayton had dinner at Clayton's London club, the RAC, and then went on to *Viktoria and her Hussar* (1930) by Hungarian composer Paul Abraham at the Palace Theatre, where it would run for 100 performances. Mayerl predictably found this Austro-German operetta-derived style stiff and Victorian, although he might have been interested in the way Abraham tried to incorporate jazzy elements into his style.

Mrs McInerney accounted for the appeal of syncopation in the 1920s in terms of the influence of radio, which went into everybody's home for the first time. *Alexander's Ragtime Band* now seemed old-fashioned after the visits of Paul Whiteman and this was where Mayerl fitted in. Syncopated styles were the latest thing and appealed to young people. Mrs McInerney identified the syncopated type as someone who looked 'with-it, alive and outgoing' and agreed that Mayerl occupied a middle ground. He appealed to people who found classical music too serious and jazz too hot. She accepted that the School's market was for these in-between people and observed: 'As jazz got more jazzy Billy Mayerl got more classical.'[22]

Mayerl's other secretary, Mrs Matkin, realized that the School's pupils were usually 'people who could play already and wanted to jazz it up'.[23] I asked Mrs Mayerl how her husband started in the education business:

At that time he used to get literally hundreds of letters from people who wanted to play like he did. That was the reason he started the School. Of course, never thinking it was going to become the great thing it was with branches everywhere. But of course the trouble was that when the war came that put a lot of stress on it because he had his offices in New Bond Street, just above Steinways. They were bombed from there. He started up again—he never was put down! He opened again further down Bond Street and they were bombed from there. Then he started again a little further down Bond Street, opposite Asprey's, and that third time the factory that made all the records, all the music, all the courses was burnt down. It was bombed and finished with and that was the end of the School. After the war he started in a

Mayerl's first secretary, Mrs E. A. McInerney, said that things were difficult until Ron Gray was appointed to the staff of the School.

Clayton made a will on 9 Sept. 1936 with Madge Howard and Fred Mayerl as witnesses. He left his gold cigarette case and lighter to Billy Mayerl, but his wife, Katherine Lily Grinling, was the principal beneficiary. Clayton's final address was in Tolworth, Surrey and he died on 1 May 1956, leaving £20,495.33 [£287,750], very close to what Mayerl would leave in 1959.

[21] 'Wimbledon Championships', *BMCM* 3/31 (July 1936) 7.
[22] E. A. McInerney (Hooper), interview with Peter Dickinson, 11 May 1992.
[23] V. Matkin (Harrison), interview with Peter Dickinson, 11 May 1992.

very poor neighbourhood and it wasn't any good and he was not very well by then and he gave it up.[24]

When reminded of this position, Mayerl's second secretary, Mrs Matkin, was able to provide a different slant, since she kept a diary:

You are quite right—the BM School was never actually bombed. What remained of the School (just me) moved from Steinway Hall (with the help of Mr. Dargie) to 10 New Bond St. on 7 February 1940. These were only small offices and most of the School's gear was stored by some arrangement with Steinway's and I believe destroyed later.

10 New Bond Street was roped off on 11 September 1940 as there was an unexploded bomb in the Arcade, Cork St., and again on the 19th when there was a time bomb in the block. I went home! Very noisy times. Raids all and every day as well as nights.

BM had a house at Maidenhead around this time and was touring a lot. The School, of course, came to an end and when BM moved to a suite at Grosvenor House I moved to his solicitors in Clarges Street in March 1941 and dodged backwards and forwards between them until I started a family.

BM actually closed the School on 3 September 1939 when war was declared. I was on holiday at the time. Then followed the telegram:

Post Office Telegram: Birmingham 19 September 1939
Harrison 23 Flambard Road Northwick Park Middlesex
= Open up School Carry on Best You Can Fix Lessons Madge
Howard Write Me Theatre Royal Birmingham Next Week Alhambra Glasgow
Keep Smiling = Billy Mayrl [sic][25]

Further information about the School's predicament at this point comes from a detailed, undated letter Mayerl wrote to Mrs Matkin when he was on tour with *Runaway Love*. The show opened at the Saville Theatre on 3 November 1939, ran for 195 performances until 30 March 1940 and then went on tour, when Mayerl must have written this letter, on the writing paper of *Runaway Love* presented by Billy Mayerl Enterprises. He writes quite formally—no first names—and since it indicates the acute stresses of the period in such detail and confirms Mrs Matkin's story it is worth quoting in full:

Next week—Grand Theatre, Blackpool
Dear Miss Harrison,
Every time I have sat down to answer your various letters some damned thing or other has cropt up. I have really had rehearsals morning noon and night, first Betty

[24] J. Mayerl, interview with Peter Dickinson, 11 Aug. 1981.
[25] V. Matkin (Harrison), letter to Peter Dickinson, 11 Mar. 1996. Mrs Matkin left her post as secretary of the School in Feb. 1938 to live in the South of France, but had returned by Jan. 1939—see V. Harrison. 'The Girl who Came Back!', *BMCM*, 6/61 (Jan. 1939), 25–6. She fortunately kept a fine set of photographs from the School instead of letting them go with other material into store—and subsequent destruction in air raids. Many are gratefully reproduced in this book.

Huntley-Wright goes then Reggie Vardell, Miss Marjorie Banks had to join her ambulance corp, I had to get another pianist, rehearsed her up and then on Saturday night she just said she didn't like the job and went back to London.

I was on the phone half the night trying to find someone and at 4 o'clock on Monday afternoon a new girl arrives—more rehearsals, I'm going nuts.

Now please don't think I have not thought about your troubles at the School. I think you have been wonderful the way you have carried on—on your own, so to speak. Regarding any future for the School, I don't know what to say as of course if you leave it all may as well pack up for good. Please do what you feel suits you best if you think there is a chance we might pull through ok if not, well Smiths and Hendersons can have the headache.

Regarding the accounts I suggest you pay Smiths £50 [£1,850] on account. Hendersons £50 and all the other little bills in full and then try to get every penny in from the Branches, pianos and instalment students. How about offering the latter a reduction for cash? Maybe that won't be any good on second thoughts.

The Mag, of course, will have to be suspended for the time being as Fred is gone and I'm stuck out on the road.

Try Steinways regarding a reduction in rent, anyway I think they will have to close very shortly, can't sell German pianos in these days!

Send Linguaphone as much stuff as you can and maybe Hendersons will give us a bit more credit for new orders, if not, I suggest you get in touch with Mr. [Henry] Bartlett [chartered accountant and Company Secretary] and ask him to liquidate the company.

I'm going completely off my head at the moment, business in the theatre is *lousey* and last week I got £2 [£70] for my salary! It if doesn't improve very quickly *Runaway Love* must also pack up and I'll have to play a piano on the streets!

Keep smiling and again thankyou for carrying on.

Very sincerely,

Billy Mayerl

I am indebted to John Archer for pointing out to me that the Billy Mayerl School (still formally known as Modern Postal Tution Ltd.) was put into liquidation at an Extraordinary General Meeting on 29 March 1940 since 'the Company cannot, by reason of its liabilities, continue its business'. As chairman, Mayerl signed the document on 4 April 1940.[26]

It looks as if Mrs Mayerl, from the perspective of 1981, simply wanted people to mind their own business. She was sensitive about the fact that she was seven years older than her husband, covering it up, and it suited her better to think of his School as bombed out rather than put into liquidation. She adjusted the facts. Either way the School got its death-blow from the war, and the destruction of London largely accounts for the lack of Mayerl materials, including unpublished works. In any case taste had moved on: the syncopation craze was an inter-war phenomenon. But we have yet to cover some of the

[26] *London Gazette*, 30 Mar. 1940.

more glamorous sides of Mayerl's teaching, pupils who did not study by post, as Mrs Mayerl remembered:

JM: He taught the Duke of Kent: he used to go to St James' Palace to teach him. They were really chums and he gave Billy a beautiful set of cuff-links with the royal cipher on, which were unfortunately stolen from one of the theatres up North somewhere where we were playing. But then he told the Duke and he replaced them!

And then he taught the Duke of Windsor—or, as he was then, the Prince of Wales—who was marvellous! He was a wonderful young man. I was very fond of him. He used to come to the theatre, up to the dressing-room. In those days some of the dressing-rooms you got up North were shocking, terrible places, dreary like little dungeons, dark with teeny-weeny windows! And he used to come there and wait for Billy. And, of course, I wasn't allowed there. I would go home—we had a car and chauffeur—and he would take Billy up to Melton Mowbray where they'd drink and play the piano and the drums.

And then the other royal, Princess Maria Christina of Spain: she used to come to the house and have lessons. Her lessons were supposed to be half an hour, but you can't tell royalty: 'it's time to get up, you've had your half hour'! We just sat down and waited. . . . It might be an hour and a half!

[From Mrs McInerney's diaries, 13 November 1929: The King of Spain's two daughters, the Infantas Beatrice and Maria Christina with their lady-in-waiting, came into the office today. They are to have personal lessons with BM.]

PD: What used to happen with the Duke of Windsor? Did he play the drums and Billy the piano?

JM: Yes. I never saw this because I wasn't there but I was very interested because he was such a friendly person, a kind person, just ordinary. He used to sit at the piano with Billy and, you know, try and play with Billy. But mostly he sat at the drums and played the drums all night!

PD: Did they meet after the Abdication?

JM: No.[27]

How fascinating to think of the Prince of Wales working out at the drums with Mayerl as his destiny led inexorably towards his Abdication on 10 December 1936 to enable him to overcome the scandal associated with his plans to marry a divorced American woman. And how rewarding that Mayerl had a little of the success with high society enjoyed so liberally by luminaries such as the Astaires, Gershwin, and Noel Coward. However, one Command Performance put on for King George V by the Green Room Club at the Theatre Royal, Drury Lane, gives less cause for satisfaction as a hangover from one of America's earliest cultural exports. Mayerl, along with famous theatrical names, had to 'black up' for a 'nigger minstrel show'. An item in the first number of the *BMCM* was headed 'A Dirty Business'—and no wonder![28]

---

[27] J. Mayerl, interview with Peter Dickinson, 11 Aug. 1981.
[28] 'A Dirty Business', *BMCM*, 1/1 (Jan. 1934), 9.

But the bulk of Mayerl's admirers came from lower down the social scale. Thanks to the start of the *BMCM* in January 1934 the whole scene can be studied in some detail. In his first editorial Mayerl explained how the Club started:

WELL, here it is at last! So many of you seem to have got together that an idea which was suggested in the first place something like six years ago has become an accomplished fact. . . . During my last tour I was really astounded at the number of friends—students most of them—who said to me, 'we have simply just got to have a Club!'[29]

From now on Mayerl was known to members as the President, with Clayton and the Birmingham representative, Howard Redley, as Vice-Presidents. Each issue contained a statement of the aims of the Club:

The Billy Mayerl Club has been founded at the request of a very large number of students of the Mayerl School. Its object is to forge a link between students and the School and between students and students. The issue of a monthly magazine represents a Club Meeting of Members which for obvious reasons, could not take place in any other manner; and the provision of exclusive new information for Club Members only, places them ahead of all other pianists.

The advantages of membership were listed:

1. Contact after formal courses are finished.
2. Exclusive provision of a transcription by Billy Mayerl every month.
3. The opportunity to keep up to date through articles in the magazine.
4. Information and advice on any musical subjects.
5. Performers of modern syncopation can unite to protect their interests.
6. Local meetings for members to get together.
7. Exchange of views and news of members' activities.

The subscription was £1. 5s. 0d. [£42] a year. Thanks to the magazine the activities of the Club and its members can now be followed in some detail right up to the declaration of war in September 1939.

---

[29] 'Our Club: Its Aims and Objects', *BMCM*, 1/1 (Jan. 1934), 9.

10

THE CLUB: PIANO TRANSCRIPTIONS

TIMES were changing for professional musicians in the 1930s, as for everyone else in Britain. The Wall Street Crash came in 1929; it impacted elsewhere through the Depression; and in 1931 constant crises led to the formation of a National Government as a coalition under Ramsey MacDonald with a massive majority. The writer Stephen Spender, a sensitive observer, said: 'From 1931 onwards, in common with many people, I felt hounded by external events. There was ever-increasing unemployment in America, Great Britain and on the Continent. The old world seemed incapable of solving its problems, and out of the disorder fascist regimes were rising.'[1]

Many musicians were out of work as a result of the arrival of talking pictures, a technical advance which was blamed on the Americans and at first resisted. Records and radio brought music into the home so that there was a decreasing need for amateur music-making and the teaching required to support it. By 1931 a third of musicians were out of work and between 1929 and 1934 the membership of the Musicians Union dropped from 20,000 to less than 8,000.[2] Sales of pianos fell sharply in favour of records, gramophones, and radios. Against this background the progress of the Billy Mayerl Club may seem a mere diversion, a kind of escapism. The pursuit of entertainment and the cheerful exchanges of members must have been a welcome contrast to the news of fascist dictators striding across Europe and the Far East.

The details of the membership can be traced from the first issue in January 1934 to the last in August 1939. In February 1934, under the New Members column it was stated:

Space does not permit us to give a full list of the original Founder Members who joined the Club prior to 1934. We hope to do this later on, but in any case they are so

---

[1] S. Spender, *World within World* (Hamish Hamilton, London, 1951), 137.
[2] C. Ehrlich, *The Music Profession in Britain since the Eighteenth Century* (Clarendon Press, Oxford 1985), 212–17.

very numerous that the list would have to be given in sections month by month. Meanwhile we propose to give additional members joining each month.[3]

When a full list of Founder Members was published in the January 1936 issue the figure was 559. The following month this was corrected by the addition of 47 names 'inadvertently mislaid' during the change of printers; in the March issue 12 more were added; and in April, with further apologies, another 5.[4] The total of Founder Members is 97 more than the monthly published lists so it seems reasonable to assume that there were 97 members before 1934. Further, comparing the lists of names of Founder Members with those published monthly indicates that the category of Founder Member was extended to everyone who joined before June 1935. But with those who had joined between June and December added in, the total was 777—not bad going for the first two years. The annual breakdown, following the original 97, is given in the table below. This means that at least 1,800 people joined altogether, although it is not known if all these kept up their membership through the full five-year period. Lists of members were not provided every month until 1936, partly because of space in the magazine, but it is still possible to come up with average monthly figures for each year:

Year	Total new members	Average monthly
Before Feb. 1934	97	
1934[a]	401	33
1935[b]	279	23
1936[c]	506	42
1937	217	18
1938	206	17
1939[d]	95	12

[a] No lists printed in July, September, and December
[b] No lists printed in March, June, and September
[c] Lists printed every month from now on
[d] Incomplete year ending with August: war declared on 3 September

The bulge in 1936 reflects the halving of subscriptions, as we shall see, but the general picture is one of declining interest.

The membership lists published in the first three months of 1934 show that 68 out of a total of 618 names were resident outside the British Isles. The largest number—16—came from India and Ceylon. Some of these reflected

---

3 New Members, *BMCM*, 1/2 (Feb. 1934), 32.

4 The first printer for the *BMCM* was the Temple Fortune Press but Henderson and Spalding Ltd. took over in June 1935. The initially thin quality of paper was improved in Sept. 1934 and, as a result, these magazines have worn well.

those serving in the far-flung outposts of the British Empire still covering a quarter of the globe, but there were Indian names as well. And there were 17 from continental European countries.

The magazine was vividly presented and designed by Leon Goodman, whose witty cartoons enlivened column headings. Mayerl School was emblazoned across the top of the cover with Club Magazine underneath on an undulating keyboard and below that a statement that it was the official organ of the Billy Mayerl Club. Each issue sported a different colour. At first it consisted of thirty-two pages, apart from December 1934 which was forty, but from October 1935 it became forty pages. At least four pages each month were required for Mayerl's own transcription and examples by students were included too. There were plenty of music examples to illustrate Mayerl's monthly lesson as well as articles with photographs. The interests of students—the constituency of the magazine—were well defined and everything fell into place around the star, Mayerl himself, and his activities. Earlier Lawrence Wright (Horatio Nicholls) had started a Social Club, which gave dinners, and on 9 April 1930 the *Era* reported the welcome he got on coming back from abroad. But the Mayerl Club offered much more—it was a teaching medium, a fan Club, and a mutual admiration society run on a democratic basis, where members could share their views in a spirit of chatty cameraderie and have their questions answered. The supporting cast in London and through the branches was also essential to the whole operation, as testimony from Mayerl's two secretaries has already shown.

The usual pattern was for branches of the Billy Mayerl School to be opened in various cities here and abroad. In April 1939 these were listed in Birmingham, Bristol, Bradford, Glasgow, Leicester, Liverpool, Manchester, Nottingham, Stoke-on-Trent, East London, North London, South London, West London, and abroad in Sweden, New Zealand, India, and South Africa.[5] The writing paper of the School was based on its principal address, 1 & 2 George St., Hanover Square, London W.1, and this mentioned branches abroad in Christchurch, New Zealand, Bombay, Berlin, The Hague, and Johannesburg. Once branches were established, Clubs would follow them in each centre. Reports of meetings were given regularly in the magazine and a calendar published in advance. In the month of November 1936, for example, the following meetings were announced:

November 6: Leicester.
November 11: Birmingham.

---

5 *BMCM*, 6/64 (Apr. 1939), 2 n. *Rhythm* (Apr. 1930) reported that Mayerl went to Germany to open the Berlin branch of the School and, whilst there, broadcast for Vox Radio Haus. Mayerl's secretaries referred to other trips to Spain, Paris, and to Holland and Luxemburg to give broadcasts.

November 13: Manchester, Liverpool, East London and Bristol.
November 16: Coventry.
November 17: South London and Surrey.
November 18: North London.[6]

A major landmark was the opening of a Club in Britain's second city, Birmingham, on 19 December 1934, with a personal appearance from both Mayerl and Clayton. Howard Redley, the energetic area representative and one of the Vice-Presidents, found that far more members planned to come than he had anticipated so it was necessary to take the Connaught Room at the Imperial Hotel to cope with an audience that turned out to be as large as 314.[7] The Midlands fans had responded to encouragement to 'make this a record attendance for Mr. Mayerl's first visit'.[8] By comparison, the Manchester meeting which Mayerl and Clayton attended on 19 April 1935, with a similar programme, was more modest, attracting over 100 people. But this was still exceptional for a Club which started with a mere handful, as the local representative, Alf Lancaster, admitted.[9]

At Birmingham Mayerl had to give an address and apologized for being a rotten speaker: 'If I read my speech—as I shall—I can't look at you. But if I look at you, I cannot read!' His written speech, which appeared in the *BMCM*, was particularly revealing about his priorities. He called the past year one of the most interesting in his career because he was surprised at the level of enthusiasm shown for the School by its members. He was flattered that students wanted to retain contact after finishing their courses and said how rare it was for both him and Geoffrey Clayton to have time away together since they were both so busy.

Mayerl generously reaffirmed his commitment to the School in spite of his habitually frenetic existence:

In spite of all this, I want to tell you tonight, and I want you to believe me when I say I place the interests of our students and interests of our Club above everything else in my mind. I do assure you that very often I have gone to great inconvenience, and possibly even to personal loss, in refusing offers which would interfere with this work, but all I want to see is the Club going on in the way it has begun.[10]

Mayerl then played for half an hour: *Four Aces Suite*; *The Joker*; Three Transcriptions: 'Smoke gets in your Eyes', 'Two Cigarettes in the Dark', 'Love in Bloom', Two 'Classical' Pieces: *Carminetta*, *Autumn Crocus*. An immediate encore was *Sleepy Piano* (*Piano Exaggerations* No. 4), described as one of Mayerl's favourites.

6 *BMCM*, 3/35 (Nov. 1936), 29.
7 'Momentous Meeting of Birmingham Club', *BMCM*, 2/13 (Jan. 1935), 3–6.
8 'Stop Press', *BMCM*, 1/12 (Dec. 1934), 21.
9 K.L., 'Impressive Gathering at Manchester', *BMCM*, 2/17 (May 1935), 3–6.
10 'Momentous Meeting', 3–6.

After an interval Mayerl performed some of his pianistic stunts, imitating a barrel-organ, an antiquated gramophone, and a boarding-house piano. Then Clayton spoke for fifteen minutes on 'Modern Popular Music and the Public's Reaction to It'. In spite of his comic persona through his tediously silly columns in the *BMCM*, he made some serious points about the musical scene, which help us to place the Mayerl fans and indicated the philosophy surrounding syncopation which he and Mayerl had put into practice so successfully for nearly ten years. As reported in the magazine:

He wanted members of the Mayerl Club to beware of the danger of getting into a 'hot' style of playing so that the melody was lost; for 80% of the public in England and 70% of the public in America, had definitely shown themselves as melody-minded. The object of syncopation was to give pleasure to those who heard it, and to take a melody and infuse it with modern rhythm to the utmost possible extent so long as that melody was not lost in a jumble of meaningless nonsense.[11]

So syncopation was a matter of giving a new look to traditional materials but retaining melodic appeal and not going too far. This fitted in precisely with Mayerl's own instructions about how to make transcriptions.[12] The approach was designed to keep in touch with the public at a time when the more advanced serious composers were finding it increasingly difficult to do so, a situation which would get worse until after the 1960s.

The *BMCM*, like other music magazines in the inter-war period, gave space to arguments between supporters and opponents of syncopated music. Mayerl dealt with some of these attacks himself, printing the charges in full and writing replies as in 'Are we wrong morally?' He himself answered a letter from Paris, in which a discontented student had given it a try, thought the decadent jazz phenomenon was coming to an end, and had simply had enough.[13]

As the 1930s progressed it began to become clear to the public that dance music was not jazz, but both types had their opponents. Ragtime had encountered similar denunciations around the turn of the century: rock 'n' roll would do so in the 1950s. Clayton took a swipe against snobbish critics and warned his listeners against thinking that the professional musical press represented popular opinion: he said it was much more important for amateur and professional pianists to give people what they wanted.

Poor Mayerl was not allowed to go home from that Birmingham meeting until he had played requests for a further hour. No wonder the *BMCM* reported the event as 'Momentous Meeting of Birmingham Club'. The whole

---

[11] Ibid.

[12] B. Mayerl, 'The Transcription Bogey No. 3', *BMCM*, 6/65 (May 1939), 8–9.

[13] B. Mayerl, 'Are we wrong morally?', *BMCM*, 1/11 (Nov. 1934), 9. For further discussion of these issues see: P. Scholes, 'The Jazz Craze', in *The Mirror of Music* (Novello/OUP, London, 1947), 519–20.

occasion emphasized the mesmeric attraction of Mayerl himself at the centre of fans who adored him and his music and wanted to benefit from his teaching.

In wartime 1940 Mayerl made a proposal to the BBC about teaching the piano by radio: 'You know—sort of brighten up the blackout, keep your lads from the pubs, play the piano and be merry and keep the old flags flying.' From that vantage point he looked back and described his pupils at the School as 'mostly the young lads, aged between 18 and 30 and the flappers of a similar age' before lamenting the loss of so many through war service.[14] But as early as the second year of its life the economic side of the BMCM had to be considered in the changing climate of the mid-1930s. Mayerl's editorial, September 1935, implies that the magazine was being run at a loss and Clayton confirmed in the following year that the School was subsidizing the Club and its Magazine.[15] However, by October 1935 Mayerl boldly announced that the subscription would be cut from £1 5s. od. [£50] to 12s. [£24] plus 2s. [£4] for postage and he urged members to interest more people in joining.[16] In his Editorial for January 1936 he said he was confident that the membership would be doubled by the end of the year. He was not far out—a membership of 772 at January 1936 was amazingly turned into 1,278 by the end of this boom year. The reduction in subscription had exactly the effect Mayerl—and no doubt Clayton—anticipated and explains the bulge in membership figures during 1935 in the table above. At first the full addresses of members were provided but this practice ceased in March 1937: 'Our attention has been called to the fact that unauthorised use is being made of this information—in certain cases by unscrupulous persons.'[17] This problem continued and the above warning was repeated in February 1939.

There were special benefits for members such as the cup awarded monthly for contributions, competitions, and various items available for purchase, such as the club tie, writing paper, bindings for the magazines, a cigarette case, and a New Mayerl School portable gramophone at £4 4s. [£165] or nine monthly payments of 10s. [£20]. The Club operated an incentive scheme offering cufflinks inscribed with the number of new members introduced—gold ones if this was twenty. A member proposed issuing records of the transcription each month with the magazine but cost prevented this—a pity since this was another pioneering idea which would have anticipated the use of CDs by several record magazines in the 1990s.[18]

---

[14] B. Mayerl, letter to D. Lawrence at the BBC, 23 July 1940. This was not a new idea since Mayerl had broadcast twice on how to play syncopated music—on 8 January and 8 June 1929 for London and Daventry 5XX.

[15] 'Report on Coventry Meeting', BMCM, 3/29 (May 1936), 8–9.

[16] B. Mayerl, 'From the President's Chair, BMCM, 2/22 (Oct. 1935), 3.

[17] New Members, BMCM, 4/39 (Mar. 1937), 40.

[18] G. Browning (letter and reply), 'Gramophone Records would Help', BMCM, 2/23 (Nov. 1935), 8.

The social side of the clubs was clearly an attraction. The Birmingham branch had a motoring section which went on outings; there were joint meetings between neighbouring clubs; and of course dinners. The Club's First Annual Dinner and Cabaret, with guests from all of the many provincial centres, was held at Pagani's Restaurant, 42 Portland Place, London W1. Tickets were 6s. [£11] each with drinks extra. When it came to dress the President had said 'boiled shirts or flannels, it doesn't matter which', so the photographs show a mixture of white tie, black tie, and just suits. This occasion was the launch of Billy Mayerl and his Claviers, including three Challens with harpishord attachment designed by Bill Evans.[19]

The Second Annual Dinner and Dance was for 200 at the Junior Constitutional Club, of which Mayerl was a member. He and Jill received the guests and Irene Ashton presented Jill with a bouquet of flowers ingeniously designed to represent the floral titles of Mayerl's pieces. The chef rose to the occasion by putting a grand piano made out of sugar on Mayerl's table and he was presented with a specially made glass fish in gratitude for his *Aquarium Suite*. The chief guests included Carroll Gibbons, who had to leave to play at the Savoy, and Jimmie Green who, as Director of the Victoria Music Publishing Company, had done so much to secure permission for Mayerl to make transcriptions of copyright material. Fred Mayerl's vivid report ends 'to talk now of next year's dinner is perhaps being a little premature'.[20] Indeed it was. In less than five months everything would change with the war and never return.

There were several ways in which the Club, as a well-focused interest group, was ahead of its time. A. E. Turner, based in Southampton and a regular contributor to the *BMCM*, used an amateur radio transmitter G 2IL on the 40-metre band to reach members in England, Holland, and Sweden on 20 March and 29 May 1938. Reception was good—at least by the standards of that time—in Holland and various parts of England, although some areas heard nothing.[21] Turner had been concerned that BBC broadcasts in those days simply disappeared, whilst radio stations in America sent out records which still survive. So he rigged up a mechanism to record off the air onto metal discs and has preserved parts of these two broadcasts.[22] What was offered was rather like local radio or aspects of the internet in the 1990s without

---

[19] 'The Club's First Dinner and Cabaret', *BMCM*, 5/52 (Apr. 1938), 3–6.

[20] F. Mayerl, 'The Second Annual Dinner and Dance', *BMCM*, 6/64 (Apr. 1939), 9–13.

[21] A. E. Turner, 'A. E. Turner Speaking', *BMCM*, 4/41 (May 1937), 13–15. And 'Calling all Members', *BMCM*, 5/52 (Apr. 1938), 7. See also 'The Life Story of a Southampton Rhythm Fiend', *BMCM*, 3/27 (Mar. 1936), 29–30.

[22] On 2 June 1991 Turner discussed his pioneering off-air recording technique with Robert Parker on BBC Radio 2 in a programme called *Jazz: the Virus* and kindly sent me a tape of this and his pre-war broadcasts.

the same rapid response. The subject-matter was parochial, the usual type of Club members' chatty news featured in the *BMCM*. But there was also a broadcast performance from Southampton member Monty Worlock, then at the start of his career as a jazz pianist.

Worlock's membership was announced in the March 1934 issue of the BMCM; his piece *Raindrops*, heavily indebted to *Nola*, was published in July 1935 and he was that month's cup winner. He won another cup in July 1937 for his article, 'This Left-hand Business', which included three music examples provocatively chosen—all by Chopin. Worlock admired Mayerl, became a pupil in July 1935, but was no satellite. Actually he preferred Carol Gibbons and pointed out how many fine pianists there were at that period, such as Bert Read. Worlock was not a typical member, but was a professional who used his connections with Mayerl and the Club to expand his horizons, in his case into jazz. He remembered that Mayerl had been known to describe jazz as 'jungle music'.[23]

Mayerl's transcriptions were at the heart of the Club magazine and he wanted to encourage other pianists to develop their own style as a way of playing popular songs. As early as 1926, in the second of his three articles for the *Melody Maker*, and didactic even at this stage, Mayerl had stressed: 'Naturally your treatment does not require to be absolutely the same as mine; remember the charm of syncopated playing is largely that of individual interpretation.'[24] He went on to compare the process with a student studying painting under a master. When one member wrote to ask why his transcriptions could not be more commercial and suitable for dancing, the reply came that the tunes were embellished in order to get away from the 'straight commercial rendering' and to make them more interesting.[25]

He was more precise in an article on transcription in 1939:

The whole matter boils down to 'good taste', and this, as near as can be summarised, consists of the following:
1. Never distort the melody so that it becomes unrecognisable.
2. Never write elaborate embellishment just for the sake of doing so, and particularly when such would alter the character of the original.
3. Always endeavour to make treatments easier if possible, if this can be done without spoiling the desired effect.
4. Always be as original as possible, and keep your work in a set style so that others will recognise the 'author' on first hearing.
5. Always bear in mind the reaction of others to a first hearing. Remember you are familiar with your work and know just how all the little 'bits' should sound, but others may not react so quickly.

[23] M. Worlock, interview with Peter Dickinson, 29 Sept. 1995 at Southampton.
[24] *Melody Maker* (Dec. 1926), 82–3.
[25] E. Snowden (letter with reply), 'Commercial Transcriptions', *BMCM*, 3/33 (Sept. 1936), 15.

6. Never 'steal' a break, passage or effect lock, stock and barrel from another writer's work. In spite of everything this certainly is 'just not done'.[26]

Mayerl wrote as a uniquely successful practitioner but he also became a pedagogue, almost as dogmatic as some of the old fogeys he came up against in his adolescence. However, his transcriptions are a remarkable contribution to the genre and a major part of his piano output. The amount of detail we have gone into about the background to the School and the Club must not be allowed to obscure this.

There are over 120 transcriptions: sixty-eight done for the *BMCM* and others published separately, not all of which may yet have been traced. There could have been more in manuscript for which copyright permission was not granted. Mayerl wanted to arrange *Tiger Rag* and *St Louis Blues*, but copyright difficulties prevented this and it is disappointing that not a single song of Gershwin is represented.[27]

Since Mayerl recorded popular songs mostly in the form of piano selections or medleys rather than the set-piece transcriptions he published, it has been difficult to get an overall idea of his contribution to the genre, which he pioneered. In another context, Gunther Schuller defines arrangement as ranging from 'strictly practical versions, primarily designed to serve commercial interests and wider professional dissemination . . . to highly creative recompositions, which transform the basic material in a specific style or manner, in itself marked by a striking originality which may even surpass the quality of the original material'.[28]

This last category fits many of Mayerl's transcriptions very well, especially where the songs themselves are now totally forgotten. The landmark in the life of the transcriptions—what became their official revival—was undoubtedly the recordings by Eric Parkin.[29] These made it clear that, although the transcriptions had a genuine educational function for the School's pupils, they were not limited to this and could vie with and even surpass the rather short-winded piano versions Gershwin published of his own songs in 1932. But Gershwin also recorded improvised treatments of his own songs, some now published in notated form, and this was the difference between him and Mayerl, who was not the same kind of improvising player. Parkin has shown himself on CD as the ideal performer in the pure 1930s style of these transcriptions. They stem from the period that W. H. Auden described in his

[26] B. Mayerl, 'The Transcription Bogey No.3', *BMCM*, 6/65 (May 1939), 8–9.

[27] B. Mayerl, 'An Analysis of the Transcription in this Issue', *BMCM*, 2/17 (May 1935), 19.

[28] B. Kernfeld (ed.), 'Arrangement', *The New Grove Dictionary of Jazz* (Macmillan, London, 1988), 32–3.

[29] P. Dickinson, reviews in *Gramophone*: Vol. I (Jan. 1995), 78; Vol. II (May 1995), 83; and Vol. III (July 1995), 86—also Editor's Choice. See also *Critics Choice* (Dec. 1995), 44.

poem, *Ist September 1939*, as a 'low dishonest decade'. He went on to say 'The lights must never go out, | The music must always play'. This is the music and it epitomizes as well as transcends its era.

The amount of detail about the transcriptions in the *BMCM* is copious. Mayerl wrote an article to go with each one, explaining how he had made his setting as well as how to perform it. There is no point in reproducing such detail here, although it is clear that as a neatly defined style study in both composition and performance all this material could have a future for students quite apart from the enjoyment of playing and hearing the pieces themselves.

Mayerl's first published transcriptions were a set of four brought out by Keith Prowse in 1926. The first is 'If you knew Susie' and Jill Mayerl's signed copy is dated 12 March 1926; the second 'I would like to know why?'; the third 'I love my baby'; and finally 'Alabamy bound'. The first three have adjacent Keith Prowse numbers KP 3005, 6 and 7; the last is KP 3034. All four are headed Billy Mayerl Transcriptions by Billy Mayerl, solo pianist to the Savoy Havana Band. They have the same cover, which is a cartoon of Mayerl rather than the matinée-idol photographs which adorn most of his transcriptions to follow. 'If you knew Susie', text by the American lyricist and producer B. de Sylva, who was soon to become part of the three-man team De Sylva, Brown, and Henderson, shows signs of having been brought out in haste: only the first three songs are listed on the front cover and there is no tempo marking. The piano style has some Mayerl fingerprints, although the left-hand tenths, at this stage, are taken from bottom to top and not vice versa as later. Typically, dominant chords tend to have raised fifths; there are some parallel fourths; and there is a bar of fairly crude right-hand *tremolando*, which would be rare later— but see *Marigold, Studies in Syncopation*, Book III, No. 16, and Mayerl's treatment of 'Sweet and lovely' in the *BMCM*, May 1935. There are two one-bar examples of the 3+3+2 rumba rhythm. 'Alabamy bound' is more original with its whole-tone scale harmony in the introduction, frequent ninth chords and cross-rhythms in 3/4 as well as 3+3+2.

These later 1920s transcriptions, before the members of the Billy Mayerl Club asked for simpler ones, tend to be elaborate. From this point of view, 'Body and soul', the standard by John W. Green, offers little to improve the original sheet music and its own wide-ranging modulations. This is a case where Mayerl's colleague, Frank Eyton, did make a hit, since he co-authored the lyric with Robert Sour and Edward Heyman. If Mayerl offered nothing very individual here, then the other transcriptions in the same Chappell volume—*Album of Famous Songs Transcribed for Piano*—which are all by Tony Lowry, have less interest.

'Balloons: who'll buy my nice balloons?' was published in 1933 but also provided for the *BMCM* in December 1934 as an extra. This is an exceptional example, since the entire piece is a rumba and Mayerl's lesson that month discusses this rhythm. He carefully explains the difference between the 3+3+2 pattern in the tango and in the rumba, which, he says, fills in all the intervening beats. 'Balloons', although difficult to play, is a most inventive piece with cross-rhythms as well as the continuous 3+3+2. Incidentally it anticipates both the Jamaican Rumba (1938) by Arthur Benjamin and the last movement of Milhaud's *Scaramouche*, Op. 165*b* (1937), which use identical rhythms. So does the last of Bartok's *Six Dances in Bulgarian Rhythm*, published in 1940, although this is a genuine 3+3+2 without a strong 4/4 backing to create a cross-rhythm.

The transcription of 'Thanks' (1933), by the American team of Arthur Johnson and Sam Coslow, is a curiosity. The introduction, marked 'tres lent', quotes the opening motif, syncopated, of Wagner's *Tristan und Isolde*; then the chorus is taken in a slow blues tempo followed by an Andante (ad lib) leading to the style-modulation into a rhythmic version of the chorus with parallel chords based on two perfect fourths. This is a successful formula which, with variations, is often the basis of Mayerl's approach.

He used it when dealing with the few standards by major figures that he was allowed to transcribe. Vernon Duke's 'April in Paris', from *Walk a Little Faster*, his first complete Broadway show of 1932, is a beautiful and original song. Mayerl rises to the occasion, taking on Duke's unusual harmonic touches, slightly simplifying them at times. The first chorus is treated as a left-hand melody; the verse is taken over a kind of waltz cross-rhythm; and the middle eight of the second chorus has plenty of Delius chromatic chords slipping down by semitones. As an afterthought Mayerl echoes the main theme *pp* and ends on an added sixth and major seventh. Parkin plays this with real under-standing, letting the verse be flexible and wisely—here and elsewhere—not taking Mayerl's *ff* markings too seriously.

One of the most popular of Mayerl's arrangements is of Kern's 'Smoke gets in your eyes', from *Roberta* (1932), published in 1934. It opens in a harmonic style close to Scriabin but soon settles to a slow treatment in strict time. This manages to be absolutely Mayerl's pace and decorative idiom but also in-escapably the mood of this song about a lost love. The song has no verse, so the second time through the melody is set in the tenor register. But with the mod-ulation—to D flat with this setting in F—Mayerl doubles the speed for con-trast before returning to a *grandioso* setting of the last eight bars of the song to finish.

'Two hearts on a tree' is another vintage transcription, this time published in the *BMCM* for November 1934. This forgotten song is by Peter Yorke, an exact contemporary of Mayerl's and also a student at Trinity College, and Mayerl cherishes it in inimitable fashion. The introduction starts over falling chromatic major thirds; in the first section the left-hand thumb anticipates the next chord, but not with the usual tenths; and the swung final section marked 'Fast Fox-trot Tempo' has a rumba rhythm and other rhythmic dislocations.

The ending, with a tonic seventh sliding down to the sixth, feels like a reflection of the last two bars of Ravel's *Pavane pour une infante défunte* (1899).

Another classic Mayerl arranged was 'Cheek to cheek', which Irving Berlin wrote for the RKO film *Top Hat* (1935) with Fred Astaire and Ginger Rogers particularly in mind. The song has a lavish layout of seventy-two bars with no verse. Mayerl follows this but just before the end of the C major song introduces a blue-note E♭. This seems to be the cue for taking off with the song's release into a whole section in the key of E flat. The transcription is in a uniform pulse throughout, which is not typical, and there is chromatic in-filling of the melody. Mayerl rightly retains the sharp eleventh-chord harmony which Berlin, or his arrangers, provided at exactly the right intoxicating moment at the end of the phrase: 'And my heart beats so that I can hardly speak'.

A distinctly unusual setting is given to 'Fatal fascination', in the *BMCM* for April 1936, a song by Harlan E. Thompson and Lewis E. Gensler, which was provided in response to members' requests for transcriptions that were easier to play. Mayerl met the situation by devising something harmonically adventurous—it might have been found easier to play but the chords would be harder to read. It is marked 'Tempo di Blues', in C minor, and opens ambiguously with chromatically descending chords derived from the whole-tone scale. The chorus slips into the major, marked 'With much Rhythm', and the sting is in the tail—a final cadence built from a fistful of notes with the fifth, sixth, seventh, ninth, and thirteenth in the dominant chord which leads to a tonic with added sixth and seventh.

Mayerl's transcription the following month, May 1936, was 'Limehouse Blues' by the British theatre-composer and conductor, Philip Braham (CD ⑲). The song was made famous by its association with Gertrude Lawrence. She launched it in London in *From A to Z* (1921) and repeated it in André Charlot's *London Revue of 1924* which went to New York in 1925. Mayerl said:

Now there are obviously many treatments that could lend themselves to a number of this nature but because of the enormous popularity of 'Limehouse Blues', more licence may be taken and less predominance of melody deemed necessary . . . Its character is very definitely Chinese, and with a slow-moving melody the scope for rhythmic deviation is enormous. Such is the case with many other old favourites, particularly those in two-four time. 'Nobody's Sweetheart now', 'Tiger Rag', and 'Whispering' all lend themselves to considerable 'mucking about'.[30]

Clayton called this transcription a 'running commentary on the melody' and in his article Mayerl goes on to provide music examples, which was unusual, to show the exact relation between his textures and Braham's sheet music for 'Limehouse Blues'. He calls the major ninth chord which opens his

---

[30] B. Mayerl, 'This Month's Lesson', *BMCM*, 3/29 (May 1936), 24–7.

setting of the chorus the 'Ravel chord' because of its use in *Ma mère l'oye* and takes off from it almost as liberally as a jazz musician. He probably knew Ellington's 1931 recording of this tune.[31]

'Limehouse Blues' is one of a handful of transcriptions Mayerl recorded himself.[32] He starts with a rhetorical flourish descending in whole tones, which is not in the score, then comes in to the printed arrangement (o′ 07″). At the Allegretto (o′ 39″), a transition leading to the verse, Mayerl does not emphasize the off-beat accents he has marked; he fails to catch every detail of the demanding left-hand leaps as written; and ends the section on a major second rather than the tonic. When we get to the chorus (1′ 18″) the elaboration gets going so that Mayerl is virtually improvising on the chords like a jazz musician. He is not quite as steady as usual but is consistently exciting and repeats the chorus at 1′ 45″ in a splendidly cumulative layout. Just before the ending everything shifts up a semitone (2′ 13″) before dropping back to the tonic to finish with a soft throwaway.

I have already referred to Mayerl's transcription of one of the finest of his own songs, 'There's a star in the sky'.[33] He included at least one treatment of his own songs in the *BMCM* every year: one in 1934; three in 1935; three in 1936; two in 1937; one in 1938; and one in the final number, August 1939.

In 1938 Mayerl called 'Thanks for the memory' 'the best tune of the year' and explained:

Here I am not speaking from a purely commercial point of view, as I am well aware that very many numbers during the past season have attained considerably greater sales than the number in question. I am looking at it purely from a musical angle, and, apart from its outstanding merit, those of you who are familiar with lyrics, will, I think, also agree that 'Thanks for the Memory' is full of very clever lines.[34]

The original song is resolutely old-fashioned, as suits such a retrospective subject. The chorus is littered with diminished seventh chords of the kind I have elsewhere castigated as clichéd but Mayerl is totally in tune with this valedictory mood. The lyric certainly is more sharply etched than the drab numbers by Frank Eyton which Mayerl was so used to and even approaches Ira Gershwin. The American team of Leo Robin and Ralph Rainger made a strong impact with this song through the advocacy of Bob Hope and Shirley Ross, who sang it in the Paramount Picture, *The Big Broadcast of 1938*, and it gained the Academy Award for that year. They recorded it and so did Bing Crosby. Throughout his setting Mayerl improves on the rudimentary

[31] D. Ellington, *Limehouse Blues/Echoes of the Jungle*, Victor 22747.

[32] B. Mayerl, 'Limehouse Blues' on *Billy Mayerl plays Billy Mayerl Favourites* ASV CD AJA 5162; also on *The King of Syncopation: Billy Mayerl* WRC/EMI SH 189 (1973).

[33] See Ch. 8 pp. 129–33.

[34] B. Mayerl, 'An Analysis of the Transcription', *BMCM*, 5/59 (Nov. 1938), 16–17.

harmony of the sheet music. He starts by transposing the song up a fourth to get a richer layout and opens unexpectedly with a chord of the supertonic plus minor seventh and eleventh rather than the original's obvious dominant thirteenth. Mayerl manages to stamp his personality on the very first bar, with a semitone rise in an inner part, and he retains the sentimental attraction of the added sixth. There is something especially poignant about transcribing a song with a text like this, since it was being made as Prime Minister Chamberlain desperately tried to appease Hitler. Soon the Long Weekend of the inter-war years would be just a memory and for millions, including Mayerl himself, things would never be the same again.[35]

Mayerl matches up to another great Kern song in his 1940 setting of 'All the things you are' from *Very Warm for May* (1939), filmed as *Broadway Rhythm* (1943). Mayerl demonstrates that there is no obvious stereotype in his approach to transcription by starting with a cadenza which at first has little obvious connection with what follows, although the falling perfect fourths of Kern's tune emerge. Mayerl retains Kern's ingenious harmonic scheme with its unusual connections between the G major verse and the same key within the A flat major chorus. He asks for the tune to be played slowly in strict time; introduces chromatic slides into the melody; and turns Kern's repeated notes into relaxed triplets. Mayerl catches the delicacy of the song's vernal scenario and, in the words of Oscar Hammerstein's text, causes the 'breathless hush of evening' to 'tremble on the brink of a lovely song'.

Finally, Mayerl made an arrangement of Noel Coward's 'Poor little rich girl' in 1956. As with 'Limehouse Blues', he was looking back to a Gertrude Lawrence hit, from André Charlot's *London Revue of 1924* (1925), but it was also sung by Alice Delysia in *On with the Dance* (1925). Mayerl is still on splendid form, avidly improving on the sheet music at all points. He starts somewhat rhetorically, in the mood of some of his orchestral pieces, but gets the skittish quality of the verse with some *scherzando* piano figuration. In the softer passages of the verse Mayerl enriches Coward's harmony and even the melody. The chorus is marked 'very rhythmic' and has two extra bars to start with. Almost every note of the tune is anticipated. Coward's instrumental filling for the last three bars of the second four-bar phrase falls flat in the sheet music, but Mayerl takes the same rising figure, starts it earlier and cuts a bar to make it work—showing Coward how to make better use of his own idea. In fact Coward needed as much help from others in getting his music down on paper as Irving Berlin. The variety of piano textures in this transcription, with crosshand effects, crotchet triplets, and a regular bass, show that Mayerl has lost none of his art.

---

35 R. Graves and A. Hodge, *The Long Weekend: A Social History of Great Britain 1918–1939* (Faber & Faber, London, 1940).

There could be no greater contrast than that between Mayerl and Coward. Both were performers whose works relied on their own delivery; both had difficulty in coping with the changed climate in entertainment from the war years onwards; but Coward survived on his talent to amuse which endeared him to the fashionable society he had courted so assiduously. Mayerl found the transition difficult to handle as he failed to get back into musical comedy, had to cope with recurrent illness, and worked in commercial light music.

11

OTHER MUSIC OF THE 1930S

MAYERL's work in the 1930s shows an extension of his series of pieces with titles based on the names of flowers and an addiction to quotation, often as some form of private joke. After *Marigold* there were ten further pieces with floral titles, apart from those in suites and in one collaborative work. The idea was not new: the name of a flower could be used to differentiate one piece from another more attractively than a title like Romance. Edward MacDowell specialised in such titles, but the popular prototype was Ethelbert Nevin's *Narcissus* (1891) and Mayerl would have known English examples such as Cyril Scott's *Asphodel* and Frank Bridge's *Rosemary*, both from 1906.

Irene Ashton recalled in 1967 that Mayerl's 'gods were Debussy, Ravel, Grieg and Delius' and later added Rachmaninov and Stravinsky.[1] Mayerl himself said on Swedish Radio in 1938: 'I've tried to be impressionist, to paint a picture of flowers, or fishes, or for that matter a pack of cards.'[2] A few years later he told the BBC:

I am a very keen gardener and actually when I first started writing tunes with flower titles, these were mostly inspired by the beautiful picture on the seed packet. Needless to say, the actual flowers never came up quite as nicely! But that did not worry me as I was much more interested in the idea suggested on the seed packet so that I could turn it into something musical.[3]

It is not surprising that Mayerl was concerned with depiction in view of his rigorous early conditioning working as a pianist for silent films. In these 1930s piano pieces, titles and bits of quotation—there are probably more to be identified—are used like puns in the manner of the period. But what is remarkable about Mayerl is that he cast his floral portraits, like most of his pieces, in a

---

[1] See Ch. 8 nn. 65 and 66.
[2] B. Mayerl, Swedish Radio interview, 2 Nov. 1938.
[3] B. Mayerl, letter from Grosvenor House, Park Lane, London W1, to E. Spear at BBC Bangor, N. Wales, 12 June 1941. See also J. Mayerl, 'Titles', *Billy Mayerl Circle Newsletter*, 1/3 (Autumn 1974), 6–7.

strict form developed from the piano rag. This would never have occurred to Scott or Bridge coming from the classical-romantic tradition. So it is worth looking at some pieces from this point of view and some others where the composing history is known. It is important to stress that the way in which Mayerl differentiated each of his pieces is related to his treatment of strain lay-out and key relationships, much as classical composers worked with the op-tions within traditional sonata form. So these details are worth observing.

Some of Mayerl's piano works published in the 1930s had been composed in the previous decade, as was revealed by the opus numbers discussed in Chapter 7. That list helped to provide an order of composition, showing his development through the 1920s. In the next decade it is possible to view the songs in the order of their shows. But for the piano music we have only the order of publication to go on, which should be more reliable than in the 1920s since Mayerl was constantly in demand with a ready publisher in Keith Prowse where, according to Osborne, he was a contracted writer.[4] The series of *Syncopated Impressions* initiated with *Marigold* continued with *Mignonette*, *Honeysuckle*, *Scallywag* (all 1931), and *White Heather* (1932), dedicated to Binnie Hale, star of *Nippy*.

The piano-writing shows familiar fingerprints as well as new develop-ments, but generally with less virtuosity. All four of these pieces have features in common. The introductions of the first three are based on a single chord in various transpositions and the main melodies of the three with floral titles are largely pentatonic. *Mignonette*, in C, has some Mayerl fingerprints, since the A strain melody is doubled in fourths and, in the B strain, the upper note of the left-hand tenth is taken by the thumb just before the beat. The C strain, in A flat major, is richly decorated in both hands including *tremolandi* at climaxes. The coda ends on a dominant major ninth chord.

Scallywag, in F, dedicated to bandleader Jack Payne, is marked 'Umoristico giocoso', its hilarity symbolized by a series of parallel dominant sevenths in the whole-tone scale dropping down more than two octaves. The C strain in A flat brings in more fourths as well as parallel chords made from two perfect fourths, originally featured in No. 13 from *Six Studies in Syncopation*, Op. 55, and thus earlier than *Marigold* in 1927: and the crazy whole-tone scale intro-duction, brought back at the end, cadences on the tonic major seventh, softly.

White Heather, another tranquil G major piece, is marked 'slowly' although Mayerl plays it fast. The anticipatory left-hand tenth technique is applied to smaller intervals immediately in the A strain. The C strain is in E flat and is simply a version of 'Loch Lomond' in Mayerl syncopation, perhaps a personal reference for the dedicatee—Binnie Hale was born in Liverpool, but *Nippy* had a trial run in Edinburgh.

---

[4] L. Osborne, interview with Peter Dickinson, 11 Aug. 1981.

Autumn Crocus (1932), in F, is the first of Mayerl's pieces since *A Lily Pond* to be described as *An Idylle*. This is the French spelling for a genre described as 'a pastoral or sentimental composition' in the *Oxford English Dictionary*, but not listed in the *New Grove*. The title goes back at least to Wagner's *Siegfried Idyll* (1870) but has also been used in solo pieces such as No. 6 of *Dix pièces pittoresques* (1881) by Emmanuel Chabrier, MacDowell's suites *Wald Idyllen* (1884) and *Idyllen: Sechs Kleine Stücke* (1887) as well as individual pieces by him and Cécile Chaminade. *Autumn Crocus* is in this tradition, a perfect salon piece. Every detail, including decoration, is in the right place in an overall ternary design. I met Mrs McInerney, Mayerl's first secretary at the School, when she was a sprightly octogenarian with perfect recall. She was in the office when *Autumn Crocus* was being composed:

Very often you'd hear him at the piano and you knew very well [he was composing]. I love *Autumn Crocus* because I can remember [it] so well. The first week I was there I was so thrilled because we had a terrible thunderstorm one day and Billy Mayerl went to the piano and he played the thunderstorm! I thought that was miraculous really. Afterwards I don't think he had very much time to do much composing like that, just off the cuff. But I do remember him composing *Autumn Crocus* because he'd be in the studio and you could just hear this few bars and then you'd hear another few bars . . . *Autumn Crocus* was lovely. [5]

Another piece involved with quotation is *Penny Whistle* (1932), in E flat, which is given a new title, *Novelette*, which goes back to Schumann's *Novelletten*, Op. 20. In the introduction realistic whistle imitations are soon followed by 'Pop goes the Weasel'. The layout of the piece, again marked 'Umoristico giocoso', is more flexible than usual, with pauses, accelerandi, and cadenzas built in. The middle section is mostly unsyncopated with a realistic cadenza for the whistle. But Mayerl's style is getting more expansive compared with the 1920s.

The *Three Syncopated Rambles* focus around the substantial central piece. The opening one, *Junior Apprentice*, is related to other G major numbers such as *Harmonica Dance*, No. 3 of *Three Dances in Syncopation*, Op. 73, and *Muffin Man*, No. 2 of *Three Miniatures in Syncopation*, Op. 76. Strain B has the left-hand parallel sixths accompaniment routine used in *Wistaria*, but the rare staccato ending is neat. The second piece is a complete surprise. It is called *Printer's Devil*, which refers to the errand boy in a printing office and is also the name of a pub in Fetter Lane, near the Lawcourts in London EC4. The subtitle is *Theme and Transcription*. A luscious sixteen-bar melody, pentatonic to begin with, harmonized with added sixths, seconds, and chromatics—Delius via Ireland and Bax, but personal too—leads to a rising figure in G minor

5 E. A. McInerney, interview with Peter Dickinson, 11 May 1992.

marked 'poco accel.'. This is a minor key version of the refrain of Mayerl's *Imaginary Foxtrot* which he used for teaching purposes.[6] After an abbreviated return of the opening theme a *tranquillo* section starts like a tribute to *Rhapsody in Blue* (the first piano entry) and develops into a Gershwinian climax. This turns out to be heralding the dramatic style-modulation to the Mayerl transcription of the theme, marked 'Blues tempo (In strict rhythm)'. This is an extraordinary movement and it seems to represent several aspects of Mayerl's life: a popular song; the foxtrot from his teaching; Gershwin; and a transcription. *Printer's Devil* could stand on its own and is far from being a mere syncopated ramble. Its power makes the last piece, *6 A.M. The Milkman: Scherzo*, a breezy trifle.

The Suite for Piano called *Four Aces* (1933), dedicated 'To my Friend "Bill" Evans', Director of the firm of Challen whose instruments Mayerl preferred, is a landmark as the most popular of the suites. Mayerl was very fond of playing cards so he chose to unify the set through this interest, adding *The Joker* (1934) later. No. 1, *The Ace of Clubs* (CD 20), in F, is marked 'Allegretto moderato (In strict tempo)'. It is a lively number with rag strain patterns still in evidence. There is a four-bar introduction followed by a till-ready; a jumping left-hand part over a tonic pedal; and catchy dotted rhythms and cross-rhythm breaks to come. The till-ready and the ending are based on subtle Debussian major seconds. But there is a lot of repetition with slightly less rhythmic invention than in the past. Mayerl makes cuts in his own recording, presumably to get two *Aces* onto each side of the 78, but Eric Parkin's recording makes complete sense of the Suite uncut.[7] Mayerl's own performance is characteristically dry and bouncy, revealing a neat finger-technique. The original 78 recordings coupled *Clubs* with *Hearts*, and *Diamonds* with *Spades* for reasons of timing, but the published order is adhered to here.

No. 2, *The Ace of Diamonds* (CD 21), in E flat, is shorter and has connections with other E flat major pieces such as *Hollyhock*: the till-ready chords are counterpointed with off-beat D♭s as blue notes, which do not recur, and its main theme, just an eight-bar phrase repeated, is decorated pentatonic. The first

---

[6] B. Mayerl, *Imaginary Foxtrot*, in *BMCM*, 2/14 (Feb. 1935), 16–19.

[7] B. Mayerl, *Four Aces Suite* (see Discography). Mayerl's 1933 performance was put onto an LP, *The King of Syncopation*, WRC/EMI SH 189 (1973), with the *Ace of Hearts* second instead of third. Mayler's cuts are as follows: (1) *Ace of Clubs* (CD 20)—Mayerl cuts the last two bars of introduction; first sixteen bars of strain B; last two bars of transition; and first sixteen bars of the repeat of strain A; (2) *Ace of Diamonds* (CD 21)—no cuts; (3) *Ace of Hearts* (CD 22)—Mayerl cuts the middle section from the end of bar 8 to bar 23; the final section loses its first twelve bars; (4) *Ace of Spades* (CD 23)—Mayerl cuts the final section after bar 5 up to the last five bars of the piece. See also Mayerl's detailed discussion of the pianistic layout of this piece—considering both the ninths in the left hand and the counter-melody—in 'This Month's Lesson', *BMCM*, 1/2 (Feb. 1934) 21–5. Parkin's recording of the *Four Aces Suite* is most unfortunately split between *Marigold: Piano Impressions of Billy Mayerl* on Chandos CHAN 8560 and *Bats in the Belfry* also on Chandos CHAN 8848.

statement is again over a tonic pedal, but the second time round it has a shifting chromatic accompaniment (o′ 20″). Then there is a contrast leading to some loud, dislocating off-beat chords and a spun-out reference to the main theme to finish with. According to Irene Ashton, No. 3, *The Ace of Hearts*, in G, (CD 22), was the composer's own favourite. Marked 'Allegro moderato', it is in a lilting 12/8 and, if the easy-going, falling two-note figure in strain A is overdone, the very typical strain B makes up for it played in a beautifully relaxed manner (o′ 40″). Here the climax, with its right-hand figures reaching upwards, is ideally placed. No. 4, *The Ace of Spades* (CD 23) breaks the pattern by starting with a free introduction which alternates tonally ambiguous cadenzas with a passage in C in 3/4 which seems to be related to Debussy's *Petite Suite* for piano duet. When this passage is repeated it shifts to D flat which becomes a dominant. The Moderato (In strict time) (o′ 48″), in G flat with much of it on the black notes, is strongly rhythmic, with the bass anticipations made into a tenor melody (1′ 36″) in the C section of an overall A–B–A–C–A–B–A rondo layout. Mayerl's own pacing in this movement is, as usual, dead right.

The cover design of the sheet music is ingenious, but may not relate to the actual compositions. It depicts the four playing cards with figures standing on them. The *Ace of Clubs* is a blindfold ballerina who looks as if she has materialized from above as a result of a magic wand brandished by an acrobat as *Ace of Diamonds*. The *Ace of Hearts* is a cherub with a quiver-full of cupid's darts. He is gesturing towards a black, cloaked Mephistophelean figure as the *Ace of Spades*. Since spades are used to dig graves, he looks like a symbol of death, seen as the ultimate end of all romance. The cover of the piano duet version of the *Ace of Spades* develops this motif further with an even more sinister, hooded figure resembling a diabolical spaceman lacking facial features and giving off flames.

The fifth piece connected to playing cards, *The Joker*, in C, is the most ingenious of all. After the eight-bar introduction, the main theme is scored in pecking three-note clusters; the B strain has dislocating, off-beat major seventh figures; and then the themes from all four previous aces emerge in the order of *Diamonds*, *Spades*, *Clubs*, and *Hearts*. The strain A material recurs softly with an upwards glissando to finish. The green cover design has a realistic joker, with cap and bells, standing on his own card and playing with a balloon on the end of a stick.

But the version of *Four Aces* as a suite for piano and dance band is a revelation. By scoring it Ray Noble did for Mayerl what Ferde Grofé did for Gershwin's *Rhapsody in Blue* ten years earlier. The skilfully manipulated instrumental colours and the interchanges between piano and band exploit all the repetitions. Even the oddly Debussian cadenzas in *The Ace of Spades*—with bitonal moments of C major against F sharp—make sense, in *Rhapsody in Blue* terms, in the recording by Raie da Costa with the New Mayfair Orchestra,

EMI's house band, under Noble.[8] He takes the Moderato of this movement rather fast ($\downarrow$ = about 144) for da Costa to cope easily with the consecutive octaves. Mayerl, just for once, was somewhat slower ($\downarrow$ = about 128) and had no trouble. Arthur Wood made a new orchestration of the Suite and this was first broadcast by the BBC Theatre Orchestra on 2 June 1935. On the back of the sheet music, it says that Noble's orchestral version was played by Henry Hall and the BBC Dance Orchestra, and Dare Lea and his Band. The Da Costa/Noble recording almost caused a problem since Mayerl wanted to be the first to record the Suite but Noble was contracted to HMV and Mayerl to Columbia. In order to get his solo recording in first, Mayerl travelled overnight from Glasgow, where *Sporting Love* was running, played the Suite for Columbia and rushed back, thus beating HMV by a month and getting in first.[9]

Mayerl made only one recording with his wife—the piano duet version of *The Ace of Spades*, recorded on 31 August 1934 and released on Columbia as the other side of their performance of *Marigold*—and it provides another slant on both pieces. The cadenza introduction of the *Ace of Spades* has fuller chording, especially in the bitonal 6/8 section. In the Moderato the mostly pentatonic rhythmic main theme is backed by a counter-melody, also pentatonic, in the lower duet part, effectively echoing the top part's rising figure in octaves, although it is subdued in the Mayerls' recording. One could guess that Jill Mayerl is playing the lower part since the familiar rhythmic dynamism comes from above.

Canaries' Serenade (1933), in C, is simply called *A Syncopation* and is marked, unusually, 'slowly con espressivo' [*sic*]. In his recording Mayerl did play at a moderate speed ranging from $\downarrow$ = 100–8. The *Serenade* is dedicated to a specific bird: to Michael—Geoffrey's Canary. Clayton was so devoted to his canary that it featured in his will made in 1936. His maid was enjoined to look after it or find someone who would. But Clayton lived another twenty years, thus surviving his pet.

The A strain in C is understandably more florid than usual, with trills and repeated-notes in the upper register, and an isolated 3+3+2 rumba rhythm. Mayerl played the trills in a scintillating, bird-like fashion. The main business of strain C is a quotation from Debussy's *Reflets dans l'eau* at the original pitch but in dotted rhythm, which Mayerl played very dry. This figure is used six times during the strain with an incongruous bluesy answering phrase, which feels like another quote. Mayerl is obviously enjoying the joke

---

[8] B. Mayerl, *Four Aces Suite*, orchestrated by Ray Noble, with Raie da Costa and the New Mayfair Orchestra/Noble on HMV B 8148–9, 2 Feb. 1934 [not listed in Rust and Forbes, *British Dance Bands*]. See also Mayerl's own enthusiastic comments on this recording in 'Congratulations to the HMV Company', *BMCM*, 1/6 (June 1934), 12. Leslie Osborne—in *Life is Nothing without Music*, 3 'The Songwriters', BBC Radio 2, 21 Apr. 1981— remembered Noble as a serious musician: they went to the Proms together and Noble took scores to the concert.

[9] 'In the News', *BMCM*, 1/2 (Feb. 1934), 11.

with these repetitions and overdoes it—for the record he cut the written-out repeat of the A and C strains. As it happens the answering phrase is the same as the opening of the verse of 'There's a star in the sky' to the words 'When I'm gazing out'. This would suit the canary in its cage but unfortunately the song was written for *Cheer up* three years later.

Another fine piece with a story behind it is *Nimble Fingered Gentleman* (1934), in E flat. It is dedicated to Coventry-based fellow pianist, Jack Wilson, who broadcast regularly on Midland Regional and apparently disliked scales. The title was Wilson's nickname and the joke is that the piece has more scales than any other Mayerl composition—in fact he hardly ever used them.[10] The barbershop harmony reappears in bar 3 of the introduction and strain A ends with a neat blue-note cadence.

There are two pieces under the title of *Stepping Tones* (1934), subtitled *Syncopations in Moderation*. This implies a reduction both in syncopation and technical difficulty, with some helpful fingering provided in both pieces. The first of these, *Fascinating Ditty*, in F, is obsessive about its principal motif which appears twenty-two times in the thirty-two-bar double A strain. Much more rewarding is *Hop-o'-my-Thumb* (1934), in A flat, dedicated to the Mayerl School teacher Madge Howard. The title means a dwarf or pigmy but it is a *double entendre* in view of the keyboard technique with left hand crossing right. The Introduction is as catchy as strain A with its falling fourths. The four phrases of strain B alternate dissonant and consonant harmonizations of the same motif. For his own recording Mayerl repeated strain A and played its last chord at the lower octave each time; in the transition to strain C, moving from A flat major to F major, Mayerl does not play the left-hand chords above the right; in the transition back to the repeat of strain A the right hand is played an octave higher and Mayerl adjusts the left hand; and he tacks an extra bass note onto the added sixth chord ending.[11]

At this point Keith Prowse published a totally unsyncopated piece, *Siberian Lament*, which harks back to the concert pieces Boosey brought out in 1928 and 1929. *Siberian Lament* started life as an orchestral piece, again scored by Arthur Wood, and was premièred in a BBC broadcast with Reginald King and his Orchestra on 5 November 1934.[12] Its combination of

---

[10] 'In the News', *The Nimble-fingered Gentleman*, BMCM, 1/2 (Feb. 1934), 12. And 'In the News—Jack Wilson', *Billy Mayerl Circle Newsletter*, 1/5 (Spring 1975), 9. See *Jack Wilson: After all these Years*, Shellwood SWCD14 (1999).

[11] B. Mayerl, *Hop-o'-my-Thumb*, Billy Mayerl, 31 Aug. 1934 (see Discography). At one time Mayerl planned to write a series called *Stepping Tones* at the rate of one per week. See 'Our President's Activities', BMCM, 1/5 (May 1934), 27.

[12] 'Stop Press', BMCM, 1/5 (May 1934) 27.

A Billy Mayerl Programme—BBC Regional, 5 November 1934, 6.30–7.15.
Reginald King and his Orchestra, Eve Becke (soprano), and Billy Mayerl (piano).

modal melodies with chromatic and whole-tone elements is close to the technique of Arnold Bax. The overall tonality is A minor—very rare for this abundantly major-key composer—but the piece is distinctly economical since the second theme, also over a tonic pedal, is simply a major version of the first. The climax is well placed, even if the sequences which precede it are rather obvious, and the reprise of the opening section interpolates delicate two-bar units in the whole-tone scale. The mood is well sustained and distinctly Russian.

Mistletoe, in D flat, published in 1935 and dedicated to the Members of the Billy Mayerl School Club, is a further *Syncopated Impression*. It was written late on the night before the BBC broadcast concert on 29 December 1934.[13] This is an unusual piece, especially if it was dashed off in a few hours under pressure, and it opens with 'The Mistletoe Bough'. Strain A is unsyncopated apart from the anticipation of the second and fourth beats of the bar, which gives the rhythm just the right lift. The repeat of strain A interpolates a mini-cadenza. Strain C, in F, is concerned with a three-note unit G–A–C, marked out over a recurring chord progression. As it happens, this motif is the same as the main theme of the slow movement of Tippett's Concerto for Double String Orchestra (1938), which has to be a coincidence.

Two more 1935 pieces were described as 'on a theme by Austen Croom-Johnson'—*Green Tulips*, in F, and *Bats in the Belfry*, in A flat. Mayerl and Croom-Johnson, a 26-year-old composer-performer-promoter-broadcaster, recorded both these collaborations on 26 August 1935 using two pianos, one with a 'harpsichord' attachment. The story appeared in the *Billy Mayerl Club Magazine*: 'Croom-Johnson, known as Ginger, had a popular radio programme called *Soft Light and Sweet Music* and was using what became strain A of *Bats in the Belfry* played on a harpsichord as its signature tune.'[14] Mayerl at once recognized both a good tune and a new gimmick and declared:

I predict a great future for one of the oldest and least-exploited instruments, the harpsichord. It lends itself so admirably to rhythmic treatment, and I think this is proved conclusively in a new record just issued by Columbia for two pianos and harpsichord. Austen Croom-Johnson and I have decided that the new tone-colour would, if handled and written for carefully, create quite a novelty. The result is rather amazing.[15]

Three Japanese Pictures—orchestra; *Ace of Clubs, Ace of Diamonds, Ace of Hearts, The Joker*—Billy Mayerl; *Three Contrasts*—orchestra; 'Have a Heart' (from *Sporting Love*), 'Sweet Indispensable' (from *Silver Wings*)—Becke and Mayerl; *Ace of Spades* and *Marigold* (piano duet)—Mayerl and King; *Siberian Lament* (first performance)—orchestra; *Hop-o'-my-Thumb*—Mayerl; *Pastoral Sketches*—orchestra.

[13] 'In the News', *BMCM*, 2/14 (Feb. 1935), 32.
[14] 'In the News: Austen Croom-Johnson finds a new Instrument', *BMCM*, 2/17 (May 1935), 25.   [15] 'A Unique Recording', *BMCM*, 2/22 (Oct. 1935), 16.

The photographs show Mayerl at a piano with two keyboards but such enthusiasm makes it surprising that he made such sparing use of the 'harpsichord' attachment. It comes only at the start, with a voice-over to explain it, and at the end of *Bats in the Belfry*. And he never came back to it, although several articles in the *Club Magazine* show how interested Mayerl always was in new keyboard developments both acoustic and electronic.

Irene Ashton interviewed Austen Croom-Johnson in 1935 just as he was about to leave for America to marry Marthe Languet from Kentucky.[16] His background was Bruton School, Somerset, and the Royal College of Music, where he studied with John Ireland and George Thalben-Ball. But he really liked hot jazz and Delius, rejected his family's plans for working in the City, and moved into entertainment and then a substantial American career.

In 1975 his widow wrote to H. Nichols of the Billy Mayerl Circle with some details of his life in America. In 1936 he was Director of Programming for NBC; two years later he set up his own firm to pioneer musical commercials with the famous *Pepsi Cola hits the Spot* and other award winners; and he 'built a personality for a station with catchy, colourful musical identifications which were credited with catapulting ratings from fourth to first place'.[17] He died suddenly in May 1964.

Croom-Johnson confirmed that Mayerl was 'intrigued by these two little themes of mine' and started to embroider them. *Green Tulips* is an oddity, starting in F major, shifting to A flat major after seven bars and B flat major four bars later. This makes the opening section fifteen bars in length with the first bar repeated eight times, the last time in a surprising bitonal setting. Mayerl comes into his own with strain B, in A flat, which is based on the same rising repeated-note figure as the excellent *Railroad Rhythm* (1938). But *Green Tulips* doesn't add up and Mayerl rightly thought this idea could be better used later.

Bats in the Belfry is quite different: every strain works and they complement each other as in the best piano rags. The two-keyboard version which Mayerl recorded with Croom-Johnson introduces further detail—the transition to strain C is particularly inventive and so is the coda—but the solo piece is just as effective. Croom-Johnson's strain A has again brought an unusual layout where a sixteen-bar unit is extended over a dominant pedal followed by transitional modulating passages. In both A and B strains the repeated off-beat single notes spice up the rhythm—Mayerl's irrepressibility—maintaining the restless jumpy quality of the piece. Strain C is unusual too. It opens with continuous right-hand figures which might have come from J. P. Johnson's *Caprice Rag* (1914), then there is 3/8 cross-rhythm dislocation lasting a bar and a half. *Bats in the Belfry* was orchestrated by George Windeatt. He, too, spices

[16] I. Ashton, 'Austen Croom-Johnson, *BMCM*, 2/23 (Nov. 1935), 3–5.
[17] 'Austen Croom-Johnson', *Billy Mayerl Circle Newsletter*, 1/8 (Winter 1975), 4–5.

up the transition before strain C, adds a counter-melody in that strain and produces a new coda, with a distinctly late 1930s cadence.[18] Mayerl apparently put words to the opening theme, 'I got tiddly in the bar last Friday!'

Croom-Johnson's view of Mayerl as seen by a bright young man in the mid-1930s is indicative: 'He's a phenomenon. Somehow he's definitely not a novelty pianist, and somehow not a dance pianist either . . . I place him in a class of his own—and a class I cannot explain.'[19]

Quotation is also a feature of *Orange Blossom*, in C, another *Syncopated Impression* (1936). Strain A is elegantly traced over a chordal bass: strain C contains a bit of 'Here comes the bride' (Wagner's *Lohengrin*), so perhaps the dedicatee Tommy Simpson was getting married. The coda sounds like a quote too. *Shallow Waters* (1936) is as fine as *Autumn Crocus* and equally unsyncopated. These are both polished salon pieces with memorable melodies in an idiom which would not have been too progressive in the 1890s. When Mayerl was writing for himself, not showing off his technique and not having to fit in with the mass demands of musical comedy, his style was relaxedly conservative. The rag strain patterns are still visible in *Shallow Waters*, but strain A has seventeen bars rather than the conventional sixteen. The opening melody spreads over nine bars, a long arc without the short fragments Mayerl normally employed. The bass descends entirely by step, allowing for octave displacements, until the climax at bar 9 on a chord of the major seventh and major ninth. Strain B relies on its harmonic changes to qualify the repetition of short phrases. The return of strain A is sheer calm and the four-bar coda, with the melody in the tenor, is perfectly gauged. *Shallow Waters* is subtitled *An Interlude* but, like *Autumn Crocus* it is also an Idyll.

As a successor to *Four Aces* Mayerl next wrote *Aquarium Suite*, which he arranged for piano and band himself. Mayerl's second secretary at the School, Mrs Matkin, arrived six months after Mrs McInerney, and she was able to provide some background for this Suite:

A year or so back he discovered the Aquarium at the Zoo. A couple of weeks later a fish-pond began to take shape in his garden, and he proudly showed me new corns and blisters on his hands each morning. Now Mrs. Mayerl says that the first thing he does when he arrives home, no matter what time, is to dash out to his pond and gaze rapturously at his pets. I shan't forget the dreadful day when a 'kind' friend left a tin of ants at the School for his fish. When Mr. Mayerl saw the closed tin he said: 'Poor little beggars: they'll be suffocated'. I suppose this was worse than being swallowed by fish! Anyway, he proceeded to stab a lot of holes in the lid, and we spent the rest of that morning crawling around collecting stray ants. And when he went home he put the tin in his pocket just as it was! I wonder if the fish had any of those

[18] B. Mayerl, *Bats in the Belfry*, in *British Light Music: Billy Mayerl*, Slovak Radio Symphony Orchestra/Carpenter, on Marco Polo 8.223514 (1994).

[19] 'Austen Croom-Johnson', *BMCM*, 2/23 (Nov. 1935), 3–5.

ants. I know I felt remarkably uncomfortable whenever I went near his desk for days after.

As a result of all this we have the *Aquarium Suite*. Believe me, it was a long time before the design for the cover of this satisfied Mr. Mayerl. The poor artist was sent down to the Zoo Aquarium to study fish and their habits, so that every detail of his drawing should be correct.[20]

Mayerl would have known where to get first-hand data since he was a member of the Zoological Society of London from 1936 to 1947.[21] The cover of *Aquarium Suite* does show particularly realistic fish in their watery environment.

Each piece is named after a fish and can be presumed to reflect some of its characteristics in detail. The first one, *Willow Moss*, in C, has a free introduction followed by a Lento section consisting of an eight-bar pentatonic melody in C repeated. Another free section, with a cadenza, follows before the pentatonic melody is treated to a swung Mayerl transcription to end with—plus two bars of Molto Lento coda. The pentatonic tune has the same intervals as Gershwin's 'I got rhythm' (*Girl Crazy*, 1930) both up and down.

Moorish Idol is Turkish to the extent that its A minor contains sharpened fourths: the middle section, in the major key as an immediate correction of the rare minor mode, is florid. Strain A of *Fantail*, in F, is another melody partly doubled in fourths: strain B uses two sharply contrasted types of figuration. There is nothing new in the high-spirited dotted rhythms of the last piece, *Whirligig*, in G. The publisher first planned to issue these pieces separately at 2s. [£3.70] each, but then decided on 3s. 6p [£6.50] for the whole set. Mayerl thought 'pianists would be pleased with the increased value'.[22]

Basically this is middle-of-the-road Mayerl, based on what might be called a *Rhapsody in Blue* approach to piano and band with cadenzas and strict numbers. In following this path Mayerl was leaving the sparkling novelty idiom behind and entering the world of light music, with its echoes of the conventions of the romantic piano concerto, a style which has retained glamour and remained popular. In their orchestral versions most of Mayerl's pieces sound like light music, especially in modern performances which lack the taut dance-band rhythms of Mayerl's own recordings. His later contributions to mood music confirm this trend, but there are still piano works on top form to come.

One of Mayerl's most popular pieces after *Marigold* was *Sweet William* (1938), in the rare key of D flat. This is another floral *Syncopated Impression*, with realistic flowers on the cover of the sheet-music, and thoroughly bouncy

---

[20] V. Matkin (Harrison), 'Ten Years with Billy Mayerl', *BMCM*, 4/45 (Sept. 1937), 16,17, and 5.

[21] K. Ferguson, letter from the librarian of the Zoological Society of London to Peter Dickinson, 17 Oct. 1994.

[22] B. Mayerl, 'From the President's Chair', *BMCM*, 4/44 (Aug. 1937), 2.

in the way that Mayerl played it. It consists of an eight-bar introduction and only two well-balanced strains in an A–B–A layout. The second bar of strain A is based on the barbershop chord of A major in the D flat context. Then the unsyncopated strain B is actually in A major but modulates back unobtrusively at the half-way point to the D flat (as enharmonic C sharp major) but much more formally at the end of the strain, making a feature of it. Added sixth chords abound and there are whole-tone formations in the fourth phrase of strain A.

The *Parade of the Sandwich-Board Men* (1938), in C, is called *A Novelty in Syncopation*. As before, the introduction specializes in one type of chord—this time root positions, which dominate strains A and C in this breezy piece. *Railroad Rhythm* (1938), in A flat (CD 24) is a fine show-piece full of zest. Jill Mayerl thought it was 'one of the most difficult of Billy's numbers to play' but Mayerl would not have agreed.[23] In the *Billy Mayerl Club Magazine* in 1939 he spent some time explaining how easy it was, as long as you slide the same fingers from the second to the third chord in the first bar, where the cross-hand technique is worthy of Ravel.[24] The layout is more lavish than usual. The first four bars, repeated, function as an introduction: the sixteen-bar strain A is also obsessed with repeated F flats as blue notes. There are repeated-note D♭s inside the texture too. Strain B is in A flat major and bounces off after the first transition, which consists of repeated added-sixth chords. Strain B (0′ 21″) is forty bars and it plays off a helter-skelter descending phrase against a catchy repeated-note figure to splendid effect—just before the return within this strain there is a hilarious rush up landing on a repeated blue note marked 'harshly', which sounds like one of Mayerl's out-of-tune piano stunts. Strain C in E flat (0′ 50″) is followed by a second transition which consists of repeated chords of the kind that opened strain B, but these are now dominants to take us back to the repeat of strain B. Strain D (1′ 19″) follows, setting up a dramatic conflict between major chords of D and A and a persistent E♭ marked 'hammer'. This leads to a repeat of the introduction followed by eight bars of strain A plus more introduction petering out slowly. But this is still not the end—the second transition is followed by strain B again plus a sixteen-bar coda based on alternating major chords of D and A flat. Two throwaway soft guitar chords finish off on A flat major with added sixth. Mayerl's own stunning performance is very fast (about ♩ = 148) but very light and he does not play the last two chords softly, adding others.[25]

Song of the Fir Tree, dedicated to Mayerl's Swedish pupil Maj Lunden, is a special case, as Dr F. S. Mooney remembered in 1994:

[23] J. Mayerl, 'Titles', *Billy Mayerl Circle Newsletter*, 1/3 (Autumn 1974), 6–7.
[24] B. Mayerl, 'Tackling a new Solo', *BMCM* 6/61 (Jan. 1939), 23–4.
[25] B. Mayerl, *The King of Syncopation*, LP on WRC/EMI SH 189.

B.M. was, of course, a shrewd businessman. The best example of this concerns his composition *Song of the Fir Tree*. B.M. had been to Sweden and was having a drink in a café where a trio of musicians was playing. One tune particularly attracted him and without delay he made enquiries about its origin. He was told that it was a traditional folk-tune. He then asked if it was copyrighted. Apparently not. He at once proceeded, on returning to England, to remedy this by copyrighting it for himself as *Song of the Fir Tree*. The story was told by B.M. himself.[26]

In 1982 Elisabeth Söderström told me that this melody was a Swedish folk-song called 'Ack Värmeland du Sköna' probably imported from the Netherlands in the eighteenth century. The words by Anders Fryzell and F. A. Dahgren celebrate the beauties of the Swedish province to the west of Stockholm. Jussi Björling used to sing it and the most recent recording is by Tito Beltran.[27] Wherever the tune came from, Mayerl recognized in it something he could use—a truly memorable melody—so he transcribed it. The introduction to *Song of the Fir Tree* (1938), which is in G minor, is more elaborate than usual. Then the main theme, which might have been harmonized by Delius, has some Mayerl characteristics—it is economical in that the wide-ranging opening four-bar phrase is used twice, then there is a two-bar phrase in the relative major before the opening phrase is used yet again. This makes a thirteen-bar period since the last bar is the moment of style-modulation, where Mayerl swings perfectly naturally into the swung version of the tune. Four bars related to the introduction finish off. That moment of style-modulation is unforgettably dramatized by Mayerl himself on a rare film clip—he has a glass of something on the piano and takes a swig before launching into the syncopated idiom!

The Song of the Fir Tree was so successful that Leslie Osborne suggested it could be turned into a song and got Alan Stranks to write the lyric.[28] This version, transposed to D minor and published in 1946, does not use the swung section and there is nothing to be said for its sentimental story about a pine tree longing to find its lost lover someday in the form of a big ship's mast.

Jill Mayerl remembered the background to *The Harp of the Winds* (1939):

Billy seemed to see and find music in almost everything. During a night of storms, gales and blinding rain, the sort of weather which depresses me terribly, the trees in the garden seemed to be moaning and sighing, but to Billy it was music and he tried to explain to me that all the sounds were like notes being played on a harp in lovely arpeggios.[29]

[26] F. S. Mooney, 'Billy Mayerl: A few Notes', *Midland Gershwin Mayerl Society Magazine*, 26 (Feb. 1994).

[27] P. Dickinson, 'Style-Modulation: An Approach to Stylistic Pluralism', *Musical Times* (Apr. 1989) 208–11. Beltran recorded this melody on Silva Classics SILKD 6009 (1996).

[28] L. Osborne, interview with Peter Dickinson, 11 Aug. 1981.

[29] J. Mayerl, 'Titles', *Billy Mayerl Circle Newsletter*, 1/3 (Autumn 1974), 6–7.

The Harp of the Winds (CD 25) is dedicated to Mario Lorenzi who, in the 1920s played the harp for Fred Elizalde and his Music and for Jay Widden and his New Midnight Follies Band (doubling clarinet and alto sax) and was harp-director of Mario 'Harp' Lorenzi and his Rhythmics in the 1930s. Mayerl's piece for this unusual performer goes back to folk sources with a subtitle, *Aeolian Harp*, an instrument which was designed to sound when activated by wind, especially out of doors. Aeolus was the Greek god of the wind.

This is a resourceful piece where the decoration is always integral. As it happens *Aeolian Harp* starts with the last two guitar chords of *Railroad Rhythm*, at the same pitch too. The opening section expands these as parallel chords, mostly added sixths, and this time the cadenzas all belong to the conception. There is one in the whole-tone scale which comes back in the syncopated version. This is another piece with a style-modulation (1′ 32″) which arrives when this original material is turned into a Mayerl transcription—a very good one too, especially in Mayerl's own performance—and, as with *The Song of the Fir Tree*, there is an unsyncopated coda.

The decade of the 1930s saw Mayerl intensely preoccupied with West End shows, touring, and the Billy Mayerl School. It is astonishing that his solo piano works show continued momentum in the face of this hectic schedule. This pace was not maintained in the years during and after the war, when Mayerl again had to meet the requirements of the market by working as a conventional bandleader in wartime and as a provider of light music in all available channels.

12

THE 1940S AND 1950S

THE Second World War brought an increase in demand for music of all kinds, especially in London. Some of this was viewed as reflecting 'the emotional pressure of war' at a time when religious belief was declining.[1] Broadcasting had been and would continue to be responsible for vastly increased access to music, along with recordings and the teaching of musical appreciation in schools, evening classes, and on the radio. After the war universities in Britain set up music departments with full-scale degree courses; international festivals were started at Edinburgh and Aldeburgh; opera and ballet were revived and the BBC opened its Third Programme (now BBC Radio 3). By the time of the Festival of Britain in 1951, when the Royal Festival Hall was opened, there was much to celebrate in British music in spite of the general climate of austerity which lasted for several years after the war was over.

The production of Benjamin Britten's opera *Peter Grimes* at Sadler's Wells on 7 June 1945 took place only a month after the German surrender and has since become a symbolic landmark in British composition. This was the more remarkable since Britain had no continuous operatic tradition. From April 1939 Britten spent three years in America and his opera with W. H. Auden, *Paul Bunyan*, was produced in New York, although it was not recognized as a remarkable achievement until much later—notably the Covent Garden revival in 1998. *Paul Bunyan* reflected influences from the American popular music scene which gained currency throughout Mayerl's lifetime and have become part of universal culture. Looking back on a career in the music business, the publisher Ernest Roth observed: 'The new entertainment music was American, and hardly ever before had music been so dominated by one well-defined type. Projected by broadcasting and gramophone records, it achieved a popularity which far outstripped that of French and Viennese light music in their heyday.'[2] Towards the end of the War American service personnel were

---

[1] *Musical Britain 1951*, compiled by the Music Critic of *The Times* (OUP, Oxford, 1951), 6.
[2] E. Roth, *The Business of Music: Reflections of a Music Publisher* (Cassell, London, 1969), 247.

present in Britain in increasing numbers. Combined with Hollywood films this influx took further the process of Americanization which we have noticed as a special kind of cultural penetration from before the First World War and through the inter-war years. But Mayerl had responded to the first wave, was no longer in the main stream, and would have new priorities.

In many ways Mayerl's fortunes had started to decline in the late 1930s. The year 1937 was unpropitious for him. First, as Irene Ashton related, he was devastated by the death of Gershwin on 11 July; then his father died suddenly on 21 November; and finally his loyal supporter in the musical theatre, Laddie Cliff, died on 8 December. Mayerl's mother died the following year. The War was the next blow and there were even difficulties about broadcasting. Mayerl's career had been launched on his instant success through radio and his post-war career also has to be seen in the context of his BBC work of all kinds. But preparations for war, changes of taste, and possible over-exposure caused him to feel he was being neglected even by the BBC, which had been—and would remain—his lifeline. In January 1939 Mayerl was surprised to discover that his fee of 15 guineas [£580] was causing him to get fewer dates and so he agreed to reduce it to 10 guineas [£390].[3] It was not put back up until 1950.[4]

When war was declared as a result of Hitler's invasion of Poland on 3 September 1939, Mayerl, who was then still only 37, was turned down for active service but was anxious to contribute to the war effort, as Leslie Osborne remembered:

Bill went to an office in Whitehall, where they put the entertainment together. It was called Stars in Battle-dress, run by George Black's two sons. Billy Mayerl went along and was interviewed by a colonel. He said, 'I'd like to do something to help the war effort.' And the Colonel said: 'What do you think you can do?' So Billy said, 'Well, I can play the piano.' So the Colonel said: 'What good do you think that's going to do to the war effort?' So Bill said: 'Could I remind you, sir, that there was a very great pianist called Paderewski who became Prime Minister of Poland?' And the Colonel said to him: 'Yes, and look at Poland now![5]

Ignacy Jan Paderewski, perhaps the only musician to become a head of state, gave up music for politics to serve his country in the years of crisis around the First World War. He was Prime Minister and Foreign Minister in 1919 for less than a year and in 1922 resumed his concert career.

3 K. A. Wright, BBC memo to Arthur Wynn, 21 Jan. 1939.
4 B. Mayerl, letter from 505 Nelson House, Dolphin Square, London SW1 on 19 Jan. 1950 to Mr Carrell, which had a successful outcome. Mayerl apologizes for the lengthiness of his letter and his penultimate paragraph reads: 'During 25 years' association with the BBC I have done many hundreds of broadcasts and never once asked for any increase in fee. In view of this it seems a little ironical that for long, and if I may say so, conscientious service, I receive a lower fee than when I first started broadcasting.'
5 L. Osborne, interview with Peter Dickinson, 11 Aug. 1981.

During the Second World War, Osborne was Progress Manager at an aircraft factory:

I used to organize litle concerts in the canteen for the vast number of employees at lunch-time as a relief from the strain and fire-watching and one of the first to volunteer his services was—of course—Billy Mayerl, who would not even allow anyone to defray his expenses. The audience loved him. The famous bass, Norman Allin, was also on the bill and sang his wonderful version of Song of the Flea [Musorgsky, 1897]. Bill accompanied him—without rehearsal.[6]

Sheila Frankel, daughter of Mayerl's colleague George Myddleton, remembered his actual war work in 1940/1:

It was the river patrol, which was the naval version of Dad's Army. Uncle Billy, my father and George Clarke (the comedian with a monocle) and two other very boozy friends used to meet at Bett's Club, which was a private drinking club. After they'd had about an hour there, they would stagger over to Boulter's Lock and do their drill. Uncle Billy never knew what to do with a rifle. He'd have it upside down and round the back of his neck and that sort of thing. Then they would stagger onto their launch, which was supposed to patrol between Boulter's Lock and Cookham Lock and defend that stretch of the river. This was quite a long distance, but they would have been working I don't think they had to do this every night. They all had their little navy blue reefer jackets and their peak caps.[7]

For most of the war Mayerl's professional work gave him and his wife the luxury as well as the anxiety of living in a central London hotel. Sydney Lipton had a long reign leading his own band at Grosvenor House Hotel, Park Lane, from 1932 until well into the 1970s.[8] When Lipton left to join the army, where he acquired a distinguished record with the Royal Artillery in North Africa and Italy, Mayerl took over at Grosvenor House from 1940 to 1944. Billy Amstell, who was a saxophonist with the band in its early days under Lipton, described it as 'a typical society band of the 1930s, playing sweet music in a rather sedate manner, as required by the management, under soft lights in elegant surroundings'.[9] Leslie Osborne, and the band's recordings, confirm this

    [6] L.Osborne, 'Notes from our President', Billy Mayerl Circle Newsletter, 1/1 (Spring 1974), 2–3.

    [7] S. Frankel, interview with John Watson, 9 Feb. 1997.

    [8] S. Lipton, Obituary in The Times, 17 Aug. 1995. No mention of Mayerl's tenure at Grosvenor House.

    [9] B. Amstell, Don't Fuss, Mr. Ambrose: Memoirs of a Life Spent in Popular Music (Spellmount, Tunbridge Wells, Kent, 1986), 22. Amstell was not paid anything like members of the Savoy bands in the 1920s. Basic pay as second alto in 1930 was £10 [£365] a week rising in 1931 to £12 [£470] as first alto plus £3 [£118] for a weekly broadcast. This was comfortable compared with wartime fees for orchestral musicians, which dropped to £3 [£93] a week in the London Philharmonic Orchestra, according to Marie Goossens in Life on a Harp String (Thorne Printing and Publishing, London, 1987).

in almost identical terms: 'typical society music of the West End, quite good, very musical, intimate but no jazz'.[10]

As it happened, the Mayerls' suite at Grosvenor House was on the same floor as the one provided for General Dwight D. Eisenhower during the war and they used to meet. As part of her war work Mrs Mayerl used to help in the offices of the American Red Cross. One night she was asked if she could wait at table since some very important people were coming for dinner:

It turned out that the guest of honour was General Eisenhower himself. I was waiting at the top table and he turned and saw me. 'Good heavens, honey', he said in astonishment, 'what are you doing here?' Afterwards, whenever we met, he made a point of pausing for a chat, which was characteristic of the man. He was a born charmer and this 'brief encounter' is one I shall always cherish.[11]

During these war years Mayerl was under contract with Grosvenor House and the band had to be referred to as Billy Mayerl and his Grosvenor House Band, but he could get permission to broadcast and take outside dates. They made two records on 24 July 1941, the second of *Nola* and *Marigold*, a good pair.[12] Mayerl wrote signature tunes and was a regular on the BBC's *Music while you Work*. For one of these sessions, on 6 December 1941, Billy Mayerl and his Band were paid only £31 [£890] to cover eleven players and Mayerl himself. He also took part in tours to entertain the troops organized by ENSA.[13] One of his BBC trips was in Variety at Bangor, replacing Billy Ternant's Orchestra for two weeks, starting on 17 August 1941. Musicians were scarce in wartime, and it was difficult to get players to go out of town. Mayerl was paid only £275 [£7,900] to cover himself and a fifteen-piece band for the whole period and they had to provide their own accommodation, but not pay for travel. Apparently Geraldo would have cost £400 [£11,500] and Peter Yorke £300 [£8,600] so that Mayerl was competitive.[14] He had to be to survive:

I thoroughly enjoyed myself whilst in Bangor, although they worked me very hard— not so much on the playing or conducting side but I was grabbed by various producers to write interpolated numbers and also by Harry Pepper to do three shows for

[10] L. Osborne, interview with Peter Dickinson, 11 Aug. 1981.

[11] J. Mayerl, 'A Few Highlights', *Billy Mayerl Circle Newsletter*, 10/2 (Summer 1976), 6–8.

[12] Major G. C. S. Black, Managing Director of Grosvenor House, letter to BBC, 25 Aug. 1942. Billy Mayerl and his Grosvenor House Band made two records for Decca on 24 July 1941. See Discography for titles and personnel.

[13] CEMA (Council for the Encouragement of Music and the Arts) and ENSA (National Service Entertainments Association) were founded by the British government in 1940 to keep the arts alive in wartime and to entertain the troops wherever they were. See R. H. Myers, *Music since 1939* (British Council, London, 1947). CEMA became the Arts Council of Great Britain in 1945.

[14] A. Brown, BBC memo from Variety Booking Manager, 1 July 1941.

Bobby Howes. Anyway this kept me out of the pubs! and I very much enjoyed doing it.[15]

Mayerl and his band were again defended as competitive since they cost £56 [£1,600] whereas Geraldo would have been over £80 [£2,300]: 'Besides all this Billy Mayerl is, of course, a great personality at the piano and, as he is well known as a composer both of straight and swing music, has a wide appeal to the listening public.'[16] Mayerl's versatility was recognized but after the war there were internal queries at the BBC about whether he was including too much of his own music in his broadcast programmes. Figures were produced for the three months October, November, and December 1948 and the results were:

Billy Mayerl Rhythm Ensemble—15 Mayerl and 59 other composers.
Mayerl Music—30 Mayerl and 128 other composers.
Solos or with other orchestras—11 Mayerl and 14 other composers.

It was accepted that his was specialized repertoire and therefore justified.[17]

By 1954 an internal BBC memo reported: 'Still the inimitable stylist but the technical dexterity is not what it was. Over 5,000 broadcasts is not a bad record though!'[18]

We shall notice what Mayerl chose to play in his later years, when he was obviously less of a virtuoso, and his broadcast repertoire is analysed in Appendix 2. Some decline would not be surprising in view of constant concern about his health for the last fifteen years of his life. Mayerl's heart condition was likely to have been the product of consistent overwork from his early teens, although there may have been a hereditary weakness since both his father and his maternal grandfather died very suddenly. Mayerl had a year away ill, forbidden to touch a piano, from mid-1944 until he resumed broadcasting on 24 May 1945. This must have been very hard to take for a man used to such constant activity.[19] And he was also out of circulation for almost a year when he and Jill went to Australia and New Zealand, initially with Stanley Holloway, on 25 March 1949.

In 1953 Mayerl got into difficulties with the powerful Musicians Union as a result of not being a member. For a few weeks he was black-listed but then agreed to join.[20] In 1954 it was the state of his health that the *Melody Maker* rather sensationally brought into the news rather than anything else about

[15] B. Mayerl, letter from Grosvenor House to Arthur Wynn, 1 Sept. 1941.
[16] A. Hayes, BBC memo, 31 Aug. 1942.
[17] D. Lawrence, BBC memo to H.M., 20 Dec. 1948.
[18] H. M. Ricketts, BBC memo of 17 June 1954.
[19] B. Mayerl, letter to Stanford Robinson from Chellow Dene, Buccleuch Road, Bournemouth, 19 Apr. 1945.
[20] 'Billy Mayerl Black-Listed by Union', *Daily Mail*, 31 July 1953; 'Billy Mayerl to Fight Boycott', *Daily Mail*, 1 Aug. 1953; and letter from the Musicians Union to John Archer, 11 Dec. 1996, confirming that Mayerl joined on 31 August.

him. He was first reported as having had two heart attacks; then improving; and then 'Billy Mayerl worse'.[21]

There must have been overwhelming expressions of concern from friends since Jill Mayerl had this note printed:

18 Avenue Mansions: October 1954
Both Billy and myself have been deeply touched by the many kind letters and messages that we have received, so many in fact, that I could not answer them all personally. Will you please accept this little card, therefore, as an acknowledgement of your letter and our sincere thanks for your kind thoughts.
Yours sincerely,
[signed Mrs B. Mayerl][22]

The nature of Mayerl's public appeal in terms of his post-war image came through in a letter to the BBC from Elizabeth Henson, who ran a singing school in Hanover Square, London. Lionel Gamlin quoted some of her letter to Mayerl himself:

What I appreciate most about the Billy Mayerl broadcasts is the air of quiet refinement which creates a happy atmosphere and I am looking forward to the next series with much keen anticipation.

There must be hundreds of thousands like myself, who find great relaxation in a refined half-hour like that—lighter style, but so well done—and I only wish that we could have such refinement in other programmes.[23]

Gamlin joked about his 'Refined Friend' but Mayerl, perhaps aware that he had exchanged virtuosity for refinement, was not too happy about his performance in that *Showboat Variety* programme: 'I didn't feel at my best on this trip as you know so please forgive me if all was not just that 100% I would like to have given you. Between now and Easter I'll go into training and then—no more wrong notes!'[24]

Elizabeth Henson was extolling very precisely the virtues of Mayerl in his newer role as a purveyor of light music, undemanding to listen to and exquisitely done. As Stephen Banfield explained in 1995:

It was not a matter of style, still less of mood—light music can be sad or cheerful, active or passive—but of stance. The one thing light music mustn't do is argue with you, be dialectical, protest, ask you questions. It must seem to reflect your mood, not try to change it, so that enthusiasm or calm is irresistible.[25]

[21]   *Melody Maker*, 11, 18, and 25 Dec. 1954.
[22]   Copy in BBC archives.
[23]   L. Gamlin, letter to Mayerl, 16 June 1951.
[24]   B. Mayerl, letter from 18 Avenue Mansions, Finchley Road, London NW3, to Lionel Gamlin on 15 Jan. 1951.
[25]   S. Banfield, *The Light Brigade*, first of four programmes for BBC Radio 3, first broadcast on 2, 9, 16, and 33 Aug. 1995.

Banfield admired William McNaught's 'nutshell definition' of light music as 'the kind for which Brahms won't do' and aptly went on to point out that British light music was written by 'top-grade professional musicians' who worked to 'impeccable technical standards'.

Mayerl increasingly identified himself with this British light music scene since he had watched the vogue for syncopation subside and a mass youth culture was exploding into rock 'n' roll. The context for light music in the first half of the twentieth century in Britain was that of incidental music for the theatre, ballet music, the musical life of seaside resorts with their municipal orchestras, and then BBC radio. Mayerl took part in the founding of the Light Music Society on 29 April 1957 and when Roy Plomley introduced him on his *Desert Island Discs* radio programme in the following year he described him in terms of his post-war image as 'a very popular composer of light music'.[26] The President of the Light Music Society was Eric Coates, the supreme exponent of the genre, succeeded after his death in the following year by Anthony Collins; the Chairman was Harry Dexter; and Mayerl was Vice-Chairman and Editor of the *Light Music Magazine*. The objects of the Society were: 'To foster the interests of Light Music throughout the world. To obtain increased facilities for those interested in this form of culture by means of broadcasting, recording and general performances.'[27] The magazine's format resembled the familiar pre-war *Billy Mayerl Club Magazine* with interviews, correspondence, cartoons, lists of members, competitions, annual dinners, and some justified special pleading.

The philosophy behind the venture was significant because Mayerl again allied himself with a cause and a type of musical expression located between classical music and jazz: 'The sober fact is that Light Music is in danger, not from direct assault, but from the fact that the lover of Light Music has no-one to speak for him. There are many societies for serious music and many for jazz but until now, none for Light Music.'[28] This campaign fitted in with Mayerl's work in light music for two contracted periods at the BBC on either side of the Australian visit of 1949–50. As part of his job he played with various groups, wrote signature tunes and made arrangements, many of which have not survived.

Mayerl's editorial in the first number of the the *Light Music Magazine* was an idealistic attempt to goad the obviously apathetic members into action at the start of what he envisaged as a campaign. Light music may not be dialectical in itself but Mayerl was starting with a polemic. But by the third issue of the

---

[26] B. Mayerl, interview with Roy Plomley.

[27] B. Mayerl, 'What is the Light Music Society's Programme?', *Light Music Magazine*, 1/1 Sept. 1957, 3.

[28] B. Mayerl, 'Why a Light Music Society?', ibid.

magazine British Light Music had sustained a blow—the death of Eric Coates, the Society's President. In a lyrical obituary editorial Mayerl set Coates's achievement into a contemporary context that he now found so totally uncongenial that it tempted him into grotesque exaggeration:

Jazz, jive, bebop, boogie, rock 'n' roll, and skiffle, all at some time or other reared their ugly heads only to die an early death because of their musical limitations and meaningless banalities. What further musical monstrosities are in store for us, I cannot say but no matter what foul noises find their way over from the USA and, while each horror lives its short and ill-conceived life, Eric Coates' music will live on for years to come.[29]

Mayerl was right to celebrate Coates's achievements. In a sense he was paying back earlier compliments from Coates, who said in 1937 that he remembered dancing to his playing with the Savoy Havana in 1925, had the greatest admiration for him as pianist and composer, and possessed every Billy Mayerl record.[30] But in his assessment of the musical world in 1957 Mayerl was looking backwards. Influences from America once launched him but their successors only two generations later were viewed as malign.

However, as with those first broadcasts in 1923, Mayerl was still in on some of the latest developments, appearing intermittently on BBC TV from 1937, although transmission ceased during the war. Some of his programmes were specially for children. But by 1958 it was felt that 'his own piano playing, though slick and accurate, has a certain monotony of tone and colour'. The idea was to use Billy Mayerl's Rhythm Players on TV instead and to suggest this deliberately in order to encourage him during what turned out to be his final illness.[31]

This generous proposal came from Kenneth Wright, who had moved from radio to TV, but had loyally supported Mayerl throughout the difficult years of struggle against illness and changing fortunes. All who value what Mayerl composed in his last two decades must pay tribute to his friends at the BBC. He would have collapsed earlier without them. It was the BBC that created unique opportunities for Mayerl in 1923 and it is to the eternal credit of this institution that it went on supporting him almost to the end.

When it comes to Mayerl's compositions of the 1940s and 1950s, there are

---

[29] B. Mayerl, 'From the Editor's Chair', *Light Music Society Magazine*, 1/3 (Mar. 1958), 4. See also: J. F. Archer, 'Billy Mayerl, Light Music Crusader', *Billy Mayerl Society Magazine*, No. 4 (Jan. 1996), 18–21, and 'The Light Music Society', *Billy Mayerl Society Magazine*, No. 8 (Feb. 1998), 3–5. The Light Music Society continued its activities sporadically into the mid-1970s and today exists as a Library of Light-Orchestral Music. This is held at the home of the Chairman, Ernest Tomlinson, Lancaster Farm, Chipping Lane, Longridge, Preston, Lancs. PR3 2NB.

[30] J. Butcher, 'Radiolympia 1937: A Review of the Show and Exhibition', *BMCM*, 4/45 (Sept. 1937), 4.

[31] K. A. Wright, BBC TV memo, 5 Nov. 1958.

fewer of them but their quality usually stands up. The decade opens with a set of four witty pieces called *Insect Oddities* (1940).[32] No. 1: *Wedding of an Ant* (CD 26) is marked 'Lightly and brightly' and is dominated by consistently dotted rhythms in repetitive figures. The C strain (0′ 36″) contains patches of rhythmic dislocation in triplets, which are a typical gesture. Mayerl's own recording of the first three pieces makes cuts in the repeats. No. 2: *Ladybird Lullaby* (CD 27) is marked unusually 'Allegretto con espressione e rubato'. This is a nostalgic waltz in D for that most elegant of insects, with much play on the barbershop key relationship. The main theme is treated with various decorations and an indulgent number of repetitions, which are convincing with the rubato style Mayerl employs for once. The middle section (0′ 40″) is distinctly Viennese with hesitations, melodies doubled in thirds, and accelerations which Mayerl pushes almost to the limits. This section climaxes with the opening theme again, thus anticipating its return at the start of the final section proper (1′ 25″). This piece is dedicated to Mayerl's old friend, John Dargie, whose widow's reminiscences have been valuable.[33] No. 3: *Praying Mantis* (CD 28), in E flat, has a thoroughly catchy A strain, anticipated in the four-bar introduction, which sports melodic split notes and slides. The main theme is underpinned by the same I–VI–II–V progression as *Marigold*. It all works so well that Mayerl changes his routine and simply makes a variation of the first strain, transposed to G major, to create the B strain (0′ 31″). He does the same thing when he repeats and varies the C strain (0′ 56″) to create the D strain (1′ 22″), but most of this is cut in Mayerl's own performance which has all his inimitable swing. No. 4: *Beetle in the Bottle* (CD 29) is a study in varied metres and could almost be by Bartok. The central section (0′ 19″) is based on the usual 3+3+2 rumba but for the outside ones the main unit is 3+3+2+2. The A sections in the A–B–A scheme are bitonal and Mayerl himself played the conflicting left hand absolutely *staccatissimo*. Mrs Mayerl wrote of this piece:

It needs very little imagination to actually see that poor frenzied beetle trying to get out of the bottle, but Billy would never have allowed it to stay there. He would have got it out somehow for he loved all animals, insects and birds and would even let snakes coil around him. It used to terrify me but he seemed to have some sort of rapport with them.[34]

---

[32] *Insect Oddities* (1940), No. 2 (KP 6059) seems to have been published first with the others following as No. 4 (KP 6062), No. 3 (KP 6063) and No. 1 (KP 6064).

[33] Major H. H. Dargie and his wife Doris both joined the Light Music Society in 1957. He was a friend of Mayerl's from the 1930s and she remained a friend of Mrs Mayerl's until her death. Mrs Dargie was included in Peter Dickinson's BBC Radio 3 documentary *Billy Mayerl: A Formula for Success*, produced by Derek Drescher with technical assistance from Robin Cherry, first broadcast on 11 Feb. 1996 and repeated on 24 Aug.

[34] J. Mayerl 'Titles', *Billy Mayerl Circle Newsletter*, 1/3 (Autumn 1974), 6–7.

The cover designer of the sheet music has caught the beetle's predicament, looking through the transparent bottle's concentric circles, in a style which anticipates the op-art movement.

From the same year, *Leprechaun's Leap* (1940) is dedicated to Stanford Robinson, who was conductor of the BBC theatre orchestra at the time: there is a piano solo version but the orchestration is by Arthur Wood. The melodies are modal in the manner of the British folk-song school of composers and this is Mayerl's fluent light-music mode with the pigmy sprite of folklore reflected in an Irish reel. There is a gap in piano pieces until *Fireside Fusiliers* (1943), which is again called a novelty piano solo. In 1974 Jill Mayerl explained its genesis: '*Fireside Fusiliers* was actually inspired when Winston Churchill was making one of his profound speeches during the war in which he used the phrase "Fireside Fusiliers". Billy was very excited and said: "Oh, what a wonderful title he has given me, I must use it!" And he did just that.'[35]

It perhaps needs explaining that Churchill, as Prime Minister and a great war leader, maintained contact with the entire population and the world outside through the medium of radio. He delivered his oratorical broadcasts to a nation which, in the winter and before the days of central heating, would literally have been listening at the fireside. Further, the principal radio in the house at that time was a focus for the entire household before transistors gave every member the chance to listen to their own programme choices wherever they happened to be. *Fireside Fusiliers* was written in this context and is a very strong piece, where Mayerl sprang into action, glad to be doing something related to the war. After an introduction of bugle-calls and a till-ready, the bouncy, irrepressible A strain melody in F takes over. After this there is a quote of 'Come to the cookhouse door, boys' leading to the lovely B strain in the barbershop-related key of D flat—a kind of Puccini melody doubling its treble in the bass. Alan Nichols made a bright orchestration.[36]

When Mayerl was ill in 1944/5, although not allowed to play the piano, he did compose, as he explained to Stanford Robinson:

Although I have done no playing I have, however, idled away my time writing and amongst other things I have completed a poem for piano and orchestra. It is called *The Forgotten Forest*, plays about eleven minutes and—strange to say—it is completely free from the jazz idiom!

Hence my reason for writing to you. I would so much like to do a first performance with you. The score and parts are all ready—may I send them to you? Keith Prowse have published it and saying so 'as shouldn't' I think it is the best 'opus' I have yet 'scraped' together.[37]

---

[35] Ibid.

[36] B. Mayerl, *Fireside Fusiliers*, on *British Light Music: Billy Mayerl*, Slovak Radio Symphony Orchestra/Carpenter on Marco Polo 8.223514.

[37] B. Mayerl, letter to Stanford Robinson, cited in n. 19.

It is worth comparing *The Forgotten Forest* with *Sennen Cove* written sixteen years earlier. Both pieces are in what Mayerl considered an appropriate idiom for serious music, although we can now identify it in terms of his light music allegiances. Whereas his early piano solos and transcriptions created an individual style, related to his own inimitable delivery and with many fingerprints, his more serious pieces simply arise out of common practice between Grieg and Rachmaninov—the light music approach. The emphasis in *The Forgotten Forest* is on the romantic concerto personality of the instrument in an orchestral context with gestures reflecting the past. The ambience is close to the film music of the period—a kind of Metro-Goldwyn Mayerl—especially *The Warsaw Concerto* by Richard Addinsell, derived from the film, *Dangerous Moonlight* (1941), where it was played by Louis Kentner. But as usual everything is clearly imagined and *The Forgotten Forest* is more coherent structurally than *Sennen Cove* and more thematically ingenious. But there has been no development in style and these pieces of the post-war years confirm that Mayerl was employing the idioms current in conservative circles soon after the turn of the century, plus the occasional bitonal chord from the Ravel of *Jeux d'eaux* or the Stravinsky of *Petrushka*.

The Forgotten Forest starts with an unaccompanied modal flute melody which acts as a motto for the whole piece. A rhetorical version of this brings in the piano and leads to some obvious solo passage-work moving towards the Andante moderato where the orchestra takes a flowing version of the motto into a longer continuous section. A second theme is not easily identified at first but one gradually emerges in an improvisatory fashion. When the motto comes back at *più mosso*, phrases from what has become a second theme are interspersed to create the climax at *molto allargando* with a touch of bitonal harmony.

The *Scherzando con licenza* is then a transformed version of the motto. With its bass drone of recurring perfect fifths and modal melodic cast, Grieg is not far away. The *tranquillo* is constantly melodic and memorable, with all its climaxes well paced, the last one before the coda landing on superimposed chords of C and F sharp major with related arpeggios to follow. On its own terms and within its limitations, *The Forgotten Forest* is like a mini-concerto that makes all its effects with skill. One can see why Mayerl was proud of it—he really had done something that other composers of novelty piano or popular songs could not have done. He might have gone further, but now it was too late.

Both *The Forgotten Forest* and *Minuet for Pamela* (1945) are available as a piano solo and in an orchestral version, presumably made by Mayerl himself at a period when recuperation gave him more time for such things. The *Minuet*, for Mayerl's god-daughter who was christened Pamela Marigold, is in a chaste, classical D major that goes back to even earlier sources than

Grieg.[38] *Minuet by Candlelight* (1956) uses similar basic diatonic materials, again with modal touches. *April's Fool* (1945), like *Postman's Knock* (1951) and *Beguine Impromptu* (1952), are rapid studies—and unsyncopated. *Crystal Clear* (1954) is another example of this style and in 1974 Jill Mayerl remembered how it came to be composed:

Crystal Clear is one of my favourites, and by sheer accident I chose the title. Billy had been playing, or as I called it 'meandering' at the piano for hours and kept on coming back again and again to a few particular bars and it sounded so fascinating I felt I could not wait to know what it was. The dexterity and clarity of every note was marvellous. I was intrigued, although I was so used to his playing, and I think he saw how I felt. He said: 'Do you like it?' I answered: 'Yes, but it sounds so difficult, not many will be able to play it'. 'But that's just it,' he said. 'Music mustn't always be easy, it must be a challenge. Now, what shall we call it, what does it sound like to you?' And for once I said the right thing. 'It sounds so crystal clear, would that be a good title?' So *Crystal Clear* it became.[39]

Evening Primrose (1946) in G, another floral title, is a perfectly turned salon piece which Cécile Chaminade could not have improved upon. It has the same type of sectional layout as Mayerl's novelty pieces and a most attractive way of dealing with the chromatically inflected third degree of the scale, usually rising but sometimes falling like a blue note. This gives the piece its capricious mood. *Shy Ballerina* (1948), also in G, has some of the same qualities of tender charm. Jill Mayerl remembered this piece too:

This title was suggested by a little girl who was asked to dance for Billy but was too shy. Just about the time he wrote this, he was asked to do a TV programme on the BBC and decided it would make a good production number. The programme was most effective with Billy at the piano and a miniature ballerina dancing on the lid. There were some wonderful shots of Billy's hands which I shall never forget.[40]

Much more ambitious is a set of five pieces called *The Big Top* (1948)—possibly a response to Stravinsky's *Petrushka*, which Mayerl had long admired, rather than Satie's *Parade*, or even a backward glance at the grandfather who played in a circus. In *The Big Top* Mayerl is well up to his old form with much more adventurous harmonies than his now accustomed light-music idiom. The conventional rag-derived framework has been expanded with uneven numbers of bars in each strain.[41] The first piece, *The*

[38] J. Mayerl, 'More Titles and Stories', *Billy Mayerl Circle Newsletter*, 1/4 (Winter 1974), 6–8.
[39] J. Mayerl, 'Titles', *Billy Mayerl Circle Newsletter*, 1/3 (Autumn 1974), 6–7.
[40] J. Mayerl, 'More Titles and Stories' as n. 38.
[41] B. Mayerl, *The Big Top*. It is worth noting the numbers of bars in each strain. No. 1, *The Ringmaster* (Intro.8–A19–B32–A17), has an unbalanced A strain with cross-rhythms which is 19 bars at first and 17 on its return. There are glissando melodic decorations in the B strain, which is in the form of a 32-bar popular song. In the second piece, *Clowning* (Intro.4–A16–B8–A8–

Ringmaster, has dissonant fanfares based on triads a tritone apart and the B strain is in the form of a thirty-two-bar popular song, with a pianistic layout very typical of Mayerl. The whole movement has an air of exuberance which Mayerl had mostly lost at this stage. The second piece, *Clowning*, is just that and there are quotations of three nursery rhymes in the C strain. The third piece, *Entrance of the Trick Cyclists*, is plainly diatonic but ventilated with comic whole-tone passages and, again, barbershop harmony. Much of this movement is built on pedal-points of tonic or dominant. The fourth piece, *Dancing Horse*, is elegant and the middle section quotes a hunting call as a reminder of a horse's life outside the circus. There is no slow movement as such—the pace of a circus was probably too busy—and finally *Trapeze* is a conventional type of toccata. *Big Top* is a well-balanced, eleven-minute concert suite which would fit easily into any piano recital. Unfortunately the composer never recorded it.

At the same time Mayerl did not neglect amateurs. He wrote four suites of three pieces each, one for each of the seasons, all called *In my Garden* (1946–7), reflecting a special interest of his.[42] From his wide experience of teaching Mayerl offers encouragement to beginners in the form of suggested fingering for the *In my Garden* pieces and explains in a prefatory note to *Wintertime*:

'Syncopated' music, in the sense of the word, has long been beyond the technical ability of the average amateur or beginner chiefly because of large left-hand stretches, intricate right-hand cadences, placing or I should say misplacing of accents the awkward 'jumps' covering most of the keyboard which are assumed necessary to display an individual style. In writing these little pieces I have endeavoured to avoid all these difficulties without losing to any large degree the desired effect.

C32–A16), the Introduction and A strain in F set the scene with dotted notes and triplets with an offbeat left hand. The B strain is half new material and half a repeat of A. But the C strain in D flat starts close to the short B strain but soon interpolates quotations—'Pop goes the Weasel', 'Here we go gathering nuts in May', and 'Three Blind Mice'—before the A strain returns.

The third piece is *Entrance of the Trick Cyclists* (Intro.4–A31–B36–A30–Coda14). The plain A flat major of the Introduction and strain A is set against links in the whole-tone scale involving flat sixth harmony. Much play is made of this in the coda, reached via an interrupted cadence. The B strain, also in A flat, is built entirely over pedal-points of tonic or dominant. The right-hand chords exploit secundal dissonances and in bar 16 the tonic chord actually contains both its major and minor third. No. 4, *Dancing Horse*, is in C (A18–B16–A18), and the middle section surely quotes the bugle-call from 'A-hunting we will go'. Finally, *Trapeze* (Intro.8–A16–B8–C8–Intro. 4–A16–C32+20+24–Intro.4–A16–Coda3) is virtually a *moto perpetuo*, especially its introduction and A strain which anticipate *Look Lively* in the same key of A. But the C strain, in D, is an extended toccata based on the kind of figuration that ends Franck's Prelude, Chorale and Fugue or, more likely, the finale of Gershwin's Piano Concerto.

  42 B. Mayerl, *In my Garden* was also the title of a record he made for Columbia on 19 May 1939 (see Discography). These are medleys to get all the tunes onto one side and *Marigold* is at top speed.

These are charming miniatures, written during 1946 and 1947, which look back to the various styles of Mayerl's great days now scaled down for children and what was left of the purely domestic market. *Japonica*, in the *Summertime* set, starts by quoting Mayerl's silly song 'Two of everything' from *Nippy* and *Alpine Bluebell* quotes the 'Swiss Yodelling Song'. All three pieces of the *Autumntime* group manage to do exactly what they set out to do, recalling Mayerl's rhythmic gambits and personal turns of phrase but all in miniature: *Amber Leaves* has a seriousness not always found in Mayerl's earlier lyrical pieces—in this key of A minor the mood is close to Gershwin's 'Summertime' (*Porgy and Bess*, 1935). *Christmas Rose* in the *Wintertime* set echoes the dotted rhythms of that old novelty war-horse, *Nola*. These are outstanding teaching pieces with real musical rewards—but inexplicably unknown, lost to generations of beginners, young or old.

Two curiosities from this period are for violin and piano: *Caprinella* (1951) for Reg Leopold; and *Blue Shadows*, probably for Max Jaffa, who broadcast it on 29 December 1953.[43] Reginald Leopold had a role in *Caprinella*:

At one period I was living right opposite Hendon Way on Finchley Road, Hampstead, and he'd moved into Avenue Mansions, which was about 200 yards down Finchley Road. I remember one morning, quite early—about 10.00 o'clock—there was a ring on the bell. It was Billy on the doorstep—unusual. 'I've come to see you because I've got something for Jeanne', my wife. 'I've just made some fudge'—he'd found out that she liked fudge. Whilst he was there he said: 'By the way, I'd like you to come back with me to the flat. I've just got the idea of writing a tune for you and I'd like you to come and see if everything's possible before I really finalise it'. So I went over there and played it over with him, looking over his shoulder. He had a wonderful flair: that was a different kind of music that didn't have any offbeat! In some way he reminded me of the lightness of Cécile Chaminade, although of course he was more inclined to get rhythmic. She had a style of her own in light music—*Autumn* was a bit more stormy here and there—otherwise she has a lot of tunes which could almost be Billy Mayerl.[44]

Caprinella could certainly have been a *morceau de salon* for the same market so stylishly supplied by Chaminade and with the same easy appeal as Elgar's *Salut d'Amour*, Op.12 (1888) all more than half a century earlier. There is certainly a suggestion of Elgar here, and even more in *Wonderment*, No. 3 of the orchestral suite *Moods in Contrast* (1954), in the same key written at the same period. *Caprinella* is touching in its use of the memorable tune and the predictable gesture: the solitary deviation from diatonic A major and its related keys is early on where the piano moves modally to a chord of G.

Blue Shadows, marked 'Andante cantabile' and also in A, is an eloquent piece

43 M. Jaffa, obituary in *The Times*, 1 Aug. 1991.
44 R. Leopold, interview with Peter Dickinson, 8 Aug. 1994.

which was published in the composer's arrangement for piano solo in 1954.[45] Jaffa played the violin and piano version beautifully, but in 1996 Reginald Leopold did not remember the piece at all.[46] Arrangements were made almost at once for brass band, trumpet/cornet and piano, and harmonica and piano, but there is not much for the piano to do in the original version. The opening theme seems to be a final tribute to Gershwin since the first six notes are the same as 'Love walked in' (*Goldwyn Follies*, 1938): then Mayerl's melody reaches upwards in different ways each time. The middle section is a kind of gypsy dance derived from Grieg. It climaxes in A minor, again inescapably recalling the rhetorical gestures and actual octave passage-work of the Grieg concerto and going back to that early appearance as a child at Queen's Hall. Mayerl's career has almost come full circle.

Look Lively (1952) is really Mayerl's answer to Zez Confrey's *Dizzy Fingers* (1923), just as breathless and in the same key of A. It was written as a signature tune for the BBC Radio feature *Hullo There!* and falls neatly into rag form.[47] The C strain is another thirty-two-bar popular song, set in the tenor register of the piano's left hand: its third and fourth bars charmingly shift up a semitone from D to E flat, colouring the melody unexpectedly.

Mayerl's association with his principal publisher, Keith Prowse, started in 1922 with the song 'Longing for You' and ended with *Balearic Episode* in 1954. The firm steadfastly supported him for over thirty years, a relationship of major importance in enabling Mayerl to reach his public. The colourful artwork on the published sheet music was typical of the period and often a neat reflection of the spirit of the music as well. For the last five years of his life Mayerl's work was spread over eleven different publishing houses. There must have been more pieces in manuscript: much has been lost in the bombing and elsewhere. For example, it never occurred to Mayerl to keep the manuscripts of his transcriptions once they were published, as Irene Ashton has confirmed.[48]

Balearic Episode is another piece for piano and orchestra but, at seven minutes, shorter than *Forgotten Forest*. The gestures are the same—this time there

---

45   B. Mayerl, *Blue Shadows*—the whole-tone chord in bar 2 of the four-bar introduction becomes a diminished seventh in the actual theme and the barbershop chord on the flat sixth is still present, featuring as its own dominant for a moment in the third bar of the introduction and creating an incident with an interrupted cadence five bars before the end.

46   R. Leopold, telephone conversation with Peter Dickinson, 27 Aug. 1996.

47   *Hullo There!* BBC Light Programme series first broadcast on 1 June 1952, 9.30–10.00, pre-recorded 29 May.

48   *BMCM*, 6/67 (July 1939), 9. According to Dr Richard Head, Mrs Mayerl gave a quantity of her husband's music to the BBC in 1959. On 14 Dec. 1972 Mr and Mrs R. W. Howarth, members of the Billy Mayerl Circle, listed 271 items. This collection is now lost, but their catalogue can be seen at the BBC Library. It shows what sheet music Mayerl possessed and how much arranging he did during his time at the BBC, including work for his own groups.

Ex. 13. Mayerl, Theme from *Balearic Episode* (1954)

are two *scherzando* sections—but the big tune in the middle has a splendid sweep to it (Ex. 13).

The first two bars rise up to a flattened leading-note but the next two bars correct that with a modulation to the dominant that might have come from Grieg. Three diatonic sequences follow: then, in the last bar here, there is a reference to the flattened leading-note in the harmony before the return to the opening phrase. Since Mayerl has been accused of not being able to write a memorable tune, this is a relevant example. The melody is almost as distinctive as the E major tune at the centre of *Rhapsody in Blue* and has a similar repetitive phrase structure, but the flat seventh now feels more like English modality than African American blues.

Mayerl's last orchestral piece is *Beyond the Hills* (1959). It consists of an Aeolian mode melody that could even be a folk-tune and the overall effect is very close to Vaughan Williams—at his best. There is also a recently discovered manuscript section of a collaborative work completed, apparently, two days before Mayerl died. This is a three-minute Finale from a work called *Alliance Variations*, where the first two movements were *Theme*, by Arthur Duckworth, and *Jig*, by Robert Docker. The *Alliance Variations* are recognizably the more bombastic orchestral Mayerl but there are some harmonic fingerprints too.[49]

Filigree (1955) is dedicated to Alfred Lancaster, who ran the Manchester branch of the pre-war Billy Mayerl School and was a teacher and Director of the revived School in London in the 1950s. It is a resourceful piece, another example where the tune is played straight then followed by a style-modulation to the swung version. It starts with a free introduction containing rhetorical statements and cadenzas based on superimposed arpeggios of major chords a tritone apart. The Andante section is as elaborate as the piece's title suggests and it is followed by the swung version marked 'slowly (strictly rhythmic)', with chordal juxtapositions derived from the bitonality of the introduction, but outlining the familiar I–VI–II–V bass pattern. Once again, and for the last time, the formula works.

By comparison *Sussex Downs*, labelled a gay gavotte, is routine—Mayerl made the orchestral version himself—and there is nothing distinctive about the waltz, *Vienna Story* (1958), which is Viennese in the usual ways. But *Funny Peculiar* (1957), marked 'With a lazy lilt', has real Mayerl character. Its A strain employs again the I–VI–II–V chord sequence which we noticed in *Marigold* thirty years earlier, which later gained wider currency through songs like 'Blue Moon' (1934) by Rodgers and Hart, or the instrumental interlude in Gershwin's *Shall we Dance* (1936) which became the piano solo, *Promenade*, or the last movement of Milhaud's *Scaramouche*.[50] The opening bars of the introduction set the mood so perfectly that Mayerl cannot resist using them for the central section too—naturally enough in the barbershop key relationship yet again. *Funny Peculiar* is a relaxed example of the kind of enjoyment which is the essence of Mayerl's music—the magic was still there.

The last piano piece we shall consider, although not the last chronologically,

---

49 B. Mayerl, Finale from *Alliance Variations* (1959), a synthesizer realization on cassette supplied by the Billy Mayerl Society with its Magazine No. 5 (Sept. 1996).

50 There are classical precedents for this chord progression too. George Pratt, in *The Dynamics of Harmony* (Open University, Milton Keynes, 1984), 38, cites the opening of the first movement of Mozart's Piano Sonata K 333, and there is, of course, 'God save the Queen' ('My Country 'tis of Thee').

is *Jill all Alone* (1955), with an uncomfortably prophetic title as Mrs Mayerl knew:

Very few people have heard of this number for the simple reason that nobody would play it. Now Billy had written violin solos especially for Reg Leopold and Max Jaffa who were both great friends of ours. *Jill all alone*, although composed for the piano, would have made a perfect violin solo for either of these performers, but both were adamant and would not even listen to it. The reason? They did not like the title.

I must add here that I was very disappointed personally. Billy had written it specially for me saying, 'It is so easy that even you could play it!' Also, incidentally, all the royalties it accrued were to be mine, which sounded very exciting at the time! That was just something which never came off.[51]

Since Jill was left alone for twenty-five years after her husband's death, the situation is desperately poignant. It must have been far worse for their close friends who could see the inevitable end coming. No wonder nobody would play a piece with such a title. The layout is: Introduction–A–A–B–B extended to climax–A–A–Coda based on B. It is very much Mayerl's G major mood, with the first four-bar phrase of strain A based on the same progression as *Evening Primrose*, with its rising chromatic bass-line. The Introduction is sixteen bars and draws on Mayerl's cadenza manner, but all in proportion. The climax is an almost Tchaikovskian outburst (Ex. 14).

As usual Mayerl never puts a foot wrong harmonically. This passage goes through the circle of fifths from C sharp–F sharp–B–E–A–D and then, quite unexpectedly, the raised fifth (enharmonically notated as flat sixth) on the dominant is harmonized as E flat minor leading back to the G major melody.

It may not be going too far to read this moment as an acute personal statement, at a time when Mayerl's fortunes were in terminal decline. His health was going, he had lost his publisher, things were less easy at the BBC, but Jill was still there. *Jill all Alone* was part of his legacy, which she and their friends understood. On its own terms and as a tribute to a remarkable woman, it is as far removed as possible from being 'something which never came off'.

We have already noticed the effect that the Grieg Piano Concerto had on Mayerl, probably the result of that childhood performance. It even affected his use of its key, A minor. Now that most of Mayerl's output has been considered, it is easy to trace key associations more widely. As might be expected from such a positive personality, he was abundantly a major key composer. Excluding pieces, or sets of pieces, which begin and end in different keys and not including the sets of studies, it is possible to come to certain conclusions. Mayerl used only four minor keys and of these only G minor and A minor were used more than once. The commonest keys, all major, are G followed by A flat,

---

[51] J. Mayerl, 'Titles', *Billy Mayerl Circle Newsletter*, 1/4 (Winter 1974), 7.

Ex. 14. Mayerl, *Jill all Alone* (1955)

E flat, and C; then A and F with all others very occasionally employed. Mayerl obviously associated certain moods with specific keys since there are similar-ities between pieces in the same key which causes them to emerge as members of the same family.

Taking matters further, Mayerl said he associated keys with colour, as he ad-mitted in response to a question in the *BMCM* in 1934:

Most certainly there is a distinct connection between colour and music. Although I have never found that a complete piece of music suggests any definite colour, I certainly have my own colour scheme for the notation on the keyboard. For instance, C is a very pale brown, D pale blue, E red, F mauve, G green, A yellow and B cream. I find that sharps and flats are a little darker or lighter, as the case may be. Although, no doubt, this is only my peculiar 'madness', I feel sure that other people, too, have their own views on this colour question.[52]

Mayerl was right that the whole question is impossibly subjective. For example, the C major that Mayerl found very pale brown was white for Rimsky-Korsakov and red for Scriabin. Mayerl found E major to be red but the two Russians were in agreement that it was blue.[53] But this does not invalidate the unusually clear connections between Mayerl's works in the same keys and the significance of his own preferences for specific major keys. These help to make his output coherent in an unusual way for a composer in the field of popular music.

[52] B. Mayerl, 'Members Air their Views', *BMCM* 1/6 (June 1934), 7.
[53] P. Scholes, 'Colour and Music', *Oxford Companion to Music* (OUP, London 1975), 204.

13

The Man and his Legacy

ONE distinctive feature about Mayerl is that he was both a pre-eminent performer and a composer of a considerable body of music. This is what sets him apart from other novelty pianists who merely wrote a few numbers. When Mayerl's piano music emerged onto CD in the 1980s and 1990s, it looked like the discovery of a neglected and somewhat isolated figure. He was not neglected, as his Performing Right Society income shows (Appendix 3), and in the 1920s and 1930s there were other performers on the flourishing British scene each with their own individuality. One of the most remarkable was the short-lived Raie da Costa, born in Cape Town and trained there and in London. In a radio interview in 1952, when most listeners would have forgotten who Da Costa was, Mayerl seemed pleased to mention her as an old pupil.[1] As a pianist with a classical background Da Costa emphasized the right hand with scintillating flourishes and she employed more rubato than Mayerl ever did. Boosey published her set of *Modernistic Pieces for the Piano* in 1930. The first of these, *Moods*, functions as variations on the initial Andante, ingeniously turning it into waltz and foxtrot versions and ending with a flourish. Da Costa had real personality as a performer but lacked the ragtime connections that were such a firm foundation for most of Mayerl, either as a performing tradition with strong rhythmic backing from the left hand or as a compositional approach based on sixteen-bar strains. Another woman pianist of this period was Patricia Rossborough. Like Da Costa she made about 100 records and published three novelties of her own. She was born in Dublin and like Mayerl, her exact contemporary, started young. She won a scholarship to the Birmingham School of Music at the age of 9 and studied under Granville Bantock. She began broadcasting in 1926 and her Mayerl recordings include her own elaborate medley *Nippy*.[2]

[1] B. Mayerl, interview on *Woman's Hour*, BBC Light Programme, 27 Aug. 1952.
[2] A. Hassan, Obituary of Patricia Rossborough in *Midland Gershwin Mayerl Society Magazine*, 20 (Jan. 1993), 6. See also *Patricia Rossborough: The Queen of Syncopation* on Shellwood SWCD 10 (1999).

The American Carroll Gibbons is often thought of as a foil to Mayerl. They both had Savoy connections but Gibbons's style was gentler, less driven by the beat. He composed a few pieces and his relaxed solo performances are always gently atmospheric. Closer to the cocktail lounge than the drawing-room, they seem content to create a mood rather than command attention in the way that Mayerl's invariably did. Charlie Kunz was another very popular American pianist who had his own manner, but it was never as distinctive as Gibbons. Another 1920s import, from the Phillipines via the USA, was Fred Elizalde, who, unlike Joplin and Gershwin, was considered close enough to jazz to get an entry in *The New Grove Dictionary of Jazz* (1988). But these were not composers on Mayerl's scale.

However, there is evidence of Mayerl's influence in the short term of the inter-war years. One of the most surprising examples is the recently revived Lothar Perl. Although born in Poland, he had a classical training in Berlin and then formed a piano duo with Rudolf Beilschowsky playing syncopated music. In 1938 he and his wife emigrated to the USA where he worked for films and TV. Perl obviously responded to the same cabaret influences as Kurt Weill but there are similarities between Perl and Mayerl that seem to go beyond coincidence. As Mike Harth has pointed out, Perl's publisher, Schott, distributed Keith Prowse's catalogue in Germany.[3]

Perl's *Cowboy* (1933) is in the same E flat major as *The Jazz Master*. There are many characteristics in common—a jumping left hand, cross-rhythms, breaks, impressionist chords, harmonic shifts to the barbershop flat sixth, melodic parallel fourths—and it is all very polished. *Rockinghorse* (1934) is very much in Mayerl's A major mood, especially *Cobweb*, No. 1 of *Three Miniatures in Syncopation*. In those cases, Mayerl's came first but Perl's *Hollywood Stars* (1932) seems to anticipate the *Imaginary Foxtrot*, in the same key of G, that Mayerl said he wrote specially for his students in 1935.[4] But there were plenty of common sources for this rising-figure cliché and, in his *Imaginary Foxtrot*, Mayerl was really only providing an exercise for his pupils. Perl's *Hollywood Stars* is one of his best pieces. Marked *Tempo di Blues* it is in the form of the piano rag. A restrained subdominant C strain has 3/8 cross-rhythms and its repeat has a *diminuendo* coda ending on a dominant seventh. The republication of eight of Perl's output of fourteen novelty pieces in 1997 has made it possible to identify him as a leading figure in this idiom after Confrey, his American contemporary Roy Bargy, and Mayerl himself. Like Mayerl, Perl obviously benefited from a sound training in classical harmony—and they both knew their ragtime.

3   M. Harth, 'Billy Mayerl Rediscoveries', CD booklet, Shellwood, Vol. 1, 1997.
4   B. Mayerl, 'This Month's Lesson', *BMCM*, 2/2 (Feb. 1935), 20. See also B. Mayerl, 'This Month's Lesson', *BMCM*, 6/68 (Aug. 1939), 24–6.

A more direct Mayerl influence can be found in *Moonbeams Dance* (1930) by Mayerl's colleague, Carroll Gibbons, written for the film of *Rookery Nook*, the 1926 comedy by Ben Travers. There are many reflections of *Marigold*. The key is the same E flat; the piece is laid out in strains ended by pat cadences; and the main melody is doubled in fourths. Exactly the same is true of *Fingerprints* (1936) by Harry Engleman, who became President of the Midland Gershwin Mayerl Society when it was founded by Terry Wilkinson in 1987.[5] Published in Cramer's Rhythmic Piano Solos series (and separately), it is another homage to *Marigold*. Engleman's *Chase the Ace !* (1936) is a strong number, with a surprising anticipation of 'Put another Nickel in' presented as a 3/8 cross-rhythm in strain B, and *Cannon off the Cush* (1935) borrows from Confrey's *Kitten on the Keys*. Engleman was a regular broadcaster on Midland Regional and recorded his pieces himself or with his Quintet. All this short-term influence came at a time when Mayerl was widening his scope, but popular piano tutors were using ominous new terms like swing. All the same, the novelty idiom was still around with just a few more years to go.

Mayerl's philosophy was encapsulated rather defensively in the introduction to his *Home Study Course in Composing Popular Music* produced in collaboration with Geoffrey Clayton around 1935:

The writing and publishing of what is known as 'popular' music always draws a sneer from that precious section of the musical world which likes to think of itself as 'high-brow'. This need not worry ordinary average persons like ourselves. Popular music is so called because it *is* popular. It is a source of pleasure to thousands of people, besides giving a means of livelihood to many others. It always has been with us and will continue as long as man wants a little cheerfulness to help him through the day. So we can ignore the cheap sneers of the few in favour of the pleasure of the many.[6]

This populist manifesto once more reflects Geoffrey Clayton's talent for embracing the consumer in a large democratic constituency. In 1932 the same team produced *The Billy Mayerl Modern Piano Method* in reaction against what they regarded as dull existing manuals. They present some brilliant ways of visualizing the keyboard in conjunction with the notation—Mayerl's contribution to musical education has not begun to be assessed. However, the chosen pieces printed as a climax to this 78-page tutor are not popular music at all, although they were well enough known, like Rachmaninov's Prelude in C sharp minor, to have been jazzed-up by popular performers: Schumann's *The Merry Peasant*; Mendelssohn's *Wedding March*; Chopin's Prelude in B minor, Op. 28 No. 6; and a Minuet in F by Mayerl. The surprise is that this Minuet is

    [5] The Midland Gershwin Mayerl Society, founded by C. T. Wilkinson in 1987, 191 Sutton Park Rd., Kidderminster, Worcestershire DY11 6LE.
    [6] *Billy Mayerl Home Study Course in Composing Popular Music* (Billy Mayerl International School of Music, no date, presumed *c.*1935).

chastely classical in an idiom closer to the eighteenth than the nineteenth century of the other three composers. In this context Mayerl saw himself humbly
fitting into established patterns of inherited common practice—that is how he
regarded classical music, as we have noticed before. Later pieces like *Minuet
for Pamela* and *Minuet by Candlelight* also reflect this neo-classical trend, but
the Minuet in F, virtually a style-study, is even more self-effacing. It has to be
accepted that the individuality that permeates Mayerl's solo piano output—
both novelties and salon pieces—is missing when he tries to be 'more serious'.
The same thing happened to Zez Confrey.

At different times Mayerl varied in his approach to the relative value of his
popular and serious works. In 1935, through the columns of the *BMCM*, he
was asked why *Marigold* was more popular than *The Legends of King Arthur* and
he gave his own account:

In my opinion, although of lesser musical quality, *Marigold* has certainly more appeal.
I have played it more than a lot of other things I have written; it is now nearly ten years
old and has had time to become established; it has an attractive title; it is moderately
easy. These are perhaps circumstances, but it was never pushed by the publishers over
and above other works; it sort of crept from one of the shelves and came to the fore,
step by step with only a fair amount of exploitation.

Over this number I think I am the biggest offender. When I had completed it,
everybody told me they liked it; I took advantage of this and played it everywhere I
went. It meant little or no difference to me whether I played *Marigold* or *The Jazz
Master* but all indications pointed to the former being more to public taste, so we all accepted the position and *Marigold* was a winner.

I wish I could write one a week. I wish I knew how to. I am still trying.[7]

That implies some apology for *Marigold* but at the same time a natural enjoyment of its popularity. And he would never have become a star merely as the
composer of *The Legends of King Arthur*.

Mayerl cared deeply about teaching people what he knew and, as we have
seen, spent valuable energies turning his own practice into a system and pro-
mulgating it through all available media. So the testimony of pupils and
friends can finally be drawn in to amplify the picture of Mayerl's personality.

Josie Franklin (now Mrs Steele) saw an advertisement for lessons with Billy
Mayerl. At the age of 17 she thought that £9 [£280] for six half-hour lessons
was expensive but she idolized her teacher. She used to go to the Mayerls' suite
at the Grosvenor House Hotel in Park Lane, which Mrs Matkin remembered
was well stocked with black-market (illegal) drink. Mayerl taught Josie Steele
there and in 1993 she recalled:

I remember Billy's immaculate hair brushed very flat and shiny—probably greased—
also his slightly bulging eyes, and even the bags beneath them which showed signs of

---

strain. His cheeks were also puffy and I wondered if he might be taking drugs. After all, he was my hero and I was concerned about his health.[8]

In the lessons Mayerl was exclusively concerned with exercises, which had to be learnt in every key until they were note-perfect. They never studied anything from sheet music. Technically he was looking for a light touch which gave everything a particular lilt. He put her at her ease, once called her 'darling', and exerted his personal magic since she was 'in a kind of dream, feeling so small beside him with his chubby fingers flying about'. There are other reports about Mayerl's hands. Bert Collings, who ran the East London Branch of the Billy Mayerl Club, confirmed that he could stretch an octave, either with the thumb and fifth finger or the thumb and fourth in the left hand, and marvelled at what he could achieve with 'small hands, almost stubby, with thickish fingers, nothing like the slenderness one imagines such a virtuoso would be blessed with'.[9] The British pianist, John Ogdon, impressed people in the same way.

Mayerl must have thought highly of Josie Steele's playing since he recommended her to ENSA to entertain the troops and she followed them as they liberated Italy in the final stages of the war. In 1993 Josie Steele, still playing in the authentic Mayerl style in Essex, felt she wanted to pass on what she had learnt from Mayerl and was certain that her investment was 'the best money I ever spent in my life'.[10] A few years earlier Mayerl's assistant, Irene Ashton, had also found him slightly intimidating at her first lesson but also 'infinitely kind and understanding'.[11] Monty Worlock was another pre-war pupil, less of a disciple since he became a jazz musician, but he found Mayerl 'a very pleasant man who made you feel at home all the time and had nothing of the schoolmaster about him'. Worlock regarded novelty as 'something out of the ordinary that's pleasing' but for a jazz-lover it was too 'airy-fairy'. He thought Mayerl was typically British and remembered that 'you could always smell his haircream—Yardley's *Brilliantine*'.[12]

As a close colleague, Mayerl's first secretary at the School, Mrs McInerny, was in an unrivalled position to assess his temperament from the mid-1920s to the mid-1930s. She described him as a Cheeky Chappie, the term used for the British comedian Max Miller, and confirmed that he loved a joke. He had a very cheerful personality and she never knew him to be miserable in spite of his range of activities, all carried on at high pressure. Mrs Matkin also saw Mayerl as a hyperactive man who enjoyed life, was nice to work for, and had golf, snooker, fish, motoring, and gardening as hobbies.

[8] J. Franklin (Steele), letter to Peter Dickinson, 1 Oct. 1993.
[9] 'In the News', *Billy Mayerl Circle Newsletter*, 3/17 (Summer 1978), 11.
[10] J. Franklin (Steele), interview with Peter Dickinson, 14 Sept. 1993.
[11] I. Ashton, 'My First Piano Lesson with Billy Mayerl', *BMCM*, 1/10 (Oct. 1934), 27–8.
[12] M. Worlock, interview with Peter Dickinson, 29 Sept. 1995.

The pianist-composer-arranger Clarence Falkener got to know Mayerl at close quarters much later in the post-war years. He found him 'very bright, extrovert' and said he sparkled. Mayerl was very modest and never talked about himself, other pianists, or his personal life. If Falkener, a great admirer, tried to turn the conversation that way, Mayerl would say: 'You want my head on a plate to take it away and study, do you?' Falkener attended broadcasting sessions at BBC Maida Vale and found that Mayerl as a performer was 'a bit like a machine, ready to go when the light was on'. But latterly he did find a piece like *The Jazz Mistress* taxing, even though he had said it was easy. Mayerl was never interested in criticizing anyone but was always businesslike and absolutely reliable. But Falkener said he found it hard to read his mind.[13]

William Davies had the experience of playing Mayerl's music in front of the composer:

I was in the BBC Maida Vale 3 Studio doing a fifteen-minute spot on the piano and played his *Ace of Spades*. I happened to glance in the control room to see BM standing there, glowering at me, so immediately the red light went off I went in expecting a ticking-off for something—and sure enough I got it. I had inserted four extra bars in the second section each time it appeared and he just said: 'You absolute so-and-so, why on earth did you not play that to me before it was published?'[14]

The violinist and band-leader Reginald Leopold was a professional colleague and friend from the time when Mayerl could be heard from the Savoy on the primitive early type of radio known as a crystal set. In 1994 Leopold remembered Mayerl as 'a wonderful businessman and a great showman who got through to an audience right away', although he remembered little about his work on the Halls or in the musical theatre. Mayerl was an excellent host who never talked shop and seemed somewhat secretive about his personal life. He loved his black Scottie, called Bogey, who did not like music and howled when Mayerl played. Apparently he once successfully sued a bar for not letting the dog in. Mayerl was fascinated by miniature bottles and appeared on TV with his collection.

Leopold found that Mayerl had a sense of fun, abundantly reflected in his music, and gave an example:

He had an impish sense of humour, bordering on the mild practical joke—a bit naughty sometimes. This adds up with his music, when you think of it. You see he'd play little tricks on anybody who was a bit pompous. He thought he'd bring him down a peg or two, make him seem a little bit small.

He had this bar with very high stools and half-way down you put your foot on the rail. The whole thing was that everybody had what they called the Mayerl Special—a secret cocktail. Nobody could get the recipe out of him however they tried. I

[13] C. Falkener, interview with Robin Cherry and John Watson, 23 Mar. 1996.
[14] W. Davies, letter to Peter Dickinson, 4 Sep. 1998.

remember him trying it out on me one time. I went up and got a drink at the bar. I had a few drinks which didn't half taste good and then I felt—ugh, ugh! Back of the neck! [makes a clunking sound] So what I did was to stay where I was for—Lord knows how long it was. I was not going to get down because I knew I would go flat on my face in the bar. So I just stayed there![15]

But overall Leopold found Mayerl 'good-tempered, kind and helpful'.

This was confirmed in 1982 by another colleague, Van Phillips, who saw most of Mayerl when they both played in the Savoy Havana in the mid 1920s:

Billy drank no more than anybody else, not as much I think. He was apt to be quiet and more self-contained. I think he was thinking more about his career. Frank Eyton used to come in and they'd stand in a corner chatting. Perhaps he'd brought him a lyric to look at or something like that.

With the chaps in normal conversation he was extremely friendly and outgoing and not at all big-headed, as he might have been because he was much more well-known than any of the rest of us except, of course, Ramon Newton.

Phillips also threw some light on Mayerl as an inventor:

Billy was, I should say, constantly on the boil. He was always busy off the bandstand in his private life working at something. One of his mad ideas, because he had punk ideas as well as good ones, was a Composing Machine. Now [laughs] this was to help—not himself because it was all he could do to explain it—but to help budding composers or, I should think, song-writers. It consisted of three concentric cardboard discs held together by a pin in the middle and you could turn each one independently of the other two. On one was the letters A, B, C, D through the notes; and on the other were the keys; and on another were the relations, if I remember this correctly, between the tonic, subdominant etc—like the three chords on the guitar today. By turning one of these wheels round a step at a time you were supposed to be able to find a new melody that nobody had ever written before. Well, as I say, the thing never got off the ground. I think it became a kind of laughing-stock. He used to leave it on the piano as a conversation piece and, believe me, there were some funny conversations![16]

Phillips also remembered with surprising precision a party in early 1928. There were three pianists present—Mayerl, Carroll Gibbons, and Fred Elizalde—and they were not too keen on each other's styles:

Naturally they drifted to the piano and eventually they were pushing each other off the stool doing imitations. Carroll was very easy to imitate because he had that trick of reversing the accent on the tenth in the left hand. Instead of doing the low note first and coming up to the thumb, he made a name for himself by reversing it, by always playing the upper note of the tenth with his thumb and the swinging down to the lower note afterwards. So he was easy to imitate. That was what started it. Fred Elizalde was very clever at imitating. Carroll was livid, of course! And then, I think it was also Fred who

[15] R. Leopold, interview with Peter Dickinson, 8 Nov. 1994.
[16] V. Phillips, interview with Peter Dickinson, 30 Sept. 1982.

played in the style of Billy Mayerl. Of course he couldn't play *Marigold*, he couldn't play any of the things because it was miles away from his style and his likes in music. But he managed to do a pop song, like 'Tea for Two' or something, as Billy would have played it in *Marigold*. It was a unique occasion!

Elizalde was an observant mimic, as his series of take-offs called *From Jazz to Rhythm* showed. It was produced as a Decca recording and appeared as sheet music in the *Melody Maker* in March 1932. Elizalde was trying to do what Jelly Roll Morton would later do in his Library of Congress recordings—document the development of style. Elizalde's selected period is from 1920 to 1933. His 1924 example, 'Too-too-tootsie', contains some of the cross-rhythm rumba breaks of the kind we have observed in Mayerl and the 1928 example is up to date harmonically with augmented triads.

A close personal friend at the opposite end of Mayerl's life was Mrs Doris Hill Dargie. Her husband, who had helped Mrs Matkin move the School in 1940, was called Howard but at their first meeting before the war Mayerl apparently insisted that he should change his name in order to be known as John. Such was the Mayerl magnetism that he did. When Jill Mayerl wrote a letter of condolence to Mrs Dargie after her husband's death in 1966 she confirmed that John was 'my darling Billy's best friend for years and years'.

Mrs Dargie, who met Mayerl in 1954 after her marriage, also became devoted to him and remembered an incident which confirmed his sense of the ridiculous:

We were staying with Billy and Jill one weekend at Beaconsfield. He had a little TV room off the lounge in his house. Jill went to make some sandwiches and we had the TV on—1950s black and white. Billy said 'Oh, there's nothing worth looking at' so he switched over and it was ballet. I don't know whether Billy liked ballet or not, but John didn't. After some ballerinas a male dancer came on and Billy said: 'Oh, look, John, he's brought his band parts with him!'[17]

Since Mrs Dargie was a seasoned observer of the lethal results of the Mayerl Special cocktail, she wisely never drank it herself. Mayerl was a confirmed whisky drinker and his choice of a luxury on his *Desert Island Discs* programme was a well-stocked bar. He was an inveterate smoker—Passing Cloud was his brand—which must have exacerbated his heart condition. His poor health gave his wife constant anxiety.

There were often distinguished visitors at the Mayerls' regular Saturday afternoon open house at Beaconsfield. In addition to luminaries from the world of show business these used to include the Russian-British pianist Benno Moiseiwitsch, but he never played there, preferring to listen to Mayerl. Back in 1925 Moiseiwitsch had been amongst the guests at the Savoy when

[17] D. H. M. Dargie, interview with Peter Dickinson, 8 Nov. 1994.

Gershwin gave the first British performance of *Rhapsody in Blue* for the BBC. *The Sound Wave* then reported him enthusiastically 'shaking the composer by the hand'.[18] The Dargies were members of the Light Music Society, which Mayerl founded and helped to run. He appreciated Grainger and one of his last enthusiasms was Robert Farnon, whom he interviewed for the magazine.[19] One can see why Mayerl admired Farnon as the composer of popular pieces like 'Jumping Bean' and 'Portrait of a Flirt'. They continued Mayerl's own tradition of colourful numbers with snappy titles.[20]

On a purely social level Mrs Dargie used to play duets with Mayerl and he'd say, 'come on, Doris, you play the bum end!' Remarkably, since he rarely spoke about his ancestry, Mayerl did tell Mrs Dargie he was of Dutch extraction, an accurate reference to the Umbachs on his mother's side of the family rather than the Austro-German Mayerls. Even in his later years she found him to be 'a man who had everything'.

In my BBC Radio 3 documentary many contributors confirmed Mayerl's pre-eminence and some of them would have known Mayerl's competitors far better than we do today. Those opinions expressed in the 1981/2 interviews now seem justified. Leslie Osborne and William Davies confirmed Mayerl's pre-eminent stature as 'the pianist's god'. And then Mayerl was a formative influence on Sir Richard Rodney Bennett, who was one of the first pianists of a later generation to take an interest in him:

When I was a child we lived in South Devon and, of course, we were dependent on the radio. At that time there were a terrific lot of novelty pianists. I loved Kay Cavendish, who was another name from that time, but best of all I loved Billy Mayerl. I used to go over to the nearest town and go to the music shop and buy all Billy Mayerl's piano solos. I couldn't play them in any way accurately as a child because they are very difficult. They really demand a lot of technique and stamina. But I did love them. When I grew up and was very high-minded and a pupil of Boulez, somehow all that music disappeared. Years later when I was approached to record the Gershwin Songbook I said I'd like to do Billy Mayerl on the other side.[21]

Bennett was attracted by a kind of vividness at a time when he felt there was less division between jazz and popular music than there would be later. Interestingly, for a composer-pianist who has made a distinguished contribution

---

[18] July 1925, 486.

[19] B. Mayerl, 'Meet Robert Farnon', *Light Music Magazine*, No. 2 (Dec. 1957).

[20] E. Parkin, *Manhattan Playboy: A Tribute to Robert Farnon* on Priory PRCD 578 (1998). Chappell published adaptations for piano solo of these two Farnon pieces in 1948 and 1949.

[21] R. R. Bennett, *Richard Rodney Bennett plays Gershwin and Billy Mayerl* on Polydor 2460–245 (Apr. 1975). See Andrew Lamb's review in *Gramophone*: 'What is here missing in Bennett's performance is the sense of throwing off the pieces and highlighting the piano technique as much as the material which Mayerl himself achieves in his own recordings'. But Bennett's advocacy was a significant step forward at this date.

both to modern music and to jazz, Bennett felt that it was Mayerl who led him to jazz. He regarded Mayerl as closely allied to jazz and appreciated his use of the piquant harmonies of French music that he always loved, especially in Poulenc. Bennett said then that he would be delighted if Mayerl's music came back in its own right and not just as nostalgia. He knew from his own experience that it is extremely difficult technically but can be played straight off the page, is very accurately notated and so there is no reason why it should not be available to concert pianists. But Bennett himself, after his recording, hardly ever played Mayerl in concerts. By the 1990s Mayerl was making headway, as the CD catalogue showed, but concert pianists were still struggling with the technical demands. As Dr Richard Head also realized:

Something often forgotten about Mayerl is the great amount of physical stamina required to play his music at speed. It varies from simple pieces like *Look lively*, which requires only minimal technique, to others like *Jasmine* or *Mignonette* which require not only physical strength but stamina. Consequently one seldom hears them played. For most of us, the only way of overcoming the difficulty is by constant practice and complete familiarity with the music which allows a certain measure of relaxation in the playing.[22]

The secret of good Mayerl playing was consistently drummed into his students:

Heavy playing is absolutely wrong from the start and will never get you anywhere. Mr Mayerl has the lightest of touches, and yet his rhythm is exceptionally clearly marked. If you play at your loudest all the time, where are you going to get that extra emphasis for accenting the beat? It is an entirely erroneous idea, but one that seems to be very prevalent, that to be a successful syncopated player you must thump. Don't bang, therefore—you are a pianist not a blacksmith![23]

The Mayerl revival on CD owes more to Eric Parkin than anyone else. Parkin's background has some similarities with that of Mayerl. He gained scholarships to Trinity College of Music and trained exclusively there, but not in the Junior Department, and immediately joined the staff. Parkin never wanted to be a band pianist but, well into his concert career, he played solo and joined Bill McGuffie's Quartet at the Mayfair Hotel. Parkin liked jazz and knew what it was like to play for dancing, both good qualifications for playing Mayerl. He later became a leading exponent of the English school of composers such as Ireland, Bax, and Bridge and has made many recordings. But it is this broad background that has made Parkin an outstanding Mayerl interpreter, aware of the different aspects of his style. Parkin assessed Mayerl: 'I feel his classical training is always there: the music (at its best—he published too

---

[22]   R. Head, letter to Peter Dickinson, 5 Feb. 1995.
[23]   B. Mayerl, *The Billy Mayerl Special Tutor-Course in Modern Syncopation* (undated), 1.

much) is perfectly proportioned, with real pianistic understanding. He was a born pianist—there's been no equal since.'[24]

More recently a number of British pianists, such as Susan Tomes, Peter Jacobs, and David Owen Norris, have regularly included Mayerl in their recitals and made recordings. In America, two pianists from the ragtime and novelty piano tradition, Tony Caramia and Alex Hassan, have taken up Mayerl and recorded his work. Hassan approaches his task with an extrovert zest which suits the rapid numbers admirably.[25]

William Davies, in 1981, prophesied that Mayerl would be revived within ten years, like Scott Joplin. He was almost right—and this was reflected by the founding of the Billy Mayerl Society in 1992 with its own headquarters, journal, and record label by a band of dedicated enthusiasts in a well-planned programme. Before that the Billy Mayerl Circle was founded by H. Nichols in 1974 with Leslie Osborne as President. It lasted for four years and attained a membership of just over 100.

At the BBC Davies found Mayerl 'gregarious, he got on with everybody, but never suffered fools gladly. He could be a hard task-master, a tyrant but charming, and he worked himself into his grave.'

He knew his own worth too, as Doris Dargie recalled:

I always remember he told us he went to Glasgow to appear there. Some titled people came in—the Laird of somewhere or other—and asked him back to their house after the show. They were giving a party. So, of course, he went there. As soon as he got in the door, they took his coat and hat and walked him over to the piano and sat him down. They said 'now play!' He walked back and said, 'Give me my hat and coat' and out he went. He walked out! He wasn't going to stand for that. He'd never even had a drink! He was furious.[26]

I put Mayerl between categories in a programme in 1990 on the BBC World Service: 'It wasn't easy to place him. He clearly wasn't an improvising jazz musician, nor was he a serious classical composer. Perhaps his music was too immediately enjoyable for that!'[27]

Back in 1935 Austen Croom-Johnson, Mayerl's collaborator in *Bats in the Belfry*, had found him neither a novelty pianist nor a dance pianist and put him

---

[24] E. Parkin, letter to Peter Dickinson, 17 Aug. 1998.

[25] See P. Dickinson, *Gramophone* (Jan. 1998), 81. Hassan's British recordings, made in 1996, are in the series from Shellwood Productions, Thames Ditton. *Billy Mayerl Rediscoveries Vol.1*—Mayerl Transcriptions; Lothar Perle Syncopations; Carroll Gibbons Medley. SWCD 1. *Billy Mayerl Rediscoveries Vol. 2*—Billy Mayerl Song Transcriptions; The Little Rascals/Billy Golwyn; Ivor Novello Medley; Burton Lane Fantasy. SWCD 6. See also, in the USA, *Phantom Fingers*—Stomp Off CD1322, P.O.Box 342, York, PA 17405.

[26] D. H. M. Dargie, interview with Peter Dickinson, 8 Nov. 1994.

[27] P. Dickinson, Recording of the Week, BBC World Service, Nov. 1990.

in a class of his own, which he found difficult to explain.[28] The difficulty that many people still have in placing Mayerl was shown by a revealing caption attached to a photograph of him at the National Portrait Gallery in 1997: 'talented composer of polite English jazz'.[29] The same could be said of Joplin's piano rags and would also miss the point. But Mayerl's first secretary, Mrs McInerney, came close to defining his position in similar terms when she said that he appealed to people who found classical music too serious and jazz too hot. She also found Mayerl's music 'lighthearted and clever' and felt it was 'classical and perfectly written'.[30] This perceptive comment brings up the Joplin–Mayerl comparison again. Joplin's rags have been described as classic since their first publication. H. Wiley Hitchcock, the American music historian, found them 'elegant, often subtle, and as sharply incised as a cameo' and he related them to dance music traditions.[31] All of this applies to Mayerl, with his background in dance music, and his compositions in the same form as Joplin's rags. They are extensions of the classical piano rag. American music is a more open field than that of any European country where stratified societies have given rise to class distinctions in art. So Joplin, like the composers of the golden age of popular song, has been given a place in the American pantheon. Billy Mayerl deserves this kind of recognition as a unique figure within British music of the period.

In 1993 Steve Race felt that Mayerl invented 'a whole enchanting musical world of his own' and that his music was fun first and foremost.[32] If the music of composers is a reflection of their temperament, then, as we have seen, the same positive enjoyment is a consistent feature of both the man and his work. In 1981 I asked Mrs Mayerl which of all his helter-skelter variety of activities was really him:

I think he liked to be at home at his own piano in his own room composing. That I'm positive, because he would go at 9.0 o'clock in the morning into his study and the rest of the day he was immune—he never heard anything, he never asked for anything. You take him in coffee, you went an hour later and it was still there. He was completely immersed in his music.[33]

This provides some sense of Mayerl's own priorities. Unlike improvising players, he wanted to be remembered as a composer with notated pieces which could be played anywhere at any time. His recordings are essential documents

---

[28] 'Austen Croom-Johnson', *BMCM*, 2/23 (Nov. 1935), 3–5.
[29] M. Jones, *Midland Gershwin Mayerl Society Magazine*, 39 (June 1997), 5.
[30] E. A. McInerney (Hooper), interview with Peter Dickinson, 11 May 1992.
[31] H. W. Hitchcock, *Music of the United States: A Historical Introduction* (2nd edn., Prentice Hall, Englewood Cliffs, NJ, 1974). Hitchcock expanded his comments on Joplin for this second edtion, following the revival of Joplin which started in the early 1970s.
[32] S. Race, 'The Marigold Man', BBC Radio 2, 9 June 1992
[33] J. Mayerl, interview with Peter Dickinson, 11 Aug. 1981.

in perpetuating his unique style but the music has a life of its own and it stems primarily from the atmosphere of the 1920 and 1930s. In 1952, during the drab post-war years of rationing and austerity, Mayerl lamented that there were no composers around like Kern and Gershwin. He referred to the happy times before the war as carefree, a spirit that had not been recaptured.[34] In spite of all its political uncertainties and threats, the inter-war period was Mayerl's heyday.

The role of his wife in providing understanding and stability, especially through the difficult later years, was essential. In 1934 Mayerl's friend C. Corti Woodcock took an early snapshot:

She is a wee soul, very charming, very pretty and full of character. To look at her you would think she had been married ten months instead of ten years; and if her photograph appeared on the Course, it would be worth a good five thousand extra pupils to the School per annum. And here's a domestic secret for you—she calls her husband Binkie. Can you imagine that, as they say in the States?[35]

Mrs Mayerl only occasionally visited the School but Mrs McInerney recalled her as 'lovely', wearing court shoes, silk stockings, and a fur coat.

In these prurient times there are sure to be queries about Mayerl's sexuality. Reginald J. Phillips was Mrs Mayerl's friend and financial adviser and he said he thought he knew her well enough for her to tell him if Mayerl had had homosexual relationships. It seems that this was not the case and that over the years his wife was more likely to have been concerned about female poppets on tour.[36] But Sheila Frankel, daughter of Mayerl's colleague George Myddleton, did not think Mayerl had affairs and thought that she would have heard such gossip if there had been any.[37] This is also the view of William Davies.[38] All the evidence points to an exceptionally happy marriage, which brings us full circle to Fred Mayerl's dictum that if anything biographically sensational was required it would have to be invented. In any case Mayerl worked incessantly and couldn't stop:

The last two years of his life were very trying. He should never have worked. He had already cut down to half his broadcasts—he was doing far too much. And then we lived in the country and it meant coming up four times a week, leave at about 6.00 in the morning to get to the studios, in case we had a puncture or there was a lot of traffic. It became too much. He couldn't give up even when he was dying—and he was dying for seven months because the specialists told me to be prepared. And then the last few days that he was in the nursing home there was a big competition going on for fourteen of

34 B. Mayerl, interview on Woman's Hour, BBC Light Programme, 27 Aug. 1952.
35 C. C. Woodcock, 'In the Lions' Den', in *BMCM*, 1/7 (July 1934), 11–13.
36 R. J. Phillips, interview with Peter Dickinson, Brighton, 3 Oct. 1994.
37 S. Frankel, interview with John Watson, 9 Feb. 1997.
38 W. Davies, letter to Peter Dickinson, 4 Sept. 1998.

the best composers to write something which would be played at the Festival Hall. Even when he was ill in bed at the nursing home he was in and out of for two years, he always had his pens and he composed. That was the last thing he wrote and it was played at the Festival Hall.[39]

It was an orchestral piece written to support the Light Music Society and called *Alliance Variations*, based on a theme by Arthur Duckworth. There were two movements: a Jig by Robert Docker and Finale by Mayerl.[40]

In 1998 Dr Richard Head remembered Mrs Mayerl's own words telling him about the circumstances of her husband's death:

I had been told by the doctors that Billy had only about six months to live, owing to a heart condition, and that on no account was I to allow him to go upstairs. He had an upright piano upstairs that he used for composing (rather than the grand downstairs) and wanted to play this one day. He went upstairs and immediately collapsed with a heart attack.[41]

So Mayerl died at home, Marigold Lodge, Pyebush Lane, Beaconsfield, Buckinghamshire, at 8.0 p.m. on Wednesday, 25 March 1959, and the death was registered by K. Roy Dolleymore. The cause of death was given as coronary thrombosis and coronary arteriosclerosis. Obituaries appeared on 27 March in the *Scottish Daily Mail*, where Cecil Wilson referred to Mayerl's 'gift for irresistibly hummable tunes', and on 28 March in *The Times*, the *Daily Telegraph and Morning Post*, the *Manchester Guardian*, the *Daily Mail*, and the *Daily Express*. The cremation took place at Golders Green, London, at 11.0 a.m. on Tuesday, 31 March. The *Melody Maker* said that Mayerl 'made syncopation his trademark' and described him as 'plump, affable and with a ready smile'.[42] Finally B. C. Hilliam, half of the comic team Mr Flotsam and Mr Jetsam, whose *Valses de Folies* Mayerl had often played, caught the mood of many of Mayerl's admirers in an obituary for the *Light Music Magazine*—and he found a felicitous way of placing Mayerl's work:

This friendly little chap—neat, cherubic, earnest in his approach to life and the profession of music—endeared himself to viewers and listeners whose tastes belong to that 'golden mean' that lies between the extremes of classic and contemporary . . . His death is painfully premature and deeply saddening to all who knew and loved him.[43]

---

[39] J. Mayerl, interview with Peter Dickinson, 11 Aug. 1981.

[40] For information about Mayerl's last composition see: J. F. Archer. 'Billy Mayerl, Light Music Crusader', *Billy Mayerl Society Magazine* No. 4 (Jan. 1996). A cassette of Mayerl's Finale was supplied with the magazine.

[41] R. Head, letter to Peter Dickinson, 28 Sept. 1998. For a more extended account see J. Archer in *Lightning Fingers* (Paradise Press, London, 1995), 50–1.

[42] C. Hayes, 'Billy Mayerl: He Taught the World', *Melody Maker*, 4 Apr. 1959.

[43] B. C. Hilliam, 'Billy Mayerl', obituary in the *Light Music Magazine* (Sept. 1959), 4.

Our final glimpse of the Mayerl impact is set in the antipodes. It was in 1949 that Billy and Jill embarked on their visit to Australia and New Zealand with Stanley Holloway. Mrs Mayerl remembered: 'After about three weeks in Sydney we went to New Zealand for three months, doing one-night stands all over the islands. Then we went back to Sydney and Stanley (breaking his contract) came home and we stayed on to the end, Billy doing four broadcasts a week.'[44] Mayerl obviously enjoyed something of his pre-war celebrity again; he made his last solo recordings there in 1949; and there was also the possibility of reopening the branches of the Billy Mayerl School. Doris Dargie knew that Mrs Mayerl had an accident falling from a tram in Sydney and hit her head, which caused her hair to go grey overnight, but she said they were wonderfully treated. Mrs Mayerl now deserves to have the last word with a symbolic anecdote which demonstrates the penetration and indestructibility of *Marigold* and the best of Mayerl's output then and into the future:

New Zealand is a wonderful country—spacious with huge, gorgeous mountains. We were in Palmerston North, where they tied the horses outside like Westerns, and were coming down to, I think, Hamilton. There were no trains and there were no flights so we had to come down on a coach which went right up in the mountains through very beautiful scenery. One day we were sitting in front with the driver. He didn't know any of the passengers: we were just passengers. And he was one of those drivers that drove with one hand and turned round and told you what you were going to see. Well, eventually we came to a place high in the mountain and there was a tiny little bit of blue. He said: 'We're going down there!' It was a lake of some sort. Eventually, a tortuous way, we got down there and as we were getting out of the coach—and this to me is even now unbelievable—we heard *Marigold* being played. Very badly. And I looked at Billy and he looked at me. I said: 'We're imagining it, you know!' We were miles away and there was nothing there. There was just a little pub, a wooden shack of a place, and we were going to have coffee, just stay there an hour and then go on. So we went in and there was a man sitting at a very old piano there and he was playing away. Billy went up to him and said: 'Where did you learn that?' 'Oh', he said, 'I've got a copy of it: it took me a long time to get. But I can't play it very well. Do you play the piano?' Billy said: 'I play a little bit'. The man said: 'I guess you can't play this!' Billy said: 'Not very well, but I'll have a go'.

And he sat down and he played *Marigold* and within about two minutes the top of the piano was filled with mugs of beer! We were there for about three hours![45]

44 J. Mayerl, interview with Peter Dickinson, 11 Aug. 1981.
45 J. Mayerl, 'Australian Adventure', *Billy Mayerl Circle Newsletter*, 1/8 (Winter 1975), 6–8, provides her written version of this story.

Appendices

Appendices

Queen's Hall Programmes*

FIRST CONCERT OF SYNCOPATED MUSIC

THE SAVOY-ORPHEANS (AUGMENTED SYMPHONIC ORCHESTRA)
THE SAVOY-HAVANA BAND & THE BOSTON ORCHESTRA
By Special Permission of the Savoy Hotel
QUEEN'S HALL, 3 JANUARY 1925, at 8.15 p.m.

THE SAVOY-HAVANA BAND

VIOLIN LEADER:	C. R. Newton		
SAXOPHONE	R. Vallee	TROMBONE	R. Tipping
SOUSAPHONE	Jim Bellamy	PIANO	Billy Mayerl
BANJO	D. Thomas	DRUMS, HARP, TYMPANI	R. Gubertini
TRUMPET	H. Thompson		

THE BOSTON ORCHESTRA

SAXOPHONE LEADER:	H. Jacobs		
VIOLIN	R. Purseglove	PIANO	C. Gibbons
BANJO	J. Brannelly	DRUMS, HARP, TYMPANI	A. Ure

THE SAVOY-ORPHEANS (AUGMENTED SYMPHONY ORCHESTRA)
CONDUCTOR: W. DEBROY SOMERS
ASSISTANT CONDUCTOR: R. Batten

VIOLIN LEADER:	C. R. Newton		
VIOLINS	Emil Vella Motylinski C. Coverman J. Coenen		
CELLO	Alberto Peretti	BANJO	Pete Mandell
STRING BASS	Jim Bellamy	SOUSAPHONE	Fred Underhaye
SAXOPHONES	Herbert Finney Al Starita Renarto Starita		
TRUMPETS	Vernon Ferry Walter Lyme		
TROMBONE	George Chaffin	BASS TROMBONE	G. Duguid

---

* Details provided as in the original publications. The programmes cost one shilling.

1st PIANO	Billy Thorburn	2nd PIANO	C. Gibbons
FLUTE	R. Murchie	OBOE	J. McDonagh
CLARINET	L. Collins	BASSOON/SARRUSOPHONE	A. Alexandra
HORNS	E. Button W. Unwin		
		HARP, TYMPANI, DRUMS	R. Gubertini

PROGRAMME

Part 1
Successes of the Past

MEMORIES	THE SAVOY-HAVANA BAND
PIANO SOLOS	W. MAYERL
ALLAH'S HOLIDAY	THE BOSTON ORCHESTRA
BEALE STREET BLUES	THE BOSTON ORCHESTRA
PIANO DUET	C. GIBBONS AND W. MAYERL
THREE O'CLOCK IN THE MORNING	THE SAVOY-HAVANA BAND
TWELFTH STREET RAG	SAVOY-HAVANA BAND AND BOSTON ORCHESTRA

Part 2
Evolution of Syncopated Music from Alexander's Ragtime Band to Symphonised-Syncopation

Great interest has been paid in the last few years to syncopated dance music, which is taking such an important part in our modern social life. It is interesting to study syncopated music from its birth and origin, through its gradual phases and improvements, finishing with the modern symphonised music of today.

Ragtime Period

Ragtime was inspired by the performances of negro musicians, who, not satisfied to keep to a set melody and rhythm, improvised on the melody and broke the rhythm in quite an original way—hence the name Ragtime.

The originality of Ragtime captured America and Europe within a year of its birth. Ragtime, like all original music, inspired a new form of dancing.

ALEXANDER'S RAGTIME BAND   Irving Berlin

Piano Solo   W. Mayerl

Banjo Bands

Ragtime eventually proving too unconventional for Ballroom dancing, an attempt was made to introduce a stricter and more suitable rhythm. Syncopated rhythm was introduced in new musical numbers about ten years ago by orchestras composed of banjos and a piano. Actually the Banjo Bands were the first orchestras to introduce syncopation in dance music. Banjos being essentially instruments of rhythm, the rhythm was perhaps emphasised to the sacrifice of the melody.

FOR ME AND MY GAL   G. W. Meyer
STRUTTERS BALL   Shelton Brooks

THE OLD BANJO BAND

Jazz!

The history of Jazz is practically the history of The Dixieland Jazz Band. About ten years ago some Chicago boys who used to meet after their work formed a five-piece band, composed then of all kinds of strange instruments.

They had heard negroes perform and wanted to improve upon them. As none of them could read music they treated the melodies they heard in their own way, each one embellishing it without paying any attention to what the other members of the Band were doing. It was hardly possible to distinguish any tune in the performance of these quaint musicians, but, strange to say, they scored a success amongst their friends and finally obtained an engagement in a leading New York café. The Dixieland Jazz Band was a great success.

The Original Dixieland Jazz Band

BLUEING THE BLUES   H. W. Ragas
BY MEMBERS OF THE SAVOY-HAVANA BAND

Part 3
Syncopated Music of Today and Tomorrow

SAHARA   H. Nicholls
THE SAVOY-ORPHEANS

Sahara is remarkable not only on account of its great and world-wide popularity, but also because it is the latest composition of Horatio Nicholls, who is one of the outstanding English composers of syncopated music. He is amongst the two or three composers in England and America with the greatest number of popular successes in syncopated music. (Publication: Lawrence Wright.)

CHALIAPINATA   F. Chaliapin

Chaliapin, a friend of the Savoy-Orpheans, has presented them with this tribute—his own composition. In June last year The Savoy-Orpheans sent Chaliapin a wire wishing him success on his opening night at the Paris Opera. Original as he always is, Chaliapin returned the compliment by writing a new syncopated composition on the back of the telegram. This he then sent to London, where it was set by the Savoy arrangers. (Publication: Chappell & Co., Ltd.)

A LITTLE COMEDY IN SYNCOPATION
'Follow the Swallow', 'Driftwood' and other well-known airs played in a strange way.
THE SAVOY-ORPHEANS AND THE BOSTON ORCHESTRA

BY THE LAKE   A. Lange
THE SAVOY-ORPHEANS

A new type of composition, written in a style reminiscent of a Barcarolle. After an introduction on flute and oboe taken from Grieg's *Morgenstimmung*, there are a few bars of smooth flowing accompaniment, following which comes a beautiful haunting melody on the violin which brings to mind a dreamboat slowly gliding along to the rhythmic accompaniment of magical oars by the shores of a fairy lake, with the suggestion of an evening bell tolling away in the distance. (Publication: Francis, Day and Hunter.)

JUST LIKE A BEAUTIFUL STORY   Earl Burnett

THE SAVOY-ORPHEANS

A striking feature of this charming composition is its symphonic orchestration. An original introduction leads to the principal theme, which is played in various keys. There is an interlude depicting Faust's love song to Marguerite, concluding with the refrain played with marked rhythmic and syncopated accompaniment. *Just like a Beautiful Story* is considered to be one of the finest compositions of Earl Burnett.

RAGGEDY ANN   Jerome Kern

THE SAVOY-ORPHEANS

SHADOWLAND   Brooks A. Ahlert

This composition conveys to the imagination all that is suggested by its title. A movement in the minor key indicates sombre shadows, and presently emerges into a delightful theme in a brighter key, gloomy thoughts are dispelled, giving the effect of strong sunlight in a deep forest. Brooks A. Ahlert, if not one of the youngest, is certainly one of the most prolific and brilliant composers of the new school. (Publication: B. Feldman & Co.)

SAVOY ENGLISH MEDLEY   Arr. Debroy Somers

THE SAVOY-ORPHEANS

THE THIRD CONCERT OF SYNCOPATED MUSIC

THE SAVOY-ORPHEANS (AUGMENTED SYMPHONIC ORCHESTRA)

THE SAVOY-HAVANA BAND & THE BOSTON ORCHESTRA

Presented by W. de Mornys by Special Permission of the Savoy Hotel

QUEEN'S HALL, TUESDAY, MARCH 8, 1925, at 8.15 p.m.

PROGRAMME

Part 1

Memories

OLD BYGONE DAYS (MEDLEY)	THE SAVOY-HAVANA BAND
SELECTION	THE BOSTON ORCHESTRA
PIANO DUET	C. GIBBONS AND W. MAYERL
OH ME, OH MY, OH YOU	THE BOSTON ORCHESTRA
I LOVE THE MOON	THE SAVOY-HAVANA BAND
BUGLE CALL RAG	THE BOSTON ORCHESTRA

Part 2

Syncopated and American Music of a Century

PIANO SYNCOPATIONS

CARROLL GIBBONS

It is generally believed that a rhythm can be syncopated in only one particular way, but this is not strictly true. Just as there are dozens of different rhythms so they can be syncopated in ways totally different from each other. Syncopation of this advanced type is enormously difficult, particularly to a soloist, and requires tremendous technical ability as well as an assured rhythmical sense. Various kinds of syncopation are demonstrated in this piano solo.

THE OLD NEGRO BAND
Some very, very old music.

Negro songs are very old; so old that it is impossible to say for how many centuries they have been sung by the negroes of the Southern States. Of recent years one has become familiar with, perhaps weary of, imitations of the negro's song. The imitations are generally much too sophisticated and the spirit of the plantations is lost. In their simplest and original forms as you will hear them now, you can trace the syncopated influence that sways the world today.

IN A MUSICAL ROOM, NEW YORK, 1849
OLD FOLKS AT HOME   Stephen Collins Foster
IN THE GLOAMING
MY OLD KENTUCKY HOME   Stephen Collins Foster
                    THE SAVOY-HAVANA BAND

A tribute to the memory of Stephen Collins Foster, the composer of 'My Old Kentucky Home', 'Swanee River' and many other songs. In spite of the fact that these songs became famous during his lifetime Foster himself died in abject poverty.

In the setting of this quaint New York room of over 70 years ago you will hear them just as Foster used to play and sing them to his friends.

HONEY DATS ALL   Van Alstyne
                    THE SAVOY-ORPHEANS

A modern piece of syncopated music.
A SUITE IN SYNCOPATED RHYTHM
M. N. Labridge[1]   Arr. Debroy Somers
                    THE SAVOY-ORPHEANS

[1] M. N. Labridge was a pseudonym for a composer who preferred to keep his identity secret when writing symphonized syncopation. Some clues were provided in *The Times* review of this concert on 11 March 1925:

SYNCOPATED RHYTHM
SAVOY ORPHEANS AT THE QUEEN'S HALL

We were lured to Queen's Hall last night by the announcement that a Suite in Syncopated Rhythm would be there produced, the work of a 'young musician, who hitherto has only been known as a brilliant executant of serious music'. We were to be told who this genius really is as soon as the work had been performed, but this latter part of the undertaking could not be fulfilled. We quite understood his reticence when we heard the music, which is frankly poor stuff. We were glad that the 'brilliant executant' who has perpetrated this suite withheld his name, for it is a name which his father made well known among musicians. He adopted the pseudonym M. N. Labridge and those who want to guess who he is may find a clue in the first two initials.

The only interesting things about the suite are the scoring [by Debroy Somers] and the playing . . . We wish to hear no more of M. N. Labridge and his like.

For the last three weeks the musical world has been guessing at the identity of the young musician who has bent his energies to composing for the Dance Band.

Syncopation has always been a feature of plantation music and was first popularised by jazz music and then by the foxtrot dance. But since the jazz period the composition of dance orchestras has changed very greatly and so has the music they play. The famous syncopated orchestras of today have not confined their attention to the Ballroom, for they have performed constantly for vast, non-dancing audiences. Up till now the tunes they have played have been extremely interesting and clever but they were all dance tunes.

Tonight we are presenting for the first time a composition which has been specially written for this orchestra. It is not dance music. This is, moreover, the first time that music of this nature, written for a Dance Band by a musician who has hitherto identified himself so completely with serious music has been heard in London. Not that this suite is not serious. It is definitely serious in that it reveals for the first time how great are the possibilities that lie in the liaison between syncopated music and the Concert Hall.

As for the Suite itself it can best tell its own story. The listener will notice a freedom from ultra-modernistic tendencies; the Suite makes its appeal rather by the light-hearted gaiety of its harmonies and the witchery of its rhythms.

Say it While Dancing   Abner Silver
                         The Savoy-Orpheans

This piece, of course, is not new. The Savoy-Orpheans have played it for month after month, but it retains its freshness to the listener or the dancer. It is certainly the most successful dance composition of the last few years.

Mr Norman Long will lecture   On Classical Music!
                              Interval

Part 3
Favourites of Today, Successes of Tomorrow

To a Wild Rose   MacDowell
                  Saxophone Solo   H. Jacobs

Shanghai   Horatio Nicholls

Shanghai is the latest composition of Horatio Nicholls, who is one of the few British composers who can compete with the American in the art of writing syncopated music. His Sahara has become famous throughout the entire world, and it is anticipated that Shanghai will prove equally successful. (Publication: Lawrence Wright.)

Me Neenyah   Fleta Jan Brown, Herbert Spencer

Me Neenya (My Little One) is the phonetic spelling of the Spanish Mi Nina. The drums and banjos immediately establish a pulsating Spanish rhythm over which a Spanish love song of delightful freshness and charm is breathed by the saxophones. Presently the theme becomes more ecstatic and exhilarating, but soon burns itself out as if with its own beauty.

A Little Comedy in Syncopation
             The Savoy-Orpheans and Boston Orchestra

ALABAMY BOUND   Bud Green, Bud de Sylva, Ray Henderson
THE SAVOY-ORPHEANS

This has never been played publicly in England until tonight. It is the most successful foxtrot that America has had for the last two years, and it is raging there like a blizzard. It ought to go through Europe like a prairie fire. Why? No one will ever know why a foxtrot becomes a success, for, like poets, they are born not made.
(Publication: Keith Prowse, Ltd.)

POEME   Z. Fibich
THE SAVOY-ORPHEANS

A waltz arrangement of this well-known work.
(Publication: Keith Prowse Ltd.)

COPENHAGEN   Charley Davis
THE SAVOY-ORPHEANS

LITTLE OLD CLOCK   Ted Fiorito
THE SAVOY-ORPHEANS

This is another foxtrot that has had an immense vogue in the United States. A quaint tick-tock effect is sustained against a captivating melody. The night seems to grow young under its rhythms, and the Little Old Clock's hands go backwards and not forwards.
(Publication: Francis Day & Hunter.)

SOME OF THE FAMOUS SAVOY MEDLEYS   Arr. Debroy Somers
THE SAVOY-ORPHEANS

2

Analysis of Mayerl's BBC Broadcasts

The works Mayerl played for his BBC broadcasts were not always specified, either in contracts or surviving letters. Programmes were often described as 'selections from repertoire' or 'own choice including . . .' However, out of thirty-four individual programmes checked from 20 July 1937 to 11 February 1950, plus a series of six called *Keyboard Cavalcade* in August 1946 and eight TV programmes, the following priorities emerge and show that he played a very limited number of his own pieces again and again. Judging from programmes given in the *BMCM*, his live performances were on similar lines and nothing from the *Pianolettes* or the *Piano Exaggerations* was featured.

Individual titles are followed by the number of times each one appeared.

Marigold	22
The Ace of Hearts	18
Sweet William	17
Song of the Fir Tree	15
Bats in the Belfry	11
Railroad Rhythm	10
Parade of the Sandwich Men	9
Ladybird Lullaby	6
Ace of Spades	6
Autumn Crocus	5
April's Fool	5
Harp of the Winds	4
Mistletoe	4
Fireside Fusiliers	4
Moorish Idol	3
From a Spanish Lattice	3
Whirligig	3
Limehouse Blues	3
Phil the Fluter	3
Willow Moss	2
Beetle in the Bottle	2
Smoke gets in your Eyes	2

The following Mayerl pieces appeared once:
Ace of Diamonds; Ace of Clubs; Scallywag; Chop-sticks; Wedding of the Ant; Orange Bossom; English Dance; Forgotten Forest; Minuet for Pamela; In my Garden (Winter); Japanese Pictures, Nos. 2 and 3; Shy Ballerina.

In these radio and TV broadcasts from 1937 to 1950, where the programme content is known, there was nothing by other composers until 29 May 1941 when a long programme contained:

Wait for the Wagon (Woodhouse)
In a Clock-store (Orde)
Harp of the Winds (Mayerl)
Railroad Rhythm (Mayerl)
Nola (with orchestra) (Arndt)
Love and Life in Holland (Joyce)
Ladybird Lullaby (Mayerl)
Marigold (Mayerl)
Yuma (Cecil Rayner)
Bats in the Belfry (with orchestra) (Mayerl)
Japanese Pictures, Nos. 2 and 3 (with orchestra) (Mayerl)
As an extra: *Roundabouts* (Arthur Wood)

After this 1941 programme, a total of ten later single radio programmes contained sixteen works by other composers. These were:

1941 *Hey Little Hen* (Butler and Gay); *Amapola* (Lacalle and Gamse); *Dolores* (Loesser and Alter), as part of a Chorus Medley.

1943 *Rhapsody in Blue* (11 minutes).

1945 *Summer Breezes* (King); *Lotus Land* and *Pierrot Triste* (Cyril Scott); *Pacific Party* (Foster); *The Darkened Valley* (Ireland).

1946 *Love Me For Ever* (Schetzinger); *Ritual Fire Dance* [twice] (Falla); the *Theme from the Warsaw Concerto* (Addinsell); *Sweet Nothings* (Rettenberg); *Valse des Follies* (Hilliam); *Shopping Tour* (Phillips).

1950 *Elfinette* (Janus).

A special case, not in the list of works above but included in my overall figures, was *Keyboard Cavalcade*, six fifteen-minute programmes which may be worth giving complete since they show Mayerl operating well outside the syncopated orbit. *Marigold* was the signature tune for all of them, which has added to its appearances in the full list. Without these, *Ace of Hearts* would be top.

26 Aug.: *Marigold*; *Valse des Follies* (Hilliam); *Stardust* (Carmichael); *Sweet Nothings* (Rettenburg); *Dreamy Afternoon* (Hartley); *April's Fool* (Mayerl).

27 Aug.: *Marigold*; *Melodie, Notturno, Butterfly, To the Spring, Wedding Day* (all Grieg).

28 Aug.: *Marigold*; *Chasing Shadows* (Silver); *Phil the Fluter's Ball* (French); *Blue Danube* (arr. Mayerl); *Smoke gets in your Eyes* (Kern); *Limehouse Blues* (Braham). [All published transcriptions]

29 Aug.: *Marigold*; *Autumn Crocus*; *Sweet William*; *Fireside Fusiliers*; *Ace of Hearts*; *Song of the Fir Tree*.

30 Aug.: *Marigold*; then *Arabesque*; *La Fille avec cheveux de lin*; *Jardin sous la pluie*; *Clair de lune* (all Debussy).

31 Aug.: *Marigold*; and then, according to Mayerl, 'the programme was a "Tune a Minute" non-stop but I can't remember all the titles'.

Mayerl's TV appearances featured his own works, included in the figures above, until 1946 when he performed works by other composers as well. In three programmes from Aug. 1946 to Aug. 1947 year he included *Valses des Follies* (Hilliam) in every one; *Star Dust* (Carmichael); *Canadian Capers* (Chandler, White, & Cohen); and *Ritual Fire Dance* (Falla).

A programme for children on 25 Oct. 1950 consisted of *Bats in the Belfry*; *Punch and Judy Polka* (Monro); *Ma Belle Marguerite* (Ellis); *Toy Piano Minuet* (Marcotte); *Buffoon* (Confrey); as well as *Shy Ballerina* (Mayerl), which Mrs Mayerl later discussed in 'More Titles and Stories', *Billy Mayerl Circle Newsletter*, 1/44 (Winter 1974), 6.

3

Mayerl's Performing Right Society Earnings, 1926–1998

Membership number 020245340

Mayerl's PRS earnings are given in pounds and pence throughout. The figures in brackets, given to the nearest pound, are based on the Retail Prices Index supplied by the Office of National Statistics. These are intended to show the approximate purchasing power of Mayerl's earnings in terms of July 1998.

Year	Earnings (£)	1998 equivalent (£)
1927	0.39	[13]
1928	3.52	[124]
1929	8.33	[294]
1930	19.13	[699]
1931	52.57	[2,061]
1932	106.11	[4,264]
1933	59.04	[2,434]
1934	88.29	[3,616]
1935	74.51	[3,013]
1936	44.46	[1,743]
1937	160.57	[6,002]
1938	183.84	[6,793]
1939	146.74	–
1940	108.12	–
1941	114.04	–
1942	125.32	–
1943	112.53	–
1944	91.80	–
1945	67.53	–
1946	96.44	[2,138]
1947	94.82	[1,967]
1948	112.54	[2,173]
1949	91.23	[1,705]
1950	65.18	[1,194]

Year	Earnings (£)	1998 equivalent (£)
1951	155.51	[2,584]
1952	805.66	[12,791]
1953	1,384.14	[21,444]
1954	886.80	[13,480]
1955	1,025.20	[15,085]
1956	1,156.20	[16,232]
1957	1,155.32	[15,706]
1958	1,152.72	[15,220]
1959	900.73	[11,772]
1960	651.89	[8,417]
1961	742.26	[9,322]
1962	853.24	[10,352]
1963	1,135.75	[13,524]
1964	713.88	[8,226]
1965	454.06	[4,999]
1966	519.71	[5,505]
1967	448.91	[4,633]
1968	609.23	[6,008]
1969	483.43	[4,525]
1970	823.26	[7,242]
1971	854.02	[6,864]
1972	804.76	[6,038]
1973	976.60	[6,716]
1974	1,180.20	[6,994]
1975	1,217.72	[5,809]
1976	1,360.15	[5,567]
1977	1,603.29	[5,664]
1978	1,311.07	[4,277]
1979	1,695.73	[4,879]
1980	1,735.21	[4,231]
1981	1,680.40	[3,663]
1982	2,014.69	[4,043]
1983	2,421.73	[4,647]
1984	2,524.94	[4,615]
1985	1,473.74	[2,539]
1986	1,347.84	[2,246]
1987	1,586.53	[2,538]
1988	1,951.51	[2,976]
1989	1,812.58	[2,564]
1990	2,725.29	[3,520]
1991	4,007.23	[4,892]
1992	3,026.44	[3,561]
1993	2,060.95	[2,387]

Year	Earnings (£)	1998 equivalent (£)
1994	3,343.78	[3,782]
1995	2,443.14	[2,671]
1996	3,584.06	[3,825]
1997	3,980.95	[4,120]

4

Mayerl's Desert Island Discs

BBC Home Service, 21 April 1958
Introduced by Roy Plomley, produced by Monica Chapman

1. Ravel, *Laideronette* (Empress of the Pagodas) from *Ma mère l'oye* (Mother Goose Suite); Philharmonia Orchestra/Guilini; Columbia 33CX 1518—side 2 band 2; 3′34″.
2. Anthony Collins, *Vanity Fair*; London Promenade Orchestra/Collins; Decca F 10337—beginning; 2′22″.
3. Stravinsky, *Le Chant du rossignol* (Song of the Nightingale); Cincinnati Symphony Orchestra/Goossens; HMV D.B. 9339—side 1; 2′19″.
4. Roger Quilter, *A Children's Overture*; London Philharmonic Orchestra/Wood; Columbia DB 951—ending; 1′34″.
5. John Ireland, *Sea Fever*; Frederick Harvey (baritone) with Orchestra/Philip Green; HMV B. 10233; one side; 2′15″.
6. Robert Farnon, *State Occasion*; Queen's Hall Light Orchestra/Farnon; Cappell C 294—beginning; 1′55″.
7. Milhaud, *Sumare* from *Saudades do Brasil*, transcribed for violin and piano by Claude Levy; Heifetz/ Arpad Sandor; HMV D.A. 1375—side 1; 1′55″.
8. Johann Strauss, *Mein Herr Marquis* (Laughing Song) from *Die Fledermaus*; Sari Barabas (soprano) with Nordwestdeutschen Rundfunk Philharmonic Orchestra/Schüchter; HMV DLP 1120—side 2; 1′42″.

DISCOGRAPHY

Compiled by John Watson

BILLY MAYERL's recording career lasted over thirty years, beginning with primitive acoustic recordings in the early 1920s and ending in the 1950s with LPs and tape. In addition to the numerous piano solos for which he is best remembered, his output also included singing, accompanying, and conducting. He was associated with several record companies, especially those under the EMI banner.

This discography concentrates on Mayerl's commercial recordings, although there are known to be a few unissued acetates and wireless broadcasts surviving in private collections. Though outside the scope here, it is hoped that this material, complemented with other additional information, together with the excluded band recordings discussed later, will be included in a definitive discography by this writer in the future.

The recording sessions here are presented in chronological order, all records being 10″ unless shown otherwise.

Mayerl also made over 100 records with the Savoy Havana Band, initially for Columbia, and later HMV. It was with them that he made his recording début in July 1922 with two obscure songs; 'Tippy canoe', a waltz by Fred Fisher; and the foxtrot 'Roaming' (Columbia 3146). The band also recorded as the Savoy Harmonists for Vocalion and under various pseudonyms for smaller labels. Though limitations of space prevent them being listed here, this information may to be found in *British Dance Bands on Record* by Brian Rust and Sandy Forbes (General Gramophone Publications, 1989.) Mayerl is also believed to have played in the Syncopated Quartet, an HMV recording group based on Havana band personnel.

On most of these records Mayerl is almost inaudible, but, fortunately, on a handful of recordings he featured a hot piano solo chorus, some notable examples being: 'Bah, bah Bartholomew'; 'Dancing honeymoon'; 'I wish I could shimmy like my sister Kate'; 'I'm knee deep in daises'; 'It ain't gonna rain no mo' '; and Confrey's ubiquitous novelty *Kitten on the Keys*.

In addition to the hit foxtrots and waltzes of the day, the band also occasionally recorded some of Mayerl's own early compositions. These include: 'Dearie, if you knew'; 'Did Tosti raise his bowler hat?'; 'I loved, I lost'; 'Just keep on dancing'; 'Longing for you'; 'Love's lottery'; 'Some day in Cambay'; 'Southern rose'; and 'Tell me in the moonlight', the latter incorporating a delightful solo by the composer.

Other important records made by the Savoy Havana Band are six titles now considered as notable examples of early British jazz. The three 12″ records, made during November 1923, and now very rare, are: Blue Hoosier Blues/Runnin' Wild (Col 952);

Henpecked Blues/Farewell Blues (Col 953); 'Tain't nobody's business if I do/ Downhearted (Col 954). Of those, the last three each uniquely feature Mayerl playing a piano solo chorus of his own personal interpretation of the blues.

Mayerl's last recording session with the Savoy Havana Band was on 17 March 1926, just over a year after their move to HMV. His departure from the band allowed him to form his own 'Vocalion' Orchestra, a new and more lucrative venture which also ensured he received more of the limelight.

Mayerl also produced special tuition records for his School. They were sold either by mail order or directly from the School and were intended to complement the written courses. The recordings were manufactured by several companies in various forms for a period of over twenty years. Unfortunately, each company either modified the existing matrixes or allocated its own numbering systems. These practices have caused much confusion for discographers, making study unnecessarily complex. For these reasons a summary is shown here.

The Billy Mayerl School first advertised its tuition courses in early 1926, but it was almost four years before the first accompanying gramophone records were made. Recorded in December 1929, the four-record set 'Personal Demonstration Course in Modern Syncopation for Pianoforte' (LO 455–0462) featured Mayerl describing and playing examples from the written lessons. His business partner, Geoffrey Clayton, acted as narrator. Of particular interest is Mayerl's playing of his own specially composed demonstration foxtrot 'Ev'ry hour of the day' in simple and transcribed versions. The course was later supplemented with a disc of the advanced Rhythm Course (LO 700–701), recorded seven months later.

Incidentally, though the School records had their own specially designed labels, the first recordings were in fact made by Vocalion, but pressed by Universal Music Co. at Hayes, Middlesex. In the spring of 1932 Vocalion was acquired by Crystalate, but the records continued to be pressed by Universal as before.

During August or September of 1931 a new five-record set, the Preliminary Course' (LO 1184–1193) was recorded. Originally aimed at the novice, its interest now is principally Mayerl's performance on the last record of Chopin's Prelude in B minor, and his own Prelude in F minor. Curiously, this set was rereleased during the early 1950s by the Times Film Company of Manchester (TF 101–110).

Late in 1934 the Personal Demonstration Course in Modern Syncopation was rerecorded, but abridged to three records. The course was then combined with the original single Rhythm Course disc, which had been relabelled as record four of that course. 'Ev'ry hour of the day' was replaced by a new, more modern 'Imaginary Foxtrot', again in simple and transcribed versions. This set was also rereleased during the early 1950s by the Times Film Company of Manchester (TF 111–118).

With the destruction of the School's remaining stock of records during the 1940s London Blitz, the post-war relaunch of the School necessitated a new set of records. These were made c.February 1950, by the Gui de Buire company of New Bond Street, with Mayerl at the piano, assisted by Bob Danvers-Walker replacing Geoffrey Clayton as narrator. Both the Preliminary Course (now G de B 1066/1–10) and the Personal Demonstration Course in Modern Syncopation—the latter renamed as the Modern Rhythmic Playing Course (now G de B 1066/11–18)—were produced. However, far from being modern, the content and format remained almost identical to the old pre-war course of *c*.December 1934, which itself mostly dated from Mayerl's heyday of the late 1920s. Though these records demonstrate his abilities as both educator and businessman, these curiosities, though unique, are now of mostly historical value.

I should like to acknowledge the assistance of the following: Frank Andrews, Arthur Badrock, Ernie Bayly, Robin Cherry, EMI Archives, Alex Hassan, John Hobbs, Hugh Palmer, Geoff Milne, Mike Sutcliffe, and Edward S. Walker.

ABBREVIATIONS

Col	Columbia	PaE	Parlophone
Dec	Decca	Voc	Vocalion
HMV	His Master's Voice		

Entries in this Discography are not indexed.

BILLY MAYERL: A DISCOGRAPHY

BILLY MAYERL, Pianoforte Solo   Hayes, Middx., 15 Sept. 1925
Solo Pianist to the Savoy Havana Band

Bb 6679–1–2	The Jazz Master (Billy Mayerl)	HMV rejected
Bb 6680–1–2	All of a Twist (Billy Mayerl)	HMV rejected
Bb 6681–1–2	Eskimo Shivers (Billy Mayerl)	HMV rejected
Bb 6682–1–2	The Jazz Mistress (Billy Mayerl)	HMV rejected

BILLY MAYERL, Pianoforte Solo   Hayes, Middx., 24 Sept. 1925
Solo Pianist to the Savoy Havana Band

Bb 6679–4	The Jazz Master (Billy Mayerl)	HMV B 2131
Bb 6680–4	All of a Twist (Billy Mayerl)	HMV B 2130
Bb 6681–4	Eskimo Shivers (Billy Mayerl)	—
Bb 6682–3	The Jazz Mistress (Billy Mayerl)	HMV B 2131

BILLY MAYERL, Pianoforte Solo   Hayes, Middx., 12 Nov. 1925
Solo Pianist to the Savoy Havana Band

| Bb 7245–1 | Jazzaristrix (Billy Mayerl) | HMV B 2203 |
| Bb 7246–2 | Virginia Creeper (Billy Mayerl) | — |

BILLY MAYERL, Pianoforte Solo   London, 3 Mar. 1926

| WA 2974–2 | Piano Exaggerations—No. 1 Loose Elbows (Billy Mayerl) | Col 3926 |
| WA 2975–1 | Piano Exaggerations—No. 2 Antiquary (Billy Mayerl) | — |

BILLY MAYERL AND HIS ORCHESTRA   London, *c*.21 May 1926
Billy Mayerl, piano, vocal, director/2 trumpets/trombone/Charlie Swinnerton and another, clarinet, soprano sax, alto sax/tenor sax/violin/banjo/brass tuba/drums.

04456–1	Wandering on to Avalon (v) (Tolchard Evans)	Voc X 9812
04457–1	Wait till tomorrow night (Leslie, Palmer, Woods)	—
04458–1	She's got forget-me-not eyes (v) (Mayerl, Helmore)	Voc X 9811
04459–1	Do you forget ? [waltz] (Reg Batten)	—

BILLY MAYERL, Pianoforte Solo   London, 4 June 1926
   WA 3366–1–2   Piano Exaggerations—No. 4 Sleepy Piano (Billy Mayerl)   Col rejected
   WA 3367–1–2   Piano Exaggerations—No. 3 Jack-in-the-Box (Billy Mayerl) Col rejected

JOE LEE, Vocal with BILLY MAYERL, Piano   [same session]
   WA 3368–1–2   Cecilia (Herman Ruby, Dave Dreyer)   Col rejected

BILLY MAYERL AND HIS ORCHESTRA   London, c.25 June 1926
   04501   Me—Myself and I (v) (Link, Bergere, Frisch)   Voc X 9824
   04502   While my pretty one sleeps (v) (Carroll Gibbons)   —
   04503–1   I wish I'd bought my missus on the hire-purchase system (v)   Voc X 9825
               (Percival Mackey, Tony Lowry)
   04504–1   Somebody's lonely (Davis)   —

BILLY MAYERL AND HIS ORCHESTRA   London, c.13 Aug. 1926
   M 05–1   I'm taking that baby home (v2) (Godfrey, David)   Voc X 9842
   M 06–1   Summer rain brings the roses again (Rule, McGhee)   —
   M   I never see Maggie alone (v) (Everett Lynton)   Voc X 9843
   M   Just a cottage small [by a waterfall] [waltz] (J. F. Hanley)   —

BILLY MAYERL, Pianoforte Solo   London, 26 Aug. 1926
   WA 3366–3   Piano Exaggerations—No. 4 Sleepy Piano (Billy Mayerl)   Col 4115
   WA 3367–3   Piano Exaggerations—No. 3 Jack-in-the-Box (Billy Mayerl)   —

BILLY MAYERL AND HIS ORCHESTRA   London, late Aug. 1926
   M 013–1   Hello, Aloha ! How are you ? (v2)
               (L. Wolfe Gilbert, Abel Baer)   Voc X 9881
   M 014–1   Who taught you this ? [Who taught you that ?] (Berg, Adler)   —
   M   Gentlemen prefer blondes (v) (Irving Berlin)   Voc X 9882
   M   Scatter your smiles (Max Kortlander, Pete Wendling)   —

BILLY MAYERL [Piano, Vocal] and GWEN FARRAR [Cello, Vocal]   London,
                                                   30 Aug. 1926
   M 017–2   Masculine Women ! Feminine Men ! (Leslie, Monaco)   Voc X 9887
   M 018–2   I'm always just a little bit not right (Kahn, Donaldson)   —
   M 019   I'm lonely without you (Harry Warren)   Voc X 9888
   M 020   Can't your friend find a friend for me ? (Lou Handman ?)   Voc X 9890

BILLY MAYERL [Piano, Vocal] and GWEN FARRAR [Cello, Vocal]   London,
                                                   c.9 Sept. 1926
   M 030   In My Gondola (Harry Warren)   Voc X 9889
   M 031   Want a little lovin' (Harry Warren)   —
   M 032   I'm a little blackbird looking for a bluebird   Voc X 9888
                (Grant Clarke, Roy Turk, George Meyer, Arthur Johnson)
   M 033   An Instrumental Excerpt (?)   Voc X 9890

BILLY MAYERL AND HIS ORCHESTRA   London, c.24 Sept. 1926
   M 051–1   That night in Araby (v) (Rose, Snyder, Nussbaum)   Voc X 9896
   M 053–2   Dreamily [waltz] (Eric Little, H. M. Tennent)   —
             Lov'- lov'- lovin' you (v) (?)   Voc X 9897
             June Rose (Billy Mayerl)   —

BILLY MAYERL AND HIS 'VOCALION' ORCHESTRA   London, Oct.–Nov. 1926
Personnel probably similar to the above, with Buddy Lee, vocal.

M 090–1	Am I wasting my time on you ? (Johnson, Bibo)	Voc X 9911
M 091–1	I ain't got nobody and I don't want nobody but you (vBL) (Abel Baer)	Voc X 9910
M 092–1	Hi-Diddle-Diddle (vBL) (Carleton A Coon, Hal Keidel)	Voc X 9911
M 093–1	Toodle-oo Sal (Billy Mayerl)	Voc X 9910

BILLY MAYERL [Piano, Vocal] and GWEN FARRAR [Cello, Vocal]   London, Nov. 1926

M 0131	Two Ton Tessie (Roy Turk, Lou Handman)	Voc X 9920
M 0132	You flew away from the nest (Bert Kalmar, Harry Ruby)	—
M 0133	Sitting around (Kahn, Saunders)	Voc X 9928
M 0134	Drink to me only with thine eyes [A Novel Interpretation] (Callcott)	—

BILLY MAYERL AND HIS 'VOCALION' ORCHESTRA   London, c.26 Nov. 1926

M 0139–1	Caring for you (vBM) (Carl Lang)	Voc X 9922
M 0140–1	I'm walking around in circles (Lewis, Young, Phillips)	—
M 0141–1	Lay me down to sleep in Carolina (Jack Yellen, Milton Ager)	Voc X 9923
M 0142–1	Where'd you get those eyes ? (v) (Walter Donaldson)	—

BILLY MAYERL AND HIS 'VOCALION' ORCHESTRA   London, c. 21 Dec. 1926
Billy Mayerl, piano, vocal, director/2 trumpets/trombone/Charlie Swinnerton and another, clarinet, soprano sax, alto sax/tenor sax/violin/banjo/brass tuba/drums/Bobby Sanders, vocal.

M 0172	Perhaps you'll think of me [waltz] (vBM) (Edgar Leslie, Billy Stone)	Voc X 9941
M 0173–1	Just a bird's eye view [of my old Kentucky home] (Gus Kahn, Walter Donaldson)	Voc X 9940
M 0174–1	I can't get over a girl like you [loving a boy like me] (vBM) (H. Ruskin, M. Broones)	—
M 0175	I've never seen a straight banana (Ted Waite)	Voc X 9941

BILLY MAYERL AND HIS 'VOCALION' ORCHESTRA   London, 21 Jan. 1927
Billy Mayerl, piano, vocal, director/2 trumpets/trombone/Charlie Swinnerton, clarinet, soprano sax, alto sax/Nat Star, clarinet, alto sax/tenor sax/violin/banjo/brass tuba/drums/Bobby Sanders, vocal.

M 0225–2	I've got the girl (Walter Donaldson)	Voc X 9973
M 0226–1	Just a rose in old Killarney [waltz] (Frank Swain)	Voc X 9957
M	Reaching for the moon (Benny Davis, Jesse Greer)	Voc X 9956
M	Cuckoo (Leslie Sarony, Jimmy Campbell, Reg Connelly)	—

BILLY MAYERL [Piano, Vocal] and GWEN FARRAR [Cello, Vocal]   London, Jan.–Feb. 1927

| M 0268–1 | I think of you (Douglas Furber, Carroll Gibbons) | Voc X 9969 |
| M 0269–2 | Mandy (Herbert) | — |

BILLY MAYERL AND HIS 'VOCALION' ORCHESTRA   London, c.11 Mar. 1927
Billy Mayerl, piano, vocal, director/2 trumpets/trombone/Charlie Swinnerton and another, clarinet, soprano sax, alto sax/tenor sax/violin/banjo/brass tuba/drums/Bobby Sanders, vocal.

M 0316–1	Blue Skies (Irving Berlin)	Voc X 9972
M 0317–1	The more we are together (v) (Irving King)	Voc X 9971
M 0318–1	When lights are low in Cairo (Sherman Myers)	—
M 0319–1	Shepherd of the hills (vBM) (Horatio Nicholls)	Voc X 9972

BILLY MAYERL AND HIS 'VOCALION ORCHESTRA'   London, late Mar. 1927
  M 0347–2   Reading between the lines (vBS) (Carl Lang)   Voc X 9989
  M 0348–2   Shalimar [waltz] (vBS) (Horatio Nicholls)   Voc X 9988
  M 0349–1   Chilly Billy Wun Lung (Wallace, Rose)   —
  M 0350–2   Since Tommy Atkins taught the Chinese how to Charleston!   Voc X 9989
        (Jimmy Campbell, Reg Connelly)

BILLY MAYERL, Pianoforte Solo   London, 19 Apr. 1927
  WAX 2605–1   The Desert Song—Piano Medley :   12″ Col 9212
        One Alone/The Riff Song/The Desert Song/It
        (Hammerstein, Romberg, Harbach)
Note: the reverse of this record is not by Billy Mayerl.

BILLY MAYERL AND HIS 'VOCALION' ORCHESTRA   London, *c*.20–1 Apr. 1927
  M 0372–1   What does it matter ? [waltz] (v) (Irving Berlin)   Voc X 10001
  M 0373–1   When the love bird leaves the nest (v) (Wade)   —
  M   Da-Da-Da (George W. Meyer)   Voc X 10000
  M   Sing a little love song (George W. Meyer)   —

BILLY MAYERL, Pianoforte Solo   London, 22 Apr. 1927
  WAX 2643–1   Whitebirds—Selection, Part 1 (George W. Meyer)   12″ Col 9215
        Three Men of Twickenham/Da Da Da/
        Oliver Twist/Flower of Spain
  WAX 2644–1   Whitebirds—Selection, Part 2 (George W. Meyer)   —
        Cuddle up/Sing a little love song/
        All the world is trying/Tomawama Land

BILLY MILTON [Vocal] with BILLY MAYERL at the Piano   London, *c*.Aug. 1927
  Z 158–2   I've got a sweetie on the radio (Mayerl, Western)   8″ Broadcast 158
  Z 159–3   The Doll Dance (Nacio Herb Brown)   —
Note: the above two sides were also issued on 8″ Unison, presumably with the same catalogue
number.

BILLY MAYERL, Piano Solo   London, 25 Aug. 1927
  WA 6063–2   Puppet's Suite—No. 2 Judy (Billy Mayerl)   Col 4676
  WA 6064–1   Puppet's Suite—No. 1 Golliwog (Billy Mayerl)   —
  WAX 3033–1   Girl Friend—Selection (Hart, Rodgers) introducing: 12″ Col 9270
        Girl Friend/Blue Room/Mountain Greenery
Note: the reverse of Col 9270 is not by Billy Mayerl.

RAMON NEWTON, Baritone [with Violin Obligato and Piano]   London,
    (WA 6281)   29 Sept. 1927

RAMON NEWTON, Baritone [with Piano] (WA 6282)
(BILLY MAYERL is the pianist but is not credited on the label)
  WA 6281–1–2   Souvenirs (Edgar Leslie, Horatio Nicholls)   Col rejected
  WA 6282–2   Old Names Of Old Flames (Howard Johnson, Irving Bibo) Col 4589
  WA 6292–1–2   Possibly (Jimmy Dyrenforth, Carroll Gibbons)   Col rejected
Note: earlier labels incorrectly state 'Baritone with Orchestra', which despite being corrected
later as shown above still did not credit Billy Mayerl as pianist on the label. 'Souvenirs' features
additional violin accompaniment to Ramon Newton's vocal. Newton was principal violinist and
vocalist with the Savoy Havana Band, but did he accompany himself here, surely a technically

difficult task, or was another violinist engaged? Unfortunately, there are no further details in the recording file.

RAMON NEWTON [Baritone with Violin Obligato and Piano]   London, 7 Oct. 1927
(Billy Mayerl is the pianist but is not credited on the label)
   WA 6281–3   Souvenirs (Edgar Leslie, Horatio Nicholls)   Col 4589
Note: see comments for the 29 Sept. 1927 session.

BILLY MAYERL, Piano Solo   [same session]
   WA 6353–2   Marigold (Billy Mayerl)   Col 4783
   WA 6354–1   Puppet's Suite—No. 3 Punch (Billy Mayerl)   Col 4677
   WA 6355–2   Hollyhock (Billy Mayerl)   Col 4783
   WA 6356–1   Chop-sticks (Billy Mayerl)   Col 4677

COLUMBIA LIGHT OPERA COMPANY conducted by   London, 7 Nov. 1927
CHARLES PRENTICE with BILLY MAYERL at the piano
   WAX 3102–2   Peggy Ann—Vocal Gems (Lorenz Hart, Richard Rodgers) 12″ Col 9267
              Hello!/Maybe it's me/A Tree in the park/
              A Country Mouse/Where's that rainbow?
   WAX 3103–2   The Girl Friend—Vocal Gems (Lorenz Hart, Richard Rodgers)   —
              The Girl Friend/Mountain Greenery/What's the use
              of talking/Blue Room/The Girl Friend

HAMILTON SISTERS AND FORDYCE [Vocal] Trio with Piano   London, 30 Nov. 1927
(Billy Mayerl is the pianist but is not credited on the label)
   WA 6617–1   Who-oo you-oo, that's you (Yellen, Ager)   Col 4698
   WA 6618–1   Zulu wail (Skinner, Bibo)   —
Note: according to the ledger, Mayerl made no other recording at this session.

BILLY MAYERL, Piano Solo   London, 7 June 1928
   WA 7459–1   Three Miniatures in Syncopation   Col 4975
              No. 1 Cobweb (Billy Mayerl)
   WA 7460–2   Three Miniatures in Syncopation   —
              No. 2 Muffin Man (Billy Mayerl)
              No. 3 Clockwork (Billy Mayerl)

BILLY MAYERL, Piano Solo   Petty France, London, 11 October 1928
   WA 7968–2   Honky-Tonk (Billy Mayerl)   Col 5154
   WA 7969–1   Rag Doll (Nacio Herb Brown)   —
   WAX 4145–2   That's a good girl—Selection (Meyer, Charig,
              I. Gershwin, Furber)   12″ Col 9594
              Sweet so and so/Tell me why/The one I'm
              looking for/Fancy our meeting/Chirp, Chirp
   WAX 4146–1   Showboat—Selection (Oscar Hammerstein II, Jerome Kern)   —
              Can't help lovin' dat man/Ol' Man River/
              Why do I love you ?/Make Believe/Ol' Man River

BILLY MAYERL [Piano, Vocal] and GWEN FARRAR [Vocal, Cello]   London,
                                30 Oct. 1928
   WA 8043–1   It don't do nothin' but rain (Cook)   Col 5186
   WA 8044–1   Funny Face—He loves and she loves (Gershwin, Gershwin)   Col 5281
   WA 8045–1   So Long Letty—Rainbow (Billy Mayerl, Frank Eyton)   —

WA 8046–1   Old Fashioned Girls (Kenneth and George Weston)   Col 5186

THE COURT SYMPHONY ORCHESTRA   Petty France, London, 16 Nov. 1928
conducted by BILLY MAYERL
    WAX 4309–1   Sennen Cove—Tone Poem [Part 1] (Billy Mayerl)   12″ Col 9688
    WAX 4310–1   Sennen Cove—Tone Poem [Part 2] (Billy Mayerl)   —

BILLY MAYERL, Piano Solo   London, 23 Nov. 1928
    WA 8139–1   Lucky Girl—Selection, Part 1 (Charig, Robin, Myers)   Col 5178
                  Lucky Girl/Where have you been all my life ?
    WA 8140–1   Lucky Girl—Selection, Part 2 (Caesar, Charig, Meyer, Kahn)   —
                  Crazy Rhythm/When I set eyes on you/
                  Under the star where I was born

THE COURT SYMPHONY ORCHESTRA   Petty France, London, 6 Dec. 1928
conducted by BILLY MAYERL
    WAX 4418–2   Pastoral Sketches (Billy Mayerl)   12″ Col 9914
                  (a) Legend/(b) Lovers' Lane
    WAX 4419–2   Pastoral Sketches (Billy Mayerl)   —
                  (c) A Village Festival

BILLY MAYERL, Piano Solo   London, 30 Jan. 1929
    WA 8487–2   Mr Cinders—Piano Selection, Part 1 (Vivian Ellis,
                  Grey, Newman)   Col 5336
                  Spread a little happiness/I've got you and you've got me/
                  On the Amazon/Spread a little happiness
    WA 8488–1   Mr. Cinders—Piano Selection, Part 2 (Vivian Ellis)   —
                  Ev'ry little moment/I'm a one–man girl (Vivian Ellis)

BILLY MAYERL and GWEN FARRAR   London, 8 Feb. 1929
    MB 3–1–2   I've got a sweetie on the radio (Billy Mayerl,
                  Kenneth Western)   Dec unissued
    MB 4–1–2   Looking for the sunshine (?)   Dec unissued

BILLY MAYERL, Piano Solo [and vocal where shown]   London, 15 Apr. 1929
    WA 8865–1   Wisteria (Billy Mayerl)   Col 5416
    WA 8866–2   The Wedding of the Painted Doll (Nacio Herb Brown)   —
    WA 8867–1   Love Lies—Medley   Col 5385
                  A house on a hilltop (Billy Mayerl, Frank Eyton)
                  You've made a difference to me (Desmond Carter, Jack Hedley)
                  I lift up my finger and I say tweet tweet (vBM) (Leslie Sarony)
    WA 8868–1   Wake up and dream—Medley (Cole Porter)   —
                  Looking at you/Let's do it, let's fall in love

BILLY MAYERL and GWEN FARRAR   Chenil Galleries, London, 24 Apr. 1929
    MB 85–1–2   Let's do it, let's fall in love (Cole Porter)   Dec rejected
    MB 86–1–2   What about me? (Billy Mayerl)   Dec rejected
    MB 87–1–2   Thinking of you (Bert Kalmar, Harry Ruby)   Dec rejected
    MB 89–1–2   A house on a hilltop (Billy Mayerl, Frank Eyton)   Dec rejected
Note: the missing matrix (MB 88) remains untraced, but is believed not to feature Mayerl and
Farrar.

BILLY MAYERL and GWEN FARRAR   Chenil Galleries, Chelsea, London,
                                                                      17 May 1929
Vocal Duet with Piano and Cello accomp.
    MB 85–4   Let's do it, let's fall in love (Cole Porter)   Dec M 27
    MB 86–4   What about me ? (Billy Mayerl)   —
    MB 87–3–4–5   Thinking of you (Bert Kalmar, Harry Ruby)   Dec unissued ?
    MB 89–3–4–5   A house on a hilltop (Billy Mayerl, Frank Eyton) Dec unissued ?

BILLY MAYERL and GWEN FARRAR   London, 21 Aug. 1929
    MB 407–1–2–3   I've got a feeling I'm falling (Billy Rose, Harry Link,
                                       Fats Waller)   Dec unissued
    MB 408–1–2   My Sin (De Sylva, Brown, Henderson)   Dec unissued

BILLY MAYERL, Piano Solo   London, 17 Sept. 1929
    WA 9500–1   Sweet Nothings (Milton J. Rettenberg)   Col 5671 Col FB 1621
    WA 9501–1   Jasmine (Billy Mayerl)   —   —

BILLY MAYERL, Piano Solo   London, 9 Sept. 1929
    WA 9510–1   Follow Through—Selection, Part 1 (de Sylva,
                                       Brown, Henderson)   Col 5605
                                       I want to be bad/Button up your overcoat
    WA 9511–1   Follow Through—Selection, Part 2 (de Sylva, Brown,
                                       Henderson)   —
                                       You wouldn't fool me, would you?/My Lucky Star/
                                       I could give up anything but you

BILLY MAYERL and GWEN FARRAR   Chenil Galleries, Chelsea, London,
                                                                     20 Nov. 1929

Vocal Duet with Pianoforte accomp. [M 107]
    MB 689–1   Dreamy Honolulu (Gumble, West)   Dec M 107
    MB 690–2   We can't blame the Bobbies for that (Billy Mayerl)   —
    MB 691–2   When the bluebirds and the blackbirds get together Dec M 98
                                       (Billy Moll, Harry Barris)

BILLY MAYERL and GWEN FARRAR   Chenil Galleries, Chelsea, London,
                                                                     11 Dec. 1929
Vocal Duet with Pianoforte accomp. [M 116]
    MB 758–2   I may be wrong [but I think you're wonderful]
                                       (Ruskin, Sullivan)   Dec M 116
    MB 759–1   In Egypt (Low)   Dec M 98
    MB 760–2   Sunshine and Rain (Frank Eyton, Billy Mayerl) Dec M 116

BILLY MAYERL, Piano Solo   Petty France, London, 17 Jan. 1930
    WA 9950–1   Three Dances in Syncopation: (Billy Mayerl)   Col DB 45 Col FB 1573
                                       1 English Dance/2 Cricket Dance
    WA 9951–2   Three Dances in Syncopation: (Billy Mayerl)   —   —
                                       3 Harmonica Dance
    WA 9952–1   Here comes the bride—Selection (Schwartz)   Col DB 16
                                       I'll always remember/I'm like a sailor/High and Low
    WA 9953–1   The House that Jack Built—Selection (Ellis, Novello, Schwartz)   —
                                       My heart is saying/The thought never entered my head/
                                       She's such a comfort to me

BILLY MAYERL and GWEN FARRAR   Chenil Galleries, Chelsea, London,
                                                                    12 Feb. 1930
Vocal Duet with Pianoforte accomp.
    MB 948–1   Indispensable you (Billy Mayerl)   Dec M 123
    MB 949–1–2   You ain't my baby now (Billy Mayerl, Bert Page)   Dec rejected

BILLY MAYERL and GWEN FARRAR   Chenil Galleries, Chelsea, London,
                                                                    27 Feb. 1930
Vocal Duet with Pianoforte accomp. [M 123]
    MB 949–4   You ain't my baby now (Billy Mayerl, Bert Page)   Dec M 123
    MB 1011–2   I'm following you (Dryer, Macdonald)   Dec M 124
    MB 1012–2   Just you, just me (Ray Klages, Jesse Greer)   —
    MB 1013–1–2 Hang on to me (Ray Klages, Jesse Greer)   Dec unissued ?

BILLY MAYERL, Piano Solo   Petty France, London, 25 Apr. 1930
    WA 10317–1   Heads Up—Selection (Rodgers)   Col DB 117
                Why do you suppose ?/Me for you/
                My man is on the make/A ship without a sail
    WA 10318–1   Cochran's 1930 Revue—Selection (Ellis, Rodgers, Nichols)   —
                The Wind in the Willows/With a song in my heart/
                The little things you do

BILLY MAYERL [as LADDIE RAY], Syncopated Piano Solos   London, June 1930
    L 0659–2   King Of Jazz—Selection (Yellen, Ager, et al)   Broadcast Twelve 5172
    L 0660–2   Puttin' on the Ritz—Selection (Irving Berlin, et al.)   —
Note: these two recordings credited to Laddie Ray are actually by Billy Mayerl, but no other
records by him under this name are known. However, research on other recordings by Laddie
Ray (always on the same label) has shown that this pseudonym was also used by Peggy Cochrane
and one other, probably Harry Bidgood. The evidence suggests that Laddie Ray was a fictitious
creation by the Vocalion Company used to disguise the true identity of various artists for contractual reasons, a common practice at that time.

BILLY STEVENS, Baritone with   Petty France, London, 24 June 1930
BILLY MAYERL at the Piano
    WA 10501–1   Sons o' guns—Why ? (Swanstrom, Davis, Coots)   Col DB 184
    WA 10503–2   Sons o' guns—Cross your fingers (Swanstrom, Davis, Coots)   —
Note: the missing matrix (WA 10502–2) does not feature Billy Mayerl.

THE NATIONAL MILITARY BAND—with VOCAL QUARTETTE   Central Hall,
                                             Westminster, London, 3 July 1930
Conducted by the Composer, BILLY MAYERL
    WA 10534–1   The Empire Parade (Frank Eyton, Billy Mayerl)   Col DB 177
Note: it is believed that Billy Mayerl is not the conductor on the reverse of this record.

BILLY MAYERL, Piano Solo   Petty France, London, 10 July 1930
    WA 10547–2   Love Race—Piano Medley (Clarke)   Col DB 188
                Don't you see ?/Take me with you/
                Frivolous Feet/Spring's in the air

BILLY MAYERL, Piano Solo with   [same session]
uncredited Clarinet, probably VAN PHILLIPS

WA 10548–1   Sons o' guns—Piano Medley (Swanstrom, Davis, Coots)   Col DB 188
Cross your fingers/Why ?/It's you I love/Let's merge

BILLY MAYERL, Pianoforte Solo with   Petty France, London, July 1930
Clarinet Solo by VAN PHILLIPS
WA 10553–1   Sing, you sinners (Harling, Coslow)   Col DB 224
introducing—In my little hope chest/Theme
Songs—*Honey*
WA 10554–2   Any time's the time to fall in love (Janis, King, Coslow)   —
introducing—Sweepin' the clouds away
Theme Songs—*Paramount On Parade*

BILLY MAYERL, Pianoforte Solo   Petty France, London, 5 Oct. 1930
WA 10737–1   Safety in Numbers—Piano Medley (Richard A. Whiting)   Col DB 287
Love is my game/The Pick-Up /
You appeal to me/My future just passed
WA 10738–1   Let's go native—Piano Medley (Richard A. Whiting)   —
It seems to be spring/My mad moment/Let's go native
WA 10739   Nippy—Piano Medley, Part 1 (Billy Mayerl, Frank Eyton)   Col rejected
WA 10740   Nippy—Piano Medley, Part 2 (Billy Mayerl, Frank Eyton)   Col rejected

BILLY MAYERL, Pianoforte Solo   Petty France, London, 22 Oct. 1930
WA 10739–3   Nippy—Piano Medley, Part 1 (Billy Mayerl, Frank Eyton)   Col DB 288
Your sunny disposition and mine/Anything/It must be you
WA 10740–4   Nippy—Piano Medley, Part 2 (Billy Mayerl, Frank Eyton)   —
The Toytown Party/Two of Everything/
While we're in love/It must be you

BILLY MAYERL, Pianoforte Solo   Petty France, London, 23 Dec. 1930
WA 11018–1   Little Tommy Tucker—Piano Selection (Ellis, Schwartz)   Col DB 380
Out of the blue/Let's be sentimental/I have no words
WA 11019–1   Ever-Green—Piano Selection (Rodgers)   —
If I give into you/Dancing on the ceiling/Dear! Dear!

BILLY MAYERL, Pianoforte Solo   Petty France, London, 16 Jan. 1931
WA 11075–1   Stand up and sing—Piano Medley (Furber, Charig, Ellis)   Col DB 406
Take it or leave it/There's always tomorrow/
I would if I could/It's not you
WA 11076–1   Blue Roses—Piano Medley (Carter, Furber, Charig, Ellis)   —
My heart's a compass/I saw the moon through the window/
If I had three wishes/Dancing in your sleep

BILLY MAYERL, Pianoforte Solo   Petty France, London, 27 Feb. 1931
WA 11263–1   Baby's Birthday Party (Ronell)   Col DB 445
WA 11264–1   Ten Cents a Dance (Rodgers)   —

BILLY MAYERL, Pianoforte Solo   Petty France, London, 8 May 1931
WA 11578–1   The Millionaire Kid—Piano Medley, Part 1 (Mayerl, Eyton) Col DB 517
Who said so?/Devonshire/Thank you most sincerely
WA 11579–1   The Millionaire Kid—Piano Medley, Part 2 (Mayerl, Eyton)   —
Life is meant for love/Dance the Polka again/
I'd be lost without you

WA 11580–1   Song Hits—Piano Medley, Part 1   Col DB 534
                   The song is done (Robert Stolz)
                   Running between the raindrops (Dyrenforth, Gibbons)
WA 11581–1   Song Hits—Piano Medley, Part 2   —
                   Fiesta (Samuels, Whitcup)/Shout for happiness (Hart, Blight)
                   Goodnight Sweetheart (Noble, Campbell, Connelly)

BILLY MAYERL, Pianoforte Solo with Vocal Chorus   London, 18 Sept. 1931
[The vocalist is PHYLLIS ROBBINS]
CA 11988–1   You can't stop me from lovin' you   Col DB 639
                   (Mann Holiner, Alberta Nichols)

BILLY MAYERL, Pianoforte Solo   [same session]
introducing Xylophone [probably RUDY STARITA]
CA 11989–1   The Match Parade (Karl Wehle)   Col DB 639

BILLY MAYERL, Pianoforte Solo   London, 23 Sept. 1931
CA 11998–1   Mignonette (Billy Mayerl)   Col DB 728   Col FB 1485
CA 11999–2   Honeysuckle (Billy Mayerl)   —   —

BILLY MAYERL, Pianoforte Solo [with chimes 'effects']   London, 17 Oct. 1931
CA 12084–1   Say it with Carols—Piano Medley, Part 1
                   (Trad., arr. Mayerl)   Col DB 668   Col FB 1182
                   The mistletoe bough/Good King Wenceslas/
                   Little brown jug/God rest ye merry gentlemen/
                   Come landlord, fill the flowing bowl
CA 12085–1   Say it with Carols—Piano Medley, Part 2
                   (Trad., arr. Mayerl)   —   —
                   My grandfather's clock/The first Nowell/Drink to me only
                   with thine eyes/Fine old English gentleman/There is a tavern
                   in the town/Auld lang syne/We won't go home till morning

COLUMBIA ON PARADE   London, 30 Oct. 1931
'In which nineteen of Columbia's greatest artists and bands provide a unique entertainment.'
includes BILLY MAYERL (Piano) and BINNIE HALE (Vocal)
CAX 6245–2   Columbia On Parade (Part 1)   12″ Col DX 299
                   The Toytown Party (Eyton, Mayerl)/Tea for Two
                   (Ceasar, Youmans)

BILLY MAYERL, Pianoforte Solo   London, 6 Feb. 1932
CA 12410–1   Have you forgotten? (Leo Robin, Dana Suesse)   Col DB 777
CA 12411–1   Helen—Piano Selection (Offenbach, arr. Korngold)   —
                   Tsing La La/Finale from Act III/Shepherd's Song/Sleep On

BILLY MAYERL, Pianoforte Solo   London, 1 Mar. 1932
CA 12490–1   By the Fireside (Ray Noble, Jimmy Campbell, Reg   Col DB 806
                   Connelly) introducing: I wouldn't change you for the world
                   (Charles Newman, Isham Jones)
CA 12491–1   Try to remember me [when you're alone]
                   (Rush, Rene, Glen, Rose)   —
                   introducing: To be worthy of you (Lou Davis, J. Fred Coots)

BILLY MAYERL, Pianoforte Solo   Abbey Road, London, 16 Sept. 1932
   CA 13035–2   Words and Music—Selection, Part 1 (Noel Coward)   Col DB 939
                Something to do with spring/The Younger Generation/
                Let's say goodbye
   CA 13036–1   Words and Music—Selection, Part 2 (Noel Coward)   —
                The Children of the Ritz/The party's over now/
                Mad about the boy

THE DAILY MAIL MYSTERY RECORD   London, Nov. 1932
[includes BILLY MAYERL, Pianoforte Solo]
'Stars from Columbia, His Master's Voice, Parlophone, Regal and Zonophone. £1,950 in prizes
for correct or most correct lists of Artists. Closing date 14 January 1933.'
   OB 4509–1   Side 1 features Ambrose and His Orchestra, Leslie Hutchinson,   RO 100
                Derickson and Brown, Binnie Hale, Doris Hare, Howard Jacobs,
                Robert Naylor, Billy Mayerl, Raie da Costa, Debroy Somers Band.
Note: Mayerl plays a 2-bar introduction and 16-bar piano solo chorus of 'Today I feel so happy'(Paul
Abraham). Following on in tempo is Raie da Costa, who plays the last 16 bars of the song.

BILLY MAYERL, Pianoforte Solo   Abbey Road, London, 3 Jan. 1933
   CA 13327–1   Please handle with care (Stride, Ballard, trans. Mayerl)   Col DB 1035
   CA 13328–1   Balloons [Who'll buy my nice balloons?]
                (Magine, trans. Mayerl)   —

BILLY MAYERL, Pianoforte Solo   Abbey Road, London, 14 Sept. 1933
   CA 13921–2   Billy Mayerl's Own Selection—Part 1
                (Billy Mayerl)   Col DB 1219 Col FB 1438
                Pennywhistle/Marigold/Wisteria/
                Chopsticks/Ace of Spades
   CA 13922–1   Billy Mayerl's Own Selection—Part 2 (Billy Mayerl)   —   —
                Ace of Hearts/Junior Apprentice/
                Hollyhock/Canaries Serenade/White Heather

BILLY MAYERL, Pianoforte Solo   Abbey Road, London, 26 Oct. 1933
   CA 14100–1   Six Miniatures—Part 1 (Billy Mayerl)   Col DB 1239 Col FB 1397
                [Billy Mayerl's Own Selection—No.2]
                Beside a Rustic Bridge/Little Lady from Spain/
                A May Morning
   CA 14101–1   Six Miniatures—Part 2 (Billy Mayerl)   —   —
                [Billy Mayerl's Own Selection—No.2]
                Many years ago/My party frock/Air de Ballet

BILLY MAYERL, Pianoforte Solo   Abbey Road, London, 12 Dec. 1933
   CA 14214–1   Four Aces—Part 1 (Billy Mayerl)   Col DB 1308 Col FB 1264
                (a) Ace of Clubs (b) Ace of Hearts
   CA 14215–1   Four Aces—Part 2 (Billy Mayerl)   —   —
                (a) Ace of Diamonds (c) Ace of Spades

BILLY MAYERL, Pianoforte Solo   Abbey Road, London, 5 Apr. 1934
   CA 14428–1   Sporting Love—Selection, Part 1 (Mayerl, Eyton, Carter) Col DB 1369
                Don't worry/I ought not to/Have a heart
   CA 14429–1   Sporting Love—Selection, Part 2 (Mayerl, Eyton, Carter) —
                A-Shooting we will go/You're the reason why/
                Those in favour

BILLY MAYERL, Pianoforte Solo   Abbey Road, London, 19 April 1934
    CA 14447–1   Billy Mayerl's Savoy Havana Memories—
                Part 1   Col DB 1419   Col FB 1181
                Kitten on the Keys (Confrey)/Ukulele Lady (Kahn,
                Whiting)/What'll I do? (Berlin)/Carolina in the
                morning (Donaldson)/Chili-Bom-Bom (Donaldson, Friend)
    CA 14448–1   Billy Mayerl's Savoy Havana Memories—Part 2   —   —
                Dancing Time (Kern)/Keep on humming (?)/
                April Showers (Silvers)/Indian Love Call (Harbach,
                Hammerstein, Friml)/I'll build a stairway to paradise (Gershwin)

MR AND MRS BILLY MAYERL, Duet on one piano   Abbey Road, London,
                                                      31 Aug. 1934
    CA 14643–1   Ace of Spades (arr. by the composer,   Col DB 1445 Col FB 1161
                Billy Mayerl)
    CA 14644–1   Marigold (arr. by the composer, Billy Mayerl)   —   —

BILLY MAYERL, Pianoforte Solo   Abbey Road, London, 25 Oct. 1934
    CA 14745–1   The Joker (Mayerl)   Col DB 1488   Col FB 1296
    CA 14746–1   Hop-o-my-Thumb (Billy Mayerl)   —   —

BILLY MAYERL, Pianoforte Solo   Abbey Road, London, 5 Feb. 1935
    CA 14903–1   Mistletoe (Billy Mayerl)   Col DB 1524   Col FB 1162
    CA 14904–1   The Nimble Fingered Gentleman (Billy Mayerl)   —   —

BILLY MAYERL, Pianoforte Solo   London, March 1935
    CAX 7496–2   Prelude in C sharp minor (Rachmaninov)   12″ Col DX 682
    CAX 7497–1   Three Preludes [Op. 28] (Chopin)   —
                No. 4 in E minor/No. 6 in B minor/No. 20 in C minor

Note: Billy Mayerl plays on 'The World's Largest Piano'. Made by Challen to celebrate the Silver Jubilee of King George V and Queen Mary, this Art Deco style grand piano was over eleven feet long.

BILLY MAYERL, Piano and Harpsichord with   Abbey Road, London, 26 Aug. 1935
AUSTEN CROOM-JOHNSON Piano and spoken introductions
    CA 15199–1   Bats in the Belfry (Austen Croom-Johnson, Billy Mayerl)   Col FB 1115
    CA 15200–1   Green Tulips (Austen Croom-Johnson, Billy Mayerl)   —

BILLY MAYERL, Pianoforte Solo   Abbey Road, London, 7 Dec. 1935
    CA 15488–1   Twenty to One—Selection, Part 1
                (Billy Mayerl, Frank Eyton)   Col FB 1276
                How'd you like your eggs fried?/I'm going to be good/
                I've never felt like that before/Hi! Taxi
    CA 15489–1   Twenty to One—Selection, Part 2 (Billy Mayerl, Frank Eyton)   —
                Rhythmic Dance/Play the Tambourine /
                I'm at your service/You've fallen in l ove

BILLY MAYERL, Pianoforte Solo   Abbey Road, London, 1 May 1936
    CA 15737–1   Orange Blossom (Billy Mayerl)   Col FB 1416
    CA 15738–1   Limehouse Blues (Furber, Braham, trans. Mayerl)   —

Billy Mayerl, Pianoforte Solo   Abbey Road, London, 25 Aug. 1936
   CA 15887–1   Over She Goes—Selection, Part 1 (Mayerl, Eyton, Carter)   Col FB 1498
                  County Wedding/The Dance Goes On/I breathe on windows
   CA 15888–1   Over She Goes—Selection, Part 2 (Mayerl, Eyton, Carter)   —
                  Mine's a hopeless case/Over She Goes/Turn on the taps

STANLEY LUPINO (Comedian) and CHORUS with the   London, 26 Oct. 1936
SAVILLE THEATRE ORCHESTRA conducted by BILLY MAYERL
   CA 16008–1   Over She Goes—Yes, No ! (Mayerl, Eyton, Lupino)   Col FB 1538

STANLEY LUPINO, LADDIE CLIFF, ERIC FAWCETT (Vocals) with the   [same session]
SAVILLE THEATRE ORCHESTRA conducted by BILLY MAYERL
   CA 16009–1   Over She Goes—Side by Side (Mayerl, Eyton, Carter)   Col FB 1538

THE SAVILLE THEATRE ORCHESTRA   Abbey Road, London, 5 Nov. 1936
conducted by BILLY MAYERL with ADELE DIXON (Soprano)
[BILLY MAYERL and GEORGE MYDDLETON Piano duet]
   CAX 7876   Over She Goes—Selection, Part 1   12″ Col DX 758
               (Mayerl, Eyton, Carter)
               Mine's a hopeless case (vAD)/Side by Side/
               The Dance Goes On/Over She Goes
   CAX 7877   Over She Goes—Selection, Part 2 (Mayerl, Eyton, Carter)   —
               I breathe on windows/Turn on the taps/
               Speed Cop—Piano duet BM, GM

BILLY MAYERL, Pianoforte Solo   Abbey Road, London, 30 Mar. 1937
   CA 16308–1   Head over Heels—Selection, Part 1
               (Mack Gordon, Harry Revel)   Col FB 1660
               Through the Courtesy of Love/Head over Heels/
               There's that look in your eyes again
   CA 16309–1   Head over Heels—Selection, Part 2 (Mack Gordon, Harry Revel)   —
               Lookin' around corners for you/
               May I have the next romance with you?

BILLY MAYERL, Pianoforte Solo   Abbey Road, London, 4 Sept. 1937
   CA 16538–1   Crazy Days—Selection, Part 1 (Mayerl, Eyton, Carter)   Col FB 1747
               Stranger in a cup of tea/Nice People/
               You're not too bad yourself
   CA 16539–1   Crazy Days—Selection, Part 2 (Mayerl, Eyton, Carter)   —
               Do/Spring/Love was born

THE SHAFTESBURY THEATRE ORCHESTRA   Abbey Road, London, 9 Sept. 1937
conducted by BILLY MAYERL (Piano) with
FRED CONYNGHAM and MARJORIE BROWN (Vocals)
   2EA 5074–1   Crazy Days—Selection, Part 1   12″ HMV C 2920
               (Mayerl, Eyton, Carter)
      Swing Clean/Spring/Love was born (vFC, MB)
   2EA 5075–1   Crazy Days—Selection, Part 2 (Mayerl, Eyton, Carter)   —
               Nice People/Everybody loves a fat man/Stranger in a cup
               of tea (vFC, MB) You're not too bad yourself/Do   HMV BD 5268
   OEA 5076–1   Crazy Days—Love was born (vFC)
               (Mayerl, Eyton, Carter)

OEA 5077-1   Crazy Days—Stranger in a cup of tea (vFC)   —
               (Mayerl, Eyton, Carter)

BILLY MAYERL (Piano) and HIS ORCHESTRA   Abbey Road, London, 27 Sept. 1937
Orchestra believed to be various members of the Shaftesbury Theatre Orchestra.
    CA 16577-1   Aquarium Suite—Part 1, Willow Moss (Billy Mayerl)   Col DB 1726
    CA 16580-1   Aquarium Suite—Part 2, Moorish Idol (Billy Mayerl)   —
    CA 16581-1   Aquarium Suite—Part 3, Fantail (Billy Mayerl)   Col DB 1727
    CA 16582-1   Aquarium Suite—Part 4, Whirligig (Billy Mayerl)   —
Note: the two missing matrixes do not feature Billy Mayerl.

BILLY MAYERL (Piano) with BILLY SCOTT-COMBER (Vocal)   Abbey Road, London,
                                                                              21 Jan. 1938
    CA 16788-1   Phil the Fluter's Ball (Percy French, trans. Mayerl)   Col FB 1880

BILLY MAYERL, Pianoforte Solo   [same session]
    CA 16789-1   Parade Of The Sandwich-Board Men (Billy Mayerl)   Col FB 1880

BILLY MAYERL and HIS CLAVIERS   Abbey Road, London, 1 Apr. 1938
[DOROTHY CARLESS, GEORGE MYDDLETON, MARION PAYNE]
    CA 16920-1   Billy Mayerl Memories—Part 1 (Billy Mayerl)   Col FB 1968
                   Sweet William/Green Tulips/Marigold
    CA 1692-1   Billy Mayerl Memories—Part 2 (Billy Mayerl)   —
                   Chop-sticks/Ace of Spades/Ace of Diamonds/Bats in the Belfry
    CA 16922-1   The Toy Trumpet (Raymond Scott)   Col FB 1937
    CA 16923-1   Clavierhapsody   —
                   Minuet (Boccherini)/Bunch of Roses (Chapi)/Czardas (Monti)

Piano solo by BILLY MAYERL   Abbey Road, London, 25 Oct. 1938
vocalist: DOROTHY CARLESS
    CA 17150-1   Heart and Soul (Hoagy Carmichael, Frank Loesser)   Col FB 2079
    CA 17151-1   Mayfair Merry-Go-Round (Jimmy Kennedy, Michael Carr)   —

BILLY MAYERL and ENID PURDY, Piano Duet   Abbey Road, London,
                                                                              28 Dec. 1938
[The Master and the Pupil]
    CA 17258-1   Amoresque (Syd Phillips)   Col FB 2119
    CA 17259-1   I've got a pocketful of dreams (Johnny Burke, James V. Monaco)   —

BILLY MAYERL, Piano Solo   [same session]
    CA 17260-2   Song of the Fir Tree (Billy Mayerl)   Col FB 2190
    CA 17261-1   Sweet William (Billy Mayerl)   —

BILLY MAYERL, Pianoforte Solo   Abbey Road, London, 19 May 1939
    CA 17454-1   The Harp of the Winds (Billy Mayerl)   Col FB 2261
    CA 17455-1   Railroad Rhythm (Billy Mayerl)   —
    CA 17456-1   In my Garden—Part 1 (Billy Mayerl)   Col FB 2229
                   Marigold/Honeysuckle/Hollyhock
    CA 17457-1   In my Garden—Part 2 (Billy Mayerl)   —
                   Jasmine/White Heather/Sweet William/Marigold

BILLY MAYERL (Novachord, Piano) AND HIS MULTITONE ORCHESTRA   London,
10 Jan. 1940

(Four Challen Multitone Pianos) with
GEORGE GEE and LUANNE SHAW (Vocals) [DR 4208]
GEORGE GEE, ERIC FAWCETT, and HAL GORDON (Vocals) [DR 4209]

DR 4208–2	Runaway Love—Selection, Part 1 (Billy Mayerl, Frank Eyton)	Dec F 7355
	Just like a cat with a mouse/Nice to know/You know me	
DR 4209–3	Runaway Love—Selection, Part 2 (Billy Mayerl, Frank Eyton)	—
	Two hearts in harmony/We can't do the things we did before/ What a jolly little honeymoon/Nice to know	

BILLY MAYERL, Syncopated Piano Solo   London, 6 May 1940

DR 4642–1	Insect Oddities (Billy Mayerl)	Dec F 7512
	Wedding of an Ant/Ladybird Lullaby	
DR 4643–1	Insect Oddities [Contd.] (Billy Mayerl)	—
	Praying Mantis/Beetle in the Bottle	

BILLY MAYERL, Piano Solo   London, 4 Sept. 1940

DR 4994–1	Fools rush in (Johnny Mercer, Rube Bloom)	Dec F 7620
DR 4995–1	Where the Blue Begins (Harry Parr-Davies, Phil Park)	—
	intro: Love, stay in my heart (Harry Parr-Davies)	

BILLY MAYERL, Piano Solo   London, 5 Nov. 1940

DR 5081–2	All the things you are (Jerome Kern, Oscar Hammerstein II)	Dec F 7662
DR 5082–1	Until you fall in love (Carr, Popplewell)	—

BILLY MAYERL, Piano Solo   London, 21 Jan. 1941

DR 5274–1	Ferry-Boat Serenade (Adamson, di Lazzaro)	Dec F 7711
DR 5275–1	Blueberry Hill (Lewis, Stock, Rose)	—

BILLY MAYERL, Piano Solo   London, 21 Mar. 1941

DR 5507–1	Room Five Hundred and Four (Maschwitz, Posford)	Dec F 7812
DR 5508–1	The last time I saw Paris (Kern, Hammerstein)	—

BILLY MAYERL, Piano Solo   London, 19 June 1941

DR 5909–1	Falling Leaves (David, Carle)	Dec F 7901
DR 5910–1	Pacific Party (Martin Foster)	—

BILLY MAYERL AND HIS GROSVENOR HOUSE BAND   London, 24 July 1941
Billy Mayerl, piano, director/Dennis Ratcliffe, Tommy Porter, trumpet/Al Roach, trombone/Ralph Wilson, Teddy Prince, clarinet, alto sax/Eddie Farge, clarinet, tenor sax, piano accordion/George Myddleton, 2nd piano/Harry Martin, string bass/Reggie Mills, drums.

DR 6044–1	Pedigree on Pomander Walk (André)	Dec F 8006
DR 6045–1	Kitten on the Keys (Zez Confrey)	—
DR 6046–1–2	Nola (Felix Arndt)	Dec F 7945
DR 6047–1	Marigold (Billy Mayerl)	—

BILLY MAYERL AND HIS FORTE FINGERS   Broadhurst Gardens, West Hampstead,
London, 25 Nov. 1942
Billy Mayerl, piano/George Elloitt, guitar/Wally Morris, bass/Reggie Mills, drums.

DR 7094–2	Ace of Hearts (Mayerl)	Dec MW 25

DR 7095–1–2	No. 35—Sweet Nothings (Milton J. Rettenberg)	Dec rejected
DR 7096–2	No. 13—Marigold (Billy Mayerl)	Dec F 8250 Dec MW 7
DR 7097–2	No. 14—Sweet William (Billy Mayerl)	— —

BILLY MAYERL AND HIS FORTE FINGERS   Broadhurst Gardens, West Hampstead,
London, 22 Jan. 1943

Personnel probably as 25 Nov. 1942.

DR 7095–4	No. 35—Sweet Nothings (Milton J. Rettenberg)	Dec F 8310 Dec MW 18
DR 7183–2	No. 21—Fireside Fusiliers (Billy Mayerl)	Dec F 8271 Dec MW 11
DR 7184–2	No. 22—Nola (Felix Arndt)	— —
DR 7185–2	No. 36—Canadian Capers (Chandler, White, Cohen)	Dec F 8310 Dec MW 18
DR 7186–2	Ace of Clubs (Mayerl)	Dec MW 25

BILLY MAYERL AND HIS FORTE FINGERS   Broadhurst Gardens, West Hampstead,
London, 26 July 1943

Personnel probably as 25 Nov. 1942.

DR 7431–1–2	Pacific Party (Martin Foster)	Dec rejected
DR 7432–1	Bats in the Belfry (Billy Mayerl)	Dec MW 104
DR 7433–1	The Dicky Bird Hop (Ronald Gourley)	—
DR 7434–1	Kitten on the Keys (Zez Confrey)	Dec MW 103

BILLY MAYERL AND HIS FORTE FINGERS   Broadhurst Gardens, West Hampstead,
London, 2 Nov. 1943

Personnel probably as 25 Nov. 1942.

DR 7431–4	Pacific Party (Martin Foster)	Dec MW 103
DR 7432–3–4	Bats in the Belfry (Billy Mayerl)	Dec rejected
DR 7433–3–4	The Dicky Bird Hop (Ronald Gourley)	Dec rejected
DR 7434–3–4	Kitten on the Keys (Zez Confrey)	Dec rejected

STANLEY HOLLOWAY, Monologue with   Sydney, Australia, mid-1949
BILLY MAYERL Piano Solo

| M 29594 B | Albert down under [Albert's Trip to Sydney] (?) | Tempo G 1 |

BILLY MAYERL, Piano Solo   [probably same session]

| M 29595 | Shy Ballerina (Billy Mayerl) | Tempo G 1 |

Billy Mayerl, Piano Solo   Sydney, Australia, late 1949

MX 30167	Smoke gets in your Eyes (Jerome Kern, trans. Mayerl)	Pacific 25–0001
MX 30168	Ace of Spades (Billy Mayerl)	—
MX 30169	Stardust (Hoagy Carmichael, trans. Mayerl)	Pacific 25–0002
MX 30170	Song of the Fir Tree (Billy Mayerl)	—

BILLY MAYERL, Piano Solo   Sydney, Australia, late 1949

MX 30375	Body and Soul (Eyton, Heyman, Sour, Green, trans. Mayerl)	Pacific 25–0004
MX 30376	Ace of Hearts (Billy Mayerl)	Pacific 25–0003
MX 30377	Love in Bloom (Leo Robin, Ralph Rainger, trans. Mayerl)	—
MX 30378	Harp of the Winds (Billy Mayerl)	Pacific 25–0004

Russell Scott and June Hamilton Vocal duet with   Sydney, Australia,
Billy Mayerl Piano Solo and Wilbur Kentwell Organ   late 1949
    MX 30486   My One and Only Highland Fling (?)   Tempo T-011

The Billy Mayerl Rhythm Ensemble   Abbey Road, London, 20 Nov. 1950
Billy Mayerl, Piano with unknown personnel
    CE 13111–1   Punch and Judy Polka (Ronnie Munro)   PaE F 2449
    CE 13112–1   Dusky Aristocrat (Norman Whiteley)   PaE F 2441
    CE 13113–1   Marigold (Billy Mayerl)   PaE F 2449
    CE 13114–3   Nola (Felix Arndt)   PaE F 2441
Note: these four recordings were reissued during the early 1950s on 7″ vinyl 45 rpm Parlophone EP GEP 8583.

Billy Mayerl and His Players   Special Recordings Dept., E.M.I. Studios,
Billy Mayerl, Piano and celeste with unknown personnel   London, *c.*July 1954
    CTP 17608–3B Merriment [Suite: Moods in Contrast, No.1]
            (Billy Mayerl)   Bosworth BC 1303
    CTP 17609–2B Wonderment [Suite: Moods in Contrast, No.3]
            (Billy Mayerl)   Bosworth BC 1304
    CTP 17610–2B Devilment [Suite: Moods in Contrast, No.2]
            (Billy Mayerl)   Bosworth BC 1303
    CTP 17611–3B Excitement [Suite: Moods in Contrast, No.4]
            (Billy Mayerl)   Bosworth BC 1304

LIST OF WORKS

Compiled by Alex Hassan

THIS list is based on published works, but it includes some arrangements available on hire but not printed. Pieces published as teaching materials for the Billy Mayerl School courses are not listed. Entries are of first printings: collections are only included if that was the only appearance of the item. Numbers given are the publishers' plate numbers, which can be take as an order of publication.

Abbreviations:

pfc = piano conductor score; NPS = Novelty Piano Solos (two albums from Keith Prowse); APT = Album of Pianoforte Transcriptions (Victoria Music Publishing Company).

The list is chronological but alphabetical within each calendar year.

1919 EGYPTIAN SUITE
Souvenir—Song of the Desert—Patrol of the Camels
Renaissance Music, Art & General Publishing Company: piano (B/5)

1922 DEARIE, IF YOU KNEW [Bert Ralton]
Boosey: song (10670); band (10670); orch. + pfc (1029)

LONGING FOR YOU [Bert Ralton]
Keith Prowse: song (2642)

1923 SOME DAY IN CAMBAY [Bert Ralton]
Boosey: song (10840); band (10840); orch. + pfc (1038)

SOUTHERN ROSE [Charles Horn]
West's: song (3034)

1924 GEORGIE PORGIE [Gee Paul]—in *The Punch Bowl*
Ascherberg, Hopwood & Crew: song (10886–2)

I LOVED, I LOST BUT WHAT DO I CARE? [Gee Paul]
West's: song (3098)

JUST A LITTLE LOVE [Gee Paul]
Worton David: song (B6)

JUST KEEP ON DANCING [Gee Paul]
Cecil Lennox: song (243); brass band

SOUTHERN ROSE [USA version: Dorothy Terriss]
Leo Feist: song (5487–3); orch. + pfc (arr. Frank Barry)

TELL ME IN THE MOONLIGHT [Gee Paul]
West's: song (3072)

1925   ALL-OF-A-TWIST (PIANOLETTES NO.4)
Keith Prowse: piano (2947)

ANY TIME, ANY PLACE, ANYWHERE (also LOVE'S LOTTERY)
[Gee Paul]—in *Charlot's Revue*
Keith Prowse: song (2875)

BABY MINE [Gee Paul]
Ascherberg, Hopwood & Crew: song (10960a); orch. + pfc (10960b)

BELLS OF ST MARY'S
Ascherberg, Hopwood & Crew: arrangement of song by Addams/Furber
(10973a)

DID TOSTI RAISE HIS BOWLER HAT, WHEN HE SAID GOODBYE? [Gee Paul]
—in *The Punch Bowl*
Keith Prowse: song (2912)

DOWN OUR WAY [Gee Paul]—in *The London Revue*
Keith Prowse: song (2964)

DRIFTING ALONG [Gee Paul]
Francis, Day & Hunter: song (17022)

ESKIMO SHIVERS (PIANOLETTES NO.3)
Keith Prowse: piano (2944)

EVERYONE OUGHTER LOVE SOMEONE [Gee Paul]—in *The London Revue*
Keith Prowse: song (2961)

HULLO LONDON [Gee Paul]—in *The London Revue*
Keith Prowse: song (2978)—in *The London Revue* piano selection only

I COULD'T LOVE HER, IF SHE CAME BACK AGAIN [William Helmore]
Keith Prowse: song (3002)

I'LL TAKE YOU TO KEW [Gee Paul]—in *The London Revue*
Keith Prowse: song (2960)

JAZZ MASTER, THE (PIANOLETTES NO.1)
Keith Prowse: piano (2943)

JAZZ MISTRESS, THE (PIANOLETTES NO.2)
Keith Prowse: piano (2946)

JAZZARISTRIX (PIANOLETTES NO.6)
Keith Prowse: piano (2949)

KEEP IT SNAPPY [Gee Paul]—in *The Punch Bowl*
Keith Prowse: song (2913)

LONDON REVUE
Keith Prowse: piano selection (2978) arr.composer

LOVE'S LOTTERY (also ANY TIME, ANY PLACE, ANYWHERE) [Gee Paul]—in
Charlot's Revue

Keith Prowse: song (2875)

NO WONDER NOBODY CARES FOR ME [Gee Paul]
Ascherberg, Hopwood & Crew: song (10907a); orch. + pfc (10907b)

SO-LONG-SU [Gee Paul]
Keith Prowse: song (2965)

SOMEHOW SOMEDAY SOMEBODY [Gee Paul]—in *The London Revue*
Keith Prowse: song (2962)

TAKE OFF A LITTLE BIT OF THIS [Gee Paul]—in *The London Revue*
Keith Prowse: song in piano selection (2978) only

THOSE MEN-IN-BLUE BLUES [Gee Paul]—in *The London Revue*
Keith Prowse: song (2963)

VIRGINIA CREEPER (PIANOLETTES No.5)
Keith Prowse: piano (2948)

1926   ALABAMY BOUND
Keith Prowse: piano transcription (3034) of song by
de Sylva/Brown/Henderson

ANTIQUARY (PIANO EXAGGERATIONS No.2)
Keith Prowse: piano (3014)

BILLY MAYERL SCHOOL OF MODERN SYNCOPATION FOR THE PIANO
Billy Mayerl School of Music: course

BILLY MAYERL BOOK OF BREAKS
Billy Mayerl School of Music: course

I LOVE MY BABY
Keith Prowse: piano transcription (3007) of song by Harry Warren

I WOULD LIKE TO KNOW WHY?
Keith Prowse: piano transcription (3006) of song by Sissle/Blake

IF YOU KNEW SUSIE
Keith Prowse: piano transcription (3005) of song by
de Sylva/Brown/Henderson

JACK-IN-THE-BOX (PIANO EXAGGERATIONS No.3)
Keith Prowse: piano (3015)

JUNE ROSE [Max Gartman]—founded on Braga's *Serenata*
Sylvester: song (123); orch. + pfc (123)

LOOSE ELBOWS (PIANO EXAGGERATIONS No.1)
Keith Prowse: piano (3013)

LULLABY BABY [Gee Paul]
West's: song (3101)

SHE'S GOT FORGET-ME-NOT EYES [William Helmore]
Francis, Day & Hunter: song (17279)

SLEEPY PIANO (PIANO EXAGGERATIONS No.4)
Keith Prowse: piano (3075)

TOODLE-OO-SAL [William H elmore]
Cecil Lennox: song (380)

1927   100 SYNCOPATED BREAKS FOR PIANO
Keith Prowse: course (3174)

BYE BYE PRETTY BABY
Keith Prowse: piano transcription (3432) of song by Gardiner/Hamilton

CHOP-STICKS, a Syncopated Impression, Op. 79
Keith Prowse: piano (3383)

DOING IT ALL FOR ENGLAND [Kenneth Western]
Cavendish/Boosey: song (12356)

HOLLYHOCK, a Syncopated Impression, Op. 80
Keith Prowse: piano (3396)

I'VE GOT A SWEETIE ON THE RADIO [Kenneth Western]
Keith Prowse: song (3380)

IN THE MOUNTAINS [Leslie Sarony]
Keith Prowse: song (3197)

MARIGOLD, a Syncopated Impression, Op. 78
Keith Prowse: piano (3335); xylophone and orch. arr. Reg Burston

NEVER STOP RAININ' BLUES [Kenneth Western]—in *Bow-wows*
Francis, Day & Hunter: song (18048)

PUPPET'S SUITE
Golliwog—Judy—Punch
Keith Prowse: piano (3221)

WHAT YOU GOING TO DO? [Leslie Sarony]—in *Whitebirds*
Campbell Connelly: song (P97)

WOULD YER? [Billy Milton]—in *Bow-wows*
Francis, Day & Hunter: song (18046)

1928   AT EVENTIDE [Frank Eyton]—in *Oh Letty!*
Chappell: song in piano selection (29871) only

DIDDY-DUM-DUM [Frank Eyton]
Chappell: song (29850)

DO YOU? [Frank Eyton]
Cavendish: song (12487); orch. + pfc (12486)

HONKY-TONK, a Rhythmical Absurdity, Op. 82
Keith Prowse: piano (3592)

JUST LIKE A MELODY OUT OF THE SKY
Keith Prowse: single page transcription of song by Walter Donaldson

MARIGOLD, a Syncopated Impression, Op. 78
Keith Prowse: orch. + pfc (3558)

NOTHING ELSE MATTERS BUT LOVE [Frank Eyton]—in *Oh Letty!*
Chappell: song (29851)

OH LETTY!
Chappell: piano selection (29871), arr. H. M. Higgs

OH MISERY, MISERY ME, OH MY [Frank Eyton]—in *Oh Letty!*
Chappell: song in piano selection (29871) only

ONE NIGHT IN JUNE [Horatio Nicholls]
Lawrence Wright: song (1459)

OUT OF THE DAWN
Keith Prowse: single page transcription (3670) of song by Walter Donaldson

PASTORAL SKETCHES, Op. 56
Legend—Lover's Lane—Village Festival
Boosey: Piano (12357); orch. + pfc (12476), arr. Arthur Wood

RAINBOW, WHERE ARE YOU NOW? [Frank Eyton]
Chappell: song (29865)

ROBOTS, a Syncopated Impression, Op. 81
Keith Prowse: piano (3557)

SO LONG, LETTY [Frank Eyton]—in *Oh Letty!*
Chappell: song (29849)

THREE MINIATURES IN SYNCOPATION, Op. 76
Cobweb—Muffin Man—Clockwork
Keith Prowse: piano (3459)

WHEN SUMMER IS GONE
Keith Prowse: one-page piano transcription (3725) of song by
Harrison/Wilhite

1929   HOUSE ON A HILL-TOP [Frank Eyton]—in *Love Lies*
Francis, Day & Hunter: song (18534)

I SHAN'T LET YOU OUT OF MY SIGHT [Gee Paul]
Chappell: song (30206); orch. + pfc (30264), arr. Van Phillips

JASMINE, a Syncopated Impression, Op. 84
Keith Prowse: piano (3842)

LEGENDS OF KING ARTHUR, The Six Impressions, Op. 64
Prelude—Merlin the Wizard—The Sword Excalibur—Lady of the Lake—
Guinevere—The Passing of Arthur
Keith Prowse: piano (3786)

LILY POND, an Idyll, Op. 12
Boosey: piano (13039); orch. + pfc (13039), arr. Fred Aldington

LOVE LIES
Francis, Day & Hunter: piano selection, arr. Henry Pether

MISS UP-TO-DATE [Frank Eyton]—in *Love Lies*
Francis, Day & Hunter: song (18543)

PICK UP THE RHYTHM [Frank Eyton]—in *Co-optimists*
Keith Prowse: song (3901)

SENNEN COVE, Poem, Op. 53
Boosey: piano (12812); orch. + pfc (?)

SHOO YOUR BLUES AWAY [Frank Eyton]—in *Darling I love you*
Francis, Day & Hunter: song (18775)

THREE CONTRASTS, Op. 24
Ladybird—Pastoral—Fiddle Dance
Keith Prowse: piano (3843)

WHAT CARE I? [Frank Eyton]—in *Co-optimists*
Chappell: song (30205)

WISTARIA, a Syncopated Impression, Op. 83
Keith Prowse: piano (3782)

1930 ANYTHING [Frank Eyton]—in *Nippy*
Chappell: song (30689)

BODY AND SOUL
Chappell: piano transcription (30434) of song by John W. Green

CO-OPTIMISTS NEW SONG ALBUM
Brush the cobwebs from your feet—Sky lady—Baby, maybe it's you—Oi
gave 'er a nod, oi gave 'er a wink—The road to fairyland—My love flew in
through the window
Keith Prowse: songs (4107)

DARLING, I LOVE YOU
Francis, Day & Hunter: piano selection (18821), arr. H. Pether

EMPIRE PARADE [Frank Eyton]
Keith Prowse: song (4082); male voices TTBB (4082), arr. Thos. J. Hewitt

EV'RY HOUR OF THE DAY [Frank Eyton]
Billy Mayerl School: song; piano transcription

EV'RY LITTLE GIRL [Frank Eyton]—in *Nippy*
Chappell: song (30652)

I FEEL SO SAFE WITH YOU [Frank Eyton]—in *Nippy*
Chappell: song (30687)

I KNOW SOMETHING THAT YOU KNOW [Gee Paul]—in *Darling I love you*
Francis, Day & Hunter: song (18776)

INDISPENSABLE YOU [Frank Eyton]—in *Silver Wings*
Chappell: song (30354)

IT MUST BE YOU [Frank Eyton]—in *Nippy*
Chappell: song (30647); orch. + pfc (30686), arr. Al Frisk

MOVE [Frank Eyton]—in *Nippy*
Chappell: song in piano selection (30672) only

NIPPY [Frank Eyton]—in *Nippy*
Chappell: song in piano selection (30672) only

NIPPY
Nippy—Your sunny disposition and mine—Two of everything—I feel so safe
with you—Move—The toytown party—It must be you
Chappell: piano selection (30672), arr. Guy Jones

PICCOLO PETE
Chappell: piano transcription (30352) of song by Phil Baxter

SILVER WINGS
Chappell: piano selection (30376)

SING YOU SINNERS
Chappell: piano transcription (30676) of song by Coslow/Harding

SIX STUDIES IN SYNCOPATION, Book 3, Op. 55
Keith Prowse: piano (4028)

SUNSHINE OR RAIN [Frank Eyton]
Campbell Connelly: song (401)

THREE DANCES IN SYNCOPATION, Op. 73
English Dance—Cricket Dance—Harmonica Dance
Keith Prowse: piano (3965)

THREE JAPANESE PICTURES, Op. 25
Almond Blossom—Temple in Kyoto—Cherry Dance
Keith Prowse: piano (4048)

TOYTOWN PARADE, THE [Frank Eyton]—in *Nippy*
Chappell: song (30646)

TWO OF EVERYTHING [Frank Eyton]—in *Nippy*
Chappell: song (30653); orch. + pfc (30696), arr. Al Frisk

WHILE WE'RE IN LOVE [Frank Eyton]—in *Nippy*
Chappell: song (30688)

YOU AIN'T MY BABY NOW [Bert Page]
Keith Prowse: song (3974)

YOUR SUNNY DISPOSITION AND MINE [Frank Eyton]—in *Nippy*
Chappell: song (30645)

1931   BILLY MAYERL SPECIAL TUTOR-COURSE IN MODERN SYNCOPATION
Billy Mayerl School/Keith Prowse: course

BUY BRITISH! [David Burnaby]
Keith Prowse: song (4422) with music by Mayerl & Philip Crook

DANCE THE POLKA AGAIN [Frank Eyton]—in *The Millionaire Kid*
Chappell: song (30904)

DEVONSHIRE [Frank Eyton]—in *The Millionaire Kid*
Chappell: song (30903)

HONEYSUCKLE, a Syncopated Impression
Keith Prowse: piano (4299)

I'D BE LOST WITHOUT YOU [Frank Eyton]—in *The Millionaire Kid*
Chappell: song (30799)

I'VE CAUGHT IT [Frank Eyton]—in *The Millionaire Kid*
Chappell: song in piano selection (30921) only

IT'S NOT FAIR [Frank Eyton]—in *My Sister and I*
Chappell: song (30798)

LIFE IS MEANT FOR LOVE [Frank Eyton]—in *The Millionaire Kid*
Chappell: song (30918)

MATCH PARADE, THE
Keith Prowse: piano transcription (4290) of song by Karle Wehl

MIGNONETTE, a Syncopated Impression
Keith Prowse: piano (4219)

MILLIONAIRE KID, THE
Dance the polka again—Thankyou most sincerely—Life is meant for love—
I'd be lost without you—Once a Devenish-always a Devenish—
Devonshire—I've caught it—We don't think such a terrible lot of that
Chappell: piano selection (30921), arr. Guy Jones

ONCE A DEVENISH—ALWAYS A DEVENISH [Frank Eyton]—in *The Millionaire
Kid*
Chappell: song in piano selection (30921) only

ORIENTAL, a Syncopated Impression, Op. 21
Keith Prowse: piano (4298)

PASTORALE EXOTIQUE
Keith Prowse: piano (4350)

SCALLYWAG
Keith Prowse: piano (4334)

SIX STUDIES IN SYNCOPATION, Book 1, Op. 55
Keith Prowse: piano (4028)

SIX STUDIES IN SYNCOPATION, Book 2, Op. 55
Keith Prowse: piano (4170)

SOMEBODY LIKES YOU [Frank Eyton]—in *The Millionaire Kid*
Chappell: song (31152)

SPEAK EASY (CUBAN DANCE)
Harms/Chappell: arrangement (30972) of song by Murphy/Simon/Gensler

SWEET AND LOVELY
Keith Prowse: piano transcription (4418) of song by
Arnheim/Tobias/Lemare

THANK YOU MOST SINCERELY [Frank Eyton]—in *The Millionaire Kid*
Chappell: song (30905); arr. orch. + pfc (30942) by Al Frisk

THREE JAPANESE PICTURES
Almond Blossom—Temple in Kyoto—Cherry Dance
Keith Prowse: orch. + pfc (4351), arr. Arthur Wood

WE DON'T THINK SUCH A TERRIBLE LOT OF THAT [Frank
Eyton]—in *The Millionaire Kid*
Chappell: song in piano selection (30921) only

WHAT MORE CAN I DO? [Frank Eyton]—in *My Sister and I*
Chappell: song (30800)

1932   AUTUMN CROCUS, an Idylle
Keith Prowse: piano (4438); orch. + pfc (4495) arr. Hermann Finck

BILLY MAYERL MODERN PIANO METHOD [with Geoffrey Clayton]
Peter Maurice: course (no number)

CARMINETTA, Chanson Espagnole
Keith Prowse: piano (4508)

HAND IN GLOVE [Frank Eyton]—in *Between Ourselves*
Keith Prowse: song (4527)

HAVE YOU FORGOTTEN?
Chappell: piano transcription (31197) of song by Suesse/Robin

LISTEN IN TONIGHT, MY DARLING [Jos. Geo. Gilbert]
Feldman: song

PENNY WHISTLE, a Novelette
Keith Prowse: piano (4592)

VALSE EUGENE [Eugene]
Eugene: song

WEEPING WILLOW, an Idylle
Keith Prowse: piano (4528)

WHAT MIGHT HAVE BEEN [Frank Eyton]—in *Between Ourselves*
Keith Prowse: song (4544)

WHITE HEATHER
Keith Prowse: piano (4419); orch. + pfc (on hire), arr. ?

1933 ACE OF SPADES (No.4 of FOUR ACES)
Keith Prowse: orch. + pfc (on hire), arr. ?

BALLOONS
Keith Prowse: piano transcription (4672) of song by Magine/Shawn

CANARIES' SERENADE, a Syncopation
Keith Prowse: piano (4692)

CLOSE YOUR EYES
Keith Prowse: piano transcription (in folio NPS 2) of song by Bern/Petkere

DID YOU EVER SEE A DREAM WALKING?
Chappell: piano transcription (31935) of song by Gordon/Revel

FOUR ACES, Suite for Piano
Clubs—Hearts—Diamonds—Spades
Keith Prowse: piano (4798)

I COVER THE WATERFRONT
Victoria: piano transcription (102) of song by John W. Green; in folio APT

LOVE LOCKED OUT
Victoria: piano transcription (103) of song by Ray Noble; in folio APT

MUSICAL MOMENTS, Six Miniatures
Beside a Rustic Bridge—Little Lady from Spain—A May Morning—Many
Years Ago—My Party Frock—Air de Ballet
Peter Maurice: piano (1233)

ON THE OTHER SIDE OF LOVERS' LANE
Peter Maurice: piano transcription (1248) of song by Carroll Gibbons

PLEASE HANDLE WITH CARE
Peter Maurice: piano transcription (1183) of song by Stride/Ballard

SING SONG SALLY [Frank Eyton]
Peter Maurice: song (1186)

THANKS
Victoria: piano transcription (104) of song by Johnston/Coslow; in folio APT

THREE SYNCOPATED RAMBLES
The Junior Apprentice (Intermezzo)—Printer's Devil (Theme and
Transcription)—The Milkman (Scherzo)
Keith Prowse: piano (4671)

1934 A-SHOOTING WE WILL GO [Frank Eyton and Desmond Carter]—in
Sporting Love
Chappell: song in piano selection (31598) only

ACE OF SPADES (FOUR ACES SUITE)
Keith Prowse: piano duet (5003), arr. composer

APRIL IN PARIS
Mayerl Club Magazine (Aug.): piano transcription of song by Harburg/Duke

ARLENE
Mayerl Club Magazine (Oct.): piano transcription of song by
Seymour/Pollack

BALLOONS
Mayerl Club Magazine (Dec.): piano transcription of song by Shawn/Magine

BILLY MAYERL HOME STUDY COURSE IN COMPOSING POPULAR MUSIC
Keith Prowse: course

CLOSE YOUR EYES
Mayerl Club Magazine (Mar.): piano transcription of number by Petkere

COME OUT [Frank Eyton and Desmond Carter]—in *Sporting Love*
Chappell: song in piano selection (31958) only

FASCINATING DITTY (STEPPING TONES NO.1)
Keith Prowse: piano (4937)

HAVE A HEART [Frank Eyton and Desmond Carter]—in *Sporting Love*
Chappell: song (31957)

HOP-O'-MY-THUMB (STEPPING TONES NO.2)
Keith Prowse: piano (4961)

I OUGHT NOT TO [Frank Eyton and Desmond Carter]—in *Sporting Love*
Chappell: song in piano selection (31958) only

IT'S NO USE SAYING I DON'T LOVE YOU [Frank Eyton]—in *Without You*
Campbell Connolly: song (832)

JOKER, THE, a Further Contribution to FOUR ACES
Keith Prowse: piano (5024)

JUNE IN JANUARY
Victoria: piano transcription (107) of song by Robin/Rainger; in folio APT

LOVE IN BLOOM
Victoria: piano transcription (105) of song by Robin/Rainger; in folio APT

LOVE THY NEIGHBOUR
Mayerl Club Magazine (Sept.): piano transcription of song by Gordon/Revel

MARIGOLD
Keith Prowse: piano duet (4956), arr. composer

MASQUERADING IN THE NAME OF LOVE
Mayerl Club Magazine (Apr.): piano transcription of song by
Sigler/Goodheart/Hoffman

NIMBLE FINGERED GENTLEMAN, a Syncopation
Keith Prowse: piano (4878)

OCEANS OF TIME
Mayerl Club Magazine (July): piano transcription of song by
Grey/Newman/Furber/Green

ROLLING IN THE HAY
Mayerl Club Magazine (June): piano transcription of song by George
Posford

SAY IT
Mayerl Club Magazine (Dec.): piano transcription of song by
Adlam/Schwartz

SIBERIAN LAMENT
Keith Prowse: piano (5014)

SMOKE GETS IN YOUR EYES
Chappell: piano transcription (32265) of song by Jerome Kern

SNAKES AND LADDERS, Rhythmic Novelty
Cramer: arrangement for two pianos (14227) of solo by Harry Engleman

SPORTING LOVE
Who asked you—I ought not to—A-shooting we will go—You're the reason
why—Come out—Have a heart—Those in favour
Chappell: piano selection (31958)

THOSE IN FAVOUR [Frank Eyton and Desmond Carter]—in *Sporting Love*
Chappell: song in piano selection (31958) only

TWO CIGARETTES IN THE DARK
Sterling: piano transcription (1029) of song by Webster/Pollack

TWO HEARTS ON A TREE
Mayerl Club Magazine (Nov.): piano transcription of song by Boyle/Yorke

WE BELONG TOGETHER
Mayerl Club Magazine (Feb.): piano transcription of song by
Hammerstein/Kern

WEEP NO MORE MY BABY
Mayerl Club Magazine (Jan.): piano transcription of song by Heyman/ Green

WHO ASKED YOU? [Frank Eyton and Desmond Carter]—in *Sporting Love*
Chappell: song (31955)

WITH MY EYES WIDE OPEN I'M DREAMING
Victoria: piano transcription (106) of song by Gordon/Revel; in folio APT

YOU'RE THE REASON WHY [Frank Eyton and Desmond Carter]—in *Sporting Love*

Chappell: song (31956); *Mayerl Club Magazine* (May): piano transcription

1935 ANYTHING GOES
Mayerl Club Magazine (Nov.): piano transcription of song by Cole Porter

BATS IN THE BELFRY (On a Theme by Austen Croom-Johnson)
Keith Prowse: piano (5226)

BE A MAN [Frank Eyton]—in *Twenty to One*
Keith Prowse: song in piano selection (5284) only

BLUE DANUBE
Mayerl Club Magazine (Aug.): piano transcription of waltz by Johann Strauss

CHASING SHADOWS
Victoria: piano transcription (109) of song by Silver/Davis; in folio APT

CHEEK TO CHEEK
Chappell: piano transcription (32518) of song by Irving Berlin

CONTINENTAL, THE
Mayerl Club Magazine (Mar.): piano transcription of song by Con Conrad

EVERYTHING'S BEEN DONE BEFORE
Keith Prowse: piano transcription (no number) of song by
Adamson/Knopf/King; in folio NPS 2

GIRL WITH THE DREAMY EYES, THE
Mayerl Club Magazine (June): piano transcription of song by Carr/Pola

GREEN TULIPS, a Syncopated Impression (on a Theme by Austen Croom-
Johnson) Keith Prowse: piano (5225)

HI-DI-HI
Mayerl Club Magazine (Sept.): two-piano transcription (with George
Windeatt) of song by Carter/Gay

HONEYMOON FOR THREE [Frank Eyton]
I'll build a fence around you—Why not madam?—Make hey! while the
moon shines
Mayerl Club Magazine (Oct.): piano medley

HOW D'YOU LIKE YOUR EGGS FRIED? [Frank Eyton]—in *Twenty to One*
Keith Prowse: song (5274)

FEEL LIKE A FEATHER IN THE BREEZE
Victoria: piano transcription (742) of song by Gordon/Revel; in folio APT

I'LL BUILD A FENCE AROUND YOU [Frank Eyton]—in *Honeymoon for Three*
Keith Prowse: song (5180)

I'M AT YOUR SERVICE [Frank Eyton]—in *Twenty to One*
Keith Prowse: song (5275); orch. + pfc (British Library uncatalogued file),
arr. Eddie Griffiths; *Mayerl Club Magazine* (Dec.): piano transcription

I'M GOING TO BE GOOD [Frank Eyton]—in *Twenty to One*
Keith Prowse: song (5273)

I'VE NEVER FELT LIKE THIS BEFORE [Frank Eyton]—in *Twenty to One*
Keith Prowse: song in piano selection (5284) only

IMAGINARY FOX-TROT (original and transcription)
Mayerl Club Magazine (Feb.): piano; also *Mayerl Circle Newsletter*, Spring

1978

LEARN TO SYNCOPATE
Mayerl Club Magazine (July): piano transcription of song by Eyton/Headley

LOVE ME FOREVER
Sterling: piano transcription (1090) of song by Victor Schertzinger

MAKE HEY! WHILE THE MOON SHINES [Frank Eyton]—in *Honeymoon for Three*
Keith Prowse: song (5179)

MISTLETOE, a Syncopated Impression
Keith Prowse: piano (5067)

OBJECT OF MY AFFECTION, THE
Mayerl Club Magazine (Apr.): piano transcription of song by Tomlin/Poe/Grier

OTHER PEOPLE'S BABIES
Mayerl Club Magazine (Jan.): piano transcription of song by Vivian Ellis

SIBERIAN LAMENT
Keith Prowse: orch. + pfc (5075), arr. Arthur Wood

SWEET AND LOVELY
Mayerl Club Magazine (May): piano transcription of song by Arnheim/Tobias/Lemare

TAMBOURINE [Frank Eyton]—in *Twenty to One*
Keith Prowse: song in piano selection (5284) only

TWENTY TO ONE
How d'you like your eggs fried?—I'm at your service—Be a man—I've never felt like this before—Tambourine—I'm going to be good—You've fallen in love
Keith Prowse: piano selection (5284), arr. composer

WHY NOT MADAME? [Frank Eyton]—in *Honeymoon for Three*
Keith Prowse: song (5178); orch. + pfc (British Library uncatalogued file) arr. Percival Mackay

YOU HIT THE SPOT
Victoria: piano transcription of song by Gordon/Revel; in folio APT

YOU'VE FALLEN IN LOVE [Frank Eyton]—in *Twenty to One*
Keith Prowse: song in piano selection (5284) only

1936 APART FROM BUSINESS [Frank Eyton]—in *Cheer Up*
Victoria: song (739)

BATS IN THE BELFREY
Keith Prowse: orch. + pfc (5374), arr. George Windeatt

CHEER UP
Mayerl Club Magazine (Aug.): piano transcription of song by Carter/Gay

COUNTRY WEDDING [Frank Eyton and Desmond Carter]—in *Over She Goes*
Victoria: song in piano selection (113) only

DANCE GOES ON, THE [Frank Eyton and Desmond Carter]—in *Over She Goes*
Victoria: song (111)

DARLING, NOT WITHOUT YOU
Mayerl Club Magazine (Feb.): piano transcription of song by
Silver/Sherman/Helman

EVERYTHING'S BEEN DONE BEFORE
Mayerl Club Magazine (Feb.): piano transcription of song by
Adamson/Knopf/King

FATAL FASCINATION
Mayerl Club Magazine (Apr.): piano transcription of song by
Thompson/Gensler

FOUR ACES, Rhythmic Orchestration
Keith Prowse: orch. + pfc (5462), arr. Ray Noble

I BREATHE ON WINDOWS [Frank Eyton and Desmond Carter]—in *Over
She Goes*
Victoria: song (110); piano transcription (753)

IS IT TRUE WHAT THEY SAY ABOUT DIXIE?
Sterling: piano transcription (1140) of song by Caesar/Lerner/Marks

LIMEHOUSE BLUES
Ascherberg, Hopwood & Crew: piano transcription (11422) of song by
Philip Braham

MARIGOLD
Keith Prowse: violin and piano (5478), arr. composer

MINE'S A HOPELESS CASE [Frank Eyton and Desmond Carter]—in *Over
She Goes*
Victoria: song (112)

ORANGE BLOSSOM, a Syncopated Impression
Keith Prowse: piano (5371)

OVER SHE GOES [Frank Eyton and Desmond Carter]—in *Over She Goes*
Victoria: song (115)

OVER SHE GOES
Mine's a hopeless case—Side by side—The dance goes on—Over she goes—
I breathe on windows—Turn on the taps—County wedding—Speed cop
Victoria: piano selection (113), arr. composer; orch. + pfc (British Library un-
catalogued file), arr. George Zalva; *Mayerl Club Magazine* (Nov.): chorus
medley for two-pianos, arr. composer

PLEASE BELIEVE ME
Keith Prowse: piano transcription (5423) of song by Jacobs

SHALLOW WATERS, an Interlude
Keith Prowse: piano (5431); orch. + pfc (5432), arr. Joseph Engleman

SIDE BY SIDE [Frank Eyton and Desmond Carter]—in *Over She Goes*
Victoria: song (114)

SPEED COP [Frank Eyton and Desmond Carter]—in *Over She Goes*
Victoria: song in piano selection (113) and chorus medley only

STEAK AND KIDNEY PUDDING [Frank Eyton]—in *Cheer Up*
Victoria: song (738)

THERE'S A STAR IN THE SKY [Frank Eyton]—in *Cheer Up*
Victoria: song (737); piano transcription (750); also in *Mayerl Club Magazine* (April); in folio APT

TORMENTED
Mayerl Club Magazine (July): piano transcription of song by Will Hudson

TURN ON THE TAPS [Frank Eyton and Desmond Carter]—in *Over She Goes*
Mayerl Club Magazine (Oct.): piano transcription; in piano selection

WILL I EVER KNOW?
Mayerl Club Magazine (Sept.): piano transcription of song by Gordon/Revel

WITHOUT A WORD OF WARNING
Mayerl Club Magazine (Mar.): piano transcription of song by Gordon/Revel

YES! NO! [Frank Eyton and Desmond Carter]—in *Over She Goes*
Victoria: song (751)

YOU HIT THE SPOT
Mayerl Club Magazine (June): piano transcription of song by Gordon/Revel

1937 AQUARIUM SUITE
Willow Moss—Moorish Idol—Fantail—Whirligig
Keith Prowse: piano (5600–5603)

AT THE BALALAIKA
Keith Prowse: piano transcription (5539) of song by George Posford

CRAZY DAYS
Spring clean—Spring—Love was born—Nice people—Stranger in a cup of tea—When a fat man passes by—You're not too bad yourself—Do!
Cinephonic: piano selection (105), arr. composer; orch. + pfc (CMO 105), arr. George Zalva

DANCE GOES ON, THE [Frank Eyton and Desmond Carter]—in *Over She Goes*
Mayerl Club Magazine (Feb.): piano transcription

DARLING, NOT WITHOUT YOU
Mayerl Club Magazine (June): piano transcription for competition of song by Silver/Sherman/Helman

DEEP HENDERSON
Keith Prowse: piano transcription (5702) of song by Fred Rose

Do! [Frank Eyton and Desmond Carter]—in *Crazy Days*
Cinephonic: song (150)

EVERYTHING'S IN RHYTHM WITH MY HEART
Mayerl Club Magazine (July): piano transcription of song by
Sigler/Goodhart/Hoffman; in folio APT

HEAD OVER HEELS
Through courtesy of love—Head over heels in love—There's that look in
your eyes—Lookin' around corners—May I have the next romance with
you?
Cinephonic: piano transcription medley (103) of songs by Gordon/Revel

I LOVE CINDERELLA [Frank Eyton]—pantomime
Cinephonic: song (348)

I NEED YOU
Mayerl Club Magazine (Apr.): piano transcription of song by H.A.P./
Botterell; in folio APT 110

I'M IN A DANCING MOOD
Mayerl Club Magazine (Mar.): piano transcription of song by
Sigler/Goodhart/Hoffman; in folio APT 110

JAZZMASTER, THE
Keith Prowse/*Mayerl Club Magazine* (Jan.): accordion, arr. Stanley Hoyle

LAMBETH WALK
Cinephonic: piano transcription (179) of song by Furber/Gay; in *Mayerl
Club Magazine* (June 1938); in folio APT 193

LOVE WAS BORN [Frank Eyton and Desmond Carter]—in *Crazy Days*
Cinephonic: song (147), piano transcription (111)

MOOD THAT I'M IN, THE
Mayerl Club Magazine (June): piano transcription of song by
Silver/Sherman

MY FIRST THRILL
Mayerl Club Magazine (Aug.): piano transcription of song by
Sigler/Goodhart/Hoffman

NICE PEOPLE [Frank Eyton and Desmond Carter]—in *Crazy Days*
Cinephonic: song in piano selection (105) only

PENNY IN MY POCKET, A
Mayerl Club Magazine (Jan.): piano transcription of song by Robin/Rainger

SITTIN' ON THE EDGE OF MY CHAIR
Mayerl Club Magazine (Oct.): piano transcription of song by
Parks/Tomlin/Poe

SO RARE
Mayerl Club Magazine (Dec.): piano transcription of song by Sharpe/Herst

SPRING [Frank Eyton and Desmond Carter]—in *Crazy Days*
Cinephonic: song in piano selection (105) only

STRANGER IN A CUP OF TEA [Frank Eyton and Desmond Carter]—in
Crazy Days
Cinephonic: song (149); piano transcription (109); orch. + pfc, arr. Ben Berlin

SWEET
Mayerl Club Magazine (Nov.): piano transcription of song by
Tomlin/Heath/Le Roux

SWING CLEAN [Frank Eyton and Desmond Carter]—in *Crazy Days*
Cinephonic: song in piano selection (105) only

THERE'S A SMALL HOTEL
Chappell: piano transcription (32874) of song by Rodgers/Hart

WHEN A FAT MAN PASSES BY [Frank Eyton and Desmond Carter]—in *Crazy
Days*
Cinephonic: song in piano selection (105) only

WITHOUT RHYTHM
Mayerl Club Magazine (May): piano transcription of song by
Sigler/Goodhart/Hoffman; in folio APT 110

YOU'RE NOT TOO BAD YOURSELF [Frank Eyton and Desmond Carter]—in
Crazy Days
Cinephonic: song (148); *Mayerl Club Magazine* (Sept.): piano transcription,
in folio APT 110

1938   AMORESQUE
Cinephonic: piano transcription of song by Sid Phillips; in folio APT 193; in
Mayerl Club Magazine (Mar. 1939)

AQUARIUM SUITE
Willow Moss—Moorish Idol—Fantail—Whirligig
Keith Prowse: orch. + pfc (5748), arr. composer

BELLS OF ST MARY'S, THE
Ascherberg, Hopwood & Crew: piano transcription (11536) of song by
Addams/Furber

CHRISTMAS MEDLEY
Little brown jug—The first Noel—Good King Wenceslas—God rest ye
merry gentlemen—Fine old English gentlemen—There's a tavern in the
town
Mayerl Club Magazine (Dec.): piano transcription

FOR ONLY YOU
Mayerl Club Magazine (Feb.): piano transcription of song by Murray/Noble

FROM A SPANISH LATTICE, a Southern Tone Picture
Keith Prowse: piano (5881)

HIGHLAND SWING, THE
Cinephonic: piano transcription of song by Grant/Johnston; in folio APT
193; in *Mayerl Club Magazine* (Jan. 1939)

I Love Cinderella [Frank Eyton]—in *Cinderella*
Cinephonic: song (348); *Mayerl Club Magazine* (Jan.): piano transcription

I'm Always in the Mood for You
Mayerl Club Magazine (Mar.): piano transcription of song by Davis/Coots

I'm Gonna Lock My Heart
Mayerl Club Magazine (Oct.): piano transcription of song by Eaton/Shand

It's a Long, Long Way to My Heart
Mayerl Club Magazine (Apr.): piano transcription of song by Pola/Brandt

Lambeth Walk
Mayerl Club Magazine (June): piano transcription of song by Furber/Gay

Me and My Girl
Mayerl Club Magazine (July): piano transcription of song by Furber/Gay

My Heaven in the Pines
Mayerl Club Magazine (Sept.): piano transcription of song by
Campbell/Sigler/Conrad; in folio APT 193

Parade of the Sandwich-Board Men, a Novelty in Syncopation
Keith Prowse: piano (5765); orch. + pfc (5784), arr. George Windeatt

Phil the Fluter's Ball
Keith Prowse: piano transcription (5736) of song by W. P. French

Railroad Rhythm, an Impression
Keith Prowse: piano (5877)

Song of the Fir Tree, a Swedish Impression
Keith Prowse: piano (5878)

Sweet Wiliam, a Syncopated Impression
Keith Prowse: piano (5747)

Thanks for the Memory
Mayerl Club Magazine (Nov.): piano transcription of song by Robin/Rainger

Turkey in the Straw
Mayerl Club Magazine (May.): piano transcription of traditional song

Two Lovely People
Mayerl Club Magazine (Aug.): piano transcription of song by
Roy/Black/Currie

1939   Blame it on My Last Affair
Mayerl Club Magazine (May): piano transcription of song by Nemo/Mills

Didn't Your Mother Tell You? [Frank Eyton]—in *Runaway
Love*
Keith Prowse: song in piano selection (5986) only

Don't Speak to me of Love [Frank Eyton]—in *Runaway Love*
Keith Prowse: song in piano selection (5986) only

From a Spanish Lattice
Keith Prowse: orch. + pfc (5961), arr. Hubert Bath

HARP OF THE WINDS, Aeolian Harp
Keith Prowse: piano (5948)

I GOT LOVE
Mayerl Club Magazine (Feb.): piano transcription of song by
Williams/Waller

I HAVE EYES
Mayerl Club Magazine (July): piano transcription of song by Robin/Rainger

LIKE A CAT WITH A MOUSE [Frank Eyton]—in *Runaway Love*
Mayerl Club Magazine (Aug.): piano transcription

MARIGOLD
Keith Prowse: piano accordion (5965), arr. C. Graves

NICE TO KNOW [Frank Eyton]—in *Runaway Love*
Keith Prowse: song (5983)

PATTYCAKE, PATTYCAKE, BAKER MAN
Mayerl Club Magazine (June): piano transcription of song by
Razaf/Johnson/Waller

RUNAWAY LOVE
Two men—Nice to know—You know me—What a jolly—Didn't your
mother—Don't speak to me—We can't do the things—Like a cat
Keith Prowse: piano selection (5986), arr. composer; orch. + pfc (5991), arr.
Harry Dexter

SONG OF THE FIR TREE
Keith Prowse: chamber orch., arr. B. Thompson; orch. + pfc (5962), arr.
Hubert Bath

THERE'S RAIN IN MY EYES
Mayerl Club Magazine (Apr.): piano transcription of song by
Ager/McCarthy/Schwartz

TWO MEN AND TWO GIRLS [Frank Eyton]—in *Runaway Love*
Keith Prowse: song in piano selection (5986) only

WE CAN'T DO THE THINGS WE DID BEFORE[Frank Eyton] in
Runaway Love
Keith Prowse: song in piano selection (5986) only

WHAT A JOLLY LITTLE HONEYMOON [Frank Eyton]—in *Runaway
Love*
Keith Prowse: song in piano selection (5984) only

YOU KNOW ME—I KNOW YOU [Frank Eyton]—in *Runaway Love*
Keith Prowse: song in piano selection (5984) only

1940   ALL THE THINGS YOU ARE
Chappell: piano transcription (34358) of song by Jerome Kern

BEETLE IN THE BOTTLE (INSECT ODDITIES No.4)
Keith Prowse: piano (6062)

FOOLS RUSH IN
Cavendish: piano transcription (15242) of song by Rube Bloom

HAPPY BIRTHDAY [Frank Eyton]—show (unpublished) including:
Do unto others—Every time I look at you—Moonlight melody—One for all

HARRY HAWK [Frank Eyton]
Noel Gay: song (110)

LADYBIRD LULLABY (INSECT ODDITIES No.2)
Keith Prowse: piano (6059)

LEPRECHAUN'S LEAP
Keith Prowse: piano (6125); orch. + pfc (BBC Music Library), arr. Arthur
Wood

MOONLIGHT MELODY [Frank Eyton]—in *Happy Birthday*
Chappell: orch. + pfc (BBC Music Library), arr. Ben Berlin

1941   PRAYING MANTIS (INSECT ODDITIES No.3)
Keith Prowse: piano (6063)

HOLLYHOCK
Keith Prowse: orch. + pfc (6141), arr. Len Manning

SCALLYWAG
Keith Prowse: orch. + pfc (6158), arr. Len Manning

MARIGOLD
Keith Prowse: orch. + pfc (6211), arr. Phil Cardew

WEDDING OF AN ANT (INSECT ODDITIES No.1)
Keith Prowse: piano (6064)

WISTARIA
Keith Prowse: orch. + pfc (6165), arr. Len Manning

1942   PLEASE ORDER YOUR LAST DRINKS! [Horatio Nicholls]
Lawrence Wright: song (2624); orch. + pfc (1947), arr. A. Nicholls

1943   FIRESIDE FUSILIERS, Novelty Piano Solo
Keith Prowse: piano (6300); orch. + pfc (6302), arr. A. Nicholls

1945   APRIL'S FOOL
Keith Prowse: piano (6458)

FORGOTTEN FOREST, a Poem
Keith Prowse: piano (6434); orch. + pfc (BBC Music Library)

MINUET FOR PAMELA
Keith Prowse: piano (6430)

1946   EVENING PRIMROSE
Keith Prowse: piano (6487)

IN MY GARDEN: AUTUMNTIME
Misty Lawn—Amber Leaves—Hollyberry
Keith Prowse: piano (6522)

IN MY GARDEN: WINTERTIME
Christmas Rose—The First Snowdrop—Evergreen

Keith Prowse: piano (6518)

RESTING [Howard Alexander]
Keith Prowse: song (6525); orch. + pfc (BBC Music Library), arr. ?

SONG OF THE FIR TREE [Alan Stranks]
Keith Prowse: song (6556)

1947   IN MY GARDEN: SPRINGTIME
Cherry Blossom—Carpet of Yellow—April Showers
Keith Prowse: piano (6607)

IN MY GARDEN: SUMMERTIME
Meadowsweet—Japonica—Alpine Bluebell
Keith Prowse: piano (6608)

ROMANESQUE
Keith Prowse: piano (6636)

1948   BIG TOP, THE, Five Circus Sketches
The Ringmaster—Clowning—Entrance of the Trick Cyclists—Dancing
Horse—Trapeze
Keith Prowse: piano (6709)

PEG O' MY HEART
Ascherberg, Hopwood & Crew: piano transcription (11938) of song by
Fisher/Bryan

SHY BALLERINA
Keith Prowse: piano (6713)

THEME FROM SWEDISH RHAPSODY
Keith Prowse: piano arrangement of song by Charles Wildman

THESE PRECIOUS THINGS [Howard Alexander]
Keith Prowse: song (6796); orch. + pfc (BBC Music Library)

WEEP NOT [Howard Alexander]
Keith Prowse: song (6802)

1949   A BIRD'S CLEAR NOTE [Howard Alexander]
Keith Prowse: song (6844)

1950   DA CAPO
Keith Prowse: piano arrangement (7060) of song by G. Boulanger

ELFINETTE
Keith Prowse: piano transcription (7013) of song by Gus Jansen

PORTSMOUTH ROAD [Ralph Howard-pseudonym]
Keith Prowse: song (7015); orch. + pfc, arr.?

TWO GLISTENING TEARS [Helena Howard-pseudonym]
Noel Gay: song (190) by Mayerl published as by 'Robert Darr & Helena
Howard'

1951   CAPRINELLA
Keith Prowse: violin and piano (7109)

HAYMAKER'S HOLIDAY
Noel Gay: piano transcription (202) of song by Colin Smith

MUSICAL EARWIG, THE
Noel Gay: piano transcription (203) of song by Eileen Kinsley

THE POMPOUS GREMLIN
Noel Gay: piano transcription (204) of song by Fred Bayco

POSTMAN'S KNOCK
Keith Prowse: piano (7117)

SATURDAY SHOWBOAT [Billy Mayerl]—signature tune in *Hello There*
Keith Prowse: song (7102)

TRANSATLANTIC LULLABY
Ascherberg, Hopwood & Crew: piano transcription (11614) of song by
Geoffrey Wright

1952   BEGUINE IMPROMPTU
Keith Prowse: piano (7178)

BLUE VELVET
Keith Prowse: piano arr. (7233) of song by Joseph Carpay

FORGET-ME-NOT, Intermezzo
Keith Prowse: piano arr. (7176) of song by Henry Richards

LOOK LIVELY—signature tune in *Hello There*
Keith Prowse: piano (7195)

TELL ME I'M FORGIVEN
Ascherberg, Hopwood & Crew: piano transcription (12285) of song by
Robert Katscher

1954   BALEARIC EPISODE
Keith Prowse: orch. + pfc (BBC Music Library); theme from Balearic
Episode, piano (7242), arr. composer

BLUE SHADOWS
Campbell Connolly: violin and piano (589); piano (610), arr. composer;
harmonica and piano (614), arr. Tommy Reilly; trumpet, cornet, and piano
(614) arr. Douglas A. Pope; brass band, arr. Douglas A. Pope

CRYSTAL CLEAR, a Rondo in Rhythm
Campbell Connolly: piano (590); orch. + pfc (no number)

ERRANT ERRAND BOY
Keith Prowse: piano (7320)

JAPANESE JUGGLER
Campbell Connolly: piano arrangement (597) of song by Alf Lancaster

MARIGOLD, Simplified Arrangement by composer
Keith Prowse: piano (7299)

MOODS IN CONTRAST: SUITE
Merriment—Devilment—Wonderment—Excitement
Bosworth: chamber orch. (21590, 21599, 21591, 21634)

SONG OF THE BUSY BEES, THE [Billy Mayerl]
Noel Gay: song (213)

1955 FILIGREE
Chappell: piano (43161)

JILL ALL ALONE
Ascherberg, Hopwood & Crew: piano (12397)

1956 BUSYBODY
Inter-Art: orch. + pfc (111), arr.?

MINUET BY CANDLELIGHT
Edwin Ashdown: piano (37120); orch. + pfc (37121), arr. composer

POOR LITTLE RICH GIRL
Ascherberg, Hopwood & Crew: piano transcription (12437) of song by Noel
Coward

WALTZ FOR A LONELY HEART
Sound Music: orch. + pfc

1957 FUNNY PECULIAR
Pickwick: piano

MAIDS OF HONOUR
Inter-Art: piano (122P)

SUSSEX DOWNS
Edwin Ashdown: Piano (37177); orch. + pfc, arr. composer

1957 VIENNA STORY
Edward Kassner: piano

1958 MINUET BY CANDLELIGHT
Edwin Ashdown: och. + pfc (37220), arr. Henry Geehl

1959 THEME FROM MAJESTIC INTERLUDE
Inter-Art: piano (154)

FINALE (ALLIANCE VARIATIONS)
Inter-Art: hire?

SELECT BIBLIOGRAPHY

PRINCIPAL WRITINGS BY BILLY MAYERL

The Melody Maker and British Metronome
   1. 'That left Hand! Or, the Secret of Syncopation on the Piano' (Nov. 1926), 55–6.
   2. 'That left Hand! Or, the Secret of Syncopation on the Piano' (Dec. 1926), 82–3.
   3. 'That left Hand! And how it should be assisted by the right' (Jan. 1927), 79–80.
'Song MSS. Reviewed', monthly feature starting Jan. 1932

The Cinema Organ Weekly
   1. 'Syncopation and the Cinema Organ', (April 1933), 45.
   2. 'Syncopation and the Cinema Organ', (June–July 1933), 151.
Tit-bits—series title 'A Master of Jazz Writes his Story for *Tit-bits*'
   1. 'High Notes in my Life of Rhythm', 19 June 1937, 3–4.
   2. 'We Played on as a Prince Lay Dying', 26 June 1937, 5–6.
   3. 'They Gave me "the Bird" in Birkenhead', 3 July 1937, 24–5.
   4. 'My Piano Fell into the Band!', 10 July 1937, 20–1.

Popular Music and Dancing Weekly
'You've got to have Rhythm!', 1/2 (Oct. 1934), 220.

Popular Music and Film Song Weekly
'Syncopating through Life', 1/9 (Dec. 1937), ii.

The Billy Mayerl Club Magazine
Mayerl was editor of this monthly published from Jan. 1934 to Aug. 1939 and contributed regular articles, editorials, and transcriptions.

The Light Music Magazine
Mayerl was editor of this quarterly published from September 1957 until shortly before his death in 1959.

The Billy Mayerl School of Modern Syncopation for the Piano
Mayerl, along with Geoffrey Clayton, produced instructional and publicity material which is not listed separately. This included various editions of the booklet, *Lightning Fingers*, not to be confused with the book edited by Mike Harth in 1995.

BOOKS ABOUT BILLY MAYERL

HARTH, M. (ed.) *Lightning Fingers* (London, 1995).
Articles and reviews are not listed separately but are fully documented in the notes to each chapter.

GENERAL BOOKS CONSULTED

AMSTELL, B., *Don't Fuss, Mr. Ambrose: Memoirs of a Life Spent in Popular Music* (Tunbridge Wells, Kent, 1986).

BADGER, R., *A Life in Ragtime: A Biography of James Reese Europe* (New York, 1995).

BANFIELD, S., *Gerald Finzi: An English Composer* (London, 1997).

BARKER, F., *The House that Stoll Built: The Story of the Coliseum Theatre* (London, 1957).

—— and JACKSON, P., *London: 2000 Years of a City and its People* (London, 1974).

BENNETT, A., *Journals of Arnold Bennett 1921–1928* (London , 1933).

BERLIN, E., *Ragtime: A Musical and Cultural History* (Berkeley, 1980).

BERNSTEIN, L., *The Joy of Music* (London, 1960).

BLADES, J., *Drum Roll: A Professional Adventure from the Circus to the Concert Hall* (London, 1977).

BOULTON, D., *Jazz in Britain* (London, 1958).

BRUNN, H. O., *The Story of the Original Dixieland Jazz Band* (London, 1963).

CLAYTON, G., *What Price Gloria* (London, 1936).

—— *Blame it on Betty* (London, 1936).

—— *Rally Round Rosalind* (London, 1937).

—— *Footnotes* (London, 1937).

—— *Reputation for Prunella* (London, 1939).

—— *Introducing Tennis* (Bognor Regis, 1946).

COATES, E., *Suite in Four Movements: An Autobiography* (London, 1953).

COCHRAN, C. B., *The Secrets of a Showman* (London, 1925).

COLLES, H. C., *Walford Davies: A Biography* (London, 1942).

COLLIER, J. L., *The Reception of Jazz in America: A New View* (Brooklyn, New York, 1988).

—— *Benny Goodman and the Swing Era* (New York, 1989).

COWARD, N., *Present Indicative* (London, 1940).

DICKINSON, P. , 'The Achievement of Ragtime: An Introductory Study with some Implications for British Research in Popular Music', in *Proceedings of the Royal Musical Association*, 105 (1978–9), 63–76.

—— *Style-Modulation as a Compositional Technique* (Goldsmiths College, London, 1996).

EHRLICH, C. , *The Music Profession in Britain since the Eighteenth Century* (Oxford, 1985).

—— *Harmonious Alliance: A History of the Performing Right Society* (Oxford, 1989).

—— *The Piano: A History* (Oxford, 1990) .

FISHER, J., *Funny Way to be a Hero* (London, 1973).

GAMMOND, P., *Oxford Companion to Popular Music* (London, 1991).

GANZEL, K., *The British Musical Theatre*, 2 vols. (London, 1986).

GRAVES, C. , *Champagne and Chandeliers* (London, 1958).

GRAVES, R., and HODGE, A., *The Long Weekend: A Social History of Great Britain 1918–1939* (London, 1940).

HALL, H. , *Here's to the Next Time: The Autobiography* (London, 1955).

HAMM, C. , *Yesterdays: Popular Song in America* (New York, 1979).

—— *Putting Popular Music in its Place* (Cambridge, 1995).

—— *Irving Berlin: Songs from the Melting Pot—the Formative Years, 1907–1914* (New York, 1997).

—— NETTL, B., BYRNSIDE, R., *Contemporary Music and Music Cultures* (Englewood Cliffs, NJ, 1975).

HARRIS, R. , *Jazz* (London,1952).

HASSE, J. E., *Ragtime: Its History, Composers, and Music* (London, 1985).

HITCHCOCK, H. W., *Music in the United States: A Historical Introduction* (Englewood Cliffs, NJ, 1974).

—— and SADIE, S. (eds.), *The New Grove Dictionary of American Music* (London, 1986).

HOARE, P., *Noel Coward: A Biography* (London, 1995).

HOLLOWAY, S. , *Wiv a little bit o' Luck* (London, 1967).

HOWARTH, R. G. (ed.), *The Billy Mayerl Circle Newsletter* (1972–8).

HUDD, R. , *Music Hall* (London, 1976).

HUGHES, S., *Opening Bars* (London, 1946).

—— *Second Movement* (London, 1951).

HUSTWITT, M. , 'Caught in a Whirlpool of Aching Sound: The Production of Dance Music in Britain in the 1920s', in *Popular Music*, 3 (1983), 7–31.

JABLONSKI, E., *Gershwin: A Biography* (London, 1988).

—— (ed.), *Gershwin Remembered* (London, 1992).

—— and STEWART, L. D. , *The Gershwin Years* (London, 1974).

JASEN, D. , *Recorded Ragtime 1897–1958* (Hamden, Conn., 1973).

—— *Tin Pan Alley: The Composers, the Songs, the Performers and their Times* (London, 1988).

—— and TICHENOR, T. J. (eds.), *Rags and Ragtime: a Musical History* (New York, 1978).

JAFFA, M., *A Life on the Fiddle* (London, 1991).

KENNEDY, M., *Portrait of Walton* (Oxford, 1990).

KERNFELD, B. (ed.), *The New Grove Dictionary of Jazz* (London, 1988).

KIRKPATRICK, J. (ed.), *Charles E. Ives: Memos* (London, 1973).

LAMBERT, C., *Music Ho!: A Study of Music in Decline* (London, 1934).

LARKIN, P., *All What Jazz* (London, 1970).

LESLIE, C., *The Life of Noel Coward* (London, 1976).

LESLIE, P., *A Hard Act to Follow* (London, 1978).

LOWE, L., *Directory of Popular Music 1900–1965* (Droitwich, Worcestershire, 1975).

LUPINO, S., *From the Stocks to the Stars: An Unconventional Autobiography* (London, 1934).

MACQUEEN-POPE, W. , *Ivor: The Story of an Achievement* (London, 1951).

—— *Night of Gladness* (London, 1956) .

MADGE, C., and HARRISON, T., *Britain by Mass-Observation* (London, 1939).

MANDER, R., and MITCHENSON, J., *British Music Hall* (London, 1965).

MANNIN, E., *Young in the Twenties* (London, 1971).

MARWICK, A. , *The Explosion of British Society 1914–62* (London, 1963).

—— *British Society since 1945* (London, 1982).

MATTHEWS, J., *Over my Shoulder: An Autobiography* (London, 1974).

MIDDLETON, R., 'Music of the Lower Classes', in *The Athlone History of Music in Britain: The Romantic Age* (London, 1981).

—— *Studying Popular Music* (Milton Keynes, 1990).

—— and HORN, D. (eds.), *Popular Music* (Cambridge, 1981–).

MILHAUD, D., *Notes without Music* (London, 1952).

MILTON, B. , *Milton's Paradise Mislaid* (London, 1976).

Music Critic of *The Times*, *Musical Britain 1951* (Oxford, 1951).

MYERS, R., *Music since 1939* (London, 1947).

NICHOLS, B., *The Sweet and Twenties* (London, 1958).

OGREN, K. J. *The Jazz Revolution: Twenties America and the Meaning of Jazz* (New York, 1989).

PEARSALL, R., *Edwardian Popular Music* (Vancouver, 1975).

—— *Popular Music of the Twenties* (Vancouver, 1976).

PERLOFF, N., *Art and the Everyday: Popular Entertainment and the Circle of Erik Satie* (Oxford, 1991).

PRATT, G., *The Dynamics of Harmony* (Milton Keynes, 1984).

RACE, S., *Musician at Large: An Autobiography* (London, 1979).

ROSE, P., *Jazz Cleopatra: Josephine Baker in her Time* (London, 1990).

ROSENBERG, D., *Fascinating Rhythm: The Collaboration of George and Ira Gershwin* (London, 1992).

ROSENFELD, P. , 'An Hour with American Music', in *Musical Impressions* (New York, 1970).

ROTH, E., *The Business of Music: Reflections of a Music Publisher* (London, 1969).

RUST, B., and FORBES, S. (eds.), *British Dance Bands on Record 1911–1945* and *Supplement* (London, 1989).

RUTLAND, H., *Trinity College of Music: The First Hundred Years* (London, 1972).

SADIE, S. (ed.), *The New Grove Dictionary of Music and Musicians* (London, 1980).

SATCHELL, T., *Astaire: The Biography* (London, 1987).

SCHIFF, D., *Gershwin: Rhapsody in Blue* (Cambridge, 1997).

SCHLEMAN, H. R., *Rhythm on Record: A Complete Survey and Register of all the Principal Recorded Dance Music from 1906–1936* (London, 1936).

SCHOLES, P., *The Mirror of Music* (London, 1947).

—— *The Oxford Companion to Music* (London, 1975).

SCHULLER, G., *Early Jazz: Its Roots and Musical Development* (New York, 1968).

—— *Musings: The Musical Worlds of Gunther Schuller* (New York, 1986).

—— *The Swing Era* (New York, 1989).

SCHWARTZ, C. M., *Gershwin: His Life and Music* (Indianapolis, 1973).

SCOTT, D. B., 'Incongruity and Predictability in British Dance Band Music of the 1920s and 1930s', in *Musical Quarterly*, 78/2 (1992), 290–315.

—— 'The Jazz Age', in *The Blackwell History of Music in Britain: the Twentieth Century* (London, 1995).

SCOWCROFT, P. L., *British Light Music: A Personal Gallery of 20th-century Composers* (London, 1997).

SEARLE, M. V., *John Ireland: The Man and his Music* (Tunbridge Wells, 1979).

SEELEY, R., and BUNNET, R. (eds.), *London Musical Shows on Record* (London, 1989).

SHEAD, R., *Constant Lambert* (London, 1973).

SITWELL, O. , *Laughter in the Next Room* (London, 1949).

Songwriters' Guild of Great Britain, *Sixty Years of British Hits* (London, 1968).

SPENDER, S., *World within World* (London, 1951).

STEARNS, M., *The Story of Jazz* (New York, 1964).

STERNE, A., and DE BEAR, A., *The Comic History of the Co-Optimists* (London, 1926).

STRAVINSKY, I., *An Autobiography* (New York, 1962).

SYMONDS, J., *The Thirties: A Dream Revolved* (London, 1960).

TOWLER, E., *British Dance Bands 1920–1949 on 12-inch long-playing records* (London, 1985).

VAN DER MERWE, P., *Origins of the Popular Style: The Antecedents of Twentieth-Century Popular Music* (Oxford, 1989).

WALDO, T., *This is Ragtime* (New York, 1976).

WHITCOMB, I. , *After the Ball: Pop Music from Rag to Rock* (New York, 1973).

WILDER, A., *American Popular Song* (New York, 1972).

WILMUT, R., *Kindly leave the Stage: The Story of Variety 1919–1960* (London, 1985).

INDEX OF COMPOSITIONS

General Index

Abraham, Paul 152
Acres, H. Morley 97
Adams, Eric 146
Addinsell, Richard 5, 196
Aeolian Hall, New York and London 49–50
Aeolian Harp 185
'After the ball was over' 119
Ahlert, Brooks A. 226
'A-hunting we will go' 198 n. 41
'Alabamy bound' 166, 228
Aldington, Fred 100 n. 2, 104
Alexander, Howard 140
Alexander's Ragtime Band 1, 4, 55, 73–5, 152
Alhambra Theatre, Glasgow 125
All alone 119
Allah's Holiday 224
Allin, Norman 188
All the things you are 170
Always 120
Amberley Wild Brooks 103
Ambrose, Bert 32, 39
American influences 5, 38, 67, 73–4, 89, 98, 112, 120, 122, 186–7
American Ragtime Octette 1, 70
Amstell, Billy 188
Amsterdam 13
Andrews, Julie 140
Andrews Sisters 141
Anjaparidze, Eteri 81 n. 20
Aquitania 145, 151
Archer, John 28, 154
Archers, The 107
Arden, Victor 79, 150
Armstrong, Louis 63
Arndt, Felix 112, 164, 189, 199, 231
Arnold, Billy 44–5
Arnold, Doris 150
Ashton, Irene 16 n. 28, 19, 62, 66, 112–13,

138, 163, 172, 176, 179, 187, 200, 210
Associated British Picture Corporation 127
Astaire, Fred and Adele 50, 97, 155, 168
Auden, W. H. 165, 186
Australia 30, 133, 190, 192, 220
Austria 14
Autumn 199

Bach, Johann Sebastian 10, 18
Badarzewska, Thekla 92
Baddeley, Hermione 118
Baker, Josephine 48
Ballets Russes 52
Bambridge, G. E. 18
Banfield, Eddie 94
Banfield, Stephen 191–2
Bantock, Sir Granville 206
barbershop chord 68, 70, 73, 75, 77, 79, 84, 96, 108, 178, 183, 194–5, 198, 200 n. 45, 202, 207
Barbirolli, Giovanni Batista (Sir John) 18
Bargy, Roy 79, 207
Bartlett, Henry 154
Bartok, Bela 49, 104, 167, 194
Barwick Green Maypole 107
Batten, Reg 223
Bax, Sir Arnold 11, 105, 174, 179, 215
Bayreuth 60
BBC, *see* British Broadcasting Company (Corporation)
BBC Dance Orchestra 177
BBC Music Library 200
BBC Theatre Orchestra 177
BBC World Service 216
Beale Street Blues 224
Beatles, The 141
Becke, Eve 178 n. 12
Bedells, Phyllis 95